HENRY MCBRIDE SERIES IN MODERNISM AND MODERNITY

The artistic movement known as modernism, which includes the historical avant-garde, produced the most radical and comprehensive change in Western culture since Romanticism. Its effects reverberated through all the arts, permanently altering their formal repertories and their relations with society at large, and its products still surround us in our workplaces and homes. Although modernism produced a pervasive cultural upheaval, it can never be assessed as an artistic movement alone: its contours took shape against the background of social, political, and intellectual change, and it was always bound up with large questions of modernity and modernization and with the intellectual challenge of sifting their meanings. Henry McBride (1867–1962) became perhaps the leading American critic of his time to write perceptively and engagingly on modern art. The Henry McBride Series in Modernism and Modernity, which focuses on modernism and the arts in their many contexts, is respectfully dedicated to his memory.

Editorial Committee

Lawrence Rainey, University of York, General Editor
Ronald Bush, Oxford University
Arthur Danto, Columbia University
Charles Harrison, Open University
Jean-Michel Rabaté, University of Pennsylvania
Jeffrey Schnapp, Stanford University
Richard Taruskin, University of California, Berkeley
Robert Wohl, University of California, Los Angeles

AN EYE ON THE MODERN CENTURY

Selected Letters of Henry McBride

EDITED BY STEVEN WATSON & CATHERINE MORRIS

YALE UNIVERSITY PRESS / NEW HAVEN & LONDON

This book has been published with assistance from the fund for the Henry McBride Series in Modernism and Modernity established by Maximilian Miltzlaff.

Designed by Mary Valencia
Set in Stone types by Keystone Typesetting, Inc.
Printed in the United States of America.

Library of Congress Cataloging-in-Publication Data
McBride, Henry, 1867–1962.
An eye on the modern century : selected letters of Henry McBride / edited by Steven Watson and Catherine J. Morris.
    p.   cm. — (Henry McBride series in modernism and modernity)
Includes bibliographical references and index.
ISBN 0-300-08326-2 (cloth : alk. paper)
1. McBride, Henry, 1867–1962—Correspondence.   2. Art critics—United States—Correspondence.   I. Watson, Steven.   II. Morris, Catherine J.   III. Title.   IV. Series.
N7483.M385 A4 2000
709'.2—dc21
[B]   00-028106

A catalogue record for this book is available from the British Library.

The paper in this book meets the guidelines for permanence and durability of the Committee on Production Guidelines for Book Longevity of the Council on Library Resources.

10 9 8 7 6 5 4 3 2 1

CONTENTS

ILLUSTRATIONS

ACKNOWLEDGMENTS

Maximilian Miltzlaff has been a primary source of support for this project. During Henry McBride's lifetime Miltzlaff helped care for his archive of letters and writings, and since McBride's death Miltzlaff has continued to keep his name in the public memory. As McBride's executor, Miltzlaff has been instrumental in granting permission to publish letters and in providing information about the figures and events.

Other people and institutions have provided information and help in a variety of ways. Libraries and institutions we would like to thank include the Yale Collection of American Literature, Beinecke Rare Book and Manuscript Library, Yale University; the Archives of American Art, Washington, D.C., especially the staff and resources at the New York branch of the archives; the New York Public Library; the Museum of Modern Art Library, New York; the Phillips Collection, Washington, D.C.; the Rosenbach Museum and Library, Philadelphia; the board of Trinity College Library, Dublin; and Knoedler Galleries, New York.

For their dedication to keeping the work of Henry McBride in the public eye, we are grateful to the late Monroe Wheeler, the late Daniel Catton Rich, and the late Lincoln Kirstein.

There are a number of individuals we wish to thank for their scholarly generosity and goodwill. At the Yale Collection of American Literature, Beinecke Library, Yale University, we thank Donald Gallup for his foresight in collecting the papers of McBride and his associates; Patricia Willis, the collection's curator; and the helpful staff led by Steven Jones. We also thank Bruce Kellner, Robert Atkins, Christien Ducker, Francis Naumann, Naomi Sawelson-Gorse, Cynthia Wells, Ingrid Schaffner, Robert and Loranda Watson, John, Janet, and Philip Watson, Thomas Morris, Elizabeth Morris, Thomas W. MacGregor, Billie MacGregor, Lawrence Smith, Thomas H. MacGregor, Felicity O'Mahoney, Ali Nematollahy, Lara Heimert, Jonathan Brent, Judy Throm, Evelyn Feldman, Dan Heaton, Ronald Pisano, Fred Baker, and Cassandra Langer.

NOTES ON THE TEXT

We have not only selected the letters and journal entries to be published here but have edited the text of some letters and journals. Sections deemed of less interest have been excised and marked thus [. . .]. Passages that have been cut frequently include apologies for not writing, quotidian details of plans to meet, discussions of health and the weather. We have included only a sampling of McBride's many letters from Marshallton, Pennsylvania. The events described are essentially unvarying—the weather is hot, the food is good, and so on—but what is lost in the present selection of letters is the country side of McBride's life.

To spare the reader irrelevant distractions, the texts of each letter and journal entry have been edited in the following ways: 1) The occasional misspellings have been silently corrected. 2) The ampersand has been changed to "and" for the sake of consistency. 3) The ellipsis dots that McBride often employed to indicate paragraph breaks—often as a frugal space-saving device, particularly for long-distance letters—have been changed to the more conventional paragraph indentation. McBride's English spelling has been retained. We have adopted these unconventional editing practices in order to provide the maximum amount of information of interest to the reader within the scope of a single volume rather than reproduce every accident of McBride's pen. While suggesting the arc of McBride's life, the edited letters emphasize his perceptions of the world in which he lived. Consistent with McBride's epistolary style, our focus is on the external rather than the internal.

Those interested in reading a larger portion of McBride's letters, or in reading correspondence to McBride, are directed to his collection at the Yale Collection of American Literature, Beinecke Rare Book and Manuscript Library, Yale University, or to microfilm of the McBride Collection available at the Archives of American Art. To supplement the understanding of these letters, readers are directed to Henry McBride's *The Flow of Art* (Atheneum, 1975, reissued by Yale University Press, 1997).

All the letters included in the current volume are housed in the Yale Collection of American Literature, Beinecke Rare Book and Manuscript

Library, Yale University (specifically, the Henry McBride papers, the Dial/ Scofield Thayer papers, the Muriel Draper papers, the Mabel Dodge Luhan papers, the Alfred Stieglitz/Georgia O'Keeffe archive, and the Carl Van Vechten papers); Marianne Moore papers, the Rosenbach Museum and Library, Philadelphia; Duncan Phillips Papers, the Phillips Collection, Washington, D.C.; James Stephens Papers, Trinity College Library, Dublin; and Maynard Walker Gallery Papers, Archives of American Art, Washington, D.C.

AN EYE ON THE MODERN CENTURY

INTRODUCTION

The Cultivation of Henry McBride

Henry McBride was an authority and a lion, and he appears in twentieth-century art history in two distinct roles. As a critic McBride is frequently invoked as an early and loyal supporter of modern art. Journalists described him as the dean of American art critics, the official beacon of the new. Marcel Duchamp recognized him as America's premier art critic. "He was a great person in 1913, '14, '15, who wrote as a great art critic in *The Sun* and different papers at the time as ever and since."[1]

McBride began writing for the New York *Sun* in 1913, at the age of forty-six, and he established his status as America's most progressive critic within his first few years at the paper. Agnes Ernst Meyer told him that the members of Alfred Stieglitz's 291 circle respected him above all other critics. During the 1920s McBride also served as *The Dial*'s art critic under the editors Scofield Thayer and Marianne Moore (1920–29), and at the beginning of the 1930s he edited the magazine *Creative Art* (1930–32). McBride's achievements as a critic are documented in his selected writings, *The Flow of Art*, which provides a survey of the ongoing opinions of a single mind about art over a period of forty years. As Lincoln Kirstein observed, McBride's longevity added an essential dimension to his identity: "For the valuable position of Henry McBride as critic depends upon his persistence in time, and his insistence over extended time on certain elements of freshness, elegance and humanity."[2] The sweeping panorama of McBride's career—beginning on the eve of the Armory Show of 1913, which introduced modernism to New York, and ending with the advent of the Abstract Expressionists—spans the rise of modernism from its School of Paris origins to its School of New York dominance after World War II. Near the end of his career as a critic during the early 1950s, McBride aptly observed, "A new cycle begins."

McBride's second role in the history of modernism is as a raconteur and

---

1. Marcel Duchamp interview with Mike Wallace, circa 1960; we are indebted to Naomi Sawelson-Gorse for transcribing and sharing this interview.
2. Lincoln Kirstein, "Henry McBride," in McBride, *The Flow of Art*, p. 3.

all-purpose champion. We would pay little attention to McBride were it not for his published work, but it is his unpublished writing, in letters and journals, that most richly fleshes out McBride's contribution to the informal history of the twentieth century. Within the art world he acquired nicknames that suggested his role as a genial defender of—and adviser to—artists. Newspaper articles referred to him as Uncle Henry. Philip Johnson recalled that in the 1930s some of his friends called him Mr. Dooby, and this affectionate nickname evoked his geniality and positive nature. Henry McBride was a critic who was also a cheerleader, a warm figure who applauded creators. The familial affection that might have been extended to his biological family found its object in his extended adoptive one, the art world.

Looking back at the end of the twentieth century, it seems that Henry McBride was born to bridge worlds, eras, and sensibilities. In his columns for the *Sun,* he conducted a thirty-seven-year-long conversation with his mythical reader, who must be prodded and cajoled and entertained into becoming more progressive and adventurous. Within the mix of the columns were references from history, from Paris, from the news. McBride always called to the attention of his dear reader pockets of grace in the larger world. "He wrote about art by believing that, in his column, two worlds met," observed the critic Sanford Schwarz. "Interpreting one for the other, he had to be nimble enough not to step on feet in either world."[3]

Henry McBride was one of the oldest figures associated with America's first avant-garde, emerging at the time of the Armory Show; he was later described as "one of the last of the pre-War 'lions.'"[4] Consider this lineup of his contemporaries, each born within barely more than a decade, all protagonists in the modernist struggle in art and literature:

Harriet Monroe (b. 1860), founding editor of *Poetry* (1912)
Arthur Davies (b. 1862), artist and chief organizer of the Armory Show
Alfred Stieglitz (b. 1864), gallerist and photographer
Robert Henri (b. 1865), artist and leader of the Independents movement
Henry McBride (b. 1867), art critic
Frank Lloyd Wright (b. 1867), architect
Baron de Meyer (b. 1868), photographer
Emma Goldman (b. 1869), revolutionary
Hutchins Hapgood (b. 1869), progressive journalist
John Quinn (b. 1870), modern art collector

3. Schwarz, *The Art Presence,* p. 211.
4. Ralph Flint, "Art and Mr. McBride," *Art News,* March 1, 1941, p. 12.

John Marin (b. 1870), painter
Florine Stettheimer (b. 1871), painter, saloneuse

Placing McBride within the company of such contemporaries—fellow movers and shakers who introduced modern ideas to America—helps to clarify his distinctive approach to modernism. McBride doesn't aspire to the rhetorical spirituality of Alfred Stieglitz, nor did he earnestly invoke art's uplifting and improving qualities, à la Harriet Monroe. McBride embraced none of the experiments in modern lifestyle of George Cram Cook or the Baron de Meyer, and as a political conservative he abhorred the radicalism of Emma Goldman and Bill Haywood. Nor did McBride's writing employ the stylistic modernism of Gertrude Stein or John Marin.

In this company, McBride seems the most middle of the road, the most widely accessible and most conventionally respectable in lifestyle. As such, McBride provided the link between conventional and avant-garde modernism; his enthusiasms were thoroughly twentieth century, even if his manners and social attitudes were nineteenth. Hutchins Hapgood entitled his autobiography *A Victorian in the Modern World,* and that title would have fit Henry McBride as well.

Shortly before he became a critic, McBride wrote in his journal: "I like the old masters as much as anyone, but we don't live like them nor dress like them nor think like them, so we can't paint like them."[5] Whatever his aesthetic preferences, McBride felt internal demands to understand the language of modern life. So completely was he identified with "putting over" modern art that a *New Yorker* cartoon appeared in the late 1930s featuring one of Helen Hokinson's archetypal matrons declaring that she simply couldn't make up her mind about modern art, because there was always "McBride saying one thing and Cortissoz another."[6]

The career of Alfred Stieglitz offers a far more stereotypical model of a crusader for modern art: loquacious, driven by modern metaphors and references, self-dramatizing, seasoning the aesthetic stew with dollops of new spirituality. McBride displayed none of these qualities. He looked with reverence and irreverence on both the past and the present. He read the classics and loved the opera. He was fascinated with the nuance of archaic social forms and the homeliest of customs and cuisine. He dressed like a gentleman, and by the time he began his full-time career as a critic, he had absorbed a great deal. As a journalist noted in 1915, "His criticisms have

5. Undated journal entry (McBride Collection, Yale Collection of American Literature, hereafter cited as YCAL, McBride).
6. Quoted in Flint, "Art and Mr. McBride," p. 12.

the deft, light touch of the master who is able after long years of life to put a few charcoal marks on paper, touch these with a colored chalk and reveal his astonishing genius."[7] One can almost hear McBride's light staccato laugh in the background, the laugh of someone in the know. Profiling McBride in *Art News*, Ralph Flint used characteristically nonacademic language to describe the critic's prose: "He seldom misses a trick, forgets a bon mot, or stops being gently oracular."[8]

McBride's lack of doctrine was a strength, but it made it more difficult for his work to weather the tidying up of history. One could not talk about a McBride school of criticism, as one could later discuss Greenbergian analysis. He proffered no formulas like "significant form" and was aligned with no academies. His advocacy was delicate and indirect, and his passions were often shaded by tones of irony and brightened by wit. "Absolutists," he wrote in his first year at the *Sun*, were puritans. He subscribed neither to the new puritanism of modernism nor to the old puritanism of the Academic Salon exhibitions. The British author Llewelyn Powys wrote that McBride's style offered a "flow of amusing observation, which kept skimming over the depths of existence with the same light assurance that a swallow shows as she dips her feathers from time to time in the mirrored surface of a duck pond."[9]

Perhaps the credo that most consistently shaped McBride's art criticism over forty years was his belief that "what pleases the 'discerning few' can please the general if the general be given a chance at it. . . . There are no closed doors to opinion and certainly there is no class distinction in thought. What Plato has thought you can think."[10]

Writing for both the "discerning few" and the general public, McBride used a language that was both broad in its references and free of jargon. He didn't hesitate, even for the general audience in the *Sun*, to incorporate references to classic literature, ancient history, nineteenth-century opera, and contemporary theater. Neither professorial nor bombastic, these references used the language of the old to introduce the new. He was specific, and his meaning was always transparently clear: As Marianne Moore wrote, "You may have premonitions but Mr. McBride has the data."[11]

Henry McBride believed in the arts as a moral force, but that force had

7. Clayton Spicer, clipping from an unspecified magazine, 1915 (YCAL, McBride).
8. Flint, "Art and Mr. McBride," p. 12.
9. Powys, *The Verdict of Bridlegoose*, pp. 141–42.
10. McBride, *The Flow of Art*, p. 15.
11. Quoted by Lincoln Kirstein, "To Honor Henry McBride" (New York: Knoedler Galleries, 1949), pp. 2–3. See also Moore, *Complete Prose*, p. 647.

little to do with improving character or upholding conventional morality. "It is not so much that artists are to be immune to the law, like the ancient aristocracy of England, but that they can only arrange their systems of value in a state that gives them complete liberty. Artists approach morality through beauty, and if they are good artists find both; but people who have no eyes for beauty are incapable of judging their processes until, as I have pointed out, history has enabled them to take a more generous attitude."[12]

PORTRAITS OF THE ART CRITIC

What can you do.
I can answer any question.
Very well answer this.
Who is Mr. McBride?

The question, posed by Gertrude Stein in "Have They Attacked Mary. He Giggled" (1917), can't be adequately answered with the usual biographical information.[13] McBride's formative years—those leading up to middle age—can be only crudely sketched. Another window on Henry McBride however—the portraits of him created by his contemporaries in pencil, paint, ink, bronze, music and words—provide more allusive and encompassing perspectives on McBride.

Peggy Bacon, Portrait of McBride, 1928

Peggy Bacon's 1928 pencil sketch of Henry McBride captures a likeness on the run, on the spot, and it looks like the most "authentic" picture of McBride. Snared in a furtive moment, teacup in hand, McBride shoots a penetrating sidelong glance, as if discovering the artist in the act of conceiving his portrait. His privacy has been invaded. He could be digesting a piece of gossip: his ears are pricked up, his mouth is fussily pursed. Bacon's tone is both satirical and affectionate—Uncle Henry as Aunt Henry, the weighty arbiter of aesthetics as gossip over tea. As the critic James Johnson Sweeney wrote at the time, the portrait had "an air of scrupulous depersonalization and yet was rife with twinkling *sous entendus*."[14] The poet Charles

12. McBride, *The Flow of Art*, p. 14.
13. Gertrude Stein, "Have They Attacked Mary. He Giggled." New York: Privately published by Henry McBride, 1917.
14. James Johnson Sweeney, "Caricatures in Pastel," *Creative Art*, spring 1931, p. 445.

1 *Henry McBride,* 1928. Peggy Bacon, graphite on paper. Courtesy of the Weyhe Gallery, New York.

Henri Ford's memory of meeting McBride at the Stettheimers' a few years later suggested the critic's receptivity: "When I knew him he was grand-fatherly, but he was always, as we say, 'with it.' Everyone around Florine was 'with it.' Henry was usually on the receiving end. Always receiving."[15]

Acting as the reporter of news and gossip for the art world, McBride genially transmitted all the news heard over tea, between acts at the opera,

15. Charles Henri Ford, conversation with Steven Watson, October 21, 1996.

and at museum openings. The title for his weekly *Sun* column, "What Is Happening in the World of Art," suggests that he was interested not only in what happened within the frame but in the reactions outside that frame. The extravagant earrings and "the Matisse dress" in the corner, the rumors circulating through the room itself, the latest gallery commerce—this was McBride's world of art. His readers felt that they were at the scene itself, and, better yet, sometimes even behind it. Years after McBride's death, Sanford Schwarz captured his chatty and conspiratorial tone: "He was much closer to his readers than art writers are now, and he alternately hovers over you like a dignified uncle or gives you pointers like a fussy aunt. In a typical piece, he moves back and forth from a throat-clearing gentlemanly dryness to a mock gossipy, confidential, this-is-between-us spirit."[16]

Gaston Lachaise, Bust of McBride, 1928

How different is Gaston Lachaise's rendition of Henry McBride! Although the bust was completed the same year as Peggy Bacon's drawing, Uncle Henry has been transformed into Mr. McBride. The cheekbones are now prominent, and the sniffing nose of Bacon's sketch becomes a noble profile, the jowls firmer. On the two-tiered square base pedestal stands the idealized Dean of American Art Critics.

16. Schwarz, *The Art Presence*, p. 207. "McBride made his points by coming through the back door, introducing difficult ideas through the language of fashion, kiddingly appealing to his audience's need to be up-to-date. His 1914 appeal for cubism, for example, begins with a humorous accounting of winning over your friends to cubism, concluding that, 'The person who doesn't like the big general art movement of the day is an old fogy.' The mild, dry humor often led into a more serious point, such as this deeply-felt conclusion a few paragraphs later. 'When an art striving or impulse keeps the world talking for six or eight years and affects all the sister arts, when emporiums spring up for the sale of works in the new system and magazines are created for its discussion, the affair may safely be called a "movement." That authoritative books upon the style have not yet been written merely means that the movement is still in progress. One never writes with authority upon a style until the style has passed. The funeral sermon is preached in the presence of the corpse.' Then, backing off from too earnest a style of direct partisanship, he glancingly delivers a knockout punch. 'Without meaning to be unnecessarily unkind, and simply in an effort to end this paragraph, we may mention that authoritative works upon the subject of impressionism have long since been at hand.' McBride rarely attacks head-on, he pokes fun. He adds his own layer of disappointment in having to deliver a disappointed judgment; he gentles his reader and puts on his gloves before delivering the blow. He wins us over as a narrator and gossiper before putting on his critical hat to address the art at hand. Sidling up to McBride, as Peggy Bacon's portrait suggests, one could get the best gossip."

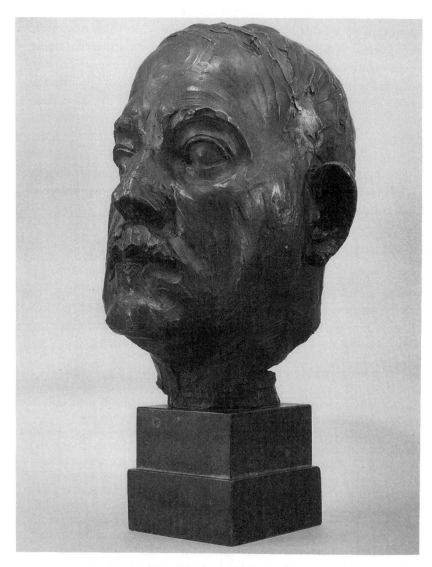

2 *Henry McBride,* 1928. Gaston Lachaise, bronze, 13⅝ × 10⅛ × 11⅛ inches.
Collection of the Museum of Modern Art, New York. Gift of Maximilian H. Miltzlaff.

When Lachaise asked McBride to sit for him in the spring of 1927, McBride initially declined, saying that he "was not the type for artists."[17] Art critics were at their lowest ebb in the spring, he added, after the annual onslaught of reviewing. Lachaise closely appraised McBride's face and found "something" there, and McBride consented, sitting several times in Lachaise's studio. By the second or third sitting, McBride saw the character emerging from the green wax. "My bust turns out to be a combination of Mussolini and Phillip II. *He* sees the heroic side of my character."[18]

By the time Lachaise finished, McBride was pleased to see that he was now "a modified form of hero." McBride wrote Lachaise: "I confess it is— Me. . . . Every time I look at it I get a different idea of myself. I have, I know, several edges to my character."[19] All traces of Mussolini had been rendered benevolent and noble: McBride became an idealized dictator of art. In fact he was widely regarded in this fashion as one of the few uncompromised and undersung saints of the art world. There were several attempts to pay homage to the critic, suggestions that he receive a laurel wreath from New York's mayor or other official accolades. The critic Jerome Mellquist wrote, "Must we always take our good men for granted?—Stieglitz, Henry McBride, poor hapless little Eilshemius—always the same."[20] Official recognition came near the end of McBride's life, when, in September 1958, he was decorated with the Legion of Honor, with the rank of chevalier.[21] It was appropriate that McBride received his greatest recognition from France, for Paris was his aesthetic home, and he loved its language both visual and verbal.

Florine Stettheimer, Two Portraits of McBride

McBride's close friend Florine Stettheimer painted a portrait, *Henry McBride, Art Critic*, in 1922, and he also appears prominently in her final, unfinished work, *Cathedrals of Art* (1942–44). Although Stettheimer had previously painted group portraits, ensemble conversation pieces, and

17. Henry McBride, "McBride's Portrait by Lachaise," *Dial,* March 1928, reprinted in *The Flow of Art,* pp. 241–242.
18. McBride to Florine Stettheimer, June 1927 (YCAL, McBride).
19. McBride to Lachaise, January 20, 1928 (Lachaise Archive, Beinecke Library).
20. Jerome Mellquist to McBride, December 23, 1943 (YCAL, McBride).
21. Though McBride wrote friends telling them of the news in his typical style: "I've had a slight headache ever since I read the letter fearing I may never be the same after this. But I shall try to live it down." McBride to Dr. and Mrs. Everett Barr, September 8, 1958 (YCAL, McBride).

portraits of family members, the fact that McBride was one of her first portraits devoted to a single friend suggests his importance within the Stettheimer circle. McBride recalled seeing her secretly sketching his out- line while visiting the Stettheimers' summer house in Seabright, New Jer- sey. At the time of the house party, a lawn tennis tournament was in progress, and at the portrait's unveiling party, McBride declared himself astonished to see a tiny version of himself seated alone viewing, or judging, the tennis competition. The lower right corner of the painting depicts McBride in a country field painting a fence. The full top third of the paint- ing presents easily decipherable allusions to the American art that McBride championed: a Winslow Homer–like palm tree, a Gaston Lachaise sculp- ture of a woman, John Marin's brightly painted buildings, a church from Charles Demuth, and a floral bouquet by Florine Stettheimer.

Within the confines of a thirty-by-twenty-six-inch canvas, Stettheimer brought together McBride's disparate worlds, accentuated by a variety of lines that divide the pictorial space—nets, fences, a tessellated wall. Mc- Bride lived in each of these worlds. He was an avid tennis fan and attended the Seabright tournament each afternoon of his visit to the Stettheimers' in order to see "the sensational new Frenchmen, Borotra, Cochet, and Lacoste," then playing for the first time in America.[22] Surrounded by sport, by the bucolic country scene, and by the highlights of American art, the largest figure of McBride is seated squarely in the center of the painting. The wings of his chair extend in such a way to suggest that McBride is an angel. What is he doing? He is keeping score. His function of aesthetic scorekeeper was especially important to an artist like Florine Stettheimer. McBride was one of the first critics, and certainly the most prominent, to recognize the importance of her work. In tennis parlance, Stettheimer served an ace.

The allusions to works of art is not surprising, but the fact that half the canvas is covered with grass is less expected, suggesting perhaps the duality of McBride's annual schedule. From October to May his life was dominated by art galleries, museums, and the New York *Sun*. But for nearly half the year, he lived in the rural setting of Marshallton, Pennsylvania. His coun- try home, Callicaste, was not a stylish retreat but a rustic home lacking the basic amenities of plumbing and electricity. McBride was not a city dweller

22. McBride, "Florine Stettheimer: A Reminiscence," *View*, October 5, 1945, pp. 13– 15.

3 *Henry McBride, Art Critic,* 1922. Florine Stettheimer, oil on canvas, 30 × 26 inches. Courtesy of Smith College Museum of Art, Northampton, Massachusetts. Gift of Ettie Stettheimer, 1951.

playing at being a country squire but a man whose country roots were essential to him. He is painting his own picket-rail fence. Brush in hand, McBride is a painter, but of the homeliest sort.

Finally, McBride stands erect on the edge of a tessellated stone wall, gazing across a storm-tossed sea. But rather than looking like a revolutionary "on the barricades," McBride is dressed in a top hat and a formal black

4 *Cathedrals of Art,* c. 1942–44, detail. Florine Stettheimer.

coat. Even when fomenting on behalf of the new tendencies of modern art, McBride retains the style and attire of a gentleman.[23]

In *Cathedrals of Art,* Florine Stettheimer's witty evocation of the art world, she portrayed Henry McBride as a figure at the foot of a grand museum stairs, as the infant Art crawls forward and up. In each hand the

23. "He liked English tailoring, and wanted his jackets short, saying it made one look taller, yet he was six feet in his stockings and athletically well-proportioned.

critic holds a round sign: STOP and GO. Stettheimer again comments on McBride's role as a reputation-maker in the art world: his critical imprimatur determined which artists would go and which would not. A retrospective look at the people McBride supported, most at the beginning of their careers, suggests his prescience: Gertrude Stein, Thomas Eakins, Stuart Davis, Charles Demuth, Gaston Lachaise, John Marin, Georgia O'Keeffe, Joseph Stella, Elie Nadelman, Oscar Bluemner, Max Weber, and later Mark Tobey, Arshile Gorky, and Jackson Pollock. The now undisputed classics—tidied into history, in Auden's phrase—were then more controversial and less tidy, and McBride was often the first critic to say GO.

But just as he was instrumental in according early attention to worthy artists, he was also philosophically and emotionally opposed to the effects of success. In a reminiscence about Florine Stettheimer he wrote, "At every opportunity I have been preaching the doctrine of seclusion of American painters, seeing how unequally they seem to be coping with the pressure that present-day publicity puts upon them."[24] McBride sounded his theme early, and it runs almost obsessively through his letters and his articles.[25] In 1913, for example, he wrote James Stephens, "I liked the 'Glass of Beer' immensely. . . . *I hope they won't be successful.* I hope you'll be poor for ten years to come, and then get rich suddenly."[26] His close friend Mildred Aldrich observed to Gertrude Stein that he had "a congenital contempt for successful people."[27]

His top coat would have the flair in the skirt like the military. Often he had his shirts made to order in London or in Paris, and later by Brooks Brothers New York. He walked very erect and in his prime weighed 200 pounds. He walked briskly, wore a dark overcoat as a rule, a black homburg hat, a plaid muffler and carried a malacca cane. He had a way of placing his pearl stud just off center in his four-in-hand. His shoes were hand-made, usually one pair tan and one pair black. He liked soft cotton and linen mixed handkerchiefs and was partial to the English manner of wearing slacks during the day. In the evening, when formal dress was prescribed, he wore the finest tailored evening clothes." Max Miltzlaff, unpublished notes.

24. McBride, "Florine Stettheimer: A Reminiscence," p. 15.

25. McBride's 1914 description of "the publicity game": "The modern machinery for publicity, although an immense affair, is also very simple, and is easily controlled by those who take the trouble to learn the system. Once you get it started the movement is almost automatic; a touch or two to the levers, occasionally, a little petrol, and there you are, almost famous" ("A Visit to Guillaumin," *The Sun*, May 3, 1914).

26. McBride to James Stephens, December 1, 1913. Trinity College Library, Dublin, James Stephens papers.

27. Aldrich to Stein, February 18, 1918 (YCAL, Stein Collection).

McBride perhaps felt immune to the effects of success, for his own relation to it was established so late in his life. But after his delayed start he moved very quickly, achieving recognition in his own profession, rising from a staff reporter in the art department to the head of the department in 1913. By June 1915 *Vanity Fair* included him as one of eight "distinguished art critics." In June 1917 Gertrude Stein's piece "Have They Attacked Mary. He Giggled" was published by *Vanity Fair,* and Henry McBride appeared in the genre piece, along with Stein and Mildred Aldrich. Perhaps the crowning accolade was Scofield Thayer's invitation to McBride to become the art critic for *The Dial* in 1920.

Toward the end of his life McBride expressed the hope that a selection of his pieces would be published. He religiously saved the tear sheets of his articles, which were stored in a little trunk in his damp stone house in Marshallton. His devoted friend Maximilian Miltzlaff discovered them in 1956—some partly chewed by silverfish—took them to New York, and sorted them in chronological order. For McBride, the desires for recognition by posterity and for éclat during one's lifetime represented vastly different impulses. McBride cared for none of the accoutrements of celebrity. He was not introverted, for he met and charmed people effortlessly and mastered the rituals of social intercourse easily. But he shunned the command performances of public life. He hated to be photographed.[28] He accepted only those honorary recognitions that were not tied to speaking. Before an audience McBride would say "Thank you" and no more.

Publishers repeatedly urged him to write memoirs and "reminiscences of the artistic world," but he declined to write anything in which he was overtly the main character. As early as January 1924 Lincoln MacVeagh of Dial Press invited such a book, and in the wake of Stein's success with *The Autobiography of Alice B. Toklas* came a wave of requests.[29] In 1946 Monroe Wheeler, director of publications at the Museum of Modern Art, pleaded that McBride "work on your memoirs which are going to constitute one of the most important documents on art in America."[30] McBride always declined, and he sometimes regarded his own achievement as fleeting. He wrote to Ettie Stettheimer, "What I have written seems so writ on water that it seems ghostly to have it recalled."[31] He didn't write in such a long

28. See, for example, McBride to Malcolm MacAdam, February 11, 1933, regarding having his picture taken by Carl Van Vechten.
29. Gorham Munson, editor at Thomas Crowell, for example, in 1935.
30. Monroe Wheeler to McBride, June 28, 1946 (YCAL, McBride).
31. McBride to Ettie Stettheimer, June 22, 1932 (YCAL, McBride).

form as a book—the length of a catalog essay was his limit, and these essays were often a struggle.

His voice in letters, journals, and articles is remarkably similar, just as the gap between the public McBride and the private McBride is small. Even when writing about himself, McBride comes across as a wryly observed figure in his own anecdote, the joke gently cracked, and often at his own expense. Anyone expecting emotional revelation will be disappointed. "He is not susceptible to self-eulogy," observed Marianne Moore. "Where feeling is deep it is not a topic."[32]

As an observer of the world around him, McBride is unparalleled. He outlived all his contemporaries in the art world—most of them by two decades—and he was the only one who continued actively writing until the end of his life. He knew the right people and he frequented the right places, and it all became fodder for his letters; as a friend noted, McBride was an "expert in ye things worldly."[33] McBride's letters provide a glimpse of his roving, anecdotal perspective on dinner parties, strolls through nineteenth-century Europe, gallery openings, royal convocations, operas, automobile races, the novelty of flying, meals good and bad, plays, and visits to friends' summer houses. The sheer expanse of years (from 1894 to 1959) vividly document the dailiness of encroaching modernity, the cultural smorgasbord of an active life. Part of the value of the letters is that they describe a social life that no longer exists, and in a voice of self-made graciousness. Marcel Duchamp described McBride's as "a marvelous style, I mean personal style in the sense of literary style; it's not commercial sounding or anything, it's perfect, it is a piece of literature really."[34] In both letters and articles his voice seems to roll effortlessly from the pen, graciously maintaining an engaging persona, though in his letters McBride is a bit freer with a barb, and is also less likely to pull his punches. The most obvious and problematic punches thrown are the instances of racism and anti-Semitism that appear in the correspondence.

At a stage of his life when McBride was vigorously trying to re-create himself, he looked to published letters as a psychological wellspring. In 1908, while reading the letters of Lafcadio Hearn, he found an epistolary model. McBride's description of Hearn provides an idealized self-portrait of McBride as well: "The character of Hearn as I get it from the letters, is completely charming. I don't know any modern literary chap who makes

32. Moore, *Collected Prose*, p. 647.
33. "Lee" to McBride, May 1920 (YCAL, McBride).
34. Duchamp, interview with Mike Wallace.

so fine a case out for himself. His constant, insistent search for beauty, for the eternal and world acceptable truth, has its effect in the imaginary portrait the reader conjures up. He seems to me so fine a gentleman. I envy him a dozen secret little touches in every letter, that betray the nobility of soul."[35]

In his letters, McBride's nuanced voice describes a similar "insistent search for beauty, for the eternal and world acceptable truth," in a world that has now vanished. Some of the rituals common to McBride's early career had already passed into history within McBride's own lifetime—the Grand Tour, the stylish Prohibition salon, high bohemia—and he came to feel that he was a relic of another age.

Just as McBride bridged the nineteenth and twentieth centuries, the publication of his letters provides a bridge from the end of the twentieth century back to its beginnings. As a journalist wrote near the end of McBride's life, "He is a survivor of a racy club of a sort we haven't any more."[36]

35. Notebook entry, February 1908 (YCAL, McBride).
36. Charlotte Devree, "Profile: Henry McBride, Dean of Art Critics," *Art in America*, October 1955, p. 42.

HENRY MCBRIDE

A Biographical Sketch

Conventional wisdom suggests that literary and artistic lives reach their climax before the onset of middle age; creativity is associated with youthful ardor and the "discovery" of oneself. The life of Henry McBride refutes this popular formulation—as well as F. Scott Fitzgerald's dictum that American lives have no second acts. In the case of McBride, we know his first forty-five years as only a sketchy prelude to his professional life. Perhaps McBride's first act was simply long delayed. On the eve of the Armory Show of 1913—the epochal moment when modern art came to America—he appears as a fully formed art critic. From then until the early 1950s, when he stopped writing in his late eighties, McBride changed remarkably little in either voice or taste. In the process, he countered his own belief that it becomes difficult, after the age of forty, to embrace the spirit of the coming generation.

CHILDHOOD AND EARLY WRITING

Henry McBride was born on July 25, 1867, the youngest of five children, to John McBride of Philadelphia and Sarah (née Pugh) McBride of Embreeville, Pennsylvania. Both parents were Quakers.[1] McBride's four siblings were much older, and by the time he reached adolescence, they were already married and settled in their own families. A key event of McBride's adolescence was the death of his mother, when he was fifteen years old. Unable to cope singlehandedly with the responsibility for his son, John McBride sent Henry to the Brintons' Boarding House in West Chester, Pennsylvania. Feeling that his immediate family had deserted him, McBride never again enjoyed a close relationship with them. No known letters to or from any member of his immediate family exist—they didn't write, or McBride didn't save them, and even references to family members

---

1. McBride's paternal grandfather came from Scotland, settled in Ballicaste, Ireland, and married Catherine McKeon.

occur only rarely. But the move to the Quaker-run residence remained a pleasant memory. It was structured and warm, and he so enjoyed some of the food (corn cut from the cob with sour cream, steamed blackberry pudding with lemon sauce) that he later considered writing an essay about those years that would be called "The Joys of Penury." At the boarding-house he came under the guidance of a fellow lodger, a distressed gentle-woman, who had lived in France and experienced court life. She taught him manners and instilled in him the desire to see Europe.

McBride, tall and athletic, was a local tennis champion. As his letters attest, he remained avidly interested in tennis, boxing, walking, and swimming, and he showed an early aptitude for drawing. The earliest photographs of McBride show an erect, attractive, personally immaculate, and slightly dandyish figure.

Around the age of eighteen, McBride began what might be called his first art and writing job: while he kept the books at the nursery owned by George Achelis in West Chester, he also wrote and illustrated the firm's seed catalogs. He continued working at the nursery for about four years, always saving money to study art. Self-sufficiency and economy were traits McBride adopted early on, and they remained core values throughout his life.

In 1889, having accumulated two hundred dollars, he moved to New York and enrolled at the Artists and Artisans Institute, studying under John Ward Stimson. The institute, at 140 West 23d Street, was highly respected for its practical studio art training. It was, according to the *New York Times,* "the most promising Art School in the country, established on the broadest and most scientific basis." The *Dry Goods Economist* called it "the most hopeful institute of its kind now in sight." Stimson, an aristocrat who was also a progressive, had studied art in Italy, Belgium, Holland, and England. He vituperated against the Royal Academy and the National Academy, hated John Singer Sargent, promoted the traditions of Ruskin and Morris, and insisted upon the important connection between art and life. This combination of aristocratic background, advanced aesthetics, and social consciousness provided a personal model for McBride, whose pencil sketches occasionally appear in his letters and journals. Most are travel sketches done on the spot, and they support Stimson's evaluation in 1892 that "McBride drew carefully, correctly and rapidly."[2] That succinct description applied not only to his drawings but to his later writing about art. In the 1890s and into the early twentieth century, when McBride's ambitions were

2. Quoted in Miltzlaff, unpublished notes.

5 Henry McBride as an art student, pictured with an unidentified friend, c. 1890. Photographer unknown.

focused on draftsmanship and becoming an artist, rather than a writer, his drawings display the competence and talent of a promising and dutiful student. The sketches that survive exhibit the more socially advanced training provided by Stimson, with illustrative qualities reminiscent of the Left Bank cabaret periodical *Le Chat Noir*. McBride's drawings tend toward a light quality of caricature that was highly popular at the turn of the century.

McBride's move to New York opened new vistas, and Manhattan was the first of the foreign territories he mastered. He lived with fellow art students, and he became attracted to the details of New York's downtown street life. Working-class neighborhoods became a staple of his international travel letters and journals. McBride didn't hide his own attraction to the vivid life of New York's slum-ridden Lower East Side, but he bridled when told that depiction of the lower classes must inevitably be tragic. In 1941, when he was scolded by a reader named Hester Huntington for his insufficient appreciation of Reginald Marsh's depiction of the tragic slums, McBride replied with uncharacteristic edge, invoking his own roots: "Did you ever live in the slums, Miss Huntington? I have, and during the years of my association with the Educational Alliance in the East Side I heard more laughter and saw more gay faces in the streets than I did when I ventured uptown to see my conventional friends. It is for this reason that I try to prod my friend Reginald Marsh to a broader viewpoint, for to insist that the slums are invariably tragic is only to know the half of it. True tragedy as the great actor Edwin Booth once remarked can only be portrayed by artists who retain their sense of humor. Fine art is a matter of keeping the proportion."[3]

McBride's first article, "Backwoods Gardens," was published in November 1890 in *American Garden Magazine*. The twenty-three-year-old McBride was still rooted in the world of George Achelis's Nursery, and the article was illustrated with his own sketches. He carried the horticultural theme into his next published piece, "One Marigold Laughed at Another." The poem, published in the winter 1894 issue of *Artist Artisan Quarterly*, speaks in an anachronistic vocabulary but foreshadows the bittersweet note McBride, then a prematurely retrospective twenty-seven-year-old, was to master as he aged:

One marigold laughed at another—
"Thy coat has a tinge of brown,"
"And thine has a tear,
To-day I felt a cold wind,
To-night crisp crickets cry,
The morrow will bring us hard weather.
But what odds, eh? We've
Had some glad weather."

McBride's other early writings suggest the twin interests that followed his horticultural phase: the Lower East Side and art. "The Lost Children of New York" was published in *Harper's* (January 1894), and in May 1901 *Das Abend Blatt* published a Yiddish translation of McBride's account of teaching on the Lower East Side. His first article about art, on the decorations and paintings of Pierre-Cécile Puvis de Chavannes, appeared in *The Art Interchange* in 1894. "Two Paintings by Manet at the Metropolitan Museum" followed in the April 1901 *Alliance Review,* and "Technical Tendencies of Caricature" was published in 1904, with illustrations by McBride's Parisian friend Gustave Verbeck. The confluence of his interest in art and the Lower East Side appeared first in an article, "Art on the East Side," published by the Eastside Artist and Educational Alliance in 1895, and

3. McBride to a Miss Huntington, April 1941 (YCAL, McBride).

6 *A Mere Growth of the Years, Aided by Expert Bargaining from Time to Time,* 1890.
Henry McBride, illustration for his article "Backwoods Gardens."

again in 1903, when the New York *Mail Express* published "Art and the East-Side Jew."

Although McBride showed early success as a writer, he ceased publishing after 1904. At the age of twenty-six he had merited publication in a journal as reputable as *Harper's* and was paid the respectable fee of $25. But from the age of thirty-seven to the age of forty-five, McBride published nothing that is known (or at least nothing that he saved, as was later the wont of a man who collected all of the "clips" of his writing).

MCBRIDE AS TEACHER

During the last years of the nineteenth century and the first years of the twentieth, Henry McBride's life was dominated by teaching. With Stimson's help and encouragement, in 1896 McBride became an instructor of an "antiques class" at the Educational Alliance, teaching each Tuesday and Thursday from 10 to 12 A.M. The Educational Alliance was an institution formed in 1889 from three separate organizations, the Hebrew Free School Association, the Young Men's Hebrew Association, and the Aguilar Free Library. Described as a "curious mixture of night school, settlement house, day care center, gymnasium and public forum," the Alliance was housed in a large five-story building at 197 East Broadway. Its mission was to serve as "an agency of American acculturation." One of the Alliance's goals was to improve its students' "standards of taste."[4] The Alliance initiated art programs in 1895, and the art school was housed within the walls of a large social service institution that also held classes in English, theater, and music.[5] The students were primarily first-generation Jewish children of Eastern European immigrants. The influx of immigrant groups with their progressive social ideals reinforced a generally accepted notion in New York that America, at the end of the nineteenth century, was in the midst of a huge social upheaval. McBride began his tenure at the Alliance with an optimistic respect for his students' potential. McBride's early support and

4. First two quotations from Irving Howe, " 'Americanizing' the Greenhorns," in Kleeblatt and Chevlowe, *Painting a Place in America*, pp. 14 and 17. The third quotation is from the Alliance's annual report at the end of its first decade, cited in Norman L. Kleeblatt and Susan Chevlowe, "Painting a Place in America: Jewish Artists in New York, 1900–1945," in Kleeblatt and Chevlowe, *Painting a Place in America*, p. 94.
5. Joan Rosenbaum, preface to Kleeblatt and Chevlowe, *Painting a Place in America*, p. 8.

encouragement of the Jewish students at the Educational Alliance became overshadowed in his later life by a politically and emotionally charged anti-Semitism that finds its voice in the letters of the 1930s. McBride's distaste for communism and socialism fostered his anti-Semitism, which became more pronounced during the Depression and the events leading up to World War II.

McBride accepted the job of instructing the students in drawing. In addition to the traditional curriculum of drawing from plaster casts, McBride added a life-drawing class to the curriculum. Drawing from the live model was to become a dominant practice in the following years.[6] The art school grew under McBride, who added courses in industrial design and painting in 1902. In 1901 McBride organized the first exhibition of works by the Art School's own students. He also wrote articles on art and his own experiences traveling in Europe for the school's magazine, the *Alliance Review*. The aesthetic sense that McBride passed along to his pupils is reflected in his own illustrations from the period. McBride's educational goals can be said to reflect the priorities that were later elucidated in his criticism: nurturing creative talent that combined a technical ability with a mature and personal creative vision.

McBride felt that his students at the Alliance possessed a talent born of their roots in European culture. His pupils were, for the most part, poor young children from families struggling to establish a foothold in their adopted country, and simultaneously facing the prospect of becoming a part of a society that didn't make much room for the traditions and cultural mores of their native lands. Many of those students came of age artistically when the influence of European culture on the developing ideas of modernism in the United States was at its peak. A few of McBride's students later showed their art in the Armory Show and became subjects of their former teacher's essays: Jo Davidson, Jacob Epstein, Samuel Halpert, and Abraham Walkowitz.

Looking back, McBride expressed affection for his teaching years on the Lower East Side. He probably identified with his ambitious students' desire for upward mobility through education, for by the early twentieth century he had notably educated himself and moved from rural Pennsylvania to New York and Europe. The warmly avuncular presence that became a trademark of his later relationships in the art world could be seen in his

6. Kleeblatt and Chevlowe, "Painting a Place in America," p. 95.

7 *Women's Drawing Class,* 1893. Henry McBride.

style at the Educational Alliance. After class, one former student recalled, McBride sometimes treated small groups to chocolate and cookies in the neighborhood.

At the turn of the century McBride took a second job, as director of the State School of Industrial Art at Trenton, New Jersey, founded by John Stimson. For several years he divided his week between the two positions, while living at 53 West 25th Street. He was highly regarded in New Jersey, where the *Trenton Gazette* quoted his description of a summer trip to Europe, even featuring his photograph on the front page. It also reported on his appearance at the Art School's annual costume dance, where Professor McBride dressed as "a king, in a long white crepe garment decorated with gold and in immense crimson togs," and was followed faithfully by a soldier in orange and black.

In contrast to the students at the Educational Alliance, who were virtually all children of European immigrants, McBride found his students in New Jersey to be aesthetically conservative. He ascribed this timidity to their tenuous connection to a European cultural tradition. McBride later told an interviewer that he decided then that Americans "faced terrible handicaps in approaching the life of art." He aspired to overcome those handicaps. He later wrote that if he had sufficient money to transform the milieu, "I know that I could guarantee an atmosphere in this country that would produce artists within ten years."[7]

To stimulate thinking, ideas, and friendship in Trenton, McBride tried to re-create the atmosphere of his friend Robertson Trowbridge's salon. He founded and participated in an organization called the Symposium, whose members gave presentations, which were followed by discussion.

By the end of McBride's tenure as the director at the Trenton school, its reputation and enrollment had risen considerably; in his final year, for example, thirty-eight students had been added. The *Gazette* reported, perhaps hyperbolically, that the school was no longer a small establishment for the study of practical arts but an institution "which is recognized by the art educators in Philadelphia and New York and other large cities of the East and West of the first class, a recognition that is indeed gratifying to educational Trenton."[8]

From these two teaching experiences McBride seems to have taken away a sense that making truly important art that could be judged against its

7. Devree, "Profile," p. 43.
8. Undated clipping (YCAL, McBride).

European peers was, at best, a difficult proposition in the United States. Or, as Lincoln Kirstein put it, "After five years he was driven to feel that, by and large, at this state in our historical development, although many Americans possessed talent, few had drive."[9] At the close of his teaching career in Trenton, McBride turned his full attention toward his own study of the cultural influences of Europe. Ten years later, when modernism finally established a permanent foothold in this country, McBride's feelings about the viability of an important school of American modernism made an about-face.

During the period of McBride's involvement with the Educational Alliance and the Trenton school of art, Robert Henri and his circle of friends were effecting radical changes in the production and exhibition of artwork, and also in its teaching. The idea of an artist being of his own time and place was probably one of the earliest modern truths a man of McBride's generation would learn. The belief in the value of the experience of the common man, also touted by Henri, probably affected McBride's work at the Alliance and at the School of Industrial Arts. He interjected into this formula his firm belief in the right of every man to better himself through experience and education. In an article in the *Alliance Review* about his travels and studies in Europe, McBride strove to teach by example the value of self-education and the benefits to be gained from exposure to European culture. This lesson remained important to McBride and made regular appearances in his writing over the next fifty years. In some sense, the American public became, for McBride, those same pupils, and his mature writing style often reflects a teacher's voice and tone.

By all apparent measures, McBride was a successful educator. But in December 1906, he fled this milieu, and his chief preoccupation over the next four years was his own re-creation through travel and writing. He later called it a "nervous breakdown," but said nothing more. What we know of the next five years is this: McBride traveled to Italy, Paris, and London with a companion named Walter Radcliff in 1906–7, and he became acquainted in 1909 with two detectives named Raymond and Reiter, and also a detective named Otto Nickli, who became a close friend. We do not know how he supported himself. Perhaps he was able to live on the money he had accumulated working two jobs.

Among the unknown elements of McBride's biography are any facts about his sexual life. There is no unambiguous evidence of any roman-

9. Kirstein, "Henry McBride," p. 4.

tic relationships with either women or men. In the years after McBride's death, several men who were themselves homosexual (Virgil Thomson, Charles Henri Ford, Philip Johnson) offered anecdotal evidence that McBride was gay. Each of them met McBride when the art critic was over sixty, and their observations concerned his sexual orientation rather than specific sexual behavior. Max Miltzlaff, a close friend and companion of McBride's from 1934 until his death, did not subscribe to the notion that McBride was homosexual. Although McBride has been described in print as "openly gay," the evidence suggests that it can be more accurately stated that he was openly not heterosexual.

The fact that McBride left no direct evidence or allusions to any sexual experience says a great deal in itself, both about the privacy of the man and the privacy of the time. Because there are at least two instances of letters having been cut with a scissors, it is possible that sexual references have been censored. Based on a combination of hearsay, McBride's homosocial networks, and minor evidence within the letters, it is clear that McBride was attuned to masculine beauty and discussed the good looks of men he encountered more than he discussed female beauty. His close friends were mostly men, many of them homosexual, and several of the social milieus with which he was associated—the Stettheimer gatherings, the Gertrude Stein salon, the Askews' parties—were open to, and sometimes dominated by, homosexual men.

MCBRIDE TRAVELS

In the summer of 1893 McBride had gone to Chicago to work in the American Pavilion of the Columbian Exposition. His three months there not only sharpened his appetite to travel abroad but also provided enough savings to pay for his first crossing to Europe. He sailed in the summer of 1894 on the SS *Laurentian,* bound for Liverpool. By the time he returned on August 15, he had visited London and stayed in the Parisian suburb of Chatillon with Gustave Verbeck, who drew for *Le Chat Noir.* McBride's letters reveal an instinct for finding his way into the most interesting networks. About the same time, McBride requested that his letters be preserved; at the age of twenty-five he showed the writerly instinct for preserving his own words. This desire reflects the era's fascination with travel writing. The preservation of his letters also documents a personal transformation.

Europe was the key site for Henry McBride's transformation. There is nothing in his drawing that suggests anything beyond highly competent

8 Henry McBride as cattle ship inspector, c. 1895. Photographer unknown.

technical proficiency, and nothing in his background (except the distressed gentlewoman) to predispose him toward the Continental. His voracious hunger for old and new culture animates the letters in the first section of this book. His itineraries include many destinations common to the Grand Tour, but there were also out-of-the-way places that reflected McBride's characteristic interest not only in the main events and the grand masterpieces but also in the colorful human events taking place in alleys and courtyards along the way.

So abiding was Europe's allure for McBride that the next winter he crossed the Atlantic on the cattle ship SS *Mentmore* as an undercover agent for the American Society for the Prevention of Cruelty to Animals, assigned the duty of reporting on the care of the cattle. Trying to understand the presence of such a refined figure in their midst, his companions on the boat speculated that he might be a fugitive from justice. Early on, McBride determined that what Europe had to offer him was worth a steep price, and in the case of his cattle ship crossing, that meant more than just traveling in steerage. The *Mentmore* departed from Baltimore in February and was so late in arriving in Liverpool that the ship was presumed lost. McBride's journals from that crossing juxtapose quotations from Ruskin with sketches of corraled animals and descriptions of how cattle fare on a transatlantic voyage.

Traveling to Europe in the summer became one of McBride's most regular and treasured practices. Over the next three decades he went almost every summer, and his letters from these trips provide our most substantial firsthand knowledge of his life at the end of the nineteenth century.

TRANSATLANTIC TRAVEL AT THE TURN OF THE CENTURY

In 1894, when McBride embarked on the first of his many trips abroad, he took with him a Victorian faith in the educational promise of European travel. That first trip, and those he took in the early part of the new century, seem to have been motivated by that most classic of reasons for undertaking the European Grand Tour: to complete his education and prepare himself for a cultured professional life.

In the seventeenth century young men traveled to Italy to acquire the qualities that made a gentleman. Even before the term "the Grand Tour" was coined by the English Catholic priest Richard Lassel in 1670, the educational pursuits undertaken during a course of study in Italy inspired generations of British gentlemen and, later, generations of American students and artists. The most common Grand Tour itineraries were shaped by the desire to study the important examples of the fine arts of painting, sculpture, architecture, and the decorative arts.

Over the course of two centuries the character of the Grand Tour gradually broadened from an obligatory educational experience for young, male British aristocrats. With industrialization and its attendant increase in wealth in the United States during the late nineteenth century, the trip abroad became a rite of passage meant to refine and edify the children—particularly the sons—of financially secure and socially prominent American families. Increasingly, young women also traveled to Europe, though the idea of "finishing" for a young woman involved a much more strictly chaperoned and social form of travel, and usually quite a bit more shopping.

As the nineteenth century wound to a close and the industrialization of the United States continued to strengthen the economy, European travel became accessible to men such as Henry McBride, who were not from even moderately wealthy families, but whose personal aspirations gave a high priority to saving the necessary funds for passage and expenses. McBride's meager budget, earned through teaching, freelance writing assignments, and various other odd jobs, dictated his means of travel. A 1955 article in *Art in America* described how for decades McBride "went abroad every summer, crossing for $50 on the one-class French Rochambeau that set wine, red and white, at the table for free. For $500 he could stay abroad for three months and buy a suit of clothes, costing less than equal time, without a new suit, in America."[10]

McBride's love of the Atlantic crossing is reflected in his letters and journals. The letters from his early trips record the excitement of watching automobile races, ordering a suit of clothes from a Saville Row tailor, taking in the tennis matches in London, walking tours of lower Germany, wandering the countryside of Spain knowing neither the language nor the customs, and socializing with the U.S. Fleet in Gibraltar after missing his boat home. McBride had some highbrow experiences as well—days in the Vatican museums or in the Prado—but he thrived on recording his experiences in the back streets, soaking up local color and observing the working-class mores of the places he visited. Through his version of the Grand Tour, McBride educated himself, studying the buildings, art, and people in the cities and towns of Europe.

On the Grand Tour one hoped to acquire a facility with Continental

10. Quoted in Devree, "Profile," p. 42.

manners, and to gain a working knowledge of the antiquated class rules that distinguished a gentleman from the common man. Important lessons—how and when to employ a marrow spoon or how to distinguish a Gothic cathedral from its Romanesque predecessor—could occupy many an hour. Henry McBride excelled in most of his self-taught etiquette and breeding, though he seems to have been most attracted by the arts of conversation and observation. Dancing and singing appear to be the refinements in which he found himself most lacking. He had at least one occasion to regret his lack of dancing ability, as he told his friend Max Miltzlaff years later. McBride "recalled a dinner followed by a dance," Miltzlaff wrote. "As he and his partner walked from the dining room to the ball room, the orchestra was playing a Viennese waltz. The lady turning to him with outstretched arms and said, 'Shall we dance?' "[11] McBride told Miltzlaff that he was never so sorry in his life that he couldn't dance. The lady was Isadora Duncan.

The polishing of manners and etiquette aside, a more important—and vocationally oriented—objective of European travel was the development of taste. Books like Henry James's *Little Tour in France* and, earlier, Nathaniel Hawthorne's *Marble Faun* inspired generations of American artists and writers to have a more broad-based experience of European culture. Toward this end, the American Grand Tour itinerary ordinarily included stops in other countries en route to that most celebrated of destinations: Italy.

McBride, like countless other youngish men before him, completed the obligatory visits to churches, galleries, and ancient monuments in Italy, France, Great Britain, Germany, and Spain, staying in modest hotels, taking night trains, and searching out inexpensive meals. The attraction of the Oriental also swayed McBride, who made one crossing to Morocco, then a colony of France.

McBride usually traveled alone but had a variety of early introductions that he later parlayed into some of the most important professional and creatively challenging relationships of his life. In Florence in 1906, when he was traveling with his friend Radcliff, he met Bernard Berenson. Through his friend Bryson Burroughs alone, McBride made the acquaintance of Henri Matisse and Roger Fry. Mildred Aldrich, another Burroughs introduction, led McBride to one of the most important relationships of his career, his friendship with Gertrude Stein.

11. Miltzlaff, unpublished notes.

MCBRIDE'S SELF-EDUCATION AND SOCIAL CIRCLES

The man who had a self-described "nervous breakdown" pursued a course of healing, primarily through reading and travel, two nineteenth-century alternatives to the psychological examination that dominated the twentieth century. Beginning about 1908 he resolved to keep notes of the most important things he read. His strategy incorporated the nineteenth-century impulse for self-improvement and the twentieth-century preoccupation with re-creating the self.

Around the summer of 1907, McBride began reading books that allowed him intimate glimpses into the lives of figures upon whom he could model himself. In his journal two years later, McBride writes directly about the connection between his reading and his hopes to refashion himself:

> During the last two years I have read Margaret Fuller's memoirs, Symonds' *Autobiography*, Lafcadio Hearn's *Letters*, and now Carlyle's *Life*. It seems to me if I could have read these books at the age of twenty, my history or lack of history would have been different. At forty-two, to ape nobility is difficult, at twenty the most natural thing in the world. Only at twenty one must have had predecessors. Of the lives of great people I have mentioned, Carlyle's and Goethe are the least encouraging to the individual of slight endowment. They were both inevitably great. Nothing apparently could have stopped them. There's a secret force that cannot be stolen or borrowed by their disciples. Hearn and Symonds are more helpful. They have arrived eventually upon pinnacles that anyone would have been content with and by their own efforts. They seem to continually tell others how the thing may be done. The reader becomes credulous and even at the age of 42, hopeful again."[12]

Around this same time, McBride participated in the gatherings of a salonlike group at the home of Robertson Trowbridge on the north side of Washington Square. Trowbridge published two books. One was a collection of sonnets, but it is his other book, an assortment of anecdotes, quotations, and recounted conversations, that suggests his métier: drawing out the conversation of others and remembering its most salient sections. In his home, the debaters of literature, music, and art included Burroughs, curator at the Metropolitan Museum, the novelist and essayist Llewelyn Powys, and art critic Fry. It was a fertile ground for the further cultivation

12. Journal entry, July 11, 1909 (YCAL, McBride). Robertson Trowbridge gave McBride Hearn's letters as a Christmas present in 1907.

of Henry McBride. After seeing McBride at Trowbridge's, Powys wrote a short sketch that suggests McBride's charm—as well as the foreboding that pops up in his letters, usually in anticipating his own death. (The first reference to his impending death occurs fifty-two years before the fact.) "Henry McBride was invariably charming to me, but I always felt that his mind, apart from its congenital frivolity, was cognizant and philosophic, was haunted in fact, by the alarming suspicion that he himself and his room at the Herald Square Hotel, with its shining hot water pipes, and indeed, for the matter of fact, that 'the great globe itself' were merely balanced in the unsatisfactory manner of a spinning top that has to fall with a sidelong rush sooner or later, later or sooner."[13]

In December 1909, at the opera, McBride met Raymond and Reiter, and shortly afterward he met Nickli. Nickli's frequent appearance in McBride's journals over the next several months reflected both his personal interest and his fascination with the underground world that Nickli saw as a detective. At the beginning the two men struck a bargain that put their relationship on a businesslike footing: McBride would criticize the untrained Otto Nickli's drawings, and Nickli would allow McBride to accompany him on his rounds. McBride's attraction to the detective echoed his affection for his young traveling companion Radcliff: drawn by the twenty-eight-year-old's energy and ambition, McBride assumed a mentoring role.[14] But the

13. Quoted in Miltzlaff, unpublished notes. See also Powys, *The Verdict of Bridlegoose,* p. 144.
14. Did McBride have romantic feelings for either or both of them? McBride actively encouraged heterosexual romances of both Radcliff and Nickli. In his journal he expressed an impassioned hope that Nickli might find a wife: "O beautiful partnership! Take my word for it, there's no such thing as single-blessedness. Not even the artist creates single-handed. He cooperates, either with his friends or the general public. The highest of lucks is to find a partner in your wife. It has been done. It can be done again." Conjoining heterosexual romance and artistic collaboration, McBride's idealized discussion may reflect his own frustrated aspirations, as well as his hopes for Otto Nickli.

The only overt discussion of homosexuality in the early journals occurs in an interchange among McBride, Nickli, Raymond, and another detective named Julian:

Nickli: Know what fairies are?
McBride: You mean . . . ?
Raymond: Yes.
McBride: Why don't you run them in?
Raymond: Oh it's not my affair.
Julian: I've a lot of sympathy with those poor sons of guns.
McBride: I suppose it's medical. More for the doctor than the jail. (YCAL, McBride)

relationship foundered when McBride unsuccessfully, and uncharacteristically, tried to introduce Nickli into the Trowbridge circle.

His participation in Nickli's detective work also provided him the content for a new kind of writing in his journal—longer pieces that incorporate more dialogue and narrative detail. These protostories represent a direction that McBride did not pursue in his writing, but the detectives' world encouraged McBride's prose experiments. Although his writing was restricted to journals and letters, some pieces from this period are more self-consciously literary; his ruminations about the intricacies of young love or the nuances in opera manners aspire to Jamesian complexity.

A few years later McBride's prose became clearly focused on art criticism. He claimed that it was accidental that he became an art critic. After James Huneker left the *Sun* in 1912, his role as art critic was assumed by Samuel Swift, who was a friend of McBride's. In fall 1912 Swift invited McBride to be his assistant, and when Swift left the paper less than a year later McBride was elevated to art critic. Thereafter he never swerved.

LETTERS

1894–1959

To Mary and Maria Pugh
August 23, 1894, London, England

Dear Mary and Maria:[1]

I know of course, you wouldn't be surprised to get a letter from me from the Moon, much less from London. I am over here on a business commission, my expenses paid and my work is almost finished and I have to enjoy a week or two and buy clothes and then return to New York. I got to London last night at five o'clock, left my bundle at the lodging house and started out to eat and go to a theatre. I took about ten steps on the street and met Wm. L. Dodge!!![2] He was rushing one way, I another. He said, "I'll see you in Paris next week, old man, ta, ta," and vanished. Feel perfectly at home and learned how to count the money in half an hour. Learned lots of things from an English chap upon the steamer. Had determined to be frugal, so stopped in a shop and bought one of Watling's pork pies (4 pence) and went to the nearest coffee-house and got a cup of coffee for a penny and ate my pie. That's the way you can do here in the tough district. I'm right near to Whitechapel and after I do up the Tower of London and all the things on this end, I shall move to the other end and see Parliament, Westminster Abbey, and the Palaces, etc.

Went to the theatre last night—the Prince of Wales. I was somewhat bored at the comic opera. I didn't think it so terribly comic. The Strand and Piccadilly and those other streets down there were fine.

Slept till ten today. Raining pitchforks and no umbrella. Saw St. Paul's Cathedral however, and Royal and Stock Exchanges and the Bank of England and that section and did a lot of shopping. Got measured for the

1. See Biographical Sketches.
2. William De Leftwich Dodge (1867–1935). Studied in Munich and Paris, where he worked in the Atelier of Gérôme. Awarded medals at the Paris Expo of 1889, by the Prize Fund Exchange, New York, 1886, and at the Columbian Exposition, Chicago, 1893, where he might have met McBride.

swellest pair of trousers you ever saw. Hope you'll see 'em Christmas time. Had a lot of writing to do. Now it is dark. I shall go take a hot bath for sixpence, get some fresh clothes on, eat and go see Whitechapel and some music-hall. Will write when I have more leisure. [. . .]

To Mary and Maria Pugh
September 9th, 1894, Chatillon, (près de) Paris

Dear Marie et Maria:
   It is cold, has been cold for two or three days. My fingers are too stiff for beautiful penmanship this morning. Gus is hustling like the deuce, trying to make enough money to come home to America with me.[1] He wants to work today, but after de'jeuner a onze heures I'm going to dress myself in my new clothes that I bought in London and go into Paris to see a nice girl I used to know in New York. I want to go over to Billy Dodge's studio, too. I have got a semi-order to write a little article when I get back and I think I can get information out of Billy. If I have the time I'll go in again to the Louvre and go see the Musée de Cluny and things like that. But in Paris here it is more fun to be on the streets than anywhere else. The streets are wide and beautiful and clean and there is always such lots to see. It is great fun to sit out along the sidewalk at the little tables and eat a stunning table d'hôte. We were in last Sunday and went to the famous Madeleine to vespers and after dinner we sat in the Jardin Royal sipping café noir et Cognac, while the band played "Carmen" and the other operas, out of sight. We went in Wednesday, too, Gus had an errand one direction and I another so we made a rendez-vous at the Bon Marché, the store that cor-responds to Wanamakers. Then we went round hunting up the fellows. There was one fellow we struck just at dinner time. We had intended going to a café called "The Hole in the Wall," a place where the students go and kick up high jinx (they say it is famous and that Thackeray used to go there), but the fellow coaxed us off to a little place he knew. We had lots of fun. There were some funny Frenchmen there and they got jolly and one commenced to sing. He turned to us and asked us what we would like. I said "Les Matelots, par example." ("Les Matelots" is the latest popular song). He pretended to get very wrothy, bowed to me very low and said,

1. Gustave Verbeck (1867–1937), an American born in Japan, was a cartoonist for the famous Left Bank periodical *Le Chat Noir*. During this trip McBride stayed at Verbeck's apartment at 131 Boulevard Montparnasse.

"Ce Monsieur, que me donnait l'honneur de me parler etc.," but we all laughed so much he had to laugh, too.

While we were eating, Louis Loeb came in and Gus and I were introduced.[2] Loeb works for *The Century,* and is considered to be somebody great. He had been commissioned by *The Century* to go to the South of France and make drawings of an out door fête there. He told us all about it and about the great French actors playing the Greek play, Oedipus-roi in the open air. He is a jolly nice fellow and good looking, but I didn't think there was much to him. He and the other fellow wanted to go off with him to play billiards, but we chased off instead to see some street fête.

Gus lives away out in Chatillon in the suburbs, way beyond the fortifications of the city, on the route to Versailles. It is fine. We are on the top of a hill and we can see beneath us the whole city of Paris, with the Eiffel Tower sticking straight up out of the middle of it. All around us are quaint farmer houses and little villages. We are half way between three, Chatillon, Fontency and Clanmart. We cook ourselves and we get our food at either village, just as it happens. We have bully things to eat. The locataire on the floor below almost everyday sends us up a soup, we have two or three vegetables of kinds you don't know, each dejeuner and dinner we have a salad and cheese and then café noir et Cognac et cigarettes. The first day when I came, I found a letter from Gus at the club telling me how to find the place. He drew out a map, locating the room, showing where the key was and said to go over to the chalet across the road, order a demi-litre du vin rouge and wait. I did it. I ordered "le petit gris" and sat at a table in the garden and watched a crowd of laborers drinking at the next table. Gus came along soon. But that wine was the best in the world and we have it every day. The Camembert cheese here is simply perfection. Gus has a quart bottle of Cognac so we burnt it into our coffee every day. At the restaurant the other night instead of café et Cognac, we had café au Marc. I like it better even.

I get along all right with my French and it is great sport. This is what amuses me. Going into town the other day, Gus and I separated and I waited alone for my car. Two or three passed in the opposite direction and two old ladies asked me if one was the car for Clanmart. It was labeled Vanues, so I explained that Vanues was near to Clanmart. They asked again, "Faut le prendre a'lors?" I was just going to ask the guard when I saw

2. Louis Loeb (1866–1907), American painter and illustrator. Known for illustrations of Mark Twain's *Pudd'nhead Wilson*.

the car for Clanmart coming, so I said, "Ah, non madame, voilà, ça viens, le vôtre." So she got in and rode away happy. I suppose she thought I know all about it.

Gus is considered great here, and so he really is. He has been working two years or so for Le Chat Noir, the swellest funny paper here.[3] And he had a play done at the Théâtre Chat Noir, which is considered away up. I am going to fetch a lot of his things back with me to illustrate an article I want to write about him.[4] It breaks me up to think I must leave France in four days. I go to London Thursday night and leave on the City of Paris, Saturday, August 15th. [. . .]

To Mary and Maria Pugh
June 16, 1902, SS. Laurentian

Chère Cousines:

This is Monday afternoon—five days out. I meant to have done a lot of things this afternoon, but have been loafing. Been having a bully time in spite of cold weather. First two days it was foggy and wet and one had not learned how to avoid the swells, so it was pretty tough—but with the fog's disappearance we felt better. It is as cold as Greenland. In fact according to the charts we seem to be just off that hospitable shore today. I have on winter flannels, winter clothes and heavy overcoat and Dud's shawl, and can't sit a moment still for the cold.[1] I have assumed charge of all amusements, of course. I invented a golf game that took lots of muscle. We used broom handles and shoved wooden-blocks along the decks from pillar to post. It was very difficult to get them over the steam pipes, which were the bunkers. We have deck-billiards and quoits also, but for two days it has been so freezing cold, we couldn't play. A ship passed this morning and signaled, asking if we had seen icebergs. We hadn't, but we're on the watch. We saw three whales spouting yesterday in the distance. The Mate found a little land bird yesterday that fell exhausted on deck. He gave it to me to

3. *Le Chat Noir* (1881–1895) was an outgrowth of Le Chat Noir Cabaret, the Montmartre landmark that existed for sixteen years and, in promoting a populist view of art, literature, performance, and music, became a symbol of avant-garde bohemian life in Paris. In addition to the journal, the visual arts activities undertaken under the umbrella name Le Chat Noir, included illustrated books, posters, prints, and menus. Between 1881 and its final edition in March 1895, the weekly journal *Le Chat Noir* was distributed each Saturday.
4. This became "The Technical Tendencies of Caricature," *Alliance Review,* undated, unpaginated (YCAL, McBride).

1. "Dud" is Dudley Carpenter; see Biographical Sketches.

9 Henry McBride, c. 1903. Photographer unknown.

care for, but it died in the night. Two children on board, about the liveliest, nicest children I have met, helped in the sad burial at sea. It was just while the funeral was going on that the steamer was sighted and we hurried up the burial and galloped to the upper deck to see the ship. I haven't been sick. Others have. But the boat started out quietly and we had no real rolling until yesterday and we are somewhat used to it now. I thought—at first I never could stand the grub, but I am learning to pick something good out of each bill of fare. The dinners are good anyway. We have ice cream every night, strawberries, raisins and nuts. Our end of the table is the lively end and when we get to the raisins and figs, everyone gets enthusiastic and feels as if the real dinner was beginning. I have to quit, and I haven't mentioned Professor Smith nor even Mrs. Professor.

After dinner 9 p.m. We've been bawling songs up on deck at the tops of our lungs, the Doctor, the two Gowans and I. Boat is rolling and most of the passengers have disappeared. Had the rails on the dinner table for the first time. The captain promises we'll be out of the Arctic Current tomorrow morning. Captain is a charming, regular old sea dog. We have formed a betting pool. Everyone puts in one cent a day and bets on the days run. Some of the girls try to worm it out of the Captain, what the run will be, and he is very staunch in his desire not to give anything away. The Doctor is a young fellow—his first voyage at sea. He is a typical Englishman. Healthy, happy and good looking. He is great fun. He seems rather shy of American girls. Two very lively ones made rather violent love to him. The first night, one girl rose rather impulsively from her seat and sat down by the Doctor saying, "Oh Doctor, won't you read aloud to us, so we can learn your lovely accent?" Poor Doctor was much embarrassed. It is great fun to hear him tell anecdotes of Mrs. Professor. He sits at the head of the table and she on his right. Prof. and Mrs. Smith think they are the only ones on board. Professor is very learned and looks rather annoyed when anyone else enters the smoking room. In fact I made myself so unpleasant he several times pointedly arose and left at my entrance. But we have tacitly sworn peace, because we have discovered we both know Prof. Seligman. Mrs. Prof. even makes advances to me but she is almost more hated than the Professor. Crowds of us get together and tell all the mean things we can of them. But the Doctor's description of how Mrs. Prof. orders her dinner is our favorite diversion. We had a concert in the salon Sunday night and I sang "Old English Songs." Barbara Allen was my most successful one. Also sang my French song.

To Dudley Carpenter
June 26, 1902, London, "Coronation Day!"

Dear Dud:

I got down from Scotland safely yesterday. The trains had been crush full, but yesterday's was empty. It was a corridor train and comfortable but my neighbors were old fogies. One had been to China for years and insisted on telling me about it. If he looked round for a moment I pretended to be asleep, but if I opened an eye even for a second, clack, clack, clack, would go his tongue, like Jane Carlyle's woman. I never encountered such a conversationalist. I was afraid I might display greenness at the station but things were easy. I had engaged my room by telegraph so I piled bag and box and my new swell steamer rug, purchased in Glasgow, into a cab, and drove off. I felt quite grand rolling up to 44 Tavistock Square, which is leafy and green and much like Grammercy Park. It seemed odd to come 3000 miles and land in so similar a spot. The house is furnished in good taste, wide stairways and soft carpets and a French butler. My rooms look into the square. Comfortable big bed, big dressing tables, etc. During the while I washed off the railway dust, four different maids knocked on my door with summonses to dinner. I finally got excited and scrambled down. Dining room is large, with large banqueting table and really nicely decorated with flowers—artistically put together. The food was good but the astonishing thing was the way I was accepted. They took me immediately to their bosoms, particularly an English Gentleman and lady, papa and mama of an apparently matrimonially inclined young lady, who likes Americans. There was positively nothing the hostess wouldn't do for me, even sitting up till 1 a.m. to let me in! The fact is every room is engaged for the coronation—and the people are not showing up. So the lady frantically clutches at straws. But I'm going to move. I can't stand being watched. They pounce on every move I make. Two seats below me at table is a lady who might have been the woolly Miss Schwarz's aunt.

It is really stupid in London. There is nothing to do. The decorations are mostly down already and the Theatres have nothing new. In desperation I'm going again to Gay Lord Quex. Went last night to Charles Wyndham in *David Garrick*.[1] Not awfully good. I always thought he was a first rate actor. But he is not in John Drew's class at all. He is a sort of poor Richard Mansfield, actorish.

This morning I went to St. Paul's to see the people attend service who were to have attended the Coronation. I think there were some substitutions and they were not such a distinguished lot as they might have been. But Henry Irving was there, pale and interesting looking, and Sir Thomas Lipton, who tried not to look great and who seemed to even smell of

1. Sir Charles Wyndham (1838–1919) played the role of David Garrick more than one thousand times in England, the United States, Germany, and Russia. During this coronation year, Wyndham was knighted by King Edward.

tea, and the Duchess of Marlborough.[2] Those were all I recognized—but a handsome young man the crowd said was Prince Adolphus of Teck.[3] A number of people drove up in Royal Coaches, but they seemed to be of no consequence—probably gentlemen of the Back Stairway.

This afternoon I walked through the park to Buckingham Palace, but nothing was to be seen there. Piccadilly was great. One hardly moved at times. Streets were full of picturesque soldiers—but they, too, are departing in every direction. The general opinion seems to be, that when the King is crowned it won't be much of a ceremonial now. I want to linger in town until Kitchener returns.[4] That will be something—but I am afraid I can't stand London so long as that. Besides it is expensive. If I go on spending at this rate, I will have to leave Italy out all together. I can't get my mail till Saturday as today and Friday are holidays.

To Dudley Carpenter
July 3, 1902, London, Hotel Metropole

Dear Dud:

W.M. has some swell friends in this hotel and I can't resist the stationary. I am tired. Been taking him around, showing him the Tower etc., which was very fatiguing. It was fun going about with those Boston fellows but after all it is a poor use of time. The Music Hall business is never exciting to me. Our dinner at the Trocadero was swell. We laughed hilariously at nothing at all, sent our cards to the leader of the band and had him play things we liked etc. We got terribly chummy by midnight and

2. Sir Henry Irving (1838–1905), born John Henry Brodribb, was an English actor and theater impresario who in 1878 founded and managed London's Lyceum Theatre. A close friend of Bram Stoker's for more than thirty years, Sir Henry is considered a source for Stoker's most famous character, Count Dracula.

Sir Thomas Lipton (1850–1931) was a British merchant and purveyor of Lipton, Ltd, who entered the tea market in 1890. In 1902 the invention of the tea bag was still two years off. Lipton introduced his ubiquitous teas to the United States market in 1909.

3. The Teck family married directly into the house of Windsor. Mary of Teck was the wife of George V, and mother of Edward VIII and King George VI.

4. Horatio Herbert Kitchener (1850–1916), the first Earl Kitchener of Khartoum, was a British field marshall most famous as a great imperial general who commanded British forces in the Boer War (1899–1902). He was then made commander in chief of the British Indian army. Made secretary of state for war during World War I, Kitchener was killed on his way to meet with Czar Nicholas of Russia when his boat hit a German mine off the Orkney Islands.

those of the party, who were going to Paris—thought I ought to join them. They all wore silk hats, frock coats and yellow gloves. One of the men knew Jeanne Langtry and his sister had been bride's maid at her wedding the day before. He saw Miss Langtry before the affair and said she was wildly excited. She had just received an exquisite diamond pin from the King with a letter written in his own hand, very shaky, beginning "My dear Jeanne." This may be stale news when it gets to you—but here it is not yet known that the King has actually written a letter.

The Queen and the Princess of Wales sat in their carriage at the review with the Princesses Maud and Victoria facing them.[1] All looked very handsome indeed. The Queen wore pale mauve with light gray—a remnant of mourning for the Queen—but they say one reason she mourns so for the Queen is that pale mauve is so becoming.[2] The Princess of Wales looked ambitious, but the other Princesses didn't. I was afraid they were going to snicker, they seemed in such a giggly state—but fortunately they didn't. The Prince of Wales was frightened, or looked so. His retinue of Crown Princes was most imposing. Earl Roberts was much cheered and so was the Duke of Connaught. He is very popular and very good looking. It is wonderful how familiar all these people are to one. I knew each one instantly and even from a distance.

A popular way of seeing processions is to line up along the route on horseback. Hundreds of swells did so. Back of me was an American girl: very good form, except that she talked a little too much to her groom, à la Daisy Miller. Beside her were two very plainly dressed women attended by a magnificent officer of the guards. He was the real thing. Suddenly in a quite distinct voice he said to the most severely dressed woman, "Oh my dear Lady Gaypuss, I really think you— etc." Everyone caught the "Lady . . ." and turned about and gave breathless attention after that to the conversation. The American girl seemed positively to stiffen in her saddle. When the Queen came along however, the American girl twisted her horse quite into the front row and poor Lady G. and her companion had to look over her shoulder.

Willie is going to dine at the Metropole. I've been fooling around and felt too dirty to go to the Humanitarian Tea. I'll go out to the Salt's Saturday.

1. Queen Alexandra was the wife of Edward VII, who had been king for less than six months, since the death of his mother, Queen Victoria, on January 22, 1901.
2. Queen Victoria died January 22, 1901, after reigning nearly sixty-five years. The Victorian era, which more than any other defined the nineteenth century, died with her.

Had a nice letter from them. They talk of the Englishman's tub as though it were a virtue. One never is clean here. It is worse than Pittsburgh. I scrub all the visible portions of my anatomy six times a day in addition to the ordinary two baths. I may go to *Paola and Francesca* tonight although I know it is n.g. I tried to get into *Merry Wives of Windsor* the other night, but didn't like to stand up, so went across the way to *Caste*. It was splendidly done and Marie Tempest is fine. She is artistic all the way through and a thorough comedienne. I haven't met any really intelligent people and so haven't encountered any one who has appreciated her. The people of the boarding house are bourgeois and the bourgeois in England are about the slowest ever. Gertrude Elliott was nice in *Mice and Men*. The play is pretty but a little amateurish at times. Not nearly so good as Robert Marshall's. Too bad they are not playing *Iris*. Really I've had tough luck all around in my London ventures. Am getting anxious to shake the soot from my heels. Will leave next Tuesday most likely.

I suppose the familiar references to Royalty in the early part of this letter will make you tired, but the English expressions I have picked up will make you tireder still. I am to be taken down the river to see some fellow's grand country house Monday. Hope to get to Hampton Court tomorrow. [. . .]

To Mary and Maria Pugh
August 2, 1902, Limbourg, Dolhain[1]

Chère Cousines:

I won't have time to tell you the sixth of what has happened in the last two days so it will be one thing to tell about, when I get home. We are just back from the great automobile race at Ardennes.[2] It was the most extraordinary affair I have ever seen, I think. We would never have gone nor have heard of it, had it not been for the Misses Centner, the two ladies who

1. McBride was on an extended stay in Belgium at the family home, called La Pépinière, of a friend named Charles, about whom little is known. The family home was based in Limbourg, but trips were made during the course of McBride's visit to the nearby cities of Antwerp and Brussels. McBride, Charles, and another friend, Andre, completed an extended walking tour across the moors to Spa and on to Cologne at the end of July.

2. Auto racing was becoming a popular pastime for the leisure class. The Le Mans automobile race was established in 1906. The allure of cars for the rich was in direct conflict with the general impression of the gizmo as a "terror creating machine." The speed limit for automobiles in London in 1903 was set at twenty miles per hour. In cities like Antwerp animals set the speed limits, and cars were prohibited from outrunning horse-drawn carriages.

speak English. The Centners are a most lively family, great friends of the Malis, and the girls are absolutely the strongest girls I have ever met. They are stronger than Mary Pugh by a long way. It may be they are not so much stronger than Miss Pugh—but they are trained athletes and know how to use their strength. In addition they are travelled and clever and witty— altogether great in fact. They came over and suggested the expedition. Their brother and his party went in automobiles starting at one a.m. and travelling all night, reaching the scene at 8 a.m. We started at six a.m. from Limbourg and got to Spa at eleven a.m. We had each little sacks for night things and for lunch, and from Spa started on a twelve mile walk, over the mountains, to another railway, which would take us to Bastogne. The Misses Centner went like the wind—we did the twelve miles in less than three hours and Charles and I were nearly dead—Charles especially, who had a nail in his boot. Long before the train got to Bastogne, queer looking people in automobile clothes, began to appear and when the train finally stopped at the station, the air was thick with the racket from hundreds of autos, cries of waiters at the hotel and people dashing around. We got ex- cited too, on the instant. People said not a bed nor pillow was to be had for love or money, but we boldly walked into one little Inn that looked decent and demanded lodging. The man looked at us as if we were crazy and replied that every inch he had, had been taken weeks ago. We had a consul- tation and the Misses Centner said they would rather sleep on the grass there at the hotel, than go twenty miles away and be comfortable. Charles and I, who were too tired to move another step, agreed with them. Then the Misses Centner had an idea; they asked to see the barn. In a moment they came back saying the hay was fine and would do magnificently and they told the garçon they would take it. The cook and the servants, who over- heard, were scandalized to think that ladies of such distinction should be put to such an outrageous inconvenience and one old man said "Tenez." He knew there were two little rooms in the police station, that he could fix up for us, if we would agree to dine at his hotel. Of course, we agreed, as we had determined to dine at that hotel anyhow—it seemed to be *the* place. So they fixed three beds on the floor for Charles, Mr. Centner and I, and the girls were squeezed into another room. We were quite comfortable and pitied the poor Dukes and Duchesses, who were paying high prices to sleep on sofas. We got in at the first table at the table d'hôte, and had the pleasure of eating a fine dinner, while hungry mortals peered in the windows and doors waiting for their turn. The people were the queerest of the world, strange types from St. Petersburg, London, Paris, New York; nobility, millionaires, sporting men, all crowded around the table d'hôte of the village inn. Outside the noises were worse than ever. A French Kirmess was making rachety music, and the fakirs and merry go rounds were thick. Racing autos were dashing along the course, testing their machines, and every moment some one would just escape a violent death. It reminded me of the night before the battle of Waterloo in Vanity Fair.

The race was to be 350 miles long and was to begin at 5 a.m., so it could be finished by noon. The course was about sixty miles in a circle, so each racer would have to go six times around. Vanderbilt, Zborovsky (of NY) and all the famous racers of the world were entered and also many new machines of 70 horse power, that were expected to make new records. Charles and I were afraid we might not get up in time—but there was no difficulty. As early as three a.m. the racket in the village street was great as that of Broadway at midday. We were eating our breakfast 4:20 a.m. and so were in plenty of time to see the start of Baron de Crawhez. Every minute there were fresh starters and fresh cries of "Attention, Attention," and fresh narrow escapes of foolish people who would always be in the way. Vanderbilt was number 76 and had not started at ten minutes of six, when there were cries that Crawhez was coming like a flash over the hill in the distance, having gone the sixty miles in less than an hour. He came with incredible speed past our station, his man shooting off pistols to warn the people of his approach and disappeared in a great cloud of dust on his second round. A moment after, young Vanderbilt started on his first round. I never saw anything so exciting. In a few moments No. 28 appeared having passed all the intervening numbers between itself and No. 1. After that something was doing every minute. One of the great racers was passing, or one of the racers was being killed, or two of the machines were colliding. It was odd how quickly we recognized the great racers. On the first round we all picked out the autos, that were to make the chief struggle. Where were the two people I wished to have with me—two people who I thought would appreciate the affair—Genevieve Peats and Uncle Caleb?[3]

We hung to the last moment to the race and so were late at lunch. I wish you could have seen our companions at the table. The racers lunched with us, some without having removed the dust and the wrinkles that the strain had put into their faces. The waiters all lost their heads and the confusion in the hotel was absolute. We waited and waited. The Baron de Caters, who

3. Genevieve Peats was a cousin of McBride's who lived in Greenwich, Connecticut; Caleb Pugh was the father of Maria and Mary Pugh, all of whom lived in McBride's house, Callicaste, in Marshallton, Pennsylvania.

10 Henry McBride, Caleb Pugh, and Genevieve Peats, c. 1905. Photographer unknown.

holds the world's record for short distances and is a splendid fellow, sat next to me. He got tired of the delay and finally, winking to us, took a soup plate and went to the kitchen. He came back immediately with it full and ate it calmly, but with intense satisfaction. Then he seized another plate and raided the kitchen again coming back with chicken and asparagus. At the sight the rest of us were roused to fury and about ten of us rushed to the kitchen. The cooks shrieked, the waiters in despair cried "Bonne volonte," "Bonne volonte," but we got our grub—or at least I got sufficient for our party. Others fared less well. Young Vanderbilt only got scraps. He is quite a fine young fellow and raced magnificently and didn't put on airs afterwards. We were quite proud of the two Americans and all our party out of politeness to me cheered them as they passed each time. The race being so far away, and starting in such a little village, made it all the finer as a spectacle. It was not the ordinary crowd. Every person there was of a type— many of them "chic" types. We of course knew all the swells and were "in it." Automobiles were going about to points of interest and returning with the news and had command of everything that was going.

We started home at six p.m. and stopped for an hour at Gouvy to change trains. There the same raid occurred on the kitchen as in Bastogne—only I led the rush instead of the Baron de Caters. It was immense fun. We got to Limbourg at midnight and C. and I slept until midday the next day. [. . .]

To Dudley Carpenter
June 1905, London, Carlton Hotel

Dear Dud:

[. . .] Part of this fatigue is due to Mary Peddle, who insists on showing me the town and as I naturally squeeze in a few events of my own the result is exhaustion.[1] The straw that broke the camel's back was the Ascot on Thursday. It is the great fashionable race of the year and I went with the Meehan boys. It was a glorious day but hot as the etc. I had breakfasted on air and tea and was ready for food when I got there, but starving as I was, I could not touch the stuff exposed for sale. Then too one was privileged to wander over the enclosure and see the nobility lunching grandly under their marquees with champagne and pâté de foie gras. I fled the moment the gold cup had been won and got a sandwich and a mug of ale at the station at four p.m. I really haven't caught up since.

The royal procession was very spectacular and we stood opposite the King and Queen most of the time. Great fun to see the Royal recognitions and the way various people took them. The gowns of the ladies were magnificent and the men were wonderfully turned out. I enjoy these open air affairs more than anything else I see—the cricket at Lords, the Ascot, and the tennis tournament at the Queens Club yesterday, for the London Championship, have been my chief events. Not so much the sport end of it as the chance to see the nicer of the English off their guard. And they are nice! Their manners are so delightful and their voices so charming, one imagines oneself in the Elysian Fields or some other refined world. The Americans won—but they had a difficult fight. The tennis was swift. After the Ascot Thursday I chased away to town, dressed, dined (it required some courage for me at first to walk along the streets in broad daylight (7 p.m.) in evening dress, the way they do here, sans overcoat, sans hat even. Going to parties and stowing away hats and coats is a nuisance—so many men go from one place to another without either), and went to the party in the studio of Miss Falk, and the sculptor Marshall, I think—out Chelsea way. Well there's no room to tell about it nor about my mash on Lady Wolseley—but you'll hear more of her . . . ta, ta. [. . .]

1. Mary Peddle was a mutual friend of McBride's and Dudley Carpenter's.

To Dudley Carpenter
July 4, 1905, Paris

Dear Dud:

Saw your letter on the floor when I arose from my couch at ten a.m. diesen morgen. First letter from America! I began to think there was no America . . . Am waiting at Credit Lyonnais for some money and it seems one way to pass the time is to write. It is hotter'n'Jno Walk's future home here. So hot one doesn't like to do anything—only be mad all the time.

Went to the opera last night and was delighted. Gluck's *Armide*. It was the most satisfactory performance of opera I have seen in years. Gorgeously mounted. Everything so solid and such stunning effects. *Parsifal* à la Conried nowhere. The music always beautiful and sung far better then I expected. They did it in such a simple way and usually at a breathless tempo, that gave lots of swing. Breval was the tragic heroine—almost too tragic. The house was full. I treated myself to a downstairs seat. During the evening the people in the largest box, just over my head, talked so loudly I turned round to look reprovingly at them. One lady in the center, who happened not to be talking (she had her back to the stage of course) caught my look and seemed to be reminded by it, that she was not doing her duty as hostess and lazily turned still further from the stage and started a conversation still louder than the others. It dawned on me who she was. She was our old friend Anna, Comtesse Boni de Castellane. After that, I watched her as much as Armide. At the end of the act the Comtesse and her guests arose, as did everyone else. One of the men stepped to the front of the loge and glared straight at me. It was Freddy Baldwin, a fellow I know slightly, but dislike much. I dislike him for one thing, because he is so superior. If *I* were to appear in the box of a Comtesse, he would appear in King Edward's or somewhere still more chic, if there be such a place.

The Opera in London is nowhere. The audience of course is far more swell—wonderfully gowned women and stunning men—but the stage management could be done as well in Embreeville. (Perhaps better now that the School of Art is there) . . .

July 5, 1905, To night I go to the Comédie Française to see Le Bargy in the *Duel*—which I have read of. It is a great success. Was disappointed not to be able to read the book. It is not yet published . . . I am tired of Paris. Never did I like it very much. Too much trouble to learn the ropes. Once learned, and with some acquaintance of course, it would be easier. But it is horrid alone. Last night I went to the Jardin de Paris. Supposed to be

American Celebration (July 4th). I didn't notice anything American. It bored me on the whole. The chief bore was the continually saying "No" to the ladies, who were incessantly bothering one. Some of them were amusing to watch, only one *couldn't* watch them, or they'd be after you in a flash. It really seems to me a stranger is not hounded quite so much in New York. In the crowd, watching four undoubtedly French ladies doing the fameux Can-Can—one extravagantly dressed American woman got separated from her husband. She cried to him across my shoulder, "Come on Jim, I don't want to be one of 'em." It struck me as funny. Particularly as she did look rather like "one of 'em."

Another thing pleased me at the Opéra. During an entr'acte on a balcony, I heard some Americans, girls and boys, holding forth about Napoléon and things French in general. When the bell sounded and we rushed for our seats, I held the door for them to pass through, and they all cried, "Messy, Monsieur," to me. Of course it wasn't funny, except that the only people who ever mistake me for French are my own countrymen. [. . .]

To Mary and Maria Pugh
July 15, 1905, Pont Aven, France, Hôtel Julia

Chère Cousines:

Dud can tell you what July 15 means. It means "the day after." July 14 was the great day in Pont-Aven. There was a continuous performance from early in the morning till long after I had gone to bed. Two curious musicians, on the order of bag-pipers, mounted two hogsheads in the open market, in the morning and at intervals there were gavottes all day. There were contests of boys getting pennies off of swinging disks, which were covered with pitch (to which pennies were stuck), by their tongues. Boys up on barrels, blindfolded would try to feed each other thick cream—getting it generally in the neck. Then crowds of young men in the river fought to catch ducks, which the mayor flung out from his boat. The old women (about Aunt Merab's age) ran sack races.[1] The old ladies cheated, I am sorry to say. Got their feet through holes and simply ran. They were made to run over again. Then there was the Gavotte of honor at six p.m., the square and illuminations, fireworks, etc. in the evening.

[. . .] Tomorrow, Sunday there is to be a village "pardon" some miles from here and everyone here seems to be going. I am not keen on it, it is

1. Aunt Merab was an African-American woman who worked as a domestic in Marshallton.

such fun here. Still I'll go if I can, I suppose. The "pardon" takes place once in seven years—processions, dances around fires, I don't know what—and wonderful Breton costumes.

A musician and poet named Berthot was here last night. Very handsome fellow, wearing Breton costume. His face was placarded all over Paris on the Kiosks, in one of the magazines. He is organizing a fête to try to revive interest in the old Breton costumes—so he had the village girls at the hotel last night—and they arranged their part in the fete, elected a queen, etc. Then they sang his songs. M. Berthot sang a number himself—exquisitely, and then we all danced Breton gavottes. Great fun. Berthot would be a great success in American should he tour. He makes the meaning perfectly clear even to those who don't speak French. The girls all wear Breton caps and costumes and they are very nice girls. The village is almost owned by the English and Americans, though. The French people in the hotel hardly cut a figure.

Julia owns an annex at the mouth of the river, quite new but built like a monastery. It is a fine place and the food is great. The water is wonderful in color. The only nuisance is the crowd of artists. I have never heard of any of 'em. At the "Gloanee," the Bohemian hotel, there is the oddest lot of 'em. One small boy has long fuzzy hair, little side whiskers, pale face, and a watch chain with about a million bangles of different sorts. He has six pupils, all as silly as himself, and they plant themselves in the middle of everything (even yesterday they were interfering with everything, continually in the way), yet they never make any sketches that one can see. They look as though gotten up for one of our Charades. [. . .]

To Dudley Carpenter
July 20, 1905, Tours, France

Dear Dud:

At the famous Hôtel de L'Univers! When one is paying $7 per day one spends one's time in doing something besides letter writing—but I'll begin it on the famous hotel's writing paper and if necessary finish it in some cheaper clime. I suppose you have never heard of it (don't writhe—no necessity for peevishness). But among the books I glanced at, the week before sailing, to prepare myself for foreign travel, was St. James' *Little Tour in France*. I opened it in the middle at a Rhapsody on Balzac, Tours, and this hotel. He said the head-waiter was the most accomplished human being, socially, he had ever met.[1] Consequently, among all the hazy ideas of what I might do in Europe this summer, there was one constant idée fixe—that I should meet that Prince of head-waiters. Well I am here. My tour may be said to be at its height. The Hotel is all Henry said it was, outwardly—but alas the prince of head-waiters has lost his job. At least the "person" who officiated in that capacity last night cannot be said to be accomplished socially, what ever Henry James may say. In the first place he looks like any other waiter only worse. He has no waist, and no waist-coat worth mentioning. His garments look as though rented for the occasion. He is for all the world like the garçon de Paris that Forain draws with three strokes of a pen.[2] The only test of his savoir-faire during the evening was when my own waiter dropped a serving spoon. A look of wild anguish passed over the countenance of the "prince." A head waiter of any social tact, under the circumstances, I think, if noticing the incident at all, would have displayed merely amused toleration. My own waiter had far more grace. I conversed with him fluently during the dinner in elegant French, and anyone who can converse with me in elegant French, had all the social ability necessary.

The dinner itself was very good, I suppose, although I only touched it here and there. I was absolutely exhausted and too tired to eat. I had travelled ever since 7:20 in the morning from Pont-Aven, with a stop of three hours in Nantes for a bad luncheon. I saw the Cathedral there and the Chateau and sent Mary a post card and then went on with my railroad.[3] It was a very hot ride, but the Loire was a very satisfactory river to ride with. It was always paintable—but seemed very familiar. I suppose I have seen so many pictures of it. Tours is a cunning little place. I didn't expect much of it, last night. I walked a little after dinner and then sat down outside a café where there was music. The place seemed so flat, and flat places rarely seem artistic! But walking about in the old part of town today, I have changed my mind. There is some variety, gotten from the

1. "There was one waiter in especial who was the most accomplished social being I have ever encountered; from morning till night he kept up an inarticulate murmur of urbanity, like the hum of a spinning top." Henry James, *A Little Tour in France* (New York: Farrar, Straus, and Giroux), 1983, p. 5. Note that James does not specify the waiter he describes as being a head-waiter.
2. Jean-Louis Forain (1852–1931) worked in the style of Degas and showed in four impressionist exhibitions. Famous as a satirist and printmaker, Forain made a living contributing cartoons to Parisian magazines.
3. The cathedral in Nantes was begun in 1434 and finished toward the end of the century. The late Gothic chateau dates from the sixteenth century. The historic residence of the dukes of Brittany, the chateau was bought, with the rest of the province, by the Duchess Anne as her dowry to Charles VIII.

crooked, narrow streets. They are tearing things down as fast as they can, and the Ancient Tower of Charlemagne, which is the thing my guide book makes the most fuss over, was plastered all over, at the base, with advertisements.[4] A thing like that shocks an American.

The Cathedral is stunning. About the most satisfactory I have seen. Not so large, but charming from every point and gives one the reverent feeling. The glass windows are beautiful and there are lots of 'em. Everywhere you turn upon some wonderful window. I had been walking steadily some hours, so sat down, to read my guide book and do my cathedral leisurely. There were some devout people on the centre aisles saying their prayers. Suddenly they stood up, and I too, for the gorgeous beadle was leading a bridal procession up the aisle. I stayed for the entire show. It was very pretty, and the organ accompaniment very well done. One new feature to me, was the collection of an offertory by the brides-maids, who were led about by the groomsmen, hand-in-hand. They had little boxes covered with ribbons and flowers in which, those requested dropped coins. The brides-maids looked very bewitching as they did it, though they didn't come to me . . . The collection may have explained the sparse attendance. I wondered what it was for. [. . .]

I did up the rest of Tours yesterday afternoon in about an hour and a half. The Musée (marked *important*) was a junk shop. A Mantegna was curious, but not wonderful. The things "envoi par l'État" were terrors. "Purchased by the Government" isn't much of a compliment after all. At three I was on the river front with nothing to do. Some dirty looking affairs floating near the bank, pretended to be swimming schools. I asked a dirty looking urchin, which he preferred, and he pointed out the dirtiest of the three as being the most enticing. On the other side of the river on a little island I suddenly saw a respectable place. A real beach and fellows racing around in the open air. I made for it of course and had a pleasant swim. Although the sun was so hot, one couldn't stay in the water as long as one does in the Brandywine. If I get back from Chenonceaux this afternoon in time I shall have another dip. It is an excellent appetizer, although I dare say, the Loire is pure poison. Marvelous to me that these rivers keep so apparently pure with all the washing of clothes that is done in them.

The guests in this hotel are the limit. As freaks they are as fine as the bohemian artists of Pont-Aven, only they are good old Americans. To do

4. The Tour de l'Horloge, the cathedral, and the Tour Charlemagne were the great landmarks of Tours that a visitor would surely seek out. The two towers (only one remains today) marked the site of the ruins of Abbey of Saint Martin, at one time the most important pilgrimage church in France.

them justice I have to admit that some of the worst of them would not seem so bad at home. There are six women being chaperoned by a queer looking man and his wife. All the six are as different from each other as possible, and to see them sitting at table together, in family intimacy, gives me a sensation every time I see them. Everyone except the chaperoned crowd and myself own an automobile. [. . .]

Dinner last night was really bully. I wear my white ducks evenings, Tours style. All the Americans dress for dinner. Because the fellow in *The Lightening Conductor* did, I suppose.[5] All these motor-car people are copying *The Lightening Conductor* in every detail.

P.S. No. 3 After lunch . . . they tell me now there's no train to Chenonceaux in the afternoons! Well, I'll go to Langeais instead. I thought to have skipped it—it was all done over, furnished throughout à la Mrs. Jack Gardner by a rich banker, who allows people to inspect.[6] I have set my heart on Chenonceaux, so I shall stay over a day for it . . . It is difficult to make the railroads suit a program like mine.

Tours is quite an elegant town. It is a garrison town for one thing. But then so is Paris and the officers and soldiers are ever so much smarter here. The type is more open-air, less blasé. One feels that one would be willing to know most of the people one meets on the streets . . . Then the café I frequent in the evenings has quite an air. And the chartreuse! We don't have chartreuse chez nous—it is varnish.

To Dudley Carpenter and Mary and Maria Pugh
July 30, 1905, Grand Hôtel de Paris, Madrid

Dear (whose ever turn it is—I forget):[1]

If I were at home I should be making a fuss over the weather—but I was lead to believe Madrid was so dreadful, that I have gotten in a state of being

5. Charles Norris Williamson (1859–1920) and A. M. Williamson, *The Lightning Conductor: The Strange Adventures of a Motor-Car* (New York: Holt, 1903).

6. Isabella Stewart Gardner (1840–1924), a bohemian, eccentric, and rich collector whose home in Boston, Fenway Court, now houses the Isabella Stuart Gardner Museum. Both Mrs. Gardner and her husband, Jack Gardner (d. 1898), came from blue blood, wealthy merchant families. Called "Boston's pre-cinema star" by her art adviser, Bernard Berenson, Isabella Stuart Gardner traveled the world collecting exotic, valuable, and rare paintings, sculpture, and decorative arts from all countries and periods. In twenty-five years she amassed more than twenty-five thousand objects from the ancient to the modern.

1. McBride's early travel letters were addressed in rotation and then shared between his cousins and Dudley.

disappointed in its being bearable at all.[2] I suppose the thermometer in the streets would be about 115 fahrenheit—still people are not dropping in their tracks. I feel rather gay myself. To be sure I am in good condition, thanks to a week's sea bathing, still I have been through an ordeal getting here. [. . .]

There is always an agonizing time catching trains for you never can tell whether to believe the hotel people or not. I have a little railroad guide and usually know the route better than the railroad people themselves. I got off at Burgos at 1:15 and walked straight for the cathedral. Two little boys bothered me continually pointing to things and pretending to be my guide. I'd look always at the opposite thing they pointed to, but they kept up a continual wail for alms—like buzzing wasps. After I had seen everything a man appeared to act as guide and chased the boys away—but I wasn't sure he was the real guide either, so gave him nothing. All are beggars and thieves apparently. While in the cathedral one of the usual horrible Spanish beggars appeared with bad boy cries in the distance. Soon he made a little run out at his tormentors and returned followed by a volley of pebbles. Local color. The beggars are outrageous. Drinking some chocolate at the swellest café of Burgos in the afternoon I was assailed by all the dirty children in the town. They would watch chances and dash in to where I was, behind the fence, shed a few tears to show how dreadfully they needed cash and then be chased out by the waiter. One little girl, with a nasty little baby in her arms, managed to get within besieging distance more than a dozen times. All this time the town had been bathed in the white glare of the sun. I raised my blue glasses once just to see how light the sun was—but I lowered them p.d.q.

In the evening all was different. All the town crowded to the boulevard and walked up and down and the cavalry band played. It played Anitras Dance, while I listened. And then at quarter to ten I set off down the road, under the trees to the station. It was very dark and I could scarcely see my way, for the first time I had the feeling of being far from home. Occasionally a form stirred in the shadow of a tree, but it didn't reassure me any. But I got to the station and got my train and rode all night in the sleeper. It was absolutely unventilated, the apartment, and boiling hot—still I slept. At seven, Madrid! The usual fearful struggle over luggage with beggars—in

2. McBride told a reporter for *The Times:* "My journey through Spain was begun with some trepidation. Everywhere I was warned against the difficulties that would confront the traveller in that country." Unidentified clipping, "Prof. McBride Sees Spanish Bull Fight: Has Some Experience With Grafting Officials and Other Doing Abroad" (YCAL, McBride).

which my tennis racket came in handily. I bang the wrong porters with the racket handle! At seven thirty the hotel—my room—chocolate and bread and butter—hot water and a bath and clean white ducks and a new London tie—then ho, for the Prado Musée.

I know the streets and the buildings without asking questions—thanks to Baedeker: It seems a pity that any one in the world should miss seeing those pictures. The Velázquez gallery actually goes ahead of expectations. *The Weavers, The Surrender of Breda,* the *Mars,* the *Drinkers!*[3] I looked at them until my eyes ached trying to memorize everything. I shall go every day, while here of course. The *Meninas* is in a room apart, where one can sit in the shadow and watch Velázquez painting the little princess and her maids. It seems to have every perfection of technique. It must be the most wonderful piece of realism in the world.[4] The figures seem really in atmosphere. Every piece of silk or still life is realized exactly and nothing seems too much so. Velázquez isn't all there is to the Prado either. Such Titians, Rubens, Tintorettos. More Titians, I almost think, than in Venice, Van Dyke, Ribera, Goyas, Murillo (I hurried out of the Murillo room—I can't control my prejudices).[5] Even Raphael and Rembrandt and Watteau masterpieces. Wonderful Holbeins, that beautiful picture Dürer made of himself in the gondolier hat—stunning Moros, etc., etc.[6] . . . I hope I can buy some good photos.

Monday, July 31, 1905 . . . Well I suppose you've got to have a description of the bull-fight. I don't feel quite well today and whether it was the horrors of the arena or drinking too much Insalus water, I can't say, but I am not in the real humor for recalling anything sickening. Bull-fighting is sickening. It quite turns the gorge (as Stevenson says) of an American.

3. *The Weavers,* by Diego Rodríguez de Silva y Velázquez (1599–1660) is now known as *The Fable of Arachne* or *Dispute Between Pallas and Arachne.* In 1905 it was more commonly known as *The Spinners.* Variously dated, it is listed as 1644–48 in the catalogue raisonné. The painting was heavily restored, with details added, in the eighteenth century. The painting called the *Drinkers* by McBride may be *Bacchus,* c. 1628–29.
4. McBride's appreciative eye for the realism of Velázquez later served as a basis for his eloquently argued support of the greatness of the American realist Thomas Eakins (1844–1916).
5. Bartolomé Esteban Murillo (1618–82) is best known for two types of painting, sentimental genre scenes of peasant children and softly rendered canvases of pious and devotional subject matters.
6. Albrecht Dürer (1471–1528), *Self-Portrait,* 1498. The panel is inscribed "1498. I painted it as I was at the age of 26. Albrecht Dürer." Dürer portrays himself elegantly and fashionably dressed, as a dandy of his time.

You have read of it all, I think, how the bulls are tormented and kept in darkness until they are in a state of frenzy and just before being released, an irritating little dart with the Spanish ribbons is stuck in their side. As the door opens, they fairly bound into the arena. The audience applauds him as though he were a great actor and then the fellows with the cloaks begin teasing him. He plunges at them only to plunge into the cloak. The spears-men on horses have their turn and nine times out of ten the bull kills the horse. Sometimes, as yesterday, tossing horse and rider over head. The horses used in this part of the combat are old broken down cobs—the kind we in refined America, use on street car lines. Their eyes are bandaged. When they have been knocked down two or three times and horned by the bull they are forced to their feet and made to do duty for another stab at the bull before they receive their coup-de-grâce. Shall I tell you something really awful? Well one poor horse yesterday was ripped open by the bull and his entrails protruded to a size larger than a man's head—but he was forced to his feet, the saddle tightened, and the spearsman forced him forward for another attack on the bull. That was one horror. Every conceivable other distraction of the kind occurred yesterday. The fight was three parts. This, in which the horseman figures and which the Spanish seem to like best—I suppose, because the bull is then at his liveliest. Then the banderillos are stuck in the beast's neck, pronged sticks that flop as the bull moves and must be frightfully painful to him. Finally the matador comes out and with his reddest cloak of all, proceeds to hypnotize the animal. Finally, when he gets him exactly as he wants him, he plunges his sword with a light graceful movement over the horns and down through the ribs to the heart. Sometimes the bull lasts a moment or two longer, sometimes he drops to earth instantly. Then the dead horses and the dead bull are dragged out, the sand sprinkled over the blood and the matador makes the circle bowing his acknowledgments. His admirers throw him cigars, anything they have. Hundreds throw their hats to him, which the assistants carefully pick up and fling back.

There are no waits. Before the matador is halfway around bowing and smirking, a new bull is wildly dashing out to the ring, and the different attendants scatter on the double quick to jump the fences. I don't want to lay the horrors on too thickly, still there was one more I must mention. Two bulls, at the second stage of their fight, instead of ordinary "bandarillos" had exploding bandarillos stuck into them. At that moment I should certainly have left the place had I been alone, but I was with a party from the hotel and had to stay it out.

Tuesday, August 1, 1905 . . . I am more refined than I had supposed. I am still a bit shaken up from the bull fight. At least I suppose it is that. Ever since I have been dying to get out of Madrid, but the trains are so awkward. I must wait over a whole day and travel all night to Seville. It takes an enormous lot of physical exertion to travel. One is either riding all night or going without one's meals or worse, having to eat bad ones en route. Between now and Saturday I am to see Seville and Granada. Córdova I must miss. It is an all day journey from Seville to Granada and an all day trip to Gibraltar. Short distances, too, apparently. [. . .]

To Mary and Maria Pugh
August 12, 1905, Tangier, Morocco[1]

Chère Cousines:

I am actually beginning to think I'm glad I missed the Princess Irene. Tangier is the most extraordinary place I have seen. If I go to the centre of China, I know I shall not seem more foreign than I do here. These filthy Moors are primitif—they haven't changed for a thousand years their habits (nor their clothes, by the looks of 'em) and you can't beat that in China.

We had the sort of landing the guide books describe yesterday. It all seems so unnecessarily inconvenient that one imagines it arranged for the comedy effect. Many people were scared to death (including a young shop-keeper from Gibraltar, who kindly volunteered to guide me through the ordeal), but as for me I roared with laughter all through the performance. There are no docks so the steamer stops out in deep water and is immediately surrounded by Moorish boatmen, who take passengers ashore. The sea was rough yesterday (it generally is I believe) and the boats bounce up and down on the waves and you really think each Moor and passenger is going to be flung overboard. My guide and I got off in the second boat—most of the passengers holding back to see how we fared. I would have given anything to have had Mary Pugh along. I would have loved to have seen her getting into the boat. One fellow, a priest was wet to the knees by a wave while waiting his turn, and the same fellow was splashed by a wave whilst in the boat. At the pier, there was a wild shouting mob of beggars

1. In 1904 England and France signed the Entente Cordiale (literally, "cordial understanding"), in which, among other agreements, France's long-term policy of "peaceful penetration" in Morocco was left intact. In 1906 Germany tried to place itself as a "protector" of Moroccan independence, and the first steps were taken toward world war.

and Moors, who try to get your luggage from you. My Gib friend walked to the hotel with me, carrying my bag. The only other way was to ride a little donkey and it seemed too sudden to immediately mount one of them—so I walked. The hotel is fine—such a comfort after the horrible affairs in Gib and I ate a good meal for the first time in a week. Pure white marble stairways, big rooms, lovely Moorish crockery, rugs, etc., everywhere.

Last evening before dinner and again this morning I went up to the great market place, where there are thousands of Moors of every kind, all crowded together, selling their produce, live cattle, chickens, everything. Each merchant squatting under his measly little ragged tent. People pushing through on donkeys, camels arriving from the desert laden with rugs, etc. Horrible beggars, who follow a foreigner everywhere, calling aloud to their kinsmen, because you don't give. Foolish fellows, who if they catch your eye, immediately perform some silly antic and claim pay for the performance. Snakecharmers, water sellers, the call of the muezzin to prayer— the whole business pushing right up against you all the time. All these people are in the most ragged of filthy brown garments and it was a hardship at first to have them come near—but there is no help for it—sometimes the only way you can get by, is to take a heavily laden donkey by the hindquarters and push him till you squeeze past. There is one specially repellent old woman, who leads an awful blind man about and who thinks she has some claim against my estate. She has a tin wash-basin for offerings, which she holds under my chin and if I walk fast the other direction she runs too, pulling the old blind man, who stumbles and cries, and everyone thinks how awful I am not to give. Yesterday this old woman, together with two strenuous boys, who have an aged cripple in tow, got me in a narrow street and I couldn't get by until I had taken 'em by the shoulders and pushed them out of my way. But I hate to touch them.

Occasionally you see the grander Moors. They are usually in white robes and give one the impression they are about to burst forth in song. They remind me of Aida, Lohengrin and other operatic people. There is a fine terrace at the hotel built right upon the beach. Wishing to clear my lungs a bit before going to dinner, I went out there—but a procession of six or eight swell Moors got in ahead of me and snapped up the choice seats. They have a way of appearing to be interested in things that are not visible to ordinary mortals that reminds me sometimes of Ivanowski. Two of 'em were entertained at luncheon by a Frenchman and I noticed their table manners were not exactly recherché.

Had a gorgeous sea bath this morning. The waves were immense and close together, so you scarcely emerged from one before the next knocked you over. My little Gib friend and I were alone in the ocean and I was a bit timid. The beach is the main road to somewhere, and streams of cattle and laden donkeys are continually passing up and down. The wind blows a gale. No storm is brewing, no cloud in the sky, yet the wind is all one can stand up against. They say it has lasted almost a fortnight. Some people at the table d'hôte were cross about it. One man said, "They advertise a continual breeze—but I don't call this a breeze—it's a hurricane." There are only a few people in the hotel. You know there was a wide spread rumor that cholera was here, so people are afraid to come. If cholera once did start I think it would leave nothing.

Mr. Perdicaris is at Idonia his country home on the mountain. Had I known in advance I was coming here I could have had an introduction to him. They tell me that Europeans here have quite given up picnics and excursions. It is hard for me to believe in the danger—but I shall not be venturesome—have no fear. Down the beach way (it looks but a stone-throw), is a beautiful house owned by a writer for the *Times,* which has been abandoned. The owner was robbed and ill-treated one night—and had to move up to town, as he could not be protected where he was. [...]

To Dudley Carpenter
December 30, 1906, Rome, Italy

Dear Dud:

I have lost track of everything. I don't know whom I owe a letter to, but if I write you, you can share with the girls—so here goes.

Have been exactly a week in Rome and am not yet wild about it. I may get to be later but I am not expecting it. There are such quantities of tourists—it is impossible to feel for a moment you are away from home. I have had no adventures, either. Being with Ratcliff prevents that.[1] Two people can't have adventures. But they can have comforts. We have stayed in mostly at nights—writing, reading. The room (Mme. Catarina's pension) is not half bad, with its Italian open stove and burning logs. The theatres are not special, they say, and the opera has been *Il Crespusculo degli Dei* by Riccardo Wagner—so we stayed home.[2] It is far warmer than I expected and I look with loathing at my big ulster, which I must tote with me all sum-

1. Ratcliff: see Bibliographic Sketches. Throughout the correspondence McBride variously refers to his travel companion as Radcliff and Ratcliff, also shortening both with apparent randomness to Rad and Rat.
2. The Italian title of Wagner's *Die Götterdämmerung* (Twilight of the gods).

mer. The pension is rich. The first night at dinner, Rat and I never said a word and had the time of our lives trying to keep our faces straight. Two boarders were dingy Englishmen, the other ten were elderly American or English ladies. I never saw such a crew outside of a play. Everyone was a character and all stars. The great joke of it was, they all seemed caricatures of other friends. One reminds me of Caroline Peddle—but Caroline would not be pleased if she know it. Another is a wild distortion of Mrs. Hackley, and so on. They perform continuously. The two maids Lisa and Maria are fine too but in a different way. Very pretty, very typical Italian girls and they are always in a giggle, when serving us in our room. Usually by the time I have made my third remark in Italian they get so hysterical they have to leave. Mme Caterina herself will give me lessons at 3 liras per. We have breakfast in our room. Six liras a day pays everything. O! firewood, enough for three nights, 70 centimes.

Monday Night. Cold today. Saw the Palazzo Farnese this morning and bought some photographs. Small morning's work so Rat thought—but we walked to the other side of Rome and back. I would have told you about Ratcliff long ago, but there was no time for letter writing. This is a poor one, you notice. Rat is across the table bothering me. He is a hustler and hustles other people as well, as I am trotted to see this palace and that on schedule time. I know more about architecture now than I ever dreamed I should know—but he has left off informing me about the "stress of beams" and "expansions of concrete" and things of that sort. He is a combination of several people I have known. Some of Tappan Adney in him, some of Carle Tefft, Bill Scattergood, and Bryson Burroughs.[3] I am very fond of him and our intercourse is exactly on basis of old, old friends. I describe him because for a while he will be in my letters. As he is only twenty-six, it is not reasonable to imagine the friendship will last forever. He is a much stronger character than I and I give in, on everything, so that I find I am running around studying buildings for all the world like a Beaux Art student. I dare say I won't be able to stand it forever, fun as it is to be with Rad. The sort of life I vaguely pictured, with curious adventures, odd theatres and speaking Italian has not commenced. I think it would be great to travel with Radcliff to Sienna, Pisa, Milan, etc., as he is the finest companion imaginable and I am loath to lose the prospect of that by cutting loose from him now. I told you, I think, that he already has standing as an architect, and the things he has already done, make my hair stand on end. It seems so wonderful to

3. Scattergood was a friend and tennis companion from Marshallton. For Burroughs see Biographical Sketches.

have done so much at his age. He is a crack athlete. First in everything, usually. Another claim to fame is that he taught May Sutton to play tennis. He says I could beat her. "O, any man can beat any woman." This will be encouraging news to Walter Scattergood. He stands in great awe of May Sutton. If by any miracle Rad and I should still be friends next fall, I will get him to come to Marshallton on his way home to California. I think I should enjoy seeing him play against the Scattergoods.

This afternoon we went to the "Gesu," where a famous service is held on December 31.[4] It is an enormous church in the form of a cross, with so many gaudy decorations that they conflict into a simplicity that is impressive. The altar was wonderfully illuminated. Candelabra with crystals, were swung in a circle high in the air at the arch of the apse, and it was thrilling to see them being lit by men who leaned far out from an upper gallery. The church was crowded (tourists of course) and the procession with candles, pushing its way through the throng was fine. The singing was the principal thing, but it was solo singing, mostly—no choir. The men soprano are astonishing. Particularly this fellow today. He sang at times like a Sembrich. Sunday we took in a concert by the National orchestra. Beethoven's Seventh Symphony and *Parsifal* music. What do you think, they encored the second movement—and it was repeated. They repeated the *Parsifal*, too. We paid 20 cents for orchestra seats. We intend to invest in them often.

Thursday Afternoon . . . By Havens! the stove is smoking. I weep as I write. If I hold the Roman Herald against the fireplace, the fire cheers up. As soon as the paper is removed—out puffs the smoke. Rad has gone to the Baths of Titus. Not so attractive a journey as you might imagine! We were both in it this morning. Rad is very nice about conceding somethings to me, which I am sure to like and then squeezing in some scientific research on the side. We went to St. Pietro in Vincoli to see Michelangelo's *Moses*— for my sake. Then having some time on our hands, dropped in on Titus— for Rad's sake. Not being so nice as Rat, I permitted myself a few airy criticisms of the dingy attractions of the ruins—and Rad's feelings were hurt. They are deep, dark cellars now—brick vaults only—very slimy and wet. Nero passed some of his vile life—as Et Pugh would say—in these baths—and the guide showed us the spot, where the *Laocoön* was found— but Baedeker says the guides lie—on this point.

4. The Gesu is the mother church of the Jesuits in Rome, built in 1568. The interior is elaborately decorated in the Baroque style.

However, I thought I would take an afternoon off—write letters, loaf, go out shopping, etc., and I persuaded Rat to go off by himself to do more baths. He has just gone—the fire, smokes—and it has begun to pour with rain. The prospect is unattractive. Still at five, Rat meets me at the café on the Corso for a cup of tea. That will be something to look forward to. It is an amusing café. Everybody in Rome drops in there about five. Most of the people eat the queerest looking ices and sweets, which we don't dare to touch for fear of interfering with our appetite for dinner.

The *Moses* is the Moses we know so well, but there was nothing thrilling about seeing the original masterpiece. I am getting cross at Rome. It is such a tawdry, cheap place—the modern Rome, I mean, and it has an effect of spoiling masterpieces. *Moses* is unimpressively placed. The church has an unchurchly air (all the churches have for that matter) and the statue is too low. Mike designed the background himself—it is said—but it is hard to believe. It is squeezed, and *Moses* ought to have a simple background—like the Venus in the Louvre.

Raphael's *Transfiguration,* which I like much better than I expected is also badly placed. Horribly silly, confused wall back of it—and nothing to make you feel that the picture is sacred.

We saw the *Apollo Belvedere,* and the *Laocoön* last Saturday and go again this week.[5] Free Saturdays! The sculptures of the Vatican are fine. Have not gone to the galleries yet. We get our permits tomorrow. Went to *Götterdämmerung* after all. Fair. Sigfried fine—but the ladies not good. Orchestra splendid. At quarter after twelve they encored an intermezzo. Ended at one o'clock. Did I tell you we saw *Mme. Butterfly,* well done, at Naples, ta, ta. [. . .]

To Dudley Carpenter
January 27, 1907, Rome Italy[1]

Dear Dud:

Ratcliff has just gone out to call upon a Duchess. I thought it might compose me a trifle to write a letter. It is very disturbing to have your friend

---

5. Champions of Greek Revival such as Winckelmann and Goethe thought *The Apollo Belvedere* the perfect example of classical beauty. At the turn of the century, plaster reproductions of the sculpture were found in virtually any serious museum, art academy, or liberal arts college. Generations of art students such as McBride were taught that it embodied the essence of the Greek spirit.

1. The original letter is incorrectly dated January 27, 1906.

call upon a Duchess. One might have a pride in it, only one couldn't mention it in the Pension Caterina. The Pension Caterina though comfortable, doesn't "compete" with Duchesses. And if one can't mention it, what's the point in knowing the noblesse. Rat was very uncertain over the business and couldn't pronounce the lady's name properly twice running and was in an agony over what he was to say, etc. Rat's greatest chum at college in California was young Lindsay, the Earl of Crawford's son. His Aunt married the Italian Duke of Sermoneta and young Lindsay sent on a very nice letter of introduction, saying to Radcliff among other things, that the Caëtani were an erratic family, but if they chose to be amiable, they could do "everything" for him. I think Rat takes that idea literally and though he is openly afraid of her, nevertheless, rather expects the Duchess to hop about and do things for him. He thinks she ought to ask him to dinner with permission to fetch me, too. It would be rather sudden, I think for the lady to meet me—so—if she happens to be in an "erratic" mood, the interview with Rat, will probably be interesting. Only no one will know of it, for Rat has no powers of description.

Ratcliff is the nicest boy! He is, I think, about the nicest person I have ever known. But he is very absorbing. That is, people who become fond of him, are apt to become mere appendages, stalactites. He is of the successful sort. He is always deep in whatever he is about and he is incessantly "at" something. He must have taken some cues from Teddy Roosevelt. I suppose there are lots of youngsters of his age who have. In all the time I have known Rat I have never seen him unoccupied a second. He is either hard at work tooth-and-nail—or sound asleep. I combat this attitude of mind both by argument and by example, but without visible results as yet. And curiously enough, he never seems to notice how little I resemble The Strenuous One. He thinks I must be a wonder, just because I am of so much service to him, I suppose. I am Rat's tutor, valet, and courier. In my departments, I have full sway. It is quite fine, how limp Rat becomes, when he collides with a problem outside his line and completely follows my lead. I can easily foresee Rad's amounting to something in the world. He has a kind of manliness I have never seen equaled, except in books. Benvenuto Cellini's jump from a sick bed to the furnace, is the kind of thing Rat can do and already has done. It would be very beautiful, I think, to go on helping him to my limit for a few months, and then step aside for some higher grade tutor, but I am not sure I am good enough for the sweetly sacrificial.

Tuesday morning . . . Rat returned at this point, completely winded but triumphant, having made a great hit with the Duchess and having run all the way home. Had been at the palace an hour, had had tea, had met the

Duke, was to go out with their party to the Castle (one of the famous ones) in motor cars, etc. We got so excited, we actually told the old ladies of the pension, who seemed as tickled over it as ourselves. As Schley said after the Battle of Santiago—there seems to be enough glory in it to go around.[2]

Rat went to the Palazzo Caëtani at four but no Duchess. Then back to a tea room on the Piazza Venèzia, followed by a mob of beggars, cabbies and small boys—for a frock coat and top hat are as scarce in Rome, as they are in Marshallton—"that was Hell all right," said Rat, telling me of it. Then again at five, the lady had not returned but at six o'clock—the flunky with a magnificent gesture which Rat imitated for me to perfection, said, "Yes—Her Grace was in." Rat, after following through endless small rooms around the usual court yard, was finally face to face with the Duchess. She proved to be very nice. Rat found he could talk to her like a streak and in a few minutes, when the Duke had been sent for and produced, he discovered he liked him too. Fortunately for Rad it happens to be one of those "united families" one sometimes hears of—and the Duchess seems really fond of Lindsay, Rad's chum. Then too, one of the Caëtani (the family name) sons is making a profession of mining engineering, at present in Idaho somewhere, so the Duke and Duchess had a natural interest in the very things that Rad is strong on. For usually, when we are "out" together, he never opens his lips, having absolutely no powers of repartee or gossip. But, once safely returned from the Palace Rat announced he was sure now of one thing he had long suspected, that the nicer people were (that is the higher class they were), the easier they were to talk to—a proposition I was willing to agree to.

After such an excitement it seemed rather tame to stay at home and read aloud something improving. Besides, after six rainy days, we had a clear one and there was a full moon. So we made for the Coliseum. When you tell people you are not wild over the Coliseum, they always say you must see it by moonlight. But there must be something wrong with me for even by moonlight the ruins did not excite me. For one thing we have to push our way in. All the star tourists were there. Even under the portals in the shadow one recognized queer but familiar headgears. There are certain freaks, who are in the foreground of everything. One gets to hate them with a fourteenth century, Florentine hatred and the moment I see one I begin to dislike the thing we are both seeing. So we weren't impressed by

2. Winfield Scott Schley (1839–1911), an admiral in the United States Navy during the Spanish-American War, in 1898 was in charge of a destructive blockade of the Santiago Harbor, which housed the Spanish fleet. Charges of unseamanlike behavior were leveled against Schley as a result of the battle.

the Coliseum. Rad vented his spirits by whistling "Dixie" as loudly as possible. Like most Englishmen who live in America he is intensely patriotic. But it was a fine night, dry and cold and the walk, there and back, was great. On the way back we stopped in the "Nationale" for an act of the *Geisha,* which is the rage here. It was stupidly given. The only amusing thing was the way the Italian actresses burlesqued the ways and walks of the English.

Another introduction of Rat's was to Miss Hogarth, granddaughter to Hogarth the Great and herself an artist.[3] She had us to tea Sunday and was very nice and is disposed to think up ways of being kind to us. She is going to give us a letter to queer Bohemian English people, who live in a palace at Florence. On Thursday we are to take tea with her again, to meet Miss Barrett (niece of Elizabeth Barrett Browning) and Dr. Ashbee, head of the British Archaeological School. If Rat should be still at the Sermoneta Castle, I should have to go alone, but his excuses would sound impressive, even to Miss Hogarth. She is a tall and mannish creature, who startles you at moments by being more womanly than most women. She was gotten up Sunday with a strange oriental damask garment flung over ordinary English dress. She had been in Athens for two years and the studio was littered with pale poster like drawings of the Grecian Remains which are to form a book soon to be published, the text of which will be by her brother. The drawings were almost good and rather clever. The outlines had all been reproduced on large sheets of water colour papers in soft outlines and Miss Hogarth was putting pale tints on them by hand! Three thousand in all I think she said, thirty to the book!!

Miss Hogarth lamented that the picturesque personalities, who used to adorn the society of Rome, were fast disappearing and that at present, there were scarcely any left, who were really worth exhibiting to strangers. It was difficult for me to keep my lack of appreciation of the city down to polite limits, but I did so. Miss Hogarth and I got on well and thanks partly to Sampson's letter to her about Rad, she is able to appreciate the urchin. Dr. Sampson is a well known authority on some subject—(I've been told forty times), geology, or hunting or something, and Rad made a famous trip with him once to some inaccessible mountain, a trip so special that even President Roosevelt wrote to them autograph letters about it. [. . .]

3. Mary Henrietta Uppleby Hogarth (c. 1861–1935) lived primarily in London. She produced two books, *Scenes in Athens* and *Fountains of Rome,* and was reputedly descended from William Hogarth (1697–1764).

To Dudley Carpenter
February 19, 1907, Perugia, Italy

To Dud:

Left Rome a week ago. This is my first attempt to write. It is the first warm hotel we have found for one thing. In spite of all the mean things I said about Rome I hated to leave, at the last, for we were knowing interesting people and having a gay time. But the allotted time had elapsed and Rad was restive, and off we went. I sulked the first three days, which were in Viterbo and didn't allow myself to enjoy it so much as I now pretend on looking back.[1] Viterbo really was a fine village. Miss Hogarth told us of it. It is very mediaeval and off the track of tourists. We were the only guests at the big hotel and the proprietor who was very nice made a tremendous fuss over us. We had wonderful wine there, excellent food and everything for comfort except heat. The wine is like the wine in *The Marble Faun,* almost as good as the Orvieto wine, where we went next.[2] I think the Orvieto is the best wine in the world. It is cheap as water, too, for it can't be transported. A journey of only a few miles changes it. While at Orvieto, Rad and I both drank our fiascos at each meal and each taste we prolonged as long as possible for we knew we were only to have a short hack at it.

The Cathedral at Orvieto is very interesting. Outside a golden mosaic, very gorgeous at sunset and inside lovely in colour. The apse without any masterpieces of decoration is, nevertheless, as handsome as possible, just from the lovely colors. Orvieto is a curious place for a town—a flat plateau on top of a steep cliff. One ascends in a funicular r.r. It took us a deuce of a time to get to Spoleto when we went there—and we were mad as hops, when we got there. Why we went, neither of us know. It crowns a mountain (all of these Italian towns do) and was freezing cold at eleven p.m. Rad and I sat close in the carriage and pulled the robe tight about us but froze just the same. At last we got to the hotel and were ushered to our room. It was about the size of St. Patrick's Cathedral and the two little beds looked lost on the brick floor. The room was up endless flights of stone steps and everything was dark, gloomy, cold, damp and scary. We got into our beds somehow and slept somehow. The breakfast chocolate was awful, the hot

1. Viterbo is a small medieval city in the province of Latium, much of it based on Etruscan foundations, northwest of Rome.
2. *The Marble Faun,* Nathaniel Hawthorne's novel of murder, intrigue, and romance among a group of American art students studying in nineteenth-century Rome, was published in 1859.

milk was goat's milk (undrinkable), the bread like metal and the tempera-
ture below freezing. We sat and cussed and ate bits of bread with our ulsters
and sweaters on, and Rat would want to know why we came to such a
blooming town and I would explain that we had only stopped there on his
account.

Assisi seemed all the more beautiful after Spoleto. It was fun driving up
the hillside, it was fun to get inside a decent hotel and meet civil waiters, it
was fun to get into the Lower Church and see the Giotto frescoes.[3] We were
lucky to have had a bright sun for the low arches of the under church require a bright light. But even in the gloom it is a great piece of decoration. I
don't think I shall admire anything more that I shall see. It is satisfying to
find a rich effect as a whole and then to examine details and find them to
be masterpieces. I got a number of photos, one for you—the *Slaughter of the
Innocents*. It is the most attractive Slaughter I have seen. As a rule they do
not appeal to me. But the chief slaughterer reminds me somehow of Bill
Scattergood and he is saying "Hi there, gimme that kid," to a lady, just
about as Bill would say it, were he to boss such a job. The lady is grandly
perturbed, about as Caroline Peddle was, in the vaudeville I wrote. I love
Giotto.

Then Assisi was my first chance to know Simone Martini.[4] His chapel is
beautiful. I knew very little about Martini, Duccio, Signorelli, Lo Spanga, or
Lorenzetti until this week. Of course we have read of 'em. By the by, Miss
Hogarth gave us letters to Berenson in Florence.[5] She doesn't like him
much, I think, for she never tells a Berenson anecdote without putting in a
ridiculous touch. She laughed particularly about his dwelling, which she
says is a very perfect affair, everything of a period, very simple and Bun-
thornish, but leading up for a grand climax to Berenson's bedroom—a very

3. The upper church of the Basilica of San Francesco at Assisi was decorated with interpretive cycles of the lives of the saint, primarily attributed to Cimabue (Cenni di
Pepi, active c. 1272–1302) and Giotto (Giotto de Bondone, c. 1277–1337). Painted
between 1296 and 1304, the twenty-eight scenes depicting the life of St. Francis
were in 1907 considered the most important examples of Giotto's early style. There
is serious art-historical debate as to Giotto's hand in the series.
4. Simone Martini (active 1315–44) of Siena began work on a series of scenes depicting the life of St. Martin in the lower church of San Francesco, probably in the
late 1320s.
5. Bernard Berenson (1865–1959) had by this time written the catalogs of Italian
Renaissance artists that earned him his initial fame. He had been the art adviser to
Isabella Stewart Gardner for many years and in 1907 began secretly working as the
adviser to the dealer Joseph Duveen. Berenson was married to Mary Smith Cos-
telloe Berenson (1891–1945).

wonderful bed-room, which Miss Hogarth thinks, too grand a setting for such a little chap as B[6] . . . It will be fun to meet him even if it be an agony. [. . .]

To Dudley Carpenter
March 2, 1907, Florence, Italy

Dear Dud:

[. . .] Florence seems pretty fine—and not the place I used to dislike. The Galleries seem more endless than ever and certainly it's the place for any-one who wants art or artistic life. Roman museums are more archeological and possibly that is why the old fogies and freaks get on better there. Freaks can get more out of archaeology than art. But Rome has the Court and the Pope, two things to attract interesting people, and give point to daily hap-penings. Rich Americans who would like to live ornamentally, can do it at Rome very easily. They can know the titled people more easily than in France or London, living is cheaper than in the great cities and so they all purchase their villas. Americans and English quite dominate the other foreigners and it is rather a toss-up, but that the Americans lead altogether. Even here it is the same.

Went to the Belle-arti yesterday and saw Botticelli's *Spring*, which I missed when here before.[1] It is very lovely—but—but Botticelli is not so tremendous to me as he used to be for some reason. I was trying to find another of his, which could be called as great or on the great style and couldn't. The next favorite is his *Annunciation*. Was quite stunned by the Perugino *Descent from the Cross*.[2] It missed being a great picture, because of the scattered composition—but the separate parts are lovelier than any-thing I have seen of Perugino. I saw photographs today of some of the separate heads and they seemed very beautiful. I shall have to buy some.

6. Bunthorne, from a Gilbert and Sullivan operetta, embodies the aesthetic movement.

1. Sandro Botticelli's (c. 1445–1510) linear style fell out of favor soon after his death. His work became fashionable again only in the second half of the nine-teenth century, when the Pre-Raphaelites and the stylization of Art Nouveau re-vived his reputation. The vogue for Botticelli would have been at its height during McBride's earliest trips to Europe, in the 1890s.

2. Pietro Vannucci Perugino (c. 1445–1523) played an important role in the forma-tion of the High Renaissance, through his influence on the young genius Raphael. Like Botticelli, Perugino, with his clarity and compositional harmony, was a major influence on the Pre-Raphaelites, and his work enjoyed a renewed popularity in the late nineteenth century.

The Uffizi I enjoyed more than the Pitti. It must be well managed, because the arrangement is so fine. Do you remember Bellini's *Sacred Conversation*? Awfully funny! Arthur Davies' things would seem Academic in comparison.[3] Then there is a battle scene in which a very round bosomed horse is kicking straight up with both hind legs, in the finest way.[4] It is equal to Richard Strauss's music.

Called to-day on the Houghtons, friends of Miss Hogarth.[5] "Very queer English people who live in a castle" was her description and she decided we ought to know them, when I told one of my favorite Atherton Curtis stories. We drove of course and after we had gotten inside the great doors the cabby insisted in going up the stone stairs to find the inhabited part. But a very nice young Englishman came down to meet us and explained, that Mr. Houghton was out of town, but that Mrs. Houghton was in, so we went up and tea was ordered straight away. The place had a suggestion of art atmosphere and we liked Mrs. Houghton and the young man, a Mr. Pynsent. The only thing, that reminded me of the Curtises, was the bread and butter. It was of fine quality but lumpy and Mrs. Houghton begged us to excuse it, because she had cut it herself. She does jewelry and showed us some interesting pieces. On Wednesday evening Mr. Houghton will have returned and they are to have a little party and we are to go. Mr. Pynsent told me that the Houghton Collection of ancient jewelry was very famous—and we are to see it. [. . .]

To Dudley Carpenter
March 6, 1907, Florence, Italy

Dear Dud:

We dined with the Berensons last night. It was grand but harrowing. We called on them last Sunday.[1] It was against my will. I felt seedy after our

3. Arthur Davies (1862–1928) is best known for organizing the Armory Show (1913); before that he painted Symbolist-influenced paintings, which were considered daring.
4. This scene, by Paolo Uccello (c. 1397–1475), is one of three large panels depicting *The Battle of San Romano,* dating from around 1456. The other two are in the Louvre and the National Gallery, London.
5. Probably Edmund Houghton, an expatriate English friend of the Berensons. A long-term resident of Florence and keen automobile owner, Houghton introduced the Berensons to motor touring in the Italian countryside—a pastime they avidly took up.

1. Other visitors the Berensons entertained that spring included Frank Jewett Mather, Jr., and Roger Fry, who was on a buying tour with J. P. Morgan. According

excursions into one night villages and wanted to wait to recuperate, before presenting Miss Hogarth's letter, but Rad (who only stays here a short time) was impatient to do it. So to be contrary, I put obstructions in the way of costume, etc., and the consequence was we ended by walking out to Settignano (3k) in our disreputable attire.[2] It is hard to know what geniuses will require of you in the way of dress. When we called on "the queer English people in a palace," the Houghtons, we found our frock coats too ornamental, as the Houghtons were very dusty in work clothes.

But, at the Berensons everything was in awe inspiring order, and a carriage was arriving, at the same time, with silk hatted callers. There was nothing for it but to brazen it out, which we did. The butler put us into a marvelous waiting room, where everything was "simple" and paralyzing and we had scarcely peeped behind two things, before Berenson Himself appeared, a dapper little man, putting his heels together military fashion, as he stiffly took Rad's hand, saying "Mr. Radcliff I believe?" He led us upstairs to the drawing room, explaining that his wife was an invalid and that the other callers were the Walcots of Colorado. Mrs. Berenson sat at the fireside, all draped in white laces, a most picturesque central figure for the drawing-room, which I felt to be superb without having a chance to look at it. She seemed a most vivacious and unpitiful invalid, though and quite sparkled, especially in repartee to B.B. as she playfully calls Mr. Berenson. Mr. Berenson, as you might imagine, loves to sparkle himself, and said many witty things I ought to have remembered, but do not. My first instantaneous instinct in regard to him was that he was a bit treacherous, a bit catty—and his occasional rallies with Mrs. Berenson had a sting, that made me feel one should be cautious with the gentleman. But his manners had been splendid all through, and he differentiated, if he differentiated at all between us and the millionaire people, rather in our favor than not, and a soft glance shone rather often from his eyes, so we regained confidence, and did succeed in escaping from the encounter without a scratch. Greatly to my surprise, he asked us to dinner for last night. One doesn't expect geniuses to do things for one, you know, especially as Miss Hogarth, who introduced us, doesn't know him very well.

---

to Fry, Bernard Berenson made every effort to show up the English art historian's lack of knowledge regarding Italian painting.

2. The villa I Tatti is situated on a hilltop between Fièsole and Settignano. The Berensons began renting the villa several months before their marriage in 1900. In 1907, as the Berensons began to negotiate its purchase, renovations of the villa were also undertaken. The villa, its collection, and its library of books and photographs are now part of Harvard University, Bernard Berenson's alma mater.

The dinner was perfect. Everything about it was memorable. The only drawback was, that we were so nervous about the showing we were making ourselves we couldn't properly attend to the details of the room and the service. The flowers were quite unusual. A low bowl of many brilliant flowers, arranged so that the colors balanced perfectly, unusual candle-sticks of silver, and remarkable knives and forks. I never saw such knives and forks. I should not have identified any had not the hostess been especially watchful to display the uses of each one in a carelessly apparent way. In all such things the Berenson's are adept hosts.

The talk was "brilliant" of course. Poor Rad was left miles behind at the soup, for he had never seen Duse, nor heard of D'Annunzio.[3] The Berenson mot is rather bitter. There was scarcely a rag left upon either Duse or D'Annunzio, by dessert. D'Annunzio is vain, the vainest person alive, he "flaunts five million peacocks' tails." And he exists for flattery; "he lives in the bottom of a treacle-well." Poor Duse is an actress—greater off the stage than on. Not of first rate order in intelligence, but capable of reproducing anything that is suggested to her. She is a business woman; the recluse idea is an advertisement. All of which I indignantly refused to believe. B.B. spoke of her once recognizing him from the stage and when I exclaimed at that and spoke of the Duse unconsciousness of audience he roared with laughter and called America the land of the naive.

I talked unusually well myself during dinner and today I have had remorse. I felt I should have worshipped rather than shone. But they are going to take us to some wonderful villa next Sunday, so perhaps, we weren't so bad, after all. Tonight the Houghtons have a little party in the palace on the via Bardi, overlooking the Arno.

Thursday p.m. The Houghtons are not clever hosts. Exceedingly kind and unselfish themselves, it doesn't occur to them, that other people are not. People were allowed to sit all evening in the seat they took on entering. The hostess would look at them once in a while to see if they were happy and of course one had to try to look happy so the hostess allowed one to stay. I sat the entire evening talking to an old lady who bored me to extinction and whom I bored. It was awful. The only thing that happened

3. Eleanor Duse (1849–1924) was one of the great actresses of the period, a noted tragedienne, often ranked next to Sarah Bernhardt. Gabriele D'Annunzio (1863–1938), was a personally flamboyant and celebrity-seeking novelist, poet, and dramatist of great talent. By 1906 he had published many highly spiced sensual novels. Berenson met him in 1896, when D'Annunzio was beginning his romantic liaison with Eleanora Duse; the two shared a villa in Settignano.

was a splendid performance by Rad. We had just entered and were standing talking in groups, when suddenly Rad propelled himself through the air for about ten feet and put out some burning laces on Mrs. Houghton's back. She had a gauzy scarf about her shoulders and inadvertently leaned against a Florentine lamp. It blazed up in an instant and would have seriously injured her, had it not been for Rad, who is as swift as lightning in emergencies.

I always feel like mighty small pickings myself when Rad is about. He is leaving to go to Venice soon, and then I will have a chance to see if my character will assert itself, left to its own devices. [. . .]

To Mary and Maria Pugh
March 15, 1907, Florence, Italy

Dear Mary and Maria:

[. . .] Last Sunday the Berensons took us to the Villa Gamberaia, one of the famous country houses of Florence.[1] (You will find Mr. Berenson's book *Florentine Painters* among my books.)[2] That is, Mrs. B. took us. Mr. B. was just going away with a lady in a big motor, as we arrived, and we were allowed to examine the house at our leisure while Mrs. Berenson was making ready for the drive. The drawing room is extremely beautiful, with interesting furniture and wonderful primitive paintings and figures in gilded wood.[3] The flowers and damask hangings were lovely. Mrs. or Mr. (I don't know whom to praise) B. has the knack of putting two or three little violets in a vase and making it seem wonderful. But we rushed out of the drawing room in the hunt for Mr. B.'s bedroom, the fame of which had spread as far as Rome. It was the last room of all and turned out to be very small and "simple." The walls were rough-white, and the rafters white. There was only one little picture on the walls, but that was a precious antique. The narrow cot, covered with a pale cobwebby green piece of old silk and the same silk made a canopy over the pillows and was used at the window.

1. The Villa Gamberaia, near Settignano, was owned by the Gambarelli, a family of important architects in the fifteenth and sixteenth centuries. The garden was created in the early years of the twentieth century by Princess Ghika, and the house, as it existed when McBride visited, dated from the eighteenth century.
2. By 1907 Berenson had published three of the four essays which encapsulated his interpretive methods: *The Venetian Painters* (1894), *The Florentine Painters* (1896), and *The Central Italian Painters* (1897). In 1907 the fourth, *The North Italian Painters,* and *The Decline of Art* were published as *Italian Painters of the Renaissance.*
3. In this usage *primitive* refers to works of art by Italian painters before c. 1400.

There was a tiny table by the bed with a book and a few precious objects, a small chair and a standing mirror—nothing else in the room. I never saw a room so chaste and my respect for Mr. B.'s courage grew,—for I, for one should never have dared to arrange so pure a sleeping room. It seemed like the abode—the cell—of some wonderful saint. Perhaps Mr. B. is one after all.

It was a lovely drive to the villa, as the day was perfect. Rad and I wore our frock coats and top hats to be swell, and were comfortable with all. At the villa we were given twenty minutes to inspect the gardens, which are pictured and described in Edith Wharton's *Italian Villas,* and then we joined our hostess, Miss Blood, at tea. The Princess Chigi, Miss Blood's friend, is not at home. But even had she been, she would not have been visible, Mrs. Berenson explained, as she is a misanthrope, though rich, young and beautiful, and never sees anyone. Miss Blood, herself is rather on the princesse order and although she dominated Mrs. Berenson completely, who is a difficult lady to quell, I, somehow, was not at all afraid of her. We got on very well, and I was invited to come again. Mrs. Hutchins Hapgood called with her little son at the same time.[4] The Hapgoods have just taken a little cottage near by.

After tea we went as far as Settignano with Mrs. Berenson and then she insisted on walking home (she is an invalid) and Rad and I were driven in state home to Florence. You might exchange letters with Dud—for this letter is a continuation of his. Horribly lonely for Rad this morning.[5] He certainly is the nicest boy! [. . .]

To Dudley Carpenter
June 4, 1907, London

Dear Dud:

[. . .] This evening our new suits come from Johnson's and we go to the "Opierroar." It is *Madame Butterfly* with Caruso and Emmy Destinn.[1] We were at Johnson's this morning buying dress suits and over coats for Rad.

4. Hutchins Hapgood (1869–1944) and his wife Neith Boyce (1872–1951) were writers; Hapgood was a progressive journalist and Boyce wrote novels and plays.
5. Radcliff had departed the day before, presumably for Venice, and had missed his train in the process.

1. The tenor Enrico Caruso (1873–1921) appeared in ten London productions in 1907. Emmy Destinn (1878–1930) played the role of Madame Butterfly (Cio-Cio San) in this revised version of Puccini's opera, originally staged to horrible response at La Scala in 1904.

You know he lost his trunk in France (care of Cooks) and has to buy everything. Rad is sure to out with something everywhere that disgraces me. This morning he told Johnson we were going to nigger-heaven at the opera tonight.[2] There was some doubt about Rad's blue suit coming by six o'clock. "You want to wear it specially tonight?" inquired Johnson. "Yes," says I, "We're going to the opera," adds Rad . . . The only place we could wear such a suit is nigger-heaven, of course. Now Rad is afraid they won't think it worth while to make his things nicely.

I had a bad attack of rheumatism last week, but the morning tub of really hot water seemed to be knocking it. First tub I've met since leaving Trento. It seems luxurious all right. Went to Mary Tempest's last night.[3] She is playing Clyde Fitch's *Truth*.[4] She could play anything, I think. She made a lot out of it. Clara Bloodgood, who they say failed in it in New York, ought to see her do it.[5] There are such lots of amusing things she does, that can't have been written in the book. And as for costumes—she is the only smartly gowned woman in London. All the swellest French actresses are wearing a new kind of skirt and Marie Tempest is the first in London to be "on." The audience hung on the play as if it were meat and drink. There was very little suggestion of American workmanship about it—it passed well enough as English. The only thing that seemed particularly American was the grand faith the husband reposed in his flighty little wife,—but the English of course don't suspect that to be an American trait. The only other play I've seen has been the revived *Liars*.[6] It should never have been revived. It is deadly. I went only on your account. You yourself would have a fit at it now. How any one could ever have accused Oscar Wilde of writing it, I can't imagine,—although it is clear enough that Jones has been imitating Wilde.

The theatres are hopeless here. Nothing to see but bum American plays. Not a single British example! Fact . . . I had not half made the rounds in Paris. France leads the world in acting. I will have stacks to tell you about them. Hated to leave Paris. I love Paris now. And as the same person can't

2. "Nigger heaven" was a term for upper balconies in segregated theaters; until the 1930s African Americans were restricted to these seats.
3. The actress Marie Tempest died in October 1942.
4. *The Truth,* a comedy by Clyde Fitch (1865–1909), ran from April 6 through July 27, 1907.
5. The actress Clara Bloodgood died late in 1907.
6. A revival of *The Liars* by Henry Arthur Jones (1851–1929) played at the Criterion Theatre for ninety-nine performances between April and July 1907. The play first opened October 6, 1897.

love both Paris and London—I'm not liking London now. Doesn't that make you tired? [. . .]

To Dudley Carpenter
June 11, 1907, London

Dear Dud:

[. . .] I took Rad to call on Mary and she sang and her friend Miss Wood played and somehow the evening dragged. Then Rad left and Mary gave me a tea party at her club. A lawyer who quizzed me about America and evidently knew more about it than I did; two sisters who talked excitedly on woman suffrage and looked bored at any other topic; and a young lady, who has almost succeeded in securing a house for respectable working girls, made up the party. My mind refused to think of anything but rheumatics and as I knew the suffragette young ladies could have no possible interest in my left shoulder blade, I had to let them entertain themselves.

[. . .] Went to the Irish Theatre last night.[1] It was great fun. Gotten up by Yeats, to exploit the Irishism, he says. In reality to exploit himself. On the program, apropos of *Shadowy Waters,* he says, "Any one can understand this little bit who understands, let us say, the love poetry of Shelley!" It sounds like Bunthorne. I don't get much out of Shelley in the first place, and as for *Shadowy Waters* it is the "lim." It is probably a worse play then my master piece *Boëtius and Chrycirce* . . . On the program were some very funny farces by Lady Gregory, which seemed genuine Irish.[2] I should love to have Jack Hodder or Bill Mulheron hear 'em. The actors are all simple working people, who carpenter and dress-make by day and grace the boards by night. Their brogues are delightful. One play, *The Playboy of the Western World,* incited a riot in Dublin. I hope to see it this afternoon. Beautiful young ladies in charming evening dress sold the books of the

1. A literary and theatrical renaissance in Dublin revolved around the Abbey Theatre, which opened in 1904 and achieved world renown for staging plays by William Butler Yeats (1865–1939), John Millington Synge (1871–1909), and Lady Augusta Gregory (1852–1932). In addition to those specified, note 2 below, other plays produced in London in July of 1907 included Synge's *Playboy of the Western World* and *Riders to the Sea* and Yeats's *The Shadowy Waters, The Hour-Glass,* and *On Baile's Strand.*
2. In 1907 Lady Gregory helped produce several plays in London at the Great Queen Street Theatre. Among the Irish plays that she had been involved in at the Abbey as playwright, dramatist, and producer were *Spreading the News, The Goal Gate,* and *The Rising of the Moon.*

play. I bought some—so will have the pleasure of reading the *Play Boy*. But Yeats is really the limit for stupidity.

To Mary and Maria Pugh
May 25, 1910, London, England

Chère Cousines:

Now that King Edward is buried, London is settling down to its usual work. For the funeral, such a crowd turned up, as has never been seen in the history of the world, I suppose. For never before was it possible for people to travel so quickly . . . The crowd at King Edward's coronation was not so big, for I was here then, too; and all agree Queen Victoria's funeral had not so big a mob.

We learned of his death at Queenstown, where some of our passengers were disembarking.[1] We were singing "Auld Lang Syne" to them when a tug appeared with flags at half mast and everybody became silent when the news was known.

It is impossible for an American to realize how completely England goes into mourning. Everybody is in black and deeply in black. On the two or three days of state ceremonials, not even a foreigner wore colour. Now that a few days have gone by some Americans are appearing in colours and a few English are wearing a bit of purple, half-mourning. But mourning for the English will go on for months. It affects all classes. Even the poorest in the slums wear black gloves or a bit of crepe around their arm.

There was a very nice Englishman, a young soldier, who shared my cabin coming over. His young sister he told me, was just "out" and a number of parties would be given for her . . . The parties were all called off, of course, and when I met the young lady she wore full and complete mourning. She like many another young woman, had laid in all her new frocks for the season, as you may imagine.

I saw the processions but had not so good a view of the funeral cortège with all the Kings, as I should have liked. For one thing, there were too many Kings and it was impossible to look at all of them and in a minute they had passed from sight . . . I was more impressed by [the] procession bearing the body to Westminster, as King George, with Kings of Norway and Denmark and all his officers of state, walked, and one had a good view of them. I saw excellently the Lying-in-State, which was most impressive.

1. McBride's ship arrived in port at Queenstown, May 11, 1910.

The line, four abreast, extended about four miles, and I joined it at two o'clock and entered exactly at five, in time to see the impressive change of guards, which took place every hour. [. . .]

PS I saw Teddy R. yesterday on his way to the Guildhall. He didn't look awfully gay as he bowed right and left, too; and never showed his teeth. I am sorry not to have met any brainy Englishman this trip. It would be interesting to know what they think of him. For one thing—he cut much less [a] figure here than the American papers make out.

The mourning for King Edward cut everything out, and among the long accounts of ceremonials one had to hunt in obscure corners for a little notice of what Mr. Roosevelt was to do or had done. In the American papers one gets an idea that Ted was the chief person present. For that matter, he may have been, but the English were really more deeply interested in King Manuel, the boy-king, than him[2] . . . Just the same I should like to hear what they say in the clubs of the Guildhall speech.

To Otto Nickli
June 8, 1910, Paris, France

Dear Otto:

Just then a rattle of thunder overhead! I very much fear we shan't dine outdoors in the Bois du Meudon tonight. Bryson Burroughs gives a dinner party to a select few (all are celebrated people but me, alas) but the invitations say, "providing it doesn't rain." But if there's a down-pour tóute-de-suite it may clear yet in time to take the train at 5:30. It has been hot and there's a thunderstorm usually every afternoon, but it clears and the evenings are bearable.

I didn't know Bryson was here yet, but two days ago I met him on the street with Roger Fry, the critic.[1] They were just getting into a victoria, so I hopped in, too. They said they would take me to a picture-show. As we drove along they said, "Where are you stopping?" I said, "a wretched place

2. Crowned in 1908 following the assassination of his father and brother, the twenty-year-old King Manuel II fled to Great Britain in 1910 after a conservative revolution. The successful coup, staged by reactionary Republican revolutionaries, ended the 270-year reign of the constitutional monarchy of Portugal, the House of Bragança.

1. One might surmise this studio visit was in preparation for the exhibition "Manet and the Post-Impressionists," which Fry (1866–1934) curated for the Grafton Galleries, London, November 8, 1910–January 15, 1911. Fry included three paintings, twelve drawings, eight sculptures, and a decorative vase by Matisse in the show.

on the Boulevard Montparnasse, I'm going to change. I don't like the people in the hotel."

"What hotel?" asks Bryson.

"The Etats-Unis," said I.

"You son of a gun," says Bryson. "Its a very good hotel, I'm stopping there myself and I like it."

Think of it. We had been in the same little hotel three days without seeing each other. Since then Bryson and I have breakfasted together in my room. The garçon fetches it at eight-thirty and Bryson, he has the room next to mine, comes in his bathrobe. Bryson being rich and celebrated has an omelette and coffee; I being poor and not celebrated have just plain chocolate and bread-and-butter. But we eat in front of the wide open window and look out on the Boulevard de Chin—and its not so bad in the hotel Etats-Unis after all.

We had an interesting afternoon that day we met. Bryson and Roger Fry were going to the village of Clanmart, to pay a visit to Matisse, the most talked of painter of the day and they took me along. Matisse is a very interesting talker and I tried to remember all he said to Fry, for he didn't say much to me. His pictures are so different from any others that have been painted within the last five hundred years that I couldn't have talked to him, had the conversation been in English. There was great uncertainty in my mind, whether the huge canvas, 12 ft. by 14 ft. with dancing figures, life size, painted flat brick red, against a flat chrome-green hill, and a flat cobalt sky, was meant as a joke or as a serious attempt at something beautiful.[2]

After we left, and Matisse did us the honor to walk to the station with us, even to run for it, for we had to run to catch our train; after we left, we all agreed that we liked him very much and thought him frank and honest. Showing that there had been doubt of his honesty in our minds.

We dined at the famous restaurant "Lavenue's," in the garden. It was charming. The company was très-distingués. There was Bryson, of course, Roger Fry, Editor of *Burlington Magazine,* and considered a great personage by many. There were Mr. and Mrs. Spicer-Simpson.[3] He is a sculptor and

2. *Dance (II)* was completed in spring 1910 and exhibited at the Salon d'Automne that fall. In spite of attacks on the painting by the press, the painting was acquired by the important Russian collector Sergei Shchukin and is now in the collection of the Hermitage Museum, St. Petersburg.

3. Both American expatriate sculptors, Theodore Spicer-Simpson (1871–1959) and his wife, Margaret (née Schmidt) Spicer-Simpson, were close friends of James Stephens (see Biographical Sketches). In 1910 Theodore Spicer-Simpson was at the

she a famous beauty. And there was last but not least, Miss Mildred Aldrich, who is sixty years at least (I tell you that at once, you are so sentimental always) and very witty.[4] She is called Mick by her friends. She is like Miss Marbury of New York an agent for poets and dramatics and consequently knows all the famous people and tells the most amusing tales of them.[5] We intended [to] have our café in the café, as the musicians play delightfully there, but we were so entertained, that at a quarter past eleven, we were still at table in Lavenue's garden! I wish I could write down all that Mick told us of Rodin, Matisse, Maeterlinck, et le reste.[6]

Tonight at Bryson's party there will be much the same company with the addition of Miss Janet Scudder, the famous sculptress, or at least famous among the women, and who is said to be "a character."[7] The restaurant is quite in the woods of Meudon, and is unknown by people in general; a charming little place that is frequented by country people chiefly.

The great heat makes the theatres uncomfortable, yet I go, for they soon close. I went to *L'Arlesienne,* at the Odeon last night, the play by Daudet, with accompanying music by Bizet. It was very good, and I shed a few tears at it. I don't expect to shed tears at the *Bois Sacre* which I mean to see tomorrow night. It is not sad! On the contrary, it, it is said, to be wicked and delightful. [. . .]

---

height of his career, and in 1911 he won a first-class medal for sculpture at the Brussels Exposition.

4. Contrary to McBride's guess, she was about 53. See Biographical Sketches.

5. Elizabeth Marbury was a high-powered literary agent who was active in the Democratic Party.

6. The sculptor François-Auguste-René Rodin (1840–1917) was by 1910 making plans with the state for the founding of the Rodin Museum in Paris, to be housed in the Hôtel de Biron, where Rodin, along with Rainer Maria Rilke, Jean Cocteau, Isadora Duncan, and Henri Matisse all had artist's studios.

The Symbolist writer Maurice Maeterlinck (1862–1949) published the popular work *L'Oiseau bleu (The Blue Bird)* in 1909. In 1911 he won the Nobel Prize for literature. Mildred Aldrich acted as Maeterlinck's American literary agent.

7. Janet Scudder (1869–1940), a sculptor primarily of figures for gardens, was the first American woman to have sculpture bought for the Luxembourg Garden, Paris. A lesbian and friend of Gertrude Stein's, Scudder also became a friend and correspondent of McBride's. Stein dubbed Scudder "The Doughboy" because she had "all the subtlety of the doughboy and all his nice ways and all his lonesomeness." Mellow, *Charmed Circle,* p. 307.

ART CRITICISM AT THE BEGINNING OF MCBRIDE'S CAREER

Critics in America have tended to fall into four major categories: moralist, social historian, formalist, or propagandist.
—Barbara Rose, 1972

During the first two decades of the twentieth century, art criticism in the United State was in its infancy. In October 1912, when Samuel Swift invited Henry McBride to write weekly, unsigned art features and criticism for the *New York Sun,* art critics in America were just beginning to establish a voice and to create an audience interested in understanding the art of the time.

In the early years of the century the vast majority of painters and sculptors in the United States adhered to the firmly entrenched traditions of the academy. Art that was experimental—either in its content or form—was rejected by the upper-class public, who were the financial supporters of the art world, and by the National Academy of Design, the monopolizing authority that governed it.[1] Based on the ideals of the French Academy, the National Academy of Design's theoreticians, including Kenyon Cox, saw art as a morally responsible medium meant to encourage virtuous refinement through noble splendor. The standards toward which American artists were taught to strive included idealized beauty, morally enriching themes, and classically inspired compositions. At the turn of the century, John Singer Sargent (1856–1925) and William Merritt Chase (1849–1916) were prime exemplars of European-trained American painters who wed modern subjects with classic beauty. The criticism of the day generally responded to the pressures and proclivities of the National Academy of Design.[2] As a result, most writing on art tended toward the party line:

---

1. Homer, *Avant-Garde Painting and Sculpture,* p. 10.
2. Much of the following information on the development of art writing in newspapers at the turn of the century is adapted from Olson, *Art Critics and the Avant-Garde.*

listing award and medal winners, observing technical accomplishment, and noting pleasing compositions.

The generation of newspaper critics who began their careers in the period before the Armory Show of 1913 established the ground rules that were in place when McBride entered the game. Several of the players continued as his colleagues for many years. Early in the century critics whose views varied as widely as Royal Cortissoz, J. N. Laurvik, Willard Huntington-Wright, and James Gibbons Huneker all found sizable popular followings in newspaper writing in New York.[3]

Before the late 1880s most art criticism was written in magazines. Time, deadlines, and space priorities didn't allow for analysis, so newspaper articles consisted mainly of notices itemizing exhibitions, naming exhibitors, listing titles, noting attendance, and offering a few brief descriptive comments on the works mentioned. As a result, bare-facts reporting rather than interpretation or assessment was the rule of the day. By the mid-1870s there were at least a dozen journals which dealt exclusively with the visual arts, though many of these included a strong focus on decorative art and design.

At the turn of the century a shift in art reporting in the New York dailies came about for reasons that were both social and technical. New lithographic technology inexpensively reproduced illustrations. Newspapers were able to use increased space for human-interest reporting. In the last years of the nineteenth century the appearance of special Saturday or Sunday editions attracted magazine readers and writers to newspapers. Space allotments for the visual arts in newspapers lagged behind the amount of space given over to the arts of literature, drama, and music. When regular art columns came into being, they would often be shuffled around, showing up on the society page, the "Ladies" page, or the amusement page, depending on space availability. Writers of newspaper columns commonly remained anonymous, as did Henry McBride in his first years at the *Sun*.

In 1908–10 leading New York newspapers such as the *Sun* and the *Times* began to support the visual arts by adding regular, signed art columns and commentaries, in addition to the standard calendars and lists. For the first time serious critics wrote for newspapers instead of magazines.

In 1912, when McBride was asked to join its staff, the *Sun* was known as "a newspaper man's newspaper" and had the reputation of being one of

3. Ibid., p. 7.

the best written of the New York dailies.[4] On the eve of the Armory Show daily newspapers in New York had begun to expand their reporting on events related to the visual arts for a variety of reasons, including production advances and increased space allotments for human interest subjects. Writing on art had begun shifting toward more critically driven writing styles, though many in the newspaper business did not take art writing—or any writing on culture—very seriously. According to an article written on McBride more than forty years later, "He arrived when the paper's cultural pretensions were petering and stayed, largely he thinks, because art was of least importance to editors and because he had the good sense to avoid them in the city room and corridors."[5]

A year later the Armory Show confirmed the need for informed authority in the press on matters of modern aesthetics. After Swift's untimely departure from the *Sun*, McBride embarked on the remarkable career that was to become synonymous with a learned and benevolent understanding of the creative implications of modernism. From the platform of his weekly newspaper column in the *Sun*, McBride became the authority by displaying an evenhanded appreciation of the strange new visual arts.

With the advent of modernism and active press coverage of the current events influencing its development, attendance at exhibitions and art-related functions increased. People wanted to know what all the fuss was about, and after reading about it, they wanted to see the art firsthand. By the late teens the influence of the press in general, and McBride in particular, is apparent in the burgeoning interest in modern art, as exemplified by the growing number of New York galleries devoted to it, such as 291, Carroll Gallery, Daniel Gallery, and Montross Gallery.

Henry McBride had the good fortune to begin his career at a moment when the institutional structure of the art world in the United States was being undermined by forces at home and abroad. On these shores, artist-initiated movements, such as Robert Henri's (1865–1929) organization of The Eight in 1908, challenged the power and relevance of a painting style that privileged allegory, history, and mythology over real-life experience. The radical new movements of postimpressionism and fauvism developing in Paris captured the attention of many young American artists studying abroad.

4. Ibid., and Frank Luther Mott, *American Journalism: A History of Newspapers in the United States Through 250 Years, 1690 to 1940* (New York: Macmillan, 1947), p. 421.
5. Devree, "Profile," p. 43.

Most significantly, the Armory Show awakened a creative and intellectual interest in people across the United States, even those who knew of it only through churlish press reports. The influx of European intellectuals, artists, writers, and musicians who arrived as World War I refugees further stimulated this interest. The unprecedented development of a critically motivated and international arts community in New York in the years immediately following the Armory Show brought unparalleled advances in the visual arts. Art writing followed the course of these developments. The artists, galleries, collectors, and patrons that made up the art community were, for the first time, supported by an active press system that critiqued and challenged the developments in the visual arts of the day.

The response of the press to the Armory Show and its aftermath reflects the emergence of critical reportage about the visual arts in the New York dailies. A new spirit in evidence at the Armory Show encouraged the discussion of radicalism as it related to modernity in all things creative— poetry, theater, politics, and even the so-called bohemian lifestyle. The press duly took note and allotted more column inches to writers on these subjects. Artists, writers, collectors, and just plain citizens were trying to define the terms and effects of modernism. Newspapers, art magazines, literary reviews, and general periodicals became the front line in the debate.

The voices for and against the European moderns being shown at the 69th Regiment Armory initiated a dialogue that was to shape the development of the critical methods for evaluating art, determine the course of the art market, and affect the entire infrastructure that supported the art of the modern period in New York and nationally. This was the fertile and confrontational moment at which McBride entered the field of art criticism. It was an opportune moment for the art world, for art journalism, and for McBride.

The following miscellany of critics from the period 1900–1918 provides an overview of McBride's art critic colleagues, their professional affiliations, and their famous (or infamous) points of view. An asterisk indicates that the critic can be considered avant-garde: a supporter of the Armory Show and modern art. A dagger denotes the derrière-garde, a critic opposed to the Armory Show and to modern art.

†John Alexander	Conservative
John Anderson	*New York Evening Journal*
†Carroll Beckwith	Conservative
†Edwin Blashfield	Conservative

Peyton Boswell	*New York Herald*
*D. Putnam Brinley	Active in supporting the Armory Show
*Christian Brinton	Freelance critic and defender of modern art. One of the few critics conversant enough with European modernism to point out during the Armory Show such missing artists and movements as Futurism and German Expressionism
James Britton	*Art News.* Writing for this conservative weekly, he "managed to present a more favorable picture of modernism than was usual."[6] A supporter of the Armory Show
*Charles H. Caffin	*New York American* and *New York Evening Post.* Prominent before World War I
Elizabeth Luther Carey	*New York Times.* A moderate who is assumed to have written the newspaper's unsigned negative review of the Armory Show
†J. Edgar Chamberlain	*New York Evening Mail*
†Royal Cortissoz	*New York Tribune.* One of the most unshakably conservative critics of the time, who proclaimed, "I have been a traditionalist steadfastly opposed to the inadequacies and bizarre eccentricities of modernism"[7]
†Kenyon Cox	*Century* and *Scribner's.* The most virulent of the antimodern critics. The reactionary all progressive critics, including McBride, loved to hate, and the perfect foil for the modern idiom
†Thomas Craven	Conservative and anti-Semitic, referred to Stieglitz as "a Hoboken Jew without knowledge of, or interest in, the historical American background"[8]
†Charles De Kay	"One of America's more ridiculous critical exhibitionists," whose *Art World: A Monthly for the Public Devoted to the Higher Ideals* has been castigated for "its excessive nationalism [that]

6. Brown, *American Painting,* p. 85.
7. Quoted in "Royal Cortissoz, Art Critic, 79, Dies," *New York Times,* October 18, 1948.
8. Quoted in Kleeblatt and Chevlowe, *Painting a Place in America,* p. 41.

	was part of a general attitude which revealed itself as a psychopathic bigotry with amazing analogies to later developments in fascist ideology"[9]
† Charles Henry Dorr	*The World,* supported the efforts of the Armory Show organizers, while voicing reservations about modernism
* Arthur Jerome Eddy	Collector and supporter of modernism, wrote the first American book on cubism, *Cubist and Post-Impressionism*
Frederick W. Eddy	*New York World, Sunday World*
James FitzGerald	Moderate promodernist in the liberal tradition of the *Sun*
* Waldo Frank	One of four editors of *The Seven Arts* (1916–17), a short-lived nationalistic magazine dedicated to fostering the development of an indigenous American cultural experience[10]
* Frederick J. Gregg	Supporter of modernism who wrote, in his preface to the Armory Show pamphlet, "To be afraid of what is different or unfamiliar, is to be afraid of life. And to be afraid of life is to be afraid of truth, and to be a champion of superstition"[11]
* Hutchins Hapgood	*New York Globe*
* Sadakichi Hartmann	Prominent before World War I
† Arthur Hoeber	*New York Globe.* Labeled by the critic Marius de Zayas one of the two most conservative critics of the time, along with Cortissoz, and the one with the more modest intellect[12]
James Huneker	*New York Sun.* Moderate/progressive, an outspoken champion of Cézanne and Matisse
Manuel Komroff	*New York Call*

9. Brown, *American Painting*, pp. 85–86.
10. Kleeblatt and Chevlowe, *Painting a Place in America*, pp. 38–39.
11. Association of American Painters and Sculptors, *For and Against: Views on the International Exhibition Held in New York and Chicago,* edited by Frederick J. Gregg (New York, 1913).
12. De Zayas, *How, When, and Why*, p. 11.

* J. N. Laurvik	*New York Times*. Also wrote books and articles for a number of different magazines, including *Century* and *International Studio*
† Frank Jewett Mather, Jr.	*New York Evening Post* and *The Nation*. In his *Modern Painting: A Study of Tendencies* (1927), said the new movements "may roughly be divided as impulsivistic or intellectualistic."[13] In *The Nation,* called postimpressionism "mostly ignorant splurge" and cubism "an occult and curious pedantry"[14]
† Roy L. McCardell	*The World*
† W. B. McCormick	*New York Press*
† Leila Mechlin	"Secretary of the American Federation of Arts, and editor of the *American Magazine of Art,* used her position to combat the threat of a modern artistic revolution, and the magazine became the most consistent and unrelenting opponent of the new developments"[15]
Harriet Monroe	*Chicago Tribune*. A progressive who maintained a distinctly nineteenth-century point of view. At the same time open to the changes wrought by the Armory Show and leery of them, wrote, "Revolt is rarely sweetly reasonable; it goes usually to extremes, even absurdities"[16]
† James Oppenheim	One of four editors of *The Seven Arts* (see entry for Waldo Frank)
* Walter Pach	Wrote during the Armory Show, "The present age in France is the equivalent of the Renaissance in Italy"[17]
* Guy Péne du Bois	Began as a defender of modernism in the pages of *Arts and Decoration*. After a break with the AAPS, however, adopted a more critical attitude toward the movement

13. Frank Jewett Mather, Jr., *Modern Painting* (New York: Garden City, 1927), p. 353.
14. Quoted in Devree, "Profile," p. 43.
15. Brown, *American Painting,* p. 85.
16. Quoted in Watson, *Strange Bedfellows,* p. 176.
17. Quoted in Devree, "Profile," p. 43.

*Duncan Phillips	Phillips's first fame is as a collector. After starting his art career as a critical detractor of modernism, became one of its most ardent supporters in the press (see Biographical Sketches)
†Paul Rosenfeld	One of four editors of *The Seven Arts* (see entry for Waldo Frank)
†F. Welling Ruckstuhl	Milton Brown called him "a rabid proto-fascist." Wrote that Manet's *Nana* was the "incarnation of the disease called 'modernism,' whose chief symptoms are commercial noise, aesthetic aberration and moral degeneration. And all such as defend, buy or condone such work are inexorably tainted with the disease"[18]
*Leo Stein	In later years a surprising voice for conservatism, wrote for the *New Republic,* which was founded by the painter-critic Robert Hallowell, with Walter Lippmann and Herbert Croly (see Biographical Sketches)
B. P. Stephenson	*Evening Post*
Samuel Swift	*New York Sun.* According to Jerome Mellquist, "wrote with a responsibility and an understanding which challenged the very best in Huneker. Not as gifted in expression, he surpassed his predecessor in depth of understanding, and his early resignation must be accounted one of the most regrettable casualties in American art criticism"[19]
†James B. Townsend	Editor of the news weekly *Art News,* which "gave modern art a largely unsympathetic but fair amount of coverage [and whose] opinion varied a great deal depending on the specific critic involved"[20]

18. "Our Creed," *Art World* 1 (October 1916), n.p.; quoted in Brown, *American Painting,* p. 86. Brown quotation is from p. 87.
19. Jerome Mellquist, *The Emergence of an American Art* (New York: Scribner's, 1942), p. 308.
20. Brown, *American Painting,* p. 85.

Henry Tyrell	*New York World*
†Louis Untermeyer	One of four editors of *The Seven Arts* (see entry for Waldo Frank)
*Forbes Watson	*New York Evening Post, The Arts,* and *New York World,* supporter and publicist of modern art
*Willard Huntington Wright	*Forum.* Published the first book in the United States on modern art, *Modern Painting: Its Tendency and Meaning* (1915)

The most articulate of the antagonists of the new art were Royal Cortissoz, Kenyon Cox, and Frank Jewett Mather, Jr., whom Milton W. Brown referred to as "the anti-modernist triumvirate."[21] McBride's relationships with these men ranged widely. Of Cox he wrote, "Upon the whole his career has been unfortunate both for himself and us. . . . He might have achieved a real reputation instead of this crumbling and shadowy one which a species of terrorism has imposed on us."[22] For Royal Cortissoz he felt a jocular affection. In his obituary of Cortissoz in 1948, McBride wrote, "It was his graciousness of manner carried over into his writing that enabled him in the recent years to dispute much of the modern art activity without giving actual offense to its perpetrators. I never knew any of them to be really angry at him. They often smiled and seemed flattered to have been thought worthy of the scolding. But it was well known that he was out of tune with them. . . . But these innovators could not have asked for a fairer opponent. They will miss him. He created the argument and when there is no argument a movement lies flat."[23]

The group of critics who attempted to understand and address the implications of the modernist movement without necessarily wholeheartedly embracing it included James FitzGerald, F. J. Gregg, and James Huneker. Defenders of Henri and the realists, these three steered a middle course. During the debate some critics changed their opinions; the art collector Duncan Phillips, for example, was a late convert to modernism. Guy Péne du Bois and Leo Stein ended by abandoning its defense, though Péne du

21. Ibid.
22. Henry McBride, "Murals by Kenyon Cox," reprinted in *The Flow of Art,* pp. 90–91. Originally printed in the *Sun,* October 17, 1915. McBride also wrote in "Philip Evergood," reprinted in *The Flow of Art,* p. 323, "Classicism died in this town with Kenyon Cox. Or possibly it is fairer to say that Mr. Cox killed classicism."
23. "The Reaper, Death! Royal Cortissoz, Henry Kent, Juliana Force, His Latest Victims," *The Sun,* October 22, 1948.

Bois had acted for a short time as the official spokesman for the American Association of Painters and Sculptors and Stein was modernism's pioneering collector from 1905 to 1910. Among the least partisan of the early explicators of modernism were Christian Brinton and J. Nilson Laurvik, whose articles appeared regularly in *Century* and *International Studio* and were reprinted in *Camera Work*.

By the beginning of World War I, Henry McBride was becoming the established voice of art writing in the daily press, having already outdistanced his colleagues in his clear understanding of the implications and long-term importance of modernism. His weekly pages for the *Sun* reflected his commitment to educating the American public on the merits of modern art, or at least engaging them in an intelligent dialogue. McBride's writing in these years also impressively and courageously lines up the group of artists whom he would champion over the course of his career.[24] In 1917 McBride wrote a series of articles on Thomas Eakins that brought this forgotten American master back into the public eye. McBride's recognition of the importance of Eakins proved not only his eye for important modern painting but his commitment to American art in the face of what amounted to the European invasion of modernism. McBride the cosmopolitan Francophile was, after all, also an orphan from West Chester, Pennsylvania.

24. Between 1913 and 1918 McBride wrote articles on Cézanne (May 18, 1913; January 16, 1916); Matisse (November 16, 1913; January 24, 1915); cubism (December 14, 1913; February 8, 1914); Brancusi (March 22, 1914); Picasso and Gertrude Stein (March 14, 1915); Demuth (November 1, 1914); Florine Stettheimer (April 28, 1918); and Stieglitz (November 30, 1913; November 8, 1914).

GERTRUDE STEIN

Henry McBride probably met Gertrude Stein in the summer of 1913, through their mutual friend Mildred Aldrich. McBride immediately recognized the importance of Stein's writing and tried to get one of her plays produced in America. That he was unsuccessful in this was not surprising, for her writing and particularly her work for the stage had no precedent, and during her lifetime only *Four Saints in Three Acts* was produced on stage. Their close friendship continued until Stein's death in 1946. The friendship was especially important to Stein in its early years, when she needed support during a time when she had difficulty getting published; McBride assured her, "There is a public for you, but no publisher." In addition to liking Stein personally, he considered her writing to be a part of the campaign on behalf of modernism. Along with Carl Van Vechten, and later Jane Heap, McBride was one of the most consistent and efficacious figures trying to connect Stein with her public. He mentioned her in his column whenever feasible and promoted *Tender Buttons* when it was published in 1914. Through his friendship with *Vanity Fair* editor Frank Crowninshield, McBride arranged for the first Stein publication in a commercial magazine; "Have They Attacked Mary. He Giggled (A Political Caricature)" was published in *Vanity Fair* in June 1917, with several lines cut. Shortly thereafter McBride arranged with Horace F. Templeton, a printer in West Chester, Pennsylvania, to print two hundred copies, using Jules Pascin's portrait of McBride on the cover.[1] McBride urged *The Dial* to publish Stein's work, and he published her during his tenure as editor of *Creative Art* ("Genuine Creative Ability," February 1930; "Thoughts on an American Contemporary Feeling," February 1932). McBride had a remarkable bond with Stein, based in great measure on their mutual interest in promoting modernism, their ability to recognize genius, and their sense of humor.[2]

---

1. McBride also saw to the booklet's distribution through the Sunwise Turn bookstore at 51 East 44th Street: McBride gave its proprietors thirty copies; by 1920 they had sold most of them, for a total of ten dollars.
2. "What differentiated her from all other collectors was the fact that she collected geniuses rather than masterpieces. She recognized them a long way off." Henry McBride, "Pictures for a Picture of Gertrude," *Artnews* 49 (February 1951), p. 18.

11 Henry McBride, Gertrude Stein, Alice Toklas, and Malcolm MacAdam, undated.
Photographer unknown.

McBride's letters to Stein have the special quality of knowing that his
correspondent knew the subjects he was talking about, appreciated his
writing, and was also safely on the other side of the Atlantic, so that he
could convey frankly and knowledgeably his opinions about art. McBride's
fears about the effects of fame became a theme in his letters to Stein when
The Autobiography of Alice B. Toklas was published. The relationship cooled
slightly when Stein became a celebrity in 1933, not because of any quarrel,
but because his role as her supporter was no longer as essential, and trips to
Paris less frequent; he last traveled to Europe in 1937. The last time Stein
and McBride saw one another in person was in 1935, during Stein's triumphant lecture tour of the United States. After her death in 1946, McBride
continued to correspond warmly with Stein's longtime companion Alice
Toklas; one of his last letters (November 1961) was written to her.

To Gertrude Stein
August 7, 1913, 33, avenue d'Antin, Paris

Dear Miss Stein:
    [. . .] Willis Polk, head of the architects, San Francisco Fair, has been here
on his way to Madrid.[1] I am going to ask him to call at the Hotel Roma on

    1. McBride was trying to catalyze a production at the 1915 San Francisco Fair of
Stein's plays, and this was only one of his several attempts. He also tried to persuade

the chance of finding you. I don't know when you arrive there, nor when he arrives, so if you meet, it will be the bon Dieu himself that directs you. I suggested it would be an outrage if some of your dramatic works were not put on, in sumptuous mounts for the delectation of the faithful. He seemed enthusiastic. . . He is not himself so wildly interesting, but nice.

Hope I see you in Madrid myself. With best wishes to you two,

To Gertrude Stein
August 28, 1913, Restaurant Weber, 21 et 25 rue Royal, Paris

Chère mademoiselle:

The Café Weber provides blank writing paper also, and some consider it more chic, but I am purposely using the printed sheets to prove I really write it here. Deficiency of style in café letters is not criminal.

You will be writing yours behind slatted windows in semi translucent darkness and the *helados* will put you in a good humor and the domino players a topic to write upon if you have no other. Here, the chaleur is more epaivantable [*sic*] than anything you will have encountered near Murcia, and the Café Weber awning is not lowered enough so the glare of the sky hits one in the eyes, and the interesting passers-by imagine you are writing out of bravado—and perhaps I am, for I have said nothing yet.[1]

You see I am slightly cross because Paris is become uncomfortable and I have to stay here instead of going to Madrid. I could have passed four days there, from the 28th (today) until the 31st, but you were not coming until September to the Hotel Roma, so I thought what's the use of such an Herculean effort, if I am to be alone. For four or five days after your letter came I had moments of wishing to appeal to you to advance your schedule one week to coincide with mine, but I overcame the weakness, which is another reason why I am cross. Virtue is certainly unpleasant in hot weather.

Minnie Ashley (Mrs. William Astor Chanler; see Biographical Sketches) to perform them, and in one of his early *Sun* columns he wrote: "When eventually a Mr. Montross, theater manager, does produce a Gertrude Stein play, involving as it will a complete departure from the technique at present in vogue, with different lights, different costumes, action and a very different tempo in speech, what fun it will be!" ("The Growth of Cubism," February 8, 1914. McBride's reference to the gallery owner N. E. Montross is not literal; the Montross Gallery had just opened its doors to cubism, and Montross thus exemplified for McBride the sort of impresario adventurous enough to produce Stein.)

1. McBride claims the dreadful heat in Paris must be a match for that in Murcia, in southeastern Spain, where Stein is spending part of her Spanish summer.

Have seen Mick (your Mildred) once or twice. Once at James Stephens' and he read aloud to us some of his things.[2] It was the first I had heard of his and I liked 'em. One called the "Three Penny Bit" not yet published, is sure to make you laugh.[3] His short sketch "Horses" is in the newest *Nation* (English) and whether Stephens knows it or not, it is "Post."[4]

I am disgusted, really, at not seeing you again. I wanted to read those plays over again and talk with you about them.[5] That man Willis Polk of San Francisco is already returned to Paris. He is Chief of the Architectural Commission for the Fair, and has some influence in a general way I imagine. I told him that the Fair should stage your plays, and that Society that plays out in the Forest should know of you. To do the gentleman justice, I must say, his eyes sparkled at the idea. . . That is some time hence, the Fair.[6] In the meantime, I still think they should be done next winter in New York, and if they are done, I hope I shall be allowed to help. . . If you see anything in the Fair, let me know and I'll nab Polk. He gave me the idea that the San Franciscans would love to be up to date or a little ahead of it, if possible.

I'm in Paris,—33 ave. d'Antin, until September 6, sailing on Rochambeau. After that in New York in care *The Sun*.[7] I think I shall have to bore you by writing occasionally. Like my friend Mr. Polk, I should like to keep up-to-date. Wishing you luck with the Palms of Murcia and kindest regards to your charming friend whose name I can't spell,

To James Stephens
December 1, 1913, *The Sun* Editor's Office, New York

My dear "Shamus":
I call you Shamus because I suspect that that gibberish you wrote upon the fly leaf of my new book is affectionate, and I respond easily to affec-

2. See Biographical Sketches.
3. "The Three-Penny Piece" was published in Stephens's book *Here Are Ladies* (London: Macmillan, 1913) and was also seen as "The Threepenny Piece" in the September 1913 issue of the *Irish Review*.
4. The poem "The Horses" was published in *Harper's* magazine in May 1913 and also appeared in *Here Are Ladies*.
5. Later published in Stein's *Geography and Plays* (introduction by Cyrena N. Pondrom, Madison: University of Wisconsin Press, 1993), the plays *What Happened* and *White Wines*, both written in 1913, were being circulated in hopes of finding performance venues.
6. The San Francisco Fair opened in 1915; it did not stage Stein's plays.
7. This was McBride's first trip abroad since starting work for the *Sun*.

tion.[1] I respond to nothing else. If it wasn't affection—I intend to find out what it means—you will hear from me next summer. I will come over there to the rue Campagne-Première with mademoiselle Germaine and the rest of my crowd and we will do you up "proper."[2] The Dublin riots will pale historically.

In the meantime I don't mind saying it's a good book. I have read but fifty-six pages so far, but these fifty-six are fine. It has the effect upon me that all good art has. It seems so easy and natural and plausible, that I find myself saying, "Why I could do that too." Of course, I can't. A sinner who sells himself all his life to the devil cannot reform at 47 and be a saint, but on the other hand, believe me, there is no one who appreciates virtue so keenly as a sinner. Sin certainly sharpens the critical faculty.

I liked the "Glass of Beer" immensely and said "O" several times at the shocking passages and the three heavy husbands and the three women who wept are very beautiful. . .[3] I *hope they won't be successful.* I hope you'll be poor for ten years to come, and then get rich suddenly. I'll tell you what. Why not turn over all of the rights of the books to Mick and tell her to keep the profit, for length of time, doling out only a pittance to you. Wouldn't that solve the problem?

Affectionately, but in great haste,

To Gertrude Stein
December 12, 1913, *The Sun,* New York

Chère mademoiselle Stein:

I was delighted to receive your post card and to know that you didn't object to the jokes. I was not quite sure I wanted you to see it, for I hoped to keep your good opinion—and I was afraid you might not, after all, know me well enough to allow me to be both gay and serious at the same time.

In this country of rural pedagogues and long faced parsons, to laugh at all is to be thought frivolous. I laugh a great deal (so do you), I laugh like an infant at what pleases me. Americans as a rule laugh bitterly, at what they hate, or at what they consider misplaced. I am sending you

1. The gift was an inscribed copy of *Here Are Ladies.*
2. In May 1913 Stephens stayed with his friends the sculptors Theodore and Margaret Theodore Spicer-Simpson at 3 rue Campagne-Premier in Montparnasse. On May 31 he moved to number 11, where he lived until September 1915.
3. "Glass of Beer" was included in *Here Are Ladies.*

this week's *Sun*. Nothing in it about you, I believe. But tomorrow's edition will have something. Kenyon Cox and Gregg, an Irish newspaper man hurled insults at each other in Philadelphia on the subject of Cubism, and William M. Chase (ridiculous old party) joined in with burlesque readings of your "Mabel Dodge."[1] I quote it sans comment. I will send it to you.[2]

By the way I read Mrs. Dodge's review of your work in the Photo-Secession Book.[3] It is fine—but I almost regret she did it. I am a rank snob in art, and I hated to see her help the mob so much. I don't like fine things going into large editions. Too many people will now understand it, or at least know how to take it, (which is the main thing). . . If you have any copies of those plays you must let me have them. I took great pleasure in them.

Why couldn't Mabel Dodge put them on?[4] I must go call upon that clever lady soon.

Regards to our mutual friends. If you hear of significant things from time to time, you must martyrize yourself and send me the tip. Best wishes, too, for the New Year!

1. Frederick James Gregg (1865–1928), Irish-born defender of modernism, was a journalist, an art adviser to the collector John Quinn, and an organizer for the Armory Show. Gregg acted as director of publicity for the Armory Show—along with Arthur B. Davies, Walt Kuhn, and Robert Chanler, he had the honor of giving Teddy Roosevelt a tour of the exhibition—and also lent several works from his own collection to the exhibition. He wrote for the *Evening Sun*.

William Merritt Chase (1849–1916) was an American painter whose long-term contribution hinges primarily on his teaching at the Chase school, which he formed in New York in 1896. Among his students were many of the artists McBride championed, including Demuth, Hartley, Sheeler, and O'Keeffe.

McBride refers to Stein's "Portrait of Mabel Dodge at the Villa Curonia," which became known through Dodge's dissemination efforts at the Armory Show. In his piece, however, McBride quotes Chase reading from Stein's "Matisse," which had been published in *Camera Work* (August 1912).

2. "The Spectre of Cubism in Philadelphia," *New York Sun,* December 14, 1913, reprinted in *Flow of Art,* pp. 49–50.

3. Mabel Dodge's "Post-Impressions in Prose" was originally published in the Armory Show issue of *Arts and Decoration* (February 1913) and reprinted in *Camera Work* (June 1913). Dodge's description of Stein was sometimes quoted: "In a large studio in Paris, hung with paintings by Renoir, Matisse and Picasso, Gertrude Stein is doing with words what Picasso is doing with paint."

4. In spite of McBride's wishes, Dodge did not stage Stein's plays at one of her Evenings at 23 Fifth Avenue.

To James Stephens
January Something 1914, The Sun Editor's Office, New York

My dear Shamus:

I meant to have enclosed instantly to you a letter printed in our paper with a silly accusation against you of plagiarizing from Rossetti lines in the apple poem, but I couldn't squeeze a moment for a note.[1] Now a few days later, a lot of replies and defenses appear, showing you have a host of sensible friends here.

The thing is not worth noticing and is only significant as proving the fact that you have friends here. . . That I had begun to notice before. You know the modern system, probably, better then I do. To appear as a subject of debate like that in a conspicuous journal is to be practically arrivée. The man who manages that section of the paper I happen to know is an admirer of yours.

When I first came back I went to Benleari, (queer name for an Irishman) asking if I could review *Here Are Ladies*. He seemed to be in a temper and hurled me from his office with insults and des injures. Later I saw a playful reference to the book in an editorial and knew Kinsbury, who manages this public-correspondence page, had written it. I asked him about it, he admitted it and chinned rapturously for half an hour upon the subject of the *Crock*.[2] I shan't tell you his words. You'd be ruined for life with vanity. This is the fellow who admitted these accusations to the paper, so I know he regards it as "good business" for you.

Nevertheless if you really mind (I'm sure you are only laughing though) anything you care to tell me will have a sure spot on the page.

As for your hard times, they are ancient history. *Here Are Ladies* the fellow at Brentano's tells me is the popular book of the day.[3] I know what that means, it means you having tea at the Pre Catalan, the Missus coming down to breakfast covered with diamonds like an American lady, and the

1. Stephens replied in a letter to McBride in March, "By the way, there were two little mistakes made in that correspondence—One that, I had stolen the poem from Rossetti, the other that Rossetti's version was better than mine. I had fancied that Sappho, that good lady, was sticking out all over that poem, that it was unnecessary to label the thing" (YCAL, McBride).
2. *Crock of Gold* (1912), one of Stephens's first published prose works, precipitated his rise to literary fame. James Joyce said of the book, "It's all right, but it isn't *written*. I don't see why anybody couldn't do that." Ellmann, *James Joyce*, p. 604.
3. The book was often reissued. In the United States alone, *Here Are Ladies* was reprinted in 1914–15, 1916–17, 1918–19, 1920–21, 1924–25, and 1928.

kiddies with six nurses each and almost forgetting who their father is. . . I suppose all is over between us.

Seriously though, you have made a real hit, here, and absolutely without puffing. The books have made their way without advertisement and I feel awfully encouraged about *us,* in consequence. I had begun to believe that this public was incapable of reading a real book or appreciating style. . . . Just the same you mustn't come here. No one can achieve style here at present, of that I am still convinced. And they'll be trying to engage you for lecture tours, and that sort of thing. You may write for our magazines for a pound a word, if you like, but nothing further.[4] Give my respectueux hommages to madame while she is still sufficiently un-rich to receive them, and consider myself, for the same term,

Yours to oblige,

To Mildred Aldrich
May 1, 1914, Fort Pitt Hotel, Pittsburgh, Pa.

Dear Mildred:

Your long charming Christmas letter, those Cahiers d'Aujourd'hui never acknowledged, letters from Mademoiselle Stein and le célèbre et fameux Monsieur Stephens never acknowledged, Margy and Theodore in town a week and never saw them, Miss Edgerton's party to which I never went—I could fill the whole page with my list of crimes—somehow I think you understand and excuse them—but nobody else does. I have never put in such a lonely winter nor such a hard working one. It is a revelation to me, the price one has to pay in these days for the little money that one earns. . . I am more convinced than ever that one cannot earn money and be decent.

But take warning, with all my crimes upon me, I'm coming to Paris. Sail about May 16 for London, and get to Paris early in June. Bryson also sails, Edith phoned me, about the same time, probably via Italy to France.

Am here in Pittsburgh, to write up the International Show.[1] Hate writing

4. In apparent reply to this or some similar entreaty from McBride to be featured in an article, Stephens responded, August 27, 1914: "I am the proprietor of a past that could not stir the heart of the great American Nation. It is tame, it is hygienic, let us hasten to forget it. Unlike Jesus Christ, I was born with the aid of a father as well as a mother. I will stir these ashes no more or I may discover other lapses from tradition of true greatness" (YCAL, McBride).

1. Into the 1930s, McBride often began, or as in this case ended (the exhibition was usually in the fall, but sometimes in the spring), his season of art writing with a trip

up institutional exhibitions. Pittsburgh inconceivably stupid. No wonder the moderns abolished hell. Pittsburgh does admirably. That reminds me of Anatole France's *Révolte des Anges!*[2] Isn't is corking? And that reminds me of James Stephens' new book of poems.[3] Please see I am down as ordering one of the first edition.

With love and thanks for your letter and books.

1914, World War I journal

Saturday July 25. Had dinner with James Stephens, talking at times of the Ulster uprising and the danger to England but never mentioning the Serbian question so little importance did it seem to have then.[1] Stephens departed on Tuesday elated at the prospect of the uprising in Dublin. Within three days of his going all Europe was planning war and Paris the scene of a rout unprecedented in magnitude—the Parisians in one day hiding all their coin gold and silver and merchants and restaurants refusing paper money. The thousands of unsuspecting tourists at once felt the inconvenience and became panic stricken adding their excitement to that produced by the mobs parading the streets. Thursday 100 f. notes were refused, Friday 50 f. notes were uncashable except at the Bank de France where 40,000 people waited all day in line. The French raided the grocery stores as well, forming in queux, storing up pâtés and tinned eatables in vivid recollection of the siege of 1870. All day and all night the taxi autos

to the Carnegie International in Pittsburgh, the annual juried exhibition of contemporary art founded by Andrew Carnegie. The eighteenth annual exhibition ran from April 30 to June 30, 1914. Jurors including Cecelia Beaux, William Merritt Chase, and Robert Henri awarded prizes to George Bellows (1882–1925) and Edward W. Redfield (1869–1965). The exhibition was suspended in 1915 because of the war, resuming in 1919 as the Annual Exhibition of Paintings.

2. Anatole France's (1844–1924) *Révolte des Anges* (1914) described, as a basis for social satire, the adventures of a band of angels wary of heaven, who decide to live as mortals in Paris.

3. In his notebook McBride writes that in Stephens's book *The Demi-Gods,* which like France's book features the close association of humans and deities, "the gods and mortals are all expressions of single aspects of an individual life." June 16, 1915 (YCAL, McBride). "Stephens' new book" probably refers to *Five New Poems* (1913).

1. The Curragh Incident took place in March 1914, when British troops voiced hesitation about the prospect of being called upon to quell a Protestant rebellion in Ulster.

On July 23 the imperial government of Austria-Hungary had issued an ultimatum to Serbia in the wake of the assassination of the Archduke Ferdinand, less than a month earlier, that the government quell its population's hostility to the monarchy. Five days later, Austria-Hungary declared war on Serbia.

rushed frantic people with baggage to the r.r. stations which were blocked with traffic, trunks piled mountain high to be lost forever probably to their owners. All this because Austria's ultimatum to the Servians in regard to the Archduke's assassination was deemed so peremptory and so impossible that war was not only inevitable but apparently wished for by Austria. In a flash everyone saw Russia defending Serbia, France assisting Russia and England helping France—millions attacking millions in a war that would destroy civilization. All the modern inventions such as the telephone, the taxi, added new terrors to the flight of a great capital, because helping it to be more swift.

Volotich the Servian gave all his money to his comrades who left for Belgrade instantly on the ultimatum so when the war was declared, Austria not deeming the Servian submission to be "sincere," Volotich was caught here. He borrowed money somewhere and on Wednesday night at dinner asked us to change his paper money for gold so that he could cross Italy to Belgrade. This we did. Not till the next night did we realize the panic was beginning and the cafés were refusing to make change. Austria had only declared war on tiny Servia and every American in Europe was making hot speed for ports and Parisians who could were getting out of Paris.

Young Kalb the German who had been here on vacation suddenly appeared. He was very cool and quiet. He collected the money due him and his belongings and on Friday night he left for Frankfurt again. Asked why returning in his soft effeminate voice he replied, "I think the war is beginning and Germans won't be safe here." Something in the extreme quietness of his voice struck me as uncanny. Since I have concluded Kalb already knew what was coming.

Miss Davey and Miss Starr began to worry about the Provence having heard a rumor she would not sail on Saturday. Since Wednesday bands of men and boys paraded the boulevards shouting Vive l'Armée and Vive la paix, with encounters by the police to further disturb those already nervous. Friday night Jaures was assassinated but the press and public took it astonishingly calmly.[2] The prospect of world wars was frightening every one and riots about the murdered socialist were not thought of. Saturday a.m., learned the Provence had not sailed. Miss Davey and Miss Starr to a

2. Jean Léon Jaures (1859–1914), leader of the socialists in the Chamber of Deputies, was cofounder and editor of *L'Humanité* (1904–14). On the eve of the war Jaures fought against all military measures and was assassinated by a fanatic on July 31, 1914. This notebook entry, while dated July 25, must have been written over the course of the following week.

hotel to be with friends saying had promise La France would sail Tuesday. Gilbertè the waiter said [he] had been summoned to mobilize Monday at Verdun. One of the nearest he said proudly. Madame said she would close Monday. We could go to Chateauraux with them, where we would be sure of vegetables to eat. Volotich gets off our train Saturday night, equipped like a Tartarien, with nickel lamp, cushions, whip, pâtés. Monsieur Paul to go Tuesday. American Express office a mass of frantic Americans clamoring for money and passage home. Saw 19 old ladies sitting in a circle on Champs Élysées, nicely dressed, pompadour hair, necklaces, quietly making plans far from the crowd shouting itself hoarse on the boulevard singing the Marseilles. They were holding a conclave they said. We have heard this and that and we don't know what to do. We'll know Monday, I told them.

In fact we knew Sunday. Robertson Trowbridge woke me at nine a.m. with the news.[3] His brow was bespangled with perspiration and he was frightened. Russia had declared war against Austria. The buses were not running and he had walked. People were dragging their belonging through the streets to the railways. Jeane wept when she brought breakfast her husband should leave for the mobilization on Monday, already declared by the French. Luncheon we served ourselves. Pierre, Mlle Germain's fiancé announcing they could not go by auto to Chateauraux as autos could not go out of the city. The mobilization proclamation gave foreigners till Sunday midnight to leave. After that everyone remaining had to have police billets. On the boulevards the mobs were smashing shops of Germans, beginning with Perlops, the Gendarmes on guard themselves laughing. Monday at eleven de Roquarols left, I alone in house, myself closed piano lid, got my trunk to sidewalk alone, found a taxi and got luggage to Sun office for 5 f. and pourboire of umbrella. No metro. Hot. Got to American Express Co., at 9 p.m. who gave me only 5 f. in silver in cashing check for $50. The rest in 50 franc notes. Monday decidedly calmer. For first time since sequence of events broken by day inaction. The German minister staying on in Paris, hoping a French minister said to put the onus of declaring war on France. More incendiaries by mobs including destruction Maggi depots, Hapenrondt, etc. Monday night first day military rules, were put forcibly out café at 9 p.m. all dark and city quiet early in consequence. All public affiches in admirable taste.

Americans weeping at consulate as form line for passports.

The fifty Americans escaping with their luggage to London via the river

3. See Biographical Sketches.

Seine to Havre seem to be in for their share of picaresque adventures. The Gentleman managing the trip does not enjoy the best of reputations. The American Ambassador in fact told everyone he was not to be trusted and in consequence instead of the 600 who were to pay 500 f. to get to London, only fifty appeared most of them ladies. Fred Howald of Columbus who is shy, minded the ignominy of the possible ridiculous ending of the affair more then the not getting to London.[4] Instead of leaving at 9:30 a.m., at 12:30 the boat was still fast to the quai d'Orsay so I said good-bye to Howalds and the nineteen old ladies from Los Angeles who at the last view were suggesting that the suspicious manager put the 250 francs each person had paid for the Rouen-London part of the trip in the hands of one member of the party who should pay it to him when the party passed Rouen. It looked like a comic opera scene. I learned afterward that a prima donna was aboard. Miss Felicie Lyme and her mother.

At the Gare du Nord later when hundreds were saying good-bye to departing soldiers and ban biene passengers were thick there was a burst of melody and eight or ten Walloon workmen with linen bags slung over their shoulders appeared singing rollickingsomely. They were somewhat drunk but extremely graceful and picturesque. The leader particularly was guileless and frank. Old Parisians said "C'est honteux," to be drunk at such a time but they were so innocent and amusing that it really wasn't honteux.[5]

Evening procession cavalry [unintelligible] and teams to Gare du Nord. Fear on sidewalk, everyone being in their own quarters at 8:30 p.m. Young Frenchman at Duvals dining. I part for the front tomorrow. 6th Cavalry. Been on sick leave. My comrades already there. I'm enjoying Paris, and in 5 days I may be dead. It's not right is it? But that's the French nature. My father says they all went laughing to the war in '70, saying à Berlin, just a man.

———

Spies Café Veinois was first to suspect assaults from marauders. Closed doors, soaped windows white. Apparently gave idea for crowd destroyed Perlops, Café Royal, Maggies, Hapenrondts, and finally Café Veinois itself. Next day every house with Germanish names affiched "Maison Française. Closed because propretaire mobilized, etc." Monday at 6 p.m. Bernheim

4. The American collector Ferdinand Howald (1856–1934) was an early avid collector of modern art, one of the few supporters of American moderns. The reclusive Howald collected alone and in almost complete anonymity, amassing one of the most extensive collections of Demuth, Hartley, Marin, and Prendergast, now housed in the museum of his hometown, Columbus, Ohio.
5. *Honteux,* disgraceful or scandalous.

Juene had such affiche. At 8:50 it was gone. Whether torn off or Bernheim had change of mind don't know.

———

Little French soldier. Champs Élysées 9:30 Sunday night. Weeping. Rendezvous my brother noon now not come, doesn't know Paris, He lost (Soldier [sans] sous) Crowd rather ashamed.

Sunday, after a day or two of comparative calmness, given over to work of readjusting ourselves to the new circumstances, making simpler habits for war time, suddenly today the entire city had become nervous again, without knowing why. Everyone talks excitedly, the taxis have gone to full speed again and there is a great deal of hurrying to and fro. Something has happened. Today everybody says so but no one knows. Two days ago it is said two trains of wounded have been in the city. The Alsace victory cost 40,000 French dead. The French say the victory was worth it. But the papers still say the affair was a trifling engagement.[6] But the bonne in my hotel knew it, the waiter at Vians knew it, Everybody knows it, but the officials say nothing.

———

On Monday first day of military rule the cafés were closed at nine p.m. and it was extraordinary the difference that resulted in the Boulevards. No tables on the sidewalks, no lighted shops, it seemed always Sunday and the crowds instead of marching in marauding processions as before went home to bed dutifully and the tired police at last had a respite. The extraordinary unanimity with which everything closed up, hotels, shops, theatres, all for the same reason, employees being gone to the front, made the city another place. One is constantly seeing suggestive sights. Nurses being dashed in autos through the streets. Damaged German shops being boarded up. Heavy loads of condensed milk being taken to Red Cross Building. Jewelers and sellers of objects de luxe packing them away in a time when superfluous. . . Shopmen carrying bulky bags of something to shops at late hours of night.

August 5. Last night I went to Gare St. Lazare to see the train off for the La France. Gendarme wouldn't let me in but I showed him my Consulate papers and as he couldn't understand them he let me pass. The great

6. The engagement in Alsace, August 4–25, 1914, failed after some initial success. The French invaded their former territory of Alsace and made some early gains, but the Germans drove the troops back and actually gained ground in the end. It was a strategic success in that it strengthened French morale and deflected German troops from the larger northern offensive.

station not animated as I expected. A few soldiers sitting on bags—no puffing engines no trains moving. No signs of pushing travelers. I saw a girl with a porter in distress. It seems she had a ticket for La France, but not the r.r. ticket to Havre. Not speaking French she had not known that r.r. tickets must be purchased day before journey. No amount of talk could sway the military in charge. . . So the train moved off and the girl and her porter toting suit cases walked back to Grand Hôtel. She took it calmly. The passengers who sat in the dark seemed stricken and did not speak. Those in lighted carriages were gay, some of them. A jew and his wife had hysterics when someone wanted them to change their places. They thought they were being put off the train.

August 5. Breakfast munching croissants read the Deschanel speech in the Chambre.[7] When he said "What am I saying are there any longer adversaries" (to the dead Jaures)? The president responding "There are now only Frenchmen" and everyone shouting, something brought the tears. I showed it to the garçon and he wept a tear too.

At 10 a.m. saw a handful of American students volunteering in the Latin Quarter marching down the street with banners to the Palais Royal. Some girls with them who meant to be nurses. Two young fellows lettering banners stretched on the Billiard table in Café du Dôme. The waiter saying to whom would listen "C'est beau. I leave tomorrow and I have two babies. But that's beau!" Another fellow fetches in a canvas with a nude and letters over it a banner.

From the notebooks
December 1914

It has already been so effectually whispered about, among the initiated that a new book by James Stephens, the Irishman, is about to appear, that perhaps it is only fair, that I who have been as busy whispering as the next one, should tell you it is to be a good book.

This I have upon the highest authority.

When I entered Stephens' rooms in the rue Campagne-Première, Paris, this last June, he rose from his table, laughing and said, "I'm just writing the last word to it."

7. Paul-Eugène-Louis Deschanel (1856–1922), statesman, author, leader of the progressive republicans, and, in 1914, in the second year of his eight-year term as president of the Chamber of Deputies.

"To what?"

"To the book, *Demi-Gods*," said he, and then he added, "It's a good book, I enjoyed writing every word of it."[1]

Thereupon we launched into one of those conversations for which Stephens' friends would love him even if he could not write, for he is one of the very best talkers in the world, and our subject was, "How can a writer hope to please the public with his writings, unless he pleases himself?"

Stephens, who is thirty years old, and about as Irish as they make them, became very restive this summer as the bulletins from Ulster reached us, and finally he could stand it no longer and packed up his wife and two small kiddies and a recent green parrot, present from the exiled Maud Gezne and left Paris for Dublin, two days before the War of Wars broke out.[2] He found upon his arrival no riots, but the peace that passeth understanding. The exact adjectives that James Stephens applied to the peace, that now reigns in Dublin are, in point of fact, scarcely quotable! He gained something by going back to Ireland though, for the great AE, the only individual of merit, whom George Moore confesses he can't quarrel with, has read the proofs to the *Demi-Gods* and pronounces it the best work Stephens has yet done.[3]

Over here in America though, the individuals who specialize upon parallels and plagiarisms will as likely as not make an out cry against the *Demi-Gods,* because angels hobnob quite casually with mortals in the new book, claiming it to be the *Révolte des Anges* over again. They will be wrong. The story is built about the delicious tale of the "Three Penny Piece" which all readers of *Here Are Ladies* will remember. And the poetry, with which the worldly adventures of the angels are surrounded is redolent of the Ould Sod, not of the Paris. But to talk of plagiarism is nonsense. It is enough to

1. *The Demi-Gods,* published by Macmillan in October 1914, was, as were so many of Stephens's books, reprinted throughout the 1920s. Stephens inscribed a copy of the book to McBride on November 14, saying, in part, "Paris is the saddest of cities. Write me, like the decent man you are, say that you are coming here soon."
2. Probably Maud Gonne (1866–1953), Irish actress, nationalist, philanthropist, and heroine to many writers of the Irish Renaissance, particularly William Butler Yeats.
3. "AE" was George William Russell (1867–1935), a poet, journalist, economist, mystic, and artist, and a member of the circle credited with instigating the Irish renaissance. *AE* was his signature for contributions to the newspaper *Irish Theosophist*. He saw Stephens's earliest poetry in the Irish publication *Sinn Fein* and introduced the younger man to George Augustus Moore (1852–1933), a novelist and dramatist, who was also a member of the Irish group who introduced native Irish drama in the English language.

say certain passages of the poetic prose in *Demi-Gods,* will be placed at once by everybody, at the top of the list of precious achievements of the Irish school and therefore at the top of English writing as well.

To Gertrude Stein
January 7, 1915, *The Sun,* New York

Dear Miss Stein:

What has become of you? What are you doing? Do please write and tell me something about yourself. I heard when I was in Paris in August that you were in Knightsbridge Hotel London but I am thinking you must have returned to Paris.[1]

In August, Paris was blue enough to get on one's nerve—and by what I hear it is even sadder now. Still apparently there is no place in the world where one can get away from the war. And so I would prefer Paris to being here.

When I got back, September 1st, the Americans were in such an affected, hypo critical attitude towards the war, that in my shame, I turned Pro-German for a time. That is, it was anything with me not to be with the Americans.

They took the whole thing as a personal affront to themselves, an insult. It interfered with their God, Business. . . In the several months since, they have grown a trifle more honest, but still the newspapers are unbearable. Their latest half-hour bulletins of new terrific battles are hard for me, at least, to read.

Secretly (and you needn't tell this to Mick) I am one of those who believe in war and out of this present one lots of things that I take pleasure in, will be revived. I mean the bigger livelier qualities of the past, the shreds of which you still see in Spain.

If you think me a barbarian, ignore my foolish remarks, but tell me about yourself. The Matisse show is due here in a short time.[2] We expect

1. When World War I broke out Gertrude Stein and Alice Toklas were staying with the English theoretical mathematician, analytic philosopher, and pacifist Alfred North Whitehead (1872–1970) and his wife Evelyn in their English country home, Lockeridge. What was to have been a weekend visit turned into an eleven-week stay.
2. The Matisse show opened at the Montross Gallery on January 20, and McBride wrote about the exhibition ("Matisse at Montross," *New York Sun,* January 24, 1915, reprinted in *Flow of Art,* pp. 75–80).

some fun. I must send you what I wrote of the other "modern" show that we had. The town is full of weird artists from all parts of the world.[3] We have become the capital of the arts!

To Gertrude Stein
March 27, 1915, *The Sun,* New York

My Dear Gertrude Stein:

I suppose people send you things like the enclosed, that are constantly appearing now over here. This is from *The Evening Sun* by a writer who signs "Don Marquis."[1] I had two things about you lately myself that I forgot to send you. I shall try to look them up for you. I am so desperately overworked however (14–18 hours a day of mechanical work) that my mind no longer plays with an idea. Hence, excuse everything that comes from me—if you can.

Just today I got a letter from a woman in Detroit asking where *Rogue* with your "Galeries Lafayette" poem could be obtained.[2] She said ecstatic things about the "Marsden Hartley Foreword" and its review, of last year.[3] It is a killing thing but do you know there are actually some people, presumed to be intelligent, who think there is no such person as Gertrude Stein! One man, one of our editorial writers actually accused me of being Gertrude Stein. I felt flattered, but denied it.

I have been meaning to ask you for a long time if you had any short pieces in your portfolio on a stereotyped art theme such as the *Laocoön,* Botticelli's *Spring* or the *Venus de Milo* that I could sling quite careless-like into my art page some sleepy Sunday before the season ends. The article

3. McBride's statement slightly anticipates the World War I emigration to New York. By the time this letter was written, Jules Pascin had arrived, and soon to arrive were the artists Marcel Duchamp, Albert Gleizes, Jean Crotti, and Francis Picabia, the composer Edgard Varese, the poet (and boxer) Arthur Cravan, and the poet Mina Loy, and New York would indeed become "the capital of the arts" for a brief period.

1. Don Marquis was a humorist, best known for "archy and mehitabel," in which there appear no capital letters or punctuation (the conceit being that because the typist, archy, is a cockroach, he cannot hit the shift key), thus the association with Stein.

2. *Rogue* was a little magazine published from March to September 1915 in New York by Allen and Louise Norton, financed in part by Walter Arensberg. Carl Van Vechten arranged for the publication of Stein's piece.

3. Sections from Stein's play *IIIIIIIII* appeared in Stieglitz's catalog for the Hartley exhibition, opening at 291 in January 1914. Although not a portrait of Hartley, this play includes among its characters MN H.

need not be stereotyped unless you insist. But it is late and I hope to end my confounded art page by the middle of May, if I can.

I'm hoping to cross to your side then for two months. Am dying to see Paris, for something in the general cussedness of the atmosphere over here has forced me to make such mistakes in the letters in which I try not to talk war talk, that I find I haven't a friend left in Europe. I'm not at all sure of you, even. James Stephens has cut me since September and I haven't heard lately from Mick. . .[4] The United States are solid for the Allies as you know. Everybody now prophesies the end by Autumn, or earlier.[5]

To Frederick J. Gregg
June 1, 1915, S.S. Malte, French Line

Dear Gregg:

If the fear of the Lord is all it is supposed to be you will certainly observe an improvement in my moral tone when next we meet. It descended upon me, I wrote you before the voyage began, and stayed with me during the trip generally in the form of a toothache. We are now at anchor just outside the mole of La Pallice, but it rains cats and dogs and the wind blows, so I can't go out on deck to see what land looks like.

The little harbor of La Pallice is so full, there is no room for us, so we may have to wait until morning to enter. If the hour of the train to Paris permits it, I will stop a half day in La Rochelle (the Station) as Captain Bataille tells me it is a quaint old walled town.

The captain proved to be a little wonder and I hope you'll be able to meet him sometime. My society was far from being cheering, but he accommodated himself to it wonderfully. He showed me his teeth which I admired unreservedly and then he told me they were false. He lost his native ivories, when he had the scurvy twenty years ago, and he is heartily thankful to the scurvy, he says, now. Of course, when you once fall into a

4. McBride shortly received a letter from Stephens, dated March 1, complaining that McBride never provides him with any address, and that he was holding the gift of a copy of *Demi-Gods* as, "you're the best of men, but America is a wide address even for Cleopatra" (YCAL, McBride).
5. In early 1915, while the war intensified, the Allies had a number of successes that people believed indicated a turning of the tide. By late 1915 ex-president Theodore Roosevelt's campaign for military "preparedness" in the United States had become a national movement, foreshadowing, instead of an end to the war, the United States' entry into it in 1917.

state of terror, everything else frightens you, too, so yesterday I actually began to think about submarines.[1] The fact is it got cold and the sky was overcast and the water took a nasty look. Although the Malte is a fine boat, there is no steam heat anywhere, and when you are chilled through and through and have a toothache, the life boats are not a pleasant thought. I could scarcely sleep last night. I tried to laugh at myself for being so silly but my Mr. Hyde replied, "It's all very well to pretend, but the next minute may come the horrid explosion," and then my Dr. Jekyll would squirm and try to think of something else. It's all very fine for you and Flannagan, sitting in Mouquins to be brave, but circumstances alter cases.

The life drill we had one day didn't reassure me a little bit. The crew didn't know it was a drill and thought something had happened. You should have seen their faces and you should have seen them! I had not seen any of the stokers, until then, but they are mediaeval beyond belief and I didn't fancy spending a night in a life boat with any of them. It was a nice bright day, that of the drill, and the scared matelots hunted for their places and fumbled with the unruly ropes and we were all very solemn about it. "See," said Captain Bataille, "We were only eight minutes getting the boats lose. A ship like this would stay afloat fifteen minutes no matter what happened." In my mind, however, I kept conjuring up a heavy list to the boat, and all of us sliding off into the sea, for there were no rails on the deck where the boats are.

I am sorry now that I got scared. When I was quite young the old people all said that I would live to be hanged, and in those days I used to say, that when my time came to be hanged, I should die with a smile on my face. That dream is o'er. I see now that my time for heroics is past. [. . .]

To Gertrude Stein
June 5, 1915, Paris, France

Chère mademoiselle:

Here I am, and delighted to be here. Even these two or three days of crippled Paris repay me, I feel, for all the nigger slavery of last winter.

Had a gorgeous trip over. Was invited guest of captain of a French liner laden to the brim with munitions of war. Was only passenger, had the royal

1. In February 1915 Britain's successful sea blockade of Germany resulted in an escalation of German submarine assaults on any ship in the waters near Britain or Ireland. Among the many international casualties was the *Lusitania,* which went down May 7 within twenty minutes of being torpedoed by a German U-boat, killing 1,198.

suite, a special valet, and the cuisine Béarnaise was superb. I was scared stiff when we got to the danger zone and never slept a wink that night, but enjoyed the fright after it was over.[1]

Please let me know your plans and future addresses. Very likely I shall run down to Spain for two or three weeks and should like to cross your paths. Much obliged to you for telling Vollard about me.[2] I went to his shop yesterday but it was closed. I hope he will give the book to me here instead of sending it. I shall try to find him.

Have not seen Mildred yet but have seen Stephens and expect to lunch with him today. He is full of amusing talk and wild ideas as usual.

But Paris is great—surtout in the dark. It may grown tiresome but at present I love the dark nights.[3]

Hoping I shall see you and Mademoiselle and with my best wishes to you both,

From the notebooks
June 15, 1915 (Chez Vollard, Art Dealer)

Vollard is a tall, awkward person, earnest simple and engrossed in linking his name with modern art history.[1] He has a trick of shutting one eye tighter than the other which gives an oblique line across the face. He has

1. In June 1915 a French boat crossing the Atlantic would enter the danger zone—where it would be most likely to run into the enemy—as soon as it approached the British Isles.
2. Ambroise Vollard (1867–1939) was a French dealer, critic, and publisher who championed the work of the early French moderns. Vollard gave Cézanne his first solo exhibition in 1895. In 1897 he took on the financial responsibility of supporting Gauguin. In 1901 he exhibited the work of an unknown foreigner named Picasso, and he went on to become the major dealer of cubism. A publisher of beautifully produced books, Vollard commissioned many of his favorite artists to make illustrations for classic and modern texts. His own writing on artists includes a biographical memoir on Cézanne, published in 1914, which is probably the book to which McBride refers.
3. Blacked-out Paris, Marcel Duchamp told a reporter, was "like a deserted mansion. Her lights are out." "French Artists Spur on an American Art," *New York Tribune*, October 24, 1915.

1. More than thirty-five years later McBride described Vollard as "very rugged and invincibly bourgeois." In the same article, about Albert Barnes and his collection, McBride recounts his pleasure at "meeting again with the Cézanne *Card Players* which I had seen many years previously in Paris at the little Vollard gallery, carelessly stacked on the floor and leaning against the wall," reprinted in *Flow of Art*, "Dr. Barnes R.I.P.," pp. 436–37.

been painted by Cézanne, Bonnard and Renoir. The Bonnard gave the background of the very room we were in, and one could recognize the Renoir on the wall. He showed us superb Degas pastels larger than any I had seen, quantities of them, and one painting of a woman in the Stevens-Manet costume at Mirror, her back in superb shadows. Very Venetian. Ought to be in a museum. Saw a fine Cézanne nude with scratches by dissatisfied artist. Lovely color. Fine still life in hot color, vase in exact center of toile. Quantities of landscapes. Vollard indefatigable in showing me. Said, "and will you make a little article sur moi?" All picture dealers are very affable now. A Mr. Strauss present, a collector of modern art, assured me prices had not tumbled since the war. He had not heard of a single instance. French were not like that. Preferred not to sell and to keep prices up. English were different.

To Gertrude Stein
August 20, 1915, Callicaste, Marshallton, Pennsylvania

My dear Gertrude Stein:
   I came away from France with a sense of failure because I didn't meet you. I only went to Paris to cure my soul and I thought that Mildred Aldrich, James Stephens and you, between you, could accomplish it. I became ill with dissatisfaction that started some years ago, but became acute last winter, when I was compelled to hear so much rot from American lips upon the subject of the war. Apparently I could not accept (or even stand) a single American utterance upon that subject. The sum of their output may be described in a phrase, for I didn't take my pen in hand to talk war talk to you, as compounded in equal parts of "ignorance of life" and of "hypocrisy."
   But this is what I really wish to write about: On the steamer coming home I met Mrs. William Astor Chanler, a conspicuous woman in society, and also president of the N.Y. Stage Society.[1] We put our heads together planning work for this society next winter. I told of those three plays I read of yours some years ago, "House to House," etc. etc.; and suggested doing them.[2] I told her a trifle of the way in which I think they could be put on,

1. See Biographical Sketches. This is the first of many appearances in McBride's letters of Minnie Ashley, or Mrs. William Astor Chanler, who would become a lifelong friend of McBride's.
2. "House to House" is the title of the third act of Stein's play *White Wines*.

and she became enchanted. I told her that part of the audience would say "This is an insult to our intelligence" and the other half would say "This is insane."

She replied, "O, we must do them. Write at once and ask for them."

Won't you permit us to do them? Won't you send me a copy of the Mss. at once. Send it and I'll guard it secretly and hold it to your orders in case the scheme falls through. But I think it will go. My idea is to have Matisse make some sketches for the scenes and costumes. His lack of knowledge of English makes it difficult of course. Is there any one else who could do them? I'd rather have bad Matisse drawings, myself, than better drawings by an unknown man, for the réclame is everything. Non è vero?

I shall write in detail how I think the play should be mounted, when you send me a copy. But the postman now awaits without.

Love to you and Mlle Alice. [. . .]

To James Stephens
December 9, 1916, *The Sun* Editorial Department, New York

My dear Shamus:

I'll try again to find out how you are. Evidently you didn't get my two letters last year, although there was nothing in them but puerile guessings on what the American policy towards last year's events was to be. Your letter with your address, written and mailed in Dublin in September (plainly postmarked) reached me *the end of April*. It had not apparently been opened by the censor.

That was not why I didn't try again though. The fact is, to suppress tiresome details, I actually thought last spring that I was going to die and I went away to the country for that purpose. It's a disgusting thing to relate, but it developed that I was not a hero—at least I wasn't last spring. . . I did nothing but cuss and hate. . . I consorted with no living people but read more or less on the sly, the letters of Shelley, Byron, and people of that sort who faced death with something like hilarity. All that I can say is, that their attitudes are totally incomprehensible to me—unless it be that Shelley and Byron were both liars. If I thought I had the slightest chance of enduring fame I know I wouldn't frankly rate myself below a hero (as I have just done).

But I am still alive and very brave again on the subject of death, (not a single ache or pain today), and immensely curious to know how your health and spirits are, and if you remember me. I wanted to write long ago to tell you how fine I thought the *Rocky Road* was.[1] It seemed immeasurably better than when you read them aloud to me at Fauquets. Write to me cher enfant, that is if you'll deign to write to a person who doesn't want to die. Would you like to see me in Dublin next summer? I'm thinking of coming.

To Gertrude Stein
February 23, 1917, New York, New York

Dear Gertrude Stein:

At last—I write! Perhaps. May be I shan't get away with it after all. . . I've not written because I've had so much to apologize for. Finally I got to the point where it would take a week to explain why I had not written. Then it got so that it would be a bore for you to read it if I wrote it. So I didn't write it. . . It all began last summer (probably Mildred told you) when I thought I was going to die and went away to the country for the purpose. But I didn't die. I never do anything I set out to do.

I loved the poem and am awful glad to think at last I'm immortalized, but I don't think it'll do for the *Sun*.[1] It would look like bragging too much. Besides it's so immoral! I thought of changing the "Who is Mr. McBride?" to "Who is Mr. Wilson?" but was afraid the subsequent line about the hotel would get me sued for libel. No one ever mentions the hotel in America.

Perhaps I'll have courage enough to let *Vanity Fair* publish it. Your play can't be done by the Stage Society (damn it) for mille reasons.

Now this is a real letter. You can't say it ain't—so you ought to be sorry for all the mean things you put in the poem. Maybe I'll see you in July.

To Gertrude Stein
Spring, 1917, Callicaste, Marshallton, Pennsylvania

My dear Gertrude Stein:

Please address your instantaneous reply to the above address. I like to have quick replies to my letters but I have never yet succeeded in making a swift answer myself, and until my rich friends burn sufficient candles to get

1. Stephens's *The Adventures of Seumas Beg/The Rocky Road to Dublin,* brought together a series of Dublin sketches written over several years. Published in London and New York by Macmillan in 1915, the American edition gave top billing to the metaphorical journey: *The Rocky Road to Dublin/The Adventures of Seumas Beg.*

1. "The poem" was "Have They Attacked Mary. He Giggled," which is also the subject of the following letter.

12 *Henry McBride*, 1918. Jules Pascin, woodcut.

me out of purgatory (the newspaper business) I dare say, I never shall. But there are real reasons why you should be quick this time. This is a business letter! I have been hesitating whether to tell you or no, that Frank Crowninshield took the portrait of us two for *Vanity Fair,* because I never will believe he'll use it until I see it in print.[1] You have had so many disappointments though that perhaps you are used to them and won't mind if this should slip the trolley, too. But he did actually say something about money, too. I

1. For Crowninshield see Biographical Sketches.

heard the sum of $40 mentioned. However we'll believe that when the cheque comes.

The fly in the ointment is this. He will only make a page out of it, therefore fifty lines have to be cut out!! I gave a reluctant consent, preferring to get the mutilated thing in print rather than nothing. You have the right to be furious—but listen.

This is what I want to do. When I get down in the country I mean to try and find a county printer who will print it à la Mabel Dodge—only in a more in a countrified style, 100 copies or so. Jules Pascin, who is one of the swellest artists alive in my opinion has consented to make a wood block of me to go with it.[2] I wish he knew you or had seen you, so he could put you in the cut, too.

But I don't want to put the separate "pages" (verses) on separate pages. It would take forty pages. In war time with paper scarce, I think we have the right to print it as you wrote it, calling them "pages" but printing them on verses several on a page. I like the look of them better so, one sees the proportion of the various verses more easily. If you forbid it I won't do it, but unless I hear to the contrary I'll carry it out according to my own feeble light.

Crowninshield took the little photo of you in the ambulance for *Vanity Fair,* so you must send me another for moi-même.

PS. If you get the chance you must tell Vollard how practical it would be for him to send me copies of his things, in summer to above address.

To Gertrude Stein
January 7, 1918, *The Sun,* New York

My dear Gertrude Stein:
You didn't send me a Christmas card this year! True, I didn't send one to you. But then I never send them to anyone, and you always do. It is clear we are becoming estranged! It is probably my fault. But I will reform. I will make New Year's resolutions. I made New Year's resolutions last year, however; and nothing much happened. . . You can't understand why I don't write letters, can you? You didn't understand why I sent the portraits of me, (or should I say "you and me") to everybody before I sent them to you, the authoress of the work? I am sure I don't understand that myself. I am in the peculiar position of being an entirely virtuous person whose life is a succession of acts of villainy!

2. For Pascin see Biographical Sketches.

How can any one be a straight, nice human being and at the same time be a journalist?

How did you like the portrait? I have the Mss. of your portrait of Braque, which I mean to publish somehow, if possible.[1] It might not be a bad idea to collect all of your portraits and make a little book of them. I hear good words spoken of your *Three Lives* from all sorts of places.[2] You are by no means forgotten, although you must understand, that nothing in the way of art that requires people to readjust their faculties, has any chance here. The war is the only topic, and the Americans have had a fright lately because of some extraordinary cold weather, the coldest ever known, and as there is no coal in town, all of us suffered, (the poor, terribly), and the *morale* of the people went to smash. It gives one an idea of the fortitude of the English, who seem to thrive upon reverses. We Americans are very Latin, and are easily affected by circumstances. But Art has to take a back seat. Poor Jacques Copeau is here with his Théâtre du Vieux-Colombier doing the most beautiful things in his theatre, and no one goes to see them, and the few that do, sit like uncomprehending little wooden blocks.[3] His Molière stuff is gorgeous, done before Gordon Craig's simplified backgrounds in grand colors.[4]

Give my kindest regards to Alice. It's hopeless I can't recall her last name. I was forced once to refer to her as Alice in the public prints lately. Isn't that shameful? But what can you do when you have no memory. I was chagrined the other day to read that wisdom was "learning well remembered." In that case I shall never be wise, for I never remember anything. I try to flatter myself by the reflection that where ignorance is bliss 'tis folly to be wise. But just the same I'm always yours. I'll send you some more portraits!

1. Georges Braque (1882–1963) was not close to Stein during the early years of her friendship with Picasso. Stein thought Braque's cubist work was ancillary to the genius of Picasso and didn't buy anything from the artist until the 1920s. While serving as an enlisted soldier in the war Braque was seriously injured. During his recovery near Avignon, Stein and Toklas visited the recuperating painter and a period of closeness followed.
2. Stein's *Three Lives* was published in 1909 by the Grafton Press, using Stein's money.
3. Jacques Copeau (1878–1949) was a French actor and theater director. In 1913 Copeau founded the Théâtre du Vieux-Colombier, where he developed new, simplified stage and set techniques.
4. Edward Gordon Craig (1872–1966) was a revolutionary stage designer who often used massive abstract forms that were a reaction against the realism of much stage design.

From the notebooks
New York to Liverpool Crossing, 1918

Americans have an idea that the worst crossings of all are upon English boats—that the Germans have their submarines eyes more upon those boats than the French, etc., etc. Everyone to whom I said good bye bid me farewell in a peculiarly solemn way. And from the time I decided to take an English boat, things began to happen that made the adventure appear more and more hazardous. First, a transport was sunk 600 miles from English shores. Then there were reports of submarines scouting in American waters. On Monday, saying goodbye to my bank cashier, he seemed more solemn than any of the others and his tones implied that I was doomed. It wasn't until I had run the gauntlet of the customs men that I caught a glimpse of the headlines saying 15 American ships had been sunk by submarines off the Jersey coast during the night. Then Malcolm appeared looking rather white about the gills, and asked me if I had heard the news.[1]

The English people, who were still struggling with the customs men, did not appear disturbed. For all one could judge they were embarking upon a pleasure journey. Apparently the ship's civilian company were largely English, the bulk of the passengers, of course, being members of Uncle Sam's army. The officers, cabin passengers, and the rank and file, about 3000 being below. The "Sammies" in khaki simply swarmed over the foredecks.[2] Probably every inch was occupied on the boat. In the evening the Sammies on the fore deck got up an impromptu concert to their great joy, and sang the newest rag time with gusto.

We lay tied up at the dock all night and until about one p-m. Tuesday. Malcolm had promised to teach me cribbage and gave a lesson every day. We were in the midst of the first one, when my instructor suddenly cried, "Look, Hank, she's moving." We sure were. Malcolm said, "You win, I concede the game," and we both rushed out on deck, Malcolm saying in a "white voice," "There's no getting off now." We swung about in midstream, and all the people on nearby boats waved to us. The ferry boat passengers waved, even some little children on a small boat waved with more than common ardor, and appeared to feel that we were people on a risky errand.

The ship at the opposite dock was camouflaged. In spite of being in New

1. Malcolm MacAdam; see Biographical Sketches.
2. "Sammies" were U.S. servicemen.

York all winter it was the first I had seen. The moment we swung into midstream for the voyage we saw others. In the lower harbor there were many small boats all camouflaged. Only one seemed to lose itself in the background and that was a boat that happened to be colored like a landscape and could hardly be seen against Staten Island. In the five days we have been at sea, I have seen the eight boats of our convoy in all sorts of atmospheric conditions but never once have I seen them much disguised. It is possible that zig-zag shadings on boats might confuse the eye that directs the torpedo, but to an amateur it would appear that the mass and outline of the ship were at all times perfectly visible. The one first and sure effect was that the boats were completely cheapened by the camouflage. The best of the boats looked like worthless hulks at the first glance.

The start was dramatic enough. From the number of boats at Sandy Hook, a certain number detached themselves into a procession, with a genuine battleship in the lead. Our boat, the Adriatic, we were pleased to observe, was in the centre of the convoy, as the chief prize of the fleet. We had scarcely started before an aeroplane began circling about us, and then a pair of them appeared, flying low and searching the waters for periscopes. Then a dirigible balloon passed over us and in the distance from a cruiser we could see a flying balloon. The aeroplanes were in the air several hours and if they lighted upon the sea, we did not see it. The dirigible circled around us until dark. Altogether there was as much entertainment from the aircraft and the maneuvering convoy, as one usually obtains from a vaudeville.

Late in the afternoon the passengers were allotted their life-boat numbers, and given a few directions in reaching them in case of accident. Most of the passengers looked extremely serious, particularly after night fall, when the lights were screened in and curtains were draped over entrances and blue lights shown in the hallways. The decks in their gloom were quite spooky and a few apparently lost souls wandered about the decks in the darkness stumbling over the deck furniture and over each other.

The group of young English and Canadian officers on board quite outshine the American officers, both in smartness of appearance and in ability to abstract a good time from the voyage. They have annexed the few pretty girls on board and they are desperately at play all day long. Malcolm and I came into contact with them on the tennis court. We had just started a game of singles, when the English colony appeared en-masse to await a turn at the court. They possessed themselves with admirable patience for our game was even and long, but when we finished they came up to us in a pretty way with compliments upon our game, etc. Today (one week out) it is raining. The English have installed a victrola on the lower stair landing and are having a dance.

The privates below decks are by far more interesting then their officers, who are with us. I never talk to one who does not supply some picturesque detail about his life. There were the two young fellows from Minnesota, who had never seen a ship until this one, and who asked how high the waves grew in a storm. When I said I had seen waves dash over a similar deck to the one we stood on, they were distinctly impressed. There was the young Texan lad, with expressive handsome face, who spoke in a simple way of the risks of war and how proud he should be to look back on it—if he survived. He was a true Walt Whitman type. This morning, a young fellow told me he was enjoying the waves and liked it better the rougher it was. He had many trips to his record and was of the sort who knows how to manage. He was in a group of soldiers, who waited on the others at table. For that he had special privileges, a room by the kitchen that was warm and aired, and he had the food that cabin passengers get. This morning all the soldiers complained of the bad fish they had had at breakfast. Coming up to life-boat-drill, there was continual mutters of fish. After drill the word was not muttered but shouted in unison. One man said to us that it was necessary to wear gas-masks to eat such fish. [. . .]

From the notebooks
July 28, 1918, Paris, France

[. . .] The rage for English is immense. One hears it being tried on all sides. Tonight in the Avenue du Bois in the dark I saw a couple walking and as I passed I heard him say in a passionately serious voice, "How many fingaires have you on your right hand?" and the pronunciation was very good, too, all except fingaires. . . The two young ladies who joined the soldiers with whom I chatted at the Café de la Paix also showed warm interest in the language. One of them had all the clippings from the Matin with the daily lesson in English, and she pronounced them aloud to her soldiers friends without, however, much relevancy. "You are biffore me," she read. "Sure," said the soldier. He added to me, "she's a lady friend. We met her the other day, and now we can't lose her."

The English and the American armies have taken the place of the former tourists. What business is done for and through them. Pensions, cafés, theaters are all Anglicized very much. With the reciprocity of the Americans who are all studying French with the assistance of the agreeable young ladies of the Bois and the Boulevards. The democratization of the languages after the war will be complete. [. . .]

From the notebooks
August 6, 1918, Paris

Down on the boulevards there seems no concern over the bombardment. People seem to feel that a shell cannot land on the Place de l'Opéra. Talking with two young American aviator-observers just up in town from finishing their instructions south in France and who felt gay at the prospect of going tomorrow to the front, suddenly espied a French friend named "Jack," hailed him and he joined us. He was one of their instructors. He had been one of the first to bring down a Zeppelin in the early days of the war, and had had wonderful adventures. But he was out of breath at first. A bomb had dropped right in front of his house in Passy and had shattered his balcony. While we were talking about it, we heard another detonation off across the rive. The noise of the bombs doesn't seem so great today as yesterday. People say it always sounds louder the first day and gradually loses its force and after the third day stops. "Jack" pointed out a young officer descending from a taxi and said he had seen him descending in flames within the German lines. He was reported officially as dead. In reality he was captured alive and after eight months escaped. Jack met him once on the boulevard and acted out the meeting amusingly.

The weather cold and rainy. Wore overcoat and heavy winter woolens. Rains very heavy. Every time Bertha sends an obus [sic] over, the clouds seem to burst again.[1] Six p-m., sun shone a minute and I started out to see the damage at the Gare des Invalides. Had gone a block when "boom," a shell dropped near. People ran out of houses. Everybody said it fell close by. But nobody could locate it. Then the rain fell in torrents and I beat a retreat homeward. I did see, however, where a bomb fell in the rue des Acacias last night.

Malcolm and I heard our first Berthas yesterday while still in bed. They fell in distant places and we weren't sure. Malcolm was not well and decided not to go to work and to stay in bed all morning. I was just beginning

1. An early long-range German cannon that shelled Paris from the German line, approximately fifty miles away. Also known as Big Bertha, the nickname came from Bertha Krupp, one of the daughters of the German munitions manufacturer, Gustav Krupp.

to dress when "bing" a loud explosion made us jump. There was no mistaking that. We knew what it was. It was the famous long distance gun. And it was near. When I went out to get a paper I saw the flower women on the Place de Termes as usual and people going about in the ordinary way. The newspaper woman told me the one at 11 a-m. hit near by on ave Monceau and did much damage, killing two Écossais.[2] After lunch I went to see the place. At three p-m. the workmen had almost finished repairing the hole and had repaved the street. All about were the remains of broken windows, etc., a tree cut down, and holes everywhere in the walls of the houses. It must have been a lively splash of cobble stones in every direction. They hit the houses with great force just about the height to get passers by. One piece of shell rebounded into the garden of the American Embassy some distance away. The young ladies let me examine the big pieces of shell that buried itself in the wall of the shop after wrecking the establishment. It was curiously heavy. After inspecting all the damage, I had less liking for Bertha than before.

2. *Écossais,* Scotsmen.

THE DIAL

Nearly forty years after Scofield Thayer and James Sibley Watson, Jr., invited Henry McBride to become *The Dial*'s art critic, he told of his time writing for the magazine in a brief introduction to an exhibition catalogue, *The Dial and the Dial Collection*. Calling it "Those Were the Days," he began the piece with an epigraph from his *Dial* colleague Kenneth Burke: "It is no dismal trick of the memory that there seem to have been gentler times in childhood." McBride was ninety-one when he wrote the catalog introduction, and he closed this, his last published piece, with a postscript. He didn't want to be identified as a gentleman stuck in the belief that past was better, he said: "I'd prefer being embalmed, when the time comes, with my fellow-spirits of the twenties. What I say now is, you understand, 'off the record.'"[1]

It was not simply that the occasion for a retrospective view—an exhibition of The *Dial* Collection at Worcester Art Museum, April 30–September 8, 1959—evoked nostalgia for more civilized times. *The Dial* simply was one of the most civilized and prescient magazines in America's history, and there was no better position for an advanced art critic during the 1920s. Just as McBride was in chronological luck to begin writing art criticism at the time of the Armory Show, so was he fortunate to write for the magazine during the period of its creative peak.

The Dial's venerable history fell into three stages. It was founded in Chicago in 1880 under the leadership of the transcendentalist Margaret Fuller and subsequently Francis Browne. The magazine moved to New York in 1918, when it was edited by Martyn Johnson, with the assistance of Robert Morss Lovett, Thorstein Veblen, and Clarence Brittin. In 1919 Thayer and Watson purchased the magazine, and their first issue, appearing in January 1920, ushered in the magazine's modernist period and also the beginning of a glittering new decade. For nine and a half years, ending with the July 1929 issue, *The Dial* was America's premier highbrow magazine.

Scofield Thayer and James Sibley Watson, Jr., had met at Harvard in the

1. Henry McBride, "Those Were the Days," *The Dial and the Dial Collection,* p. 5.

early 1910s.[2] Between the two of them they possessed sufficient money to support an advanced magazine in style. Watson was a tolerant, hands-off publisher. An index to his catholic range is the fact that he became an important medical researcher and one of the first American avant-garde filmmakers, directing the 1928 silent short *The Fall of the House of Usher*. Thayer was the driving editorial force, and he was an extraordinary and unstable editor. He was exacting and compulsively detailed; McBride remarked that Mondrian went through less trouble with his paintings than did Thayer and Bruce Rogers in designing the magazine's cover. Van Wyck Brooks jibed that "the editors of *The Dial* were aesthetic or nothing."[3] But McBride saw this attention to aesthetics as indications that Thayer was more than a gentleman, he was a prince with a lofty nature, "so princely in his attitudes towards his writers that he never eliminated a comma from their copy without first consulting them by telephone."[4]

The Dial had the sensibility of a little magazine and the elegance of design and production of *Vanity Fair*. Thayer and Watson wrote that they hoped to publish the magazine "without any intention of making money, or truckling to popular prejudice, or of undertaking propaganda for any school of art."[5]

Thayer and Watson approached McBride in about December 1919. Sibley Watson recalled what they valued in McBride's columns in the *Sun:* "They revealed a spontaneous gift for gentle kidding, together with wonderfully complete information, amiability, and good sense."[6] McBride was ill when they first visited, and he did not initially feel up to additional writing duties. He suggested publishing a play by Stein, but Thayer declined. From July 1920, when McBride's first piece appeared, he became a fixture. By the end of the decade he was not only its oldest regular contributor but an exemplar of the magazine's spirit. Nicholas Joost, who wrote two books on *The Dial,* concluded that after Thayer and Watson, McBride was most responsible for shaping the magazine's enthusiasm for modernism. The magazine introduced a new section called "Modern Forms" in

---

2. Thayer graduated cum laude in 1913, then went on to Magdalen College, Oxford, to study the classics and philosophy.

3. Joost, *Scofield Thayer and* The Dial, p. 11, quoting Van Wyck Brooks, *Days of the Phoenix,* 1957.

4. McBride, *Flow of Art,* p. 435.

5. Quoted in Joost, *Scofield Thayer and* The Dial, p. 46.

6. Quoted in Max Miltzlaff, unpublished notes.

July 1920, warning: "This department of The Dial is devoted to the exposition of the less traditional types of art."[7] Altogether appropriately Henry McBride was enlisted to introduce the new section. "Modern Forms" was abandoned after six months, but McBride continued to honor its manifesto. He wrote seventy-three pieces of art commentary for *The Dial*, in addition to other essays and reviews. His work appeared in most issues, except during the summer months. His essays together formed "an index," Joost wrote, "to the consolidation of a certain kind of taste."[8]

Thayer highly respected McBride's eye and ability to evoke a work of art, and he repeatedly said that McBride's columns were always "delightful." The other art critic to appear most often in the magazine was Thomas Craven. Although Craven was not a supporter of modernism, Thayer considered him "the only writer upon the theory of painting in America today whom one cares to read."[9] But Thayer thought that Craven lacked aesthetic perception and he showed his loyalty to McBride when Albert Barnes approached with a proposition to bankroll an annual $2,000 prize to art, so long as Craven received the first award. Thayer declined.

The editorial mix of *The Dial* was transcontinental and it included images as well as words. An advertisement for *The Dial* suggests how the magazine saw itself, and how it positioned itself in the 1920s marketplace of ideas: "*The Dial* is that fastidious, unaverage instance of substantial judgment you have wished for—an aesthetic Gibraltar manifesting love for art and an expertise to present it. The elsewhere defrauded reader finds here a fearlessness which both assails and saves him—a sympathy with unacknowledged excellence and unsympathy with carelessness, confusion, and insensibility paraded as 'consistency.' *The Dial* is generous, agile, unencased, and open to conviction. It has fondness for learning, not for a leaning towards learning."[10]

Looking back on the magazine near the end of his life, Henry McBride wrote his own recollections of *The Dial* and its editors:

> My first impression is not only of their youthful daring and bravado but of their unquestioning confidence in ideas and values that must have seemed hazardous to conventional amateurs then, but which are no

7. *The Dial* 69 (July–December 1920), p. 36.
8. Joost, *Scofield Thayer and* The Dial, p. 136.
9. Quoted in Joost, *Scofield Thayer and* The Dial, p. 139.
10. Advertisement in *Creative Art,* 1927.

longer disputed by anybody. There is no sense of strain, no faintest shadow of a doubt but that Benedetto Croce, Oswald Spengler, Thomas Mann, and George Santayana were conspicuously doing the thinking for their world; that Matisse, Picasso, Léger, Braque, and Miró were treading closely on the heels of the already immortalized Cézanne, Van Gogh, and Gauguin; and that it was quite all right to place e. e. cummings, Paul Rosenfeld, Edmund Wilson, Marianne Moore, T. S. Eliot, and even Ezra Pound side by side in *The Dial* pages with the best things by James Joyce, Willie Yeats, Lytton Strachey, Virginia Woolf, and James Stephens. Beside all that there was some missionary work to be done for the native artists, and Thomas Eakins, Gaston Lachaise, John Marin, Charles Demuth, and Elie Nadelman were hoisted upon pedestals from which they have not since been detached. That was truly missionary work, for art and literature had been looked upon by most American reviews as unrelated activities and though we did have illustrated magazines we had few writers who dared to have an opinion upon pictures or a bit of sculpture."[11]

With Thayer spending more time in Europe, Alyse Gregory became acting editor of the magazine in February 1924. She continued through June 1925, when Marianne Moore left her position at the Hudson Park Branch of the New York Public Library on April 27 and was officially named acting editor on June 26. Scofield Thayer left *The Dial* permanently on July 22, 1925. He seems to have suffered a breakdown in the wake of a fight with Barnes. "It appeared that Dr. Barnes was at war with *The Dial*," McBride later recalled, "threatening death and destruction, to the magazine and ready to use any means to accomplish his ends, and as a matter of fact, it is to the strain of this conflict that I have always attributed the nervous collapse of Scofield Thayer."[12] He was soon hospitalized—his contemporary diagnosis sounds like what would now be called paranoid schizophrenia—and he remained incapacitated for the rest of his life.

The advent of Marianne Moore as the magazine's editor marked the beginning of a relationship that proved to be one of the happiest and most enduring in McBride's life. Although not marked by intimacy or frequent contact, it was buoyed by mutual affection and by the collegial bond to an enterprise that was, for each of them, a high point in their professional

11. McBride, "Those Were the Days," p. 3.
12. McBride, *Flow of Art*, p. 435.

lives. It began as a writer-editor relationship, rooted in their mutual literary respect and strict observance of editorial manners. Moore's recollections of McBride are as poetic as they are astute. She described "his punctuality and his punctuation, each comma placed with unaccidental permanence, and the comfortable quality of his pitiless ultimatums. One does not lose that sense of 'creeping up on the French,' of music, of poetry, of fiction, of society sparkle, that came with his visits to the office. He did not 'specialize in frights,' nor in defamation, nor nurse grudges; and too reverent to speak in religious accents often, could not trust himself to dwell on personal losses, sentiment with him was so intense."[13] On another occasion, she ruminated at length on the critic's contribution to the magazine:

> With regard to Mr. McBride and his Modern Art commentary in *The Dial,* mere fact in the way of editorial gratitude has the look of extravagance. It is hard to credit Mr. McBride's innate considerateness as synonymous with his unfailing afflatus, thought so substantial as coincident with gaiety, and so wide a range of authority as matched by ultra-accuracy.
>
> Each month, usually in the morning, Mr. McBride would bring his three pages of Modern Art Commentary to *The Dial,* visit without hurry, but briefly, and infect routine with a savor of heretic competence. The word "competent" may have connotations of mildness, but not in this connection. Mr. McBride and insight are synonymous. You may have gone to the fair and come away with a gross of green glasses, but not Mr. McBride. As he said of Elie Nadelman: "Directly in proportion to the vitality of an artist's work is the reluctance of the public to accept it." You may have premonitions but Mr. McBride has the data, is succinct and matter-of-fact,—be your investigations in what field they may—: houses, furniture, dress, printing, painting, dancing, music, verse, sculpture, the camera, movies, the drama. Wit that is mentality does not betray itself and Henry McBride is adamant to the friend of a friend desiring encomiums. He is not susceptible to self-eulogy. Where feeling is deep it is not a topic. Reverence that is reverence is a manifestation, and has never been proved better than by Mr. McBride.[14]

Near the end of McBride's life, Marianne Moore sent his *Dial* clippings to him. McBride's pleasure in rereading his columns is reflected in his letter

13. Moore, *Predilections,* p. 111.
14. Quoted by Lincoln Kirstein, "To Honor Henry McBride" (New York: Knoedler Galleries, 1949), pp. 2–3. See also Moore, *Complete Prose,* p. 647.

to Moore: "I look at them in astonishment and ask myself 'did I write those?' and then blush a little and try to suppress the tide of vanity I feel surging within though not entirely defeating the thought that those things are not 'too bad' and might do, in a book."[15]

To Gertrude Stein
January 5, 1920, Herald Square Hotel, New York

Dear Gertrude Stein:

I almost wrote to you in the middle of December and I almost sent you a Christmas present but I didn't do either one, did I? It was this way: A young man I happened to know, Scofield Thayer, rich, and something of a Shelleyian socialist, bought *The Dial,* and set out to run a magazine. He honored me with an invitation to write something—but I was laid flat upon my pallet of straw at that time with my interesting but unnamed malady. They came each day to see me, my only visitors, and finally I thought of your Alsatian play and suggested that.[1] The young man turned away sadly, for he was exceedingly rich, as the Scriptures have it, and said me nay. Hence no Christmas gift for you. I thought it would have been a nice Christmas gift to have told you your poem was to appear in a high brow, serious magazine along with an essay by George Santayana. . . But it seems you are cast for the role of martyr at present. The out look is discouraging here, and the present is blank. There seems to be nothing doing in art and I have the devil's own time in pretending to write art stuff. In fact I don't even pretend. That's why I don't sent any of my pages because I know myself they are empty. I'll send you this week's as it is given over to a letter by Max Weber protesting against excluding the modern art from the American Show at the Luxembourg.[2] Can't you induce some of your friends to see that the facts of the underhand suppression of these pictures gets into some Paris papers? "Pinturicchia" in the Carnet de la Semaine usually likes such morceaux. I didn't see the things, and I dare say our modernists are all

15. McBride to Moore, July 17, 1959 (Marianne Moore papers, Rosenbach Museum and Library, Philadelphia).

1. *Accents in Alsace: A Reasonable Tragedy* (1918) was written after Stein's and Toklas's experiences in Alsace, where they assisted the American Fund for the French Wounded to provide help and supply assistance to World War I refugees.
2. The Musée du Luxembourg was the only museum in Paris that housed and exhibited work by living artists, making it the only "modern" museum in the capital.

replicas of Paris originals, just as our impressionists works are, but the principle of the thing is bad. It is a chance to knock Benedite on the head. . . As it happens the French art sent over here and now at our museum, is rotten beyond belief.[3] It is avowedly meant to advertise Paris art schools, as the French want the pupils to come over again; but it is so amazingly stupid it has the contrary effect. . . Somewhat to my own surprise there seems to be no reaction towards photographic art. Even the photographic battle scenes attract no one. I suppose it's because the people prefer the *actual* photos and have been educated in photos, and so can't stand the pseudo-realistic painting.

New York seems amazingly prosperous and decidedly the capital of the world. Where the people come from no one knows, but the problem of obtaining a bed is very difficult. Every hotel is packed and rooms can't be had except at outrageous prices. About the minimum for two rooms and a bath is $1500 a year. I can earn my living and in a year or two I see myself hiring out as a cook or waiter. I tell Malcolm, who seems in line to belong to the new aristocracy, he'll have to take me on as a valet.

The place is full of all the literati of Europe and most of 'em come to grief. Lord Dunsany has just gone home in a sulk.[4] People didn't like him. I thought him something of a boor, myself. Cher Maurice is very likely in for a smash, too.[5] Oh, if he isn't really married to the new Mme. Maeterlinck, there'll be trouble. It's all very funny though. Ibáñez, the man who coined money with the *Four Horsemen of the Apocalypse* is now said to be an out and out crook and plagiarist. . . Send the Maeterlinck article to Mildred, please; she'll be amused.

Am somewhat better this week past but have a hard time working. The doctors now say I have "nerves." If any funny little reviews come along, with interesting matter, make Malcolm MacAdam get them for me.

So, best regards to Alice and yourself.

3. In 1919 three gallery exhibitions brought European modern art to New York: The Annual Exhibition of Modern Art at Bourgeois Galleries, May 3–24; French Art at Arden Galleries in May; and European Modern Art at Modern Gallery. See Judith K. Zilczer, "Modern Art and Its Sources: Exhibition in New York, 1910–1925, A Selective Checklist," in Homer, *Avant-Garde Painting and Sculpture*, pp. 166–70.
4. Edward John Lord Dunsany (1878–1957) was an Irish poet and dramatist who served in the Boer War and was injured during World War I. Dunsany won recognition as a playwright in 1909, when W. B. Yeats produced his *Glittering Gate* at the Abbey Theatre.
5. Maurice Maeterlinck did relief work in France and Belgium during the war and wrote against German rule in Belgium. His first U.S. lecture tour took place in 1921.

To Alfred Stieglitz:
April 5, 1920, The Coffee House, New York, New York[1]

Dear Stieglitz:[2]

The three lovely Marins arrived safely and I feel like a nouveau riche just landed in high society and not knowing how to act. But Americans are adaptable (or at least we say we are) and perhaps I'll get the smirk off my face in time and behave as though it were a natural thing to have Marins on your walls. . . They do look grand. . . It was however an imposition to borrow three as I feel a premonition I'm going to keep the smashing green thing—I don't actually know why—for, as a critic, I'd probably give the best write-up to the cool blue sea-piece in the latest manner. . . It will be fun to have all three for a week or two and I look forward to hearing what the chambermaid says tomorrow when she sees them. I set great value on chambermaid's opinions. They always give it to you straight.

Thank Marin, also yourself. It was a fine and surprising thing to do. It isn't generally done, I may tell you.[3]

Faithfully your friend,

PS. I want to see you in regard to a Marin for the Scofield Thayer proposition.[4] I'll try on Friday.

To Gertrude Stein
November 13, 1920, The Coffee House, New York, New York

Dear Gertrude:

Your letter which doesn't breathe fire and brimstone as I expected (and deserved) has just come. Also *Three Lives*. I read it through again with the

1. The Coffee House, founded in 1915, was a gentlemen's social club located at 54 West 45th Street. *Vanity Fair* editor Frank Crowninshield was a key figure at the club, which was founded to support connections between people in the arts. McBride remained a member throughout his life and wrote many letters on Coffee House stationery.
2. See Biographical Sketches.
3. Marin made a gift of a watercolor to McBride, allowing him to select one from among three he admired. Over the course of his career, McBride added several Marins to his personal collection.
4. "*The Dial* Portfolio of Contemporary Art," called "Living Art," was a project Thayer undertook early in the 1920s to earn revenue for the magazine by selling a portfolio of high quality reproductions of drawings and paintings and photographs of sculpture by important artists. Published late in 1923, the portfolio of living art included work by Matisse, Picasso, Demuth, Marin, Lachaise, Maillol, Derain, Chagall, Kokaska, Vlaminck, de Chirico, and Archipenko.

same empressement as before. I don't review books but I'll try and sneak a little announcement of it into my page.

Last spring I dined with Walter Arensberg and Duchamp and we talked of a new book of your things and the best way to put it over etc.[1] My opinion was that you ought to print it privately at your own expense (Heavens! Don't tell any one) and once a thousand volumes were printed they could be sold somehow. I think in the end it would pay for itself. You see you are handicapped by writing in a language that is behind in the arts. *There is a public for you but no publisher.*[2] The war has hurt the American cubists somewhat and the experimenters have lost courage. For all that a writer who already has so many followers as you have is safe in assuming the expense of publishing. Only don't be impatient. Let the books that don't sell at once wait in your trunk and every new book you get out helps sell the old ones. Don't throw 'em away as you did the first issue of *Three Lives,* all of which *could* have sold eventually.

I've just met Arensberg again. He says he's getting out a crazy book proving Dante was a cryptogramist—at his own expense. He says it's much—the expense—and to tell you to publish yours in France or Italy—a better volume for less. Now don't necessarily publish a huge volume—but something—just for the form of appearing and being criticized, etc.

Now I know you won't like this advice—but economize somehow—go with one less chapeau this winter—and do as I tell you. Make Alice do with one less chapeau, too. (You know how Wagner borrowed from Liszt!), and give her my love.

I was to have written this last spring but I collapsed seriously and my feeble correspondence stopped automatically—can't write without a head, you know. I stayed in the country all summer, mowed the grass and chopped wood, and now am much, much better and can look at a pen

1. Walter Arensberg (1878–1954) and Marcel Duchamp were instrumental figures in "putting over" modernism. Arensberg and his wife Louise (1879–1953) were prominent collectors, but most relevant to Stein, Arensberg had financially supported two little magazines, *Others* and *Rogue,* and could help get Stein's work published. The previous July, McBride had written a typically droll yet supportive article on the Arensbergs and their collection of conceptual work by Duchamp ("The Walter Arensbergs," *The Dial,* July 1920). In fall 1920 the Arensbergs ended their famous salons by packing up and moving to California.
2. At this moment experimental publishers were at a low point. Around 1917 *Poetry* had taken a conservative turn; *The Little Review* was dominated by Stein's rival, James Joyce, whose *Ulysses* the review was serially publishing; *Rogue* ceased publication in 1916, *Others* in 1919.

without prostration. This is a brand new one—the first letter with it—it looks like a ghost's writing. Next summer I hope to get to Paris.

Have you seen Bet Burroughs?[3] She is a lovely girl. Being a student and having a corking time. You remember her Pa, of course. We die with rapture and pride over her letters.

Well—so long. If you come across any amusing art things in the papers kindly clip them out and sent 'em along. There is absolute famine of news here. [. . .]

To Alfred Stieglitz
April 4, 1921, Herald Square Hotel, New York, New York

My dear Alfred Stieglitz:
You were evidently annoyed—and after promising me you never would be annoyed at anything I might say! I'm sorry.[1]

I always hate to write about people I'm fond of, such as you, Bryson Burroughs, etc., for I know no other way to write but the detached one—to forget the friendship and thresh the idea out for what will come of it.

I heard a discussion of my article the other day that astonished me, for the speakers put interpretations upon it I never thought of. For instance, that last part about anonymity. I don't counsel it for you. I regard it as your duty to try to put yourself and your ideas over, but I do think anonymity the ultimate end of democracy. I was arraigning the times we live in—not you. (I was shocked in early infancy at the idea of the millennium as it was taught to me. When the lion and the lamb lie down together it seems to me that both will have lost their essential characteristics. They might both be considered sheep.)

The part of my article you had a right to be cross about—that about the old shoes—you let pass. It was a mistake of hasty writing. Two or three words in it would have made it inoffensive. . . As for the $5000. That was

3. See Biographical Sketches.

1. In his April 1921 "Modern Art" column in *The Dial,* McBride wrote about Stieglitz's scandalous exhibition of photographic nudes of Georgia O'Keeffe that opened February 7, 1921, at the Anderson Galleries. In his article McBride noted the gossip, speculation and voyeurism that swirled around the show: "Someone ran down Fifth Avenue crying that Alfred Stieglitz had put a price of $5,000 on one of the photographs, a nude. . . . Gracious Heavens! $5,000 for a mere photograph! And then everyone had to see the exhibition over again, the crowd about the nude being particularly dense." He also affectionately describes Stieglitz as "a dear, delightful duck."

nonsense of course. It was the gossip; and fitted in with the accusation of coastlines, but was not intended seriously. You will never find "facts" in my articles. And in conclusion—I didn't pay income tax, either.

You may believe I'm a tough customer, but you might as well believe I love you just the same.

To Gertrude Stein
October 29, 1921, Herald Square Hotel, New York

Dear Gertrude:

By luck I was able to get a "Have They Attacked Mary. He Giggled" (you forgot your own titles!) to Mr. Bram. My cousins who are still at my place, sent me ½ dozen and I send you three to Paris. I still have more but they are hid somewhere in the garret at Callicaste. I meant whilst there to look them up but the fact was it was such lovely weather all the time and there was so much to do out doors that I never thought of books. The mending of fences and chopping trees benefited me decidedly and I had a happy time. I must be nearer normal than usual as an extra quantity of work was piled upon me by fate when I got to New York and so far it has not killed me. By this time last year I was already a dead one. Two articles for *The Dial* and two catalogue introductions for stupid artists (Had to write them) besides the ocean of newspaper stuff.

Have reviewed Marsden Hartley's new book.[1] It's not bad. Almost literature. He might write if he didn't paint. You have nothing to learn from it nor had I—but foreigners may be surprised to learn that an American had been dabbling in so many nice directions. You must read it.

We are awfully poor here. It was a surprise to me to come home from France, where one got the effect that people had money to come home to this rich country and find everybody distinctly hard up. Near me in Pennsylvania the mills had shut down and tramps were again running the roads and asking for meals. Here in New York you are begged from every minute and the small parks are filled up with the unemployed. Such sights have not been seen since before the war. The present generation which forgets easily, seems to regard tramps as a new phenomenon in history—one more

1. The painter Marsden Hartley (1877–1943) had recently returned to New York after years spent in Berlin and Paris. In 1920 his poetry was included in *The Dial*, while his first book, *Adventures in the Arts,* was published in New York by Boni and Liverwright, circa 1921, to generally good reviews. It was published in Paris in 1922.

reproach to the new detested war. So the signs all point to a troubled winter.

Did you know the Spicer-Simpsons came home on my steamer? Margy told me her version of the story. Oh, why didn't I write you a steamer letter when conversation was fresh in my mind? It was rich.

Do write me about the Autumn Salon—and don't forget, when photos of the portrait by Lipchitz are printed, that I'm to have one.[2]

Love to Alice and you.

PS. I wrote to Bram also. Hope he comes across.

To Malcolm MacAdam
February 28, 1922, New York

Dear Malc:

I really think I got one on you this time. Whom do you think I lunched with yesterday? Doug Fairbanks. And Doug turns out to be a high-brow. It's a fact; he quoted Huxley to me. Doug and I [are] very intimate and Doug invited me to come out to Hollywood and visit him and Mary. Now what you got to say? Doesn't that give you a pain in the neck?

I was at the Coffee House reading a paper under a reading lamp, when I heard voices approaching and Frank saying, "Well I sure brought you to the right place—here's Henry McBride, the only critic in America, who gave you a rating of 'Plus 25'. . .[1] Douglas, let me present you to Henry Mc-Bride."[2] Doug grinned and showed the teeth that always look so well in the films and shook hands heartily. After I "et" my lunch, there was a vacant chair next to him and I went over and took it and told him all the flattering things about the *Three Musketeers* that I already wrote to you and, believe me, Doug was pleased. I began by saying, "I dare say you are fed up with compliments but perhaps you can stand one more," and Douglas replied, "From you, I certainly can." He gave me a cigar, which I very carefully put

2. Jacques Lipchitz (Chaim Yakob) (1891–1973) made two sculptural portraits of Stein. Lipchitz said the first, done in 1920, showed her as "a massive, inscrutable Buddha," while claiming the second, done in 1938, showed her more as a rabbit with a cap on; and he lamented, "The massive, self-confident Buddha has become a tired and rather tragic old woman." Lipchitz, *My Life in Art*, p. 63.

1. "Frank" is Frank Crowninshield.

2. "The New Order of Critical Values" (*Vanity Fair*, April 1922) enlisted ten critics to rate a variety of subjects from −25 to +25. The critics included H. L. Mencken, Edmund Wilson, George Jean Nathan, and Henry McBride. The subjects ranged from Dante and Kant to Maxwell Bodenheim and Krazy Kat.

away. It's a Corona, of course, and you should have it were you here. But if you're not coming over till 1923, it won't keep, will it. I don't know anybody else who is worthy of smoking Doug Fairbanks' cigar. What shall I do with it? We talked for a full hour—Doug doing most of the talk, telling me all about the business, and about the new film they are working on of *Robin Hood* and about how he'd like to do *Benvenuto Cellini*. He spoke nicely about Charley Chaplan, but said that Charles had only lately begun to get an education. [. . .]

To Malcolm MacAdam
March 31, 1922, New York

Dear Malc:

[. . .] I'm sending *Vanity Fair,* with the critic's opinions, etc. It made a great stir. All the critics who weren't asked to join in, are furious and all the people, who got slammed, are more furious still. I send one thing from the *Globe,* but the *Tribune*'s account was worse yet. I'm told there was something scathing about me in particular, in one of the Sunday papers, but I didn't see it. I just received today from Crowny a stunning cigarette case as a souvenir of the affair. It's pigskin like yours, otherwise I'd send it on to you. If you had two you'd be sure to give one of 'em away, which wouldn't be nice. I know you Al.[1] It has a little knob at the bottom, which you press, when presenting the case to a friend, and the cigarettes are pushed up so they are easy to take hold of.

I went to a few dinners last week, but nothing notable. I was one of the judges of prize winning costumes at the fancy dress ball of the Society of Independents, at the Waldorf.[2] I had two tickets, one of which would have been yours, had you been here, as I think you would have liked the party. Oscar Cesare, the cartoonist of the Tribune, was the swellest thing by far, in a Russian costume, but he didn't get the prize. I couldn't make the other pigheaded jurors see it. The funniest thing was a fellow who came with Helen Westley, the actress of the Theatre Guild. He had blue damask around his body, and wore a damask headdress with feathers, but legs, shoulders, arms, bare. After dancing with Helen once or twice, he unwrapped the veil from his body, and was practically nude, except for the

1. The allusion is to Ring Lardner's collection of stories *You Know Me Al.*
2. The Society of Independent Artists was founded in 1917 as an alternative to the commercial and salon systems, on the principle of "No juries, no prizes." Its participants paid a flat fee and exhibited their work.

little blue damask jockstrap. Nobody seemed to mind, much, but after awhile a serious individual in evening dress touched him on the shoulder and motioned for him to withdraw. He retired to a corner of the room and I saw Helen helping put on his wraps. After that they danced some more, always in bare legs, as at first.

I meant to have told you in my Doug Fairbanks letter, that Doug's photographer, who was along, told me that in Paris at the Folies-Bergère, there was an extraordinary, naked coon act that was the limit. I was going to forbid you to go. But apparently I'm too late, and now I suppose, my little blond, butterfly correspondent will never be the same again. Gee how I wish I was going out to Villennes with you this week.

THE STETTHEIMER SISTERS

Henry McBride was introduced to the world of the three Stettheimer sisters through a painting by Florine Stettheimer. The bright oil painting, *La Fête à Duchamp,* depicted Marcel Duchamp's thirtieth birthday, which took place on July 28, 1917, at the Stettheimer sisters' summer residence near Tarrytown, New York. She exhibited the painting at the 1918 Society of Independents exhibition, and McBride admitted that it was the first time he had heard of her, or indeed the first time he heard of many figures depicted in the painting, who his former student Abraham Walkowitz assured him were famous in Greenwich Village's advanced circles—they included not only Duchamp and the Stettheimers but Carl Van Vechten, Leo Stein, Fania Marinoff, Henri-Pierre Roché, Avery Hopwood, and Francis Picabia. McBride closed his positive review by writing, "The more I think of it, the more miffed I am that I wasn't asked to that party."[1]

Soon thereafter McBride was not only invited to the Stettheimers' parties but became one of their most regular guests, the subject of one of Florine Stettheimer's portraits, and a close friend of the three sisters for the rest of their lives. The Stettheimers—Carrie (c. 1870–1944), Florine (1871–1944), and Ettie (1874–1955)—conducted a salon that began about 1915 and continued until 1935. Their sumptuous parties were the longest-lived gatherings of New York's avant-garde, and the guests included transatlantic visitors, artists, writers, and musicians, among them Van Vechten, Philip Moeller, Paul Rosenfeld, Muriel Draper, the Askews, Alfred Stieglitz, Georgia O'Keeffe, Joseph Hergesheimer, and Virgil Thomson.

Carrie, Florine, and Ettie (christened Henrietta) were not the only Stettheimer siblings; an older sister, Stella, and an older brother, Walter, lived on the West Coast. The three younger sisters made up a tight family group, observing the tacit family rule that they would never leave their mother alone. Each of the three also had a vocation: Florine painted; Carrie created a fantastic dollhouse, which included miniatures by her friends and now resides in the Museum of the City of New York; Ettie wrote two books, *Philosophy* (1917) and *Love Days* (1923). After her two sisters died, within

1. *New York Sun,* April 28, 1918, reprinted in *Flow of Art,* p. 152.

six weeks of one another, Ettie wrote that each of the three had worked in "strict singleness." But only Florine practiced her vocation throughout her adult life.

McBride was friends with all three, whom he sometimes joking called "the committee," but he shared a special bond with Florine, through his support of her painting, and with Ettie, with whom he had one of his longest-lasting relationships. McBride wrote at length about the Stettheimers on three occasions; his catalog essay for Florine's retrospective at the Museum of Modern Art in 1946 and essays in *View* (1945) and *Town and Country* (1946). He was the ideal writer to evoke their world: an insider to their circle, he shared their transcontinental perspective and their nineteenth-century sensibility in a modern world.

To Malcolm MacAdam
May 15, 1922, New York

Cher Malc:

[. . .] As for my reputation, it has gained I think. Frank's putting me in that list of critics in *Vanity Fair* was a help, for we were supposed to be the pick of the critics, See? Right away I noticed that my dinner invitations jumped from three a week to five. I don't think I ever dined out so much as I did this winter. But it's the only thing I do, I don't go to cards, teas or dances.

Last night I went to see Grasso and Mimi Agulia, do *Othello* in Italian, at the Irving Place theatre. These are Sicilian players that are all the rage among us highbrows. The Stettheimer girls were there and Fania Marinoff, and the Harveys and lots more.[1] Scenery shabby and the troupe wretched, but Grasso was pretty fine. Carl Van Vechten has written a book called *Peter Whiffle* that has a lot about art and Paris in it, and that amuses us chiefly because he had mentioned so many of the people we know in it.[2] There is a funny character in it called Clara Barnes, who is a failure as a

1. Carrie, Florine, and Ettie Stettheimer; see Biographical Sketches. Fania Marinoff (1887–1971) was an actress; she debuted at eight, performed frequently on the stage and in films until the 1920s. She was married to Carl Van Vechten from 1914 to 1964.
2. *Peter Whiffle* (Knopf, 1922) was the first of Van Vechten's novels. He wrote a string of seven popular books during the 1920s; the best known was the notorious best-seller *Nigger Heaven* (1926). He stopped writing novels after *Parties* (1930). The heroine of *Peter Whiffle*, Edith Dale, was based on Mabel Dodge, and Van Vechten himself was a character.

singer but who is always bragging about how great she is. Well I met Van Vechten in a book shop the other day, and he told me that in the next book he was going to mention me. I said, in that case put in a whole lot more about Clara Barnes, because I thought she was fun. He said, "I'll tell you what, I'll marry you to Clara Barnes." So Malc, I presume I may say I'm engaged at last.

The Stettheimers have a big house on the coast in New Jersey and have invited me to a house party there in the summer. Carl Van Vechten says he is coming down to stay with the Joseph Hergesheimers who live near us in the country, in June, and will run over to see me.³ This is a terrible éventuellement, for we expect to tear up the floors June first. Besides Carl has an evil reputation. He was in jail once.⁴ Didn't pay alimony to his first wife and married Fania Marinoff. Of course, you know, it's the style here, for wives not to take their husband's names? You seem so shocked at poor Else Peterson smoking a simple little cigarette in public.⁵ What would you say if you saw the things that they do and heard the things they say, in our smart set? But don't you forget, kid, that we are the ones that set the fashions now. Don't you let any of those passé French bourgeoisie try to put anything over on you. Else Peterson is a mighty nice girl, in spite of what you say. You ought to hear her sing. She sings well. She used to be a pupil of Edith Burroughs and we have always liked her. I'm dying to read all that stuff to Betts, and I think I will. Always the best parts of your letters, you say, now don't you blab this. This letter was a very nice letter all the way through.

PS. [. . .] Got to take tea this afternoon at the Ritz with Madeleine McKay, my former fiancée, you remember? She asked me once before and I forgot and she was furious. At the Stettheimer's Saturday, there was a Mrs. Locker, just back from a winter in Paris.⁶ Said what first impressed her on landing,

3. Joseph Hergesheimer (1880–1954) was a popular American novelist during the years between World War I and the Depression, at which point his novels fell out of fashion. He was a close and long-term friend of Van Vechten, introduced through their mutual publisher, Alfred Knopf.

4. Van Vechten was incarcerated in December 1914 for failure to pay his first wife, Ann Snyder Van Vechten, back alimony. He entered the jail whistling a passage from Debussy's *Peleas and Melisande* (the corresponding words: "So the walls do not a prison make nor iron bars a cage"). "He wore a Byronic collar, an oxblood tie and a silken shirt of many colors" (*Morning Telegraph*, December 9, 1914).

5. Else Peterson, living in Paris, and friend of McBride's. A trained singer, she took lessons from Edith Burroughs.

6. Probably Beatrice Locher, wife of Robert Locher (see Biographical Sketches), subject of a word portrait by Gertrude Stein.

were; the bright sun, legs and shiny automobiles. She said she died of cold in Paris.

To Florine Stettheimer
July 3, 1922, Callicaste, Marshallton, Pennsylvania

Chère mademoiselle:

Don't be furious at my silence. I wasn't fit to speak. My famous tonsillitis, that kept me from your nice dinner party, laid me low for a week after my quasi arrival here.[1] Since then it's been carpenters, tinsmiths and Sam Bonsall. Sam Bonsall is 78 years old and puts up our new picket fence. He is an engrossing and disturbing personage. Requires some one to be always with him to hand him things and is forever losing his hatchet. Stepped on his rule and broke it and remarked, "That's 50 cents gone to Hell." He had borrowed it from old Joe Cunningham, 81 years old, mending the roads near by, and he would be obliged to return it. With Sam Bonsall about I couldn't write, you understand. Since Sam left I've been painting the fence. Every try painting a 500 rail fence? Marcel must have told you about the Society Anonyme printing a brochure by me.[2] It's to be like an index and some what stunty. I am dying with impatience to see it. [. . .]

To Gertrude Stein
June 14, 1923, Callicaste, Marshallton, Pennsylvania

Dear Gertrude:

[. . .] You are powerful good natured. That review was rotten but I couldn't help it. It came at a time when circumstances were too much for me and Mildred will explain to you that circumstances pile high in newspaper

1. "The committee" had invited McBride to a dinner party June 29 at their summer home in Red Hook, New Jersey.
2. Henry McBride and Marcel Duchamp collaborated on a publication called *Some French Moderns Says McBride*. The collaboration consisted of McBride contributing art columns from 1915–21, including pieces on Cézanne, Rodin, Brancusi, Matisse, Dufy, Signac, Segonzac, Gleizes, Villon, Duchamp, Gaughin, Picasso, Picabia, Van Gogh, Derain, and Marie Laurencin. Duchamp, using his pseudonym Rrose Sélavy, designed the book (and copyrighted the format) in the spirit of New York Dada, so that the size of the type increased every few pages and eventually only a few words fit on a page. Photographs of art were taken by Sweeler, a pseudonym for the American precisionist painter and photographer Charles Sheeler (1883–1965). Published by the Société Anonyme in 1922 and printed by Melomine Publications in New York, it consisted of an edition of two hundred hand-constructed and numbered books.

offices sometimes. However, you are obliged to me for the review in *The Dial,* even though it wasn't so tumultuously enthusiastic as it might have been. But I insisted there should be one and was gratified to see I had so much influence. One thing about it—he compared you with Milton. I believe he blamed you both. Still it is not so bad to be damned into the same hell with Milton. I should be quite content with that myself.

I shall be eager to hear your news and can pay you back with a few choice morsels in regard to Mabel Dodge.[1] Of course you must have got some reverberations from her latest exploits but in case you haven't the details I can supply them.

With love to you both.

To Malcolm MacAdam
July 14, 1923, Paris, France

c.a.:[1]

[. . .] I got through it better than expected. That is to say, I lived. I expected it would kill me. I mean my visit to Mildred. [. . .]

Mildred was all in white, very chic, and looked as fit as ever—but she says it is all façade. We had sirop de fraise in water, with cake, and started the talk that lasted for the next 24 hours. She has had another piece of luck. Its a secret, but I'll tell you. She has had a play accepted by George Tuler for production this fall in New York and has received some advance cash. Otherwise she would have been on the rocks. Isn't that just like her? The garden is lovely. So is Robert the gardener. Charming person. But it irritates me to think of that immense garden and those tons of legumes, all for just Mildred. Of course the whole commune lives off her, the money going into Amelie's pocket.[2] Mildred adores Amelie, but I detest her, She is in full charge, as the retrenchment has obliged Mildred to fire the other domestiques, and as Amelie is a poor cook and not overly clean (she detests the Cuisine) it is one of the agonies of visiting Mildred. I only put 15 frs. in her palm as I said good-bye (Amelie's palm of course), but I begrudged her even that. The air at Hilltop, however, is fresh, though hot, and the blessed

1. Upon marrying her fourth husband, the Tiwa Indian Antonio Luhan, she became Mabel Ganson Evans Dodge Sterne Luhan. She lived with Luhan for the next four decades.

1. Abbreviation for "cher ange"—"dear angel"—McBride's frequent salutation to MacAdam.
2. Aldrich's cook and housekeeper.

absence of taxi toots was such a relief, that my nerves quieted perceptibly and I slept the sleep of the just.[3] I came back to Paris Thursday in time for dinner, finding the town was as torrid and horrid as ever. Mildred told me one thing you'll like. It was of Edgerly. Edgerly wrote at the time of the marriage, that the Count vowed to make her the mother of a new civilization but Mildred remarked to Gertrude, that she guessed it would be a fausse-couche.[4] Mildred nearly died at my story of the countess' teeth.

Another supplice begins today. I am to entertain, or be entertained by Miss Williams. At any rate I am to go with her to hear her lesson chez M. Lortat. I have been disciplining her lately. I have not been sitting at her table at the Alpes. I find she is no help to nerves. Miss W. asked me if I ever addressed you as Petit Choux. I said "Certainly not" . . . "He answers to it," was her reply.[5] She is horrified at the idea of your going to Shanghai. Says it will kill you. Climate is not only dreadful, but vampires, to which you seem peculiarly susceptible, abound. She wants me to go with you. Says she will feel safer if I go with you. In the presence of Mrs. Coleman she remarked that she didn't want to be made a widow within a year. Mrs. Coleman said you were one of the most charming of men. Miss Williams and I said you were *The most*. I beat Miss Williams slightly to it. She thinks now of giving in her demission and hurrying to America. You might arrange to have her lodge with Clara and Elizabeth. [. . .]

To Malcolm MacAdam
July 21, 1923, Paris, France

c.a.:

J'ai fait les noces hier soir. A mon âge, ça c'est going some, n'est-ce-pas? Pascin me donnait un banquet dans le quartier latin. Il y avaient vingt personnes à table—toutes les plus distinguées parmi les bohémiens du quartier.[1] I got to Pascin's apartment in the Place Pigalle, just as several children (one of them a petite et chic mulattress) were coming out with their

3. Hilltop—or La Creste in Huiry—was Aldrich's house, which she immortalized in her best-selling World War I memoir *Hilltop on the Marne*.
4. *Fausse couche*, miscarriage.
5. *Mon petit chou*, my little darling or sweetheart; literally, my little cabbage.

1. "I did the town last night. At my age, that's going some, isn't it? Pascin gave me a banquet in the Latin Quarter. There were twenty people at the table—all from the most distinguished bohemians of the Quarter." McBride immortalized this evening in "The Banquet by Pascin," *Dial*, November 1923. This letter apparently serves as a rough draft for the piece. See *Flow of Art*, p. 175.

parents and bonnes. I was introduced. It seems the parents and the young mulattress were to be of the banquet, so we all piled into two taxis and had a merry ride across town to the Café du Dôme. We had a chaleureuse reception at the Café du Dôme you can imagine.[2] All the hungry students there are envious of Pascin's great fame and regarded his party with extreme interest. Without wishing to boast, I may say, I shared the honors with the young mulattress. Before we found seats, there was a stream of people coming up to greet me. Mahonri Young who was overcome with emotion, when I presented him to Pascin, then Man Ray with an invitation from Mme. Picabia for that evening, which I could not accept; then Else Peterson; and then Mme. Pascin the most extraordinary looking woman in Paris (which is saying something) arrived, and our particular crowd (Else fled, of course) sat down and all had aperitifs sauf moi, who had tilleul.[3] Were we looked at by the horde of students? I'll say we were. We dined over near the Bal Bullier, outside behind a hedge and although a cold night, I did not unduly suffer. At eleven, we were all (or most all) piled into a big touring car of the man who had charge of the twelve year old mulattress and we went to the Café Suedois. There we found more riotous students rioting, including several who insisted on knowing me. But at minuit I beat it for the Palais d'Orsay. [. . .]

In the morning Gertrude had taken me in her Ford to Montmartre to call on Braque in his studio and while we were there, Erik Satie the famous composer came in.[4] He was charming. Then back for one of Alice's magnificent luncheons. Would you like to know the menu? Some kind of hot pâté to begin with, surrounded by very fine but peculiar macaroni. Then a wonderfully roasted loin of pig and for legume, mallots, that I liked for the

2. *Chaleureuse,* warm, animated, cordial.
3. A nonalcoholic lime drink. Mahonri M. Young (1877–1957), the grandson of the Mormon leader Brigham Young, was a social realist sculptor committed to glorifying the dignity of the working man. Man Ray, born Emmanuel Radnitzki (1890–1976), was a photographer, painter, sculptor, and little-magazine editor. He knew the art critic Gabrielle Buffet-Picabia from c. 1917 through the Arensberg circle. Buffet-Picabia (1881–1985) was the first wife of Francis Picabia. Her invaluable memoir of New York Dada is a primary source about this period. She and Picabia separated in the spring of 1920.
4. Erik Satie (1866–1925) played piano in various Montmartre cabarets after abandoning his studies at the Paris Conservatoire in 1884. Often the serious intent of his music was concealed by his absurdly witty titles. Satie's eccentricity, humor, harmonic innovations, and seemingly revolutionary theories won him numerous devoted admirers among musicians, including a group of young composers known as Les Six.

first time in my life,—both with rare sauces. Then a salad with cheese, and then a carameled pudding with little cakes. Café in the salon. Have had some grand eats at Gertrude's. Have the final one next Monday, for I'm clearing out for Rouen, Caen and places north. Can't stand the place here. Have refused invitations for lunch or dinner from Mme. Picabia, Mina Loy, Waldo Pierce, Miss Williams, Man Ray, Paul Ullman and George Biddle.[5]
[. . .]

To Gertrude Stein and Alice B. Toklas
July 28, 1923, Grand Hôtel du Casino, Cherbourg, France

Dears Gertrude and Alice:

After all I think you are lucky to have a Lady Godiva.[1] Little voyages in France, I am beginning to think, are not so easy as they used to be, owing to a scarcity of porters. At Caen, for instance, there were two, divided among 150 passengers. I engaged the attention of one of them, but it would have been better for my piece of mind, if I had not—for he left me until among the last with mes baggages out on the street, and at the final rush only flung my bags on the train and allowed me to hunt for a seat myself. It used not to be like that. At smaller places, such as Serquigny, etc., there are none at all. . . Next time I shall do my touring with a small sac I can handle myself.

5. Mina Loy (1882–1966) was best known as a poet (*Lunar Baedeker* 1923), and she also exhibited paintings in Paris (the Salon d'Automne from 1904 to 1906) and New York (Julien Levy's gallery, 1933). In 1918 she married the poet–boxer–editor–Dada icon Arthur Cravan. When he disappeared in 1919, she was emotionally devastated. She returned in the 1920s to Paris, where she ran a studio producing lampshades of her own design, supported in part by Peggy Guggenheim.

Waldo Pierce (1884–1970), an American painter born in Bangor, Maine, and educated at Harvard University. An ambulance driver during World War I, Pierce became a close friend of Ernest Hemingway's in the late 1920s.

The painter Eugene Paul Ullman (b. 1877) was a pupil of William Merritt Chase, lived in Paris and exhibited at the Salon des Independents. Highly regarded in his lifetime, Ullman received many awards and medals.

George Biddle (1885–1973) was a social realist painter born to a wealthy and socially prominent Philadelphia family. He was an important participant in the mural painting movement in the United States. He took an active part in the WPA Federal Art Project and received the mural assignment for the Department of Justice Building in Washington, D.C. His autobiography, *An American Artist's Story,* was published in 1939.

1. Stein and Toklas called their Ford Lady Godiva because of its lack of ornamentation.

Caen went to my heart. After all I like people rather than places and the Caennais are charming and it is they who make the place charming and not the cathedral. They are *clean,* clever, honest and good looking, and one can appreciate these qualities the more after coming from Rouen, where I could not apply them to the Rouennais. I hated Rouen. But why go into that, further than to say that I now understand perfectly, why Marcel Duchamp had to be a cubist.[2]

Last night about nine, I turned a corner and found St. Pierre's illuminated for choir practice. I heard the singing but could not get in. But it is the first time I ever saw a great church with cathedral pretensions illuminated at night—and *I did not like it.* The glass windows destroyed all sense of architecture and the result was a cheap effect recalling the candy illuminated churches of my childhood. I wonder if this is always so—or only a defect of this church. [. . .]

2. Duchamp's mother was a native of the Norman town Rouen; the artist was born and raised in Blainville-sur-Crevon, fifteen miles northeast of Rouen. Duchamp began his career as a member of the Puteaux cubists, a group founded by Duchamp's two older brothers, Raymond Duchamp-Villon and Jacques Villon, whose approach to cubism was less intuitive and more geometric than that of Picasso and Braque.

MALCOLM MACADAM

McBride met MacAdam, who was several years his junior, on New Year's eve 1917, while having dinner at a restaurant near his 23d Street residence. McBride (who uncharacteristically had a cocktail with his dinner that evening) initiated a conversation with MacAdam and began a friendship that would last forty years. A graduate of Syracuse University, MacAdam was an accountant for Standard Oil, and he was often sent on auditing assignments overseas. He spent most of the years 1922–52 working in various cities in Asia. His travels over that span offered McBride—who wrote every week or so—the opportunity to write many of his most intimate, forthright, and unfettered letters. MacAdam saved the letters and returned them to McBride in the late 1950s.

Before MacAdam began his travels, he and McBride were frequent companions. In 1921, when McBride moved into the Herald Square Hotel (where he would spend his winter "seasons" until the end 1946), MacAdam was a regular visitor.

When MacAdam was in New York he lived near Columbus Avenue on West 80th Street. In his final years he lived with a male companion on East 55th Street. When MacAdam and McBride were in the city, they would meet on Sunday mornings to spend time together and have lunch, a weekend ritual that continued until just before MacAdam's death of a heart attack in July 1957, just a few days shy of his eighty-fifth birthday.

Few of MacAdam's letters to McBride survive, though many references to the "unprintable" notes "Malc" favored pepper McBride's replies to him. It appears that McBride, after sharing MacAdam's letters with friends, would often announce, "We had better tear that one up right away."[1] Max Miltzlaff said that MacAdam's usual choice of words was "as bad as the language used by Henry Miller."[2]

1. Miltzlaff, conversation with Steven Watson, January 17, 1999.
2. Miltzlaff, unpublished notes.

To Malcolm MacAdam
September 21, 1923, Callicaste, Marshallton, Pennsylvania

Cher Malc:

[. . .] I went to the tennis championships at Manheim the day before the semi-finals, and saw four grand matches. The Tilden-Alonso match was wonderful—at least Tilden's part in it.[1] He is the greatest I've ever seen and he was greater that day, than I had ever seen him. He is a genius and the people glue their eyes to his every movement the way they used to glue their ears to Caruso. Billy Johnson who is almost as strong lacks genius, and is not really exciting to watch.[2]

Suppose you had heart failure at the Dempsey-Firpo prize fight. The Martins got it over the radio, and Dick said the announcer was so excited he could hardly get the facts over the wire. Probably there will be more disputes over the fight then any in history. I only hope Dempsey will find a clever Montgomery to safeguard his money for him.[3] I am on Dempsey's side, you know; also Babe Ruth's.

To Malcolm MacAdam
June 20, 1924, Callicaste, Marshallton, Pennsylvania

Dear Malc:

[. . .] PS . . . "Branwell was rather a handsome boy with 'tawny' hair, to use Miss Brontë's expression for a more obnoxious colour," (I had to look it up too, when I came across it in E. Dickinson). Well, some day you'll read *Shirley* again and like it the more for knowing Charlotte's life.[1] It's extraordinary to everybody how those quiet, sedate Brontë girls could have written the way they did—but everybody forgets, that such qualities depend

1. William Tatum Tilden (1893–1953) known as "Big Bill" ruled the world of tennis in the 1920s. Known as the game's "absolute master," Tilden became the first American to win England's Wimbledon championship in 1920. In the late 1920s he spent time in prison for having sex with an underage young man, and he died in poverty, ostracized for his homosexuality. The Spaniard Manuel Alonso was ranked eighth in the world in 1923, but would drop out of the top ten in the 1930s.
2. William Johnson was "Little Bill" to Tilden's "Big Bill."
3. Montgomery handled Malcolm MacAdam's finances.

1. *Shirley*, by Charlotte Brontë (1816–1855) was published in 1849. Set in Yorkshire at the beginning of the nineteenth century, the novel describes the relationship between two heroines and the two brothers they marry. Charlotte Brontë's sister Emily (1818–48), who died of tuberculosis the year before the book was published, served as the model for the title heroine of the novel.

upon an exercise of the imaginative faculty. The May Sinclairs and Rebecca Wests of today try fornication and every other device in order to learn the difference between love and passion—without, however, arriving at any where near the fire and vitriol of *Jane Eyre*.[2] You who have such an artistic disposition should ponder over this! Heavens knows I try to bring you up right. It won't be my fault if you go bad.

To Alyse Gregory
July 3, 1924, Callicaste

My dear Alyse Gregory:

I was about to call you an angel when it occurred to me to look the word up. Webster says: "A celestial being, superior to man in power and intelligence; spirit; demon." Upon the whole I will let the word stand. I agree with Webster. You are one. More books and more kindness were the last things I expected. I actually feared to open your letter. I thought it would say "Where are those Briefer Mentions? Where are those reviews? Where, in fact, are the simple acknowledgments of my past favors?" But nothing of that, only nice kindly sentiments usually quite foreign to editors. Did Scofield instruct you to take as your motto "Forgive, that ye may be forgiven?" But did you notice that Webster adds "demon"? He must have been thinking, of course, of your Sherwood Anderson review! However the general celestialness that emanates from *The Dial* offices is a mystery to me, and always has been.

[. . .] Lewellyn's book is truly grand. I am bowled over completely. Why can't some one write a really firm laudation of it, for once saying that a book is a work of genius the moment it appears! Why wait till the stupid ones catch on?

Gratefully, affectionately,

To Malcolm MacAdam
October 3, 1924 Callicaste, Marshallton, Pennsylvania

Cher Malc:

Last Sunday the Martin ladies took Mary Pugh to Marshallton Church. The preacher was a Rev. Mr. Heck. Nothing remarkable about this. But

2. May Sinclair, British writer (1865–1946); Rebecca West (1892–1983, born Cicily Isabel Fairfield), an English critic and novelist who took her pseudonym from Ibsen's *Rosmersholm*.

when Mary Pugh returned, there seemed much confab between the two Miss Pughs. "I don't see he looks like Harry at all," was one remark I overheard. "Oh, that's just Sadie for you. She says that just for something to say. She says she always likes to shake hands with Mr. Heck, because it always seems like shaking hands with Harry."

Hereupon I asked who this Mr. Heck was. Both Miss Pughs, in hushed voices, said: "Anna's son." Fancy that!

But of course you don't know who Anna was. She was a Pugh, a first cousin, and I well remember the fuss there was, though I was a small boy at the time, when she was seduced by a Louis Heck. It was the first event of its kind in our family connection and, I may boast, the only one: but it did make a stir. I vaguely understood what the fuss was all about, but grasped that nothing so startling had occurred since the Lisbon earthquake. We lost track of that branch of the family, not because of the shame, but because we didn't like 'em anyhow, and for years I have never heard them mentioned. But since Sunday they have been restored to the map. The Miss Pughs seem to gloat over every detail of Mr. Heck's personality. "He has Uncle Josh's hair," says Mary. "Well he comes by it honestly," says Maria, etc. etc. "He has her eyes," etc. etc. The fact that this illegitimate fruit of love has become a preacher seems to mend the whole matter. [. . .]

To Malcolm MacAdam
June 2, 1925, Callicaste, Marshallton, Pennsylvania

Cher a.:

Yesterday was hot, today hotter. Pauvre Malc, dans la ville Brooklyn, audessus les vitrines de bureau! Mais laissons ça de côté. Ici, c'est assez agreable.[1] Everything much as it was. The mortality of the winter less than usual and so far my cousins have not trotted out many horrors. The Dain boys quite as usual, if not more so.[2] Miner helped me carry my trunk up to my room and by way of recompense I gave him a mouth organ, that I meant to have given him last year, but forgot. As soon as Jack drove in sight Miner blew a blast on the instrument and without saying a word, Jack, who is the stronger, went up to him, wrestled with him, took it away from him, put it in his own pocket, and went into the house. By the next day, Miner, who is foxy if not strong, had it back again: Up on our porch conversing in

1. "Poor Malc, stuck in the office in Brooklyn. But we'll leave that alone. Here it is quite pleasant."
2. The Dains, including the brothers Jack and Miner, were a local family.

the evening, Miner suddenly shrieked out, "Oh, Harry, you want to see me tomorrow. In my new suit of clothes. I'm a regular sheik, I am. Ain't I Maria?"

I couldn't make any deal with Jack for services in exchange for my old Gillette razor. He has three, an auto-strop, a star, and a something else; but he admits he'd like to have a gold plated one. I asked if Miner shaved yet and in a tone of great scorn he asked, "Do women shave?" There is nothing in the way of insult they don't hurl at each other. I asked Jack where Miner was, but wishing to speak in vernacular, I said, "Where is bag-ears?" And Jack said, "Oh, you mean monkey-face. I don't know where he is." But neither of them are sensitive much to insult. They talk a lot of their cousin Anne Martin's young husband, who is a State Trooper and who is visiting and only beat Jack at tennis by six to four, but can blow the best bugle you ever heard in your life. Miner has been lent a clarinet and after he has had a few lessons, he intends to join the terrible Marshallton band, in which Jack plays the alto horn.

Miner stopped in on the way to Sunday school to get a flower for his boutonniere. He really did look like a sheik. His sheik suit turned out to be a golf suit not unlike yours. Jack, you will be scandalized to learn, has been fired from school, or allowed to quit, for not passing his exams. It's all because he gets no help at home. He is not stupid and could have learned with the ordinary encouragement. But not a member of his family ever reads a book, and not even his mother ever tried to read over his lessons. This means that Jack had to go into the uneducated classes of the future, and the next generation, I imagine, will demand more in the way of education than this one has. You may think you're getting more than your share of Jack and Miner stuff, but there is no other news. [. . .]

To Gertrude Stein
June 25, 1925, Callicaste, Marshallton, Pennsylvania

Dear Gertrude:

Do you accept pittances for your fund for Mildred?[1] I enclose one which I am ashamed of but thought at least I must be on your list. . . As usual I am hard up, and at this moment the prospects are that I shall be still harder

1. In 1924 the Mildred Aldrich Memorial fund was named and organized by Gertrude Stein, Alice Toklas, and Janet Scudder to ensure Aldrich's financial stability. Stein was happy with McBride's "pittance" and responded that they had gathered $3500.

up. . . I had thought of coming over, (this is my year), but one of my old cousins dropped flat into the helpless kind of rheumatism ten days ago and I have been nursemaid, housemaid and gardener ever since. There seems no Paris on the horizon. . . I had intended coming steerage, figurez-vous, I who love comfort moderne, but they tell me it is a steerage altogether modern and not too revolting to people of delicate susceptibilities. . . However!!

I am delighted about the book.[2] I gave it an announcement in the *Sun* and I slip those little notices into letters to likely people. Two or three of my friends have signified their intention of subscribing. It behooves one to drum up trade, you see, since you are giving me one. I hope it appears early enough for me to review it before I actually start winter work on October 15. It is, of course, sure to be a success.[3]

My summer seems to start off badly. I not only have the slavery obliged by my cousin's illness (made stranger by the fact that there is no affection between these old cousins and me—one of those odd family entanglements that occur in America in the country) but the likelihood that the establishment itself must be brought to an end before autumn. For a nervous wreck the immediate future is not alluring. . . "However," as I said before!

I am glad fate has been staved off from Mildred by your and Alice's grand efforts. Tell me how the situation stands. I am on the point of writing her but shan't mention it. Also news of the artists I crave. Mark in your address book my address, as above, until October. Will write all you wish this summer to make up for my laxities next winter.

Love to Alice and yourself.

To Gertrude Stein
November 26, 1925, Herald Square Hotel, New York

Dear Gertrude:

It seems to be a case of type-writer or nothing. I suppose Alice will be horrified but you must persuade her to forgive it. Here it's being done,

2. Stein's *The Making of Americans* was published by Robert McAlmon's Contact Editions in 1925 in Paris. Stein considered it her masterpiece and one of the three masterpieces—with *Ulysses* and *Remembrance of Things Past*—of the twentieth century.
3. The book was not financially successful. By December 1926, 103 copies had sold, including one with deluxe binding and twenty-eight bound in leather. McAlmon threatened to pulp the remainder, but didn't.

though I confess I'm always slightly irritated when an actual friend machines his thoughts in this fashion. . . Send me the book here, to this hotel.
I'm here and hate it but I suppose I shall stay on through the winter,
having hated the Herald Square Hotel for six years I think.[1] In any case it
doesn't seem safe to send a book to me to *The Sun*. I get letters, but not
always books. I prefer even my letters to come here as I only go down to the
office once a week and sometimes not even then. I look forward with great
expectations to the book which I shall enjoy but scarcely expect to master.
You have always been very discreet about it yourself but the others, May
Knoblauch, Carl Van Vechten, always look interrogation points whenever
they speak of it. You will at least have satisfied your ambition to match
Lord Macauley size for size.

I am just back in town and have seen, so far, only Mabel Dodge. There is
a break in your relation but you know all her activities, I daresay. She is in
town for a short stay at the Brevoort and goes back in a few days to her
Indian.[2] Did I tell you she asked me to visit her at Taos last summer? She
thinks her Aborigine and I would get along but of course she doesn't know
me very well. We lunched together but there was a strange woman along, a
fanatic who thinks artists are unfitted to cope with modern life and is
going to do something about it and she effectually prevented any personal
gossip and so spoiled the lunch for me. All I got was that Mabel had forcibly
moved Bobby Jones out of the old Lafayette Hotel where he has been
miserable for years, into a little apartment in Greenwich Village which—I
understand—she personally furnished. . .[3] Mabel seems happy, healthy,
but as much a myth to me as ever. I heard so much about her before I ever
met her and it is impossible now to match the apparently simple individual I meet with the fabulous person of report. She probably hasn't changed
in the least since your day but I suspect her to be fluid and that people read
into what they wish.

1. McBride moved into the Herald Square Hotel in fall 1921 and spent twenty-five
seasons there, finally moving on in 1946.
2. The large and fashionable Hotel Breevort, at Fifth Avenue and Eighth Street, was
a block south of Mabel Dodge's previous apartment at 23 Fifth Avenue, the site of
her "evenings" (1913–15).
3. The Hotel Lafayette at University Place and 9th Street. Robert Edmond Jones
(1887–1954) was a prominent and revolutionary stage designer, beginning in June
1913 with his designs for the Paterson Strike Pageant and continuing with his work
for the Provincetown Players. Dodge had given him financial support for many
years.

The town is terrifying. There seem to be such appalling numbers of people. The increase in quantity and the pace is now visible from year to year. It is impossible to look at the millions of uninteresting people on the streets without conjecturing what the next five years even may have in store. The thought of a 35,000,000 city is so unpleasant that I might eventually, that is to say, soon, imitate you and fly the country—although I consider it, tell Alice, a highly immoral thing to do. But all of our millions have money. Poverty is obsolete. Do you still have poverty in Paris? And happiness?

Love to Alice and Mildred.

To Katherine Dreier
December 8, 1925, Herald Square Hotel

Dear Miss Dreier:[1]

I am not contributing to your society nor to any other this winter for the simple reason I cannot afford it. I don't know what my status with you is but at the last account I was upon your advisory board. As it is an equivocal position I therefore resign it.[2] With best wishes for your success,

To Malcolm MacAdam
June 7, 1926, Aboard S.S. "Lancastria"

Dear Malc:

[. . .] It's a hell of a trip so far, but it may become easier as it goes on. The English are not artists enough to arrange for the first impression and certainly on Saturday I thought once of jumping overboard and ending it all. By today, Monday, I discovered this decent reading room and a fairly comfortable portion of deck. The French would have shown them off first thing.

1. McBride's unusually blunt tone may have been a response to Dreier's manner. Dreier (1877–1952) was renowned for being tyrannical in her devotion to her dual obsessions—the Société Anonyme, and Marcel Duchamp. In a letter to Dreier's assistant, May Knoblauch (April 20, 1922), McBride candidly wrote, "Please don't allow yourself to be browbeaten by Miss. Dreier" (YCAL, McBride).
2. In a letter dated December 10, 1925, Dreier accepted McBride's resignation, saying, "You know, I think that we will be better friends. One of the odd situations in life is an equivocal position and the moment the atmosphere is cleared, there is room for better understanding" (YCAL, Dreier).

I won't detail objections, further than a smelly cabin, a terribly smelly dining room, and still smellier stewards. One look at the stewards and I lost all interest in food. Nice enough people on board. My favorites are the jazz-band; a group of six or eight Columbia boys, full of pep, and pretty good jazzers. One very still Englishman, something like my Mr. Nichol, doesn't like them. I heard him complaining that the jazz was intolerable and that he'd have to have his meals in the smoking room. He raised such a row, they agreed to serve him there. Today this Englisher came and sat near me and engaged me in conversation. He came over on this same Lancastria, was four days on landing seeing Niagara, Toronto, the St. Lawrence, Philadelphia and New York; and returns rather pleased with himself.

My cabin mate is also English, clean, decent, docile mechanic employed in the shipyard at Newport News. The Lancastria seems to be steady, and is making 16 knots so far, but oh that food, I simply can't touch the vegetables, which are so necessary for a person in my interesting condition. [. . .]

I have the blues. I ask myself what on earth can I do in Paris. I am in no mood to hunt a good time or even accept it if it came my way. These last six weeks of misery of all sorts have used up all my courage. The episode of my brother was just one item.[1] Everything goes the wrong way. My not seeing you was another item. But if you had known how everything that day, including the queer getaway in the bus, had gone wrong, you would have considered the accidents as portents and have advised me to give the voyage up. I only noticed by chance on the train, that my boat sailed at midnight. The one bit of luck was, that my bank let me in after closing hours at 4:30, gave me money and even American Express Cheques. At the Herald Square Hotel there was an entire change of Hotel clerks, who didn't know me and who wouldn't cash a cheque. [. . .]

Wednesday. . . When near a book shop get Lewellyn Powys new book, *The Verdict of Bridlegoose.* You must have heard enough intimate details of all the people spoken of, to appreciate the plain speaking; besides you've met some of them. He says I'm "congenitally light minded." I was to have reviewed it for *The Dial,* but Marianne Moore got shocked by it and said it shouldn't be reviewed at all. Still feel suicidal. [. . .]

1. This is one of McBride's few mentions of his immediate family. In an earlier, unpublished letter to Malcolm (June 1, 1926), McBride wrote from Callicaste, "When I arrived Friday my brother seemed to be taking a turn for the worse. . . I am practically waiting to be present at the end, and since he is in a state of coma, it is only a technicality."

To Malcolm MacAdam
June 16, 1926, Hôtel Continental—Paris, France

Dear Malc:

I am still ill and you must accustom yourself to complaining letters. I have no one else to complain to and I don't expect to be scolded in return. I expect consolation of some sort. At present I do not see how I can live until my sailing date July 31 and then make that terrible journey home. I suppose by that time, if I do survive, this disease will have fastened on me for life and had I stayed at home, I should have been well by this time. But enough of this—if you get the idea I am really sick!

A few impressions: Paris is unprecedentedly cold and expensive. The cold ocean weather continues here and how the tennis players did anything at all I don't see. Not only are the intervals between rains short, but the air is frosty. I went to the Palais d'Orsay expecting my 28f room to have doubled, but the clerk looked me in the eye and said "165 frs. par jour." I said bonjour and heard the clerk laughing as I departed. I tried the Quai Voltaire, which was full and then, as it was raining, accepted a room in the Hôtel Intendant on the rue de l'Université for 45 frs. on the sixieme. It is a forlorn little hotel, not at all the style of the Palais d'Orsay or the Hotel Celtic, and the three lower floors are like an ice house, so that there is no place I can lounge. As soon as I had washed and shaved I went to the Café de la Paix and sat under the awning during the down pour and had a chocolate and two brioches for 8 frs. A steamer acquaintance joined me and also a stranger with dirty finger nails and a monocle. In spite of the fact that I talked with my acquaintance, the monocled stranger joined in. He asked did I like Paris, I said "No," which is the literal truth, but he was not to be rebuffed. He pulled out an awful looking watch, said he had no money to pay his hotel bill and would I give him 60 frs. for it. I said I had a watch. Then he turned to my friend, held up his malacca cane and said, "Give me two dollars for this." I finally got cross and said "C'est assez. Taisez-vous," and after apparently shedding a veritable tear the crook departed. I merely tell you the episode that you may see that Paris, in its essentials, is much the same. The same taciturn, bald-headed man pours the coffee at the Café de la Paix, and the man that makes the little, worsted puppy wriggle on his arm, is still here. The puppy is now 15 frs. [. . .]

I got a Veron tie for 60 frs.!! The shop windows are as alluring as ever, but the prices are fabulous. I wonder who is rich enough to buy these luxuries. I think I have given you enough prices to show that the old game of a poor American coming here and pretending to be rich for a month or so, is finished.

Went to Gertrude Stein last night. I was tired to death, but thought Gertrude would have a fire, and she did. But a lot of relatives came in and I had to leave as I wasn't up to conversation. This morning my chocolate and croissants seemed to cause internal disorders and I have been extra unhappy since. I never-the-less went to the Alpes for luncheon and ate heartily and feel a little easier now. Met Janet Scudder on the street and got asked to tea this afternoon . . . but I don't feel up to it. [. . .]

Wednesday [. . .] Went to the Palais Royal last night. Had heard nothing of it, but like King Alfonso of Spain, I always go to the Palais Royal first thing on arriving. Paid 35 frs. and landed on a strapontin.[1] I guess its the last strapontin, I'll sit on for a while. By luck I found myself next to Mme. Samaroff and a woman friend. (She's Alice Garrett's friend and music critic for the *Evening Post*.) The farce was very gay and wonderfully well acted. I don't recall as good acting in anything I saw in New York last winter with the exception of the Russian players. Albert Brasseur was the star, but all were good—and we laughed every minute. I defeated the vestiaires for once, for I wore my overcoat all evening. The little Palais Royal is an adorable theatre—all the "assistance" looked like pictures. Olga Samaroff tells me I must see *Monsieur St. Obin,* too, at the Variétés, she says it funny.

Thursday. My society life begins. Gertrude threw a tea for me yesterday and the great Juan Gris came, also Romaine Brooks and her friend Natalie Barney.[2] They have asked me for tea Friday. Today I went to the Picasso

1. Folding seat.
2. Juan Gris (José Victoriano González, 1887–1927) came to Paris in 1906. In addition to his painting, Gris excelled at the papier collé technique developed at the height of cubism. He also made sculptures and book illustrations and worked with Diaghilev, making stage sets and costumes for his ballet.

Romaine Brooks (née Goddard, 1874–1970), was an eccentric portrait painter born in Rome to a wealthy and unstable American mother. She studied art in Paris and Rome, and when her brother and mother died, she inherited a fortune. She entered into a marriage of convenience with John Brooks, a homosexual dilettante from Capri. Best known for her stark and penetrating portraits, Brooks also gained notoriety as a decorator of austere black, white, and gray interiors. She painted D'Annunzio and Jean Cocteau, as well as many portraits of Natalie Barney, her partner of forty years.

Barney (1876–1971) was a wealthy American who settled in Paris in 1899 and did not return to the United States until 1946. Barney wrote poetry, drama, fiction, and essays, and the afternoons she organized at her home at 20, rue Jacob celebrated

show and saw a whole crowd of Americans I know, including Else Peterson, Mahonri Young and Albert Gallatin.[3] Gallatin asked me to lunch tomorrow at the Crillon. Saturday afternoon we all go to hear Antheil's concert in the Théâtre Champs-Élysées, in which a feature is his *Ballet Mécanique* and which it is hoped, will provoke a riot.[4] Gertrude and Alice are going out to Mildred's on Sunday and maybe I will, too. I dread going alone, as I don't feel equal to coping with Mildred. Apparently Gertrude is at her patience's end. She says the fund only gives Mildred 1000 frs. a month and she won't live within that. They want her to give up her gardener but she won't. Instead she gave up her own maid and cooks her own meals.

This is a dull letter and more than you will read, but I write in order to distract my mind from the conditions of life which are dûr.

I am so conspicuous in my straw hat. Nobody else had one and I have nothing else. . . Romaine Brooks says she'll send her chauffeur up with an electric stove to warm up my room. I half hope she remembers to do so. And Natalie Barney has asked me to play tennis.

To Malcolm MacAdam
June 21, 1926, Paris, France

Cher ange:

You didn't know I had become a moving picture actor, did you? Yes, I make my debut on the screen tomorrow night at Albert's charming and cute little house on the rue Bassane.[1] We shot the pictures Sunday. Gerald was taking me to lunch at Prunier's, back of the Étoile, and Ruth, who brought him to the Hotel, said she would take us as far as Albert's in her Hispano . . ., but when we got there, we had to go in for a minute to see the house, and Albert who has a little moving-picture camera you carry in one

---

lesbianism and literature; her group was called l'Académie des Femmes. Besides Romaine Brooks, Barney's lovers included Liane de Pougy and Renée Vivien.
3. An exhibition of Picasso's work of the previous twenty years was held in June 1926 at Paul Rosenberg's gallery. For Gallatin see Biographical Sketches.
4. George Antheil's (1900–1959) *Ballet Mécanique,* with its use of airplane propellers and dissonance, aroused controversy at its Paris premiere. Fernand Léger created a film to be shown in synchronization with the ballet, and the libretto was by William Carlos Williams. The work aroused controversy in Europe but was a fiasco in its U.S. debut at Carnegie Hall in 1927. Barbara Haskell, *Charles Demuth* (New York: Whitney Museum of American Art and Harry N. Abrams, 1987), p. 187.

1. Albert Rothbarth was a New York financier who attended high bohemian gatherings.

hand, insisted he had to shoot a picture of us down in the courtyard, and so we hastily arranged a little comedy with Ruth on the stairs, and all the domestiques looked out of the window at us and roared with laughter, so the comedy must be good. At any rate . . . we'll know tomorrow night, for Albert is to give a moving picture party and dinner, and show all the films they shot in Morocco.

To hear Gerald's tales of their adventures in Morocco is to die. They made the acquaintance of Colette the writer, on the way down, and as Colette was on a mission, she let them into all the grand palaces and introduced them to all the sultans.[2] The time Gerald and Ruth took a bain turc is the high spot of the tale. I have decided, ange, that when you come abroad next year, you are to go straight to Gibraltar and Morocco. Gerald says two months won't be enough. Gee, but Prunier gives you good food. It is one of the most frequented places in Paris, but new since I was here last. Gerald and I spent the hot afternoon in the Bois, enjoying the first sunshine of two months, and then dined at the Grand Pic on the ave. d'Antin, also new and very good. Gerald's frivolous and semi-naughty conversation cheered me up from the depression I fell into after going to the concert Friday night with Romaine Brooks, Natalie Barney and the Duchesses of Clermont-Tonnere.[3] They are all high-brows, and you can say what you like, but high-brows tire me. [. . .]

Wednesday. Quel Chagrin! I look terrible in the movies. So fat and flabby. Great rolls of flesh between the jaw and the ear, when I laugh, like a rhinoceros. Royal was right—I *am* a behemoth. But all the others thought me good and free from the sin of self-consciousness. Albert said with great enthusiasm, that I could sign a contract any day I chose. It would have to be for Fatty Arbuckle parts. [. . .]

To Malcolm MacAdam
July 2, 1926, Paris, France

Cher a.:

[. . .] Clara Thomas called early yesterday morning. The maid said, "Mlle Tomah vous demande," but I knew who it was, so I told her to say I would

2. Sidonie-Gabrielle Colette (1873–1954) French writer of two dozen sensual novels written intimately from a woman's perspective.
3. Elisabeth de Gramont, the duchesse de Clermont-Tonnerre (1875–1954), was a friend of Gertrude Stein's and the author of several volumes of memoirs, travel books, and works on Proust.

descend in an instant. Clara looked like a chit of twelve, in a pale blue summer dress; and said she wanted me to go to Boutet de Monvel's studio, at 3:30.[1] In reality she wanted to get me into her own show of maquettes at Seligmans, just around the corner from de Monvel's; and sure enough, just as soon as Gerald, Mrs. Force, Flora Whitney and Mrs. Whitney got thorough seeing de Monvel's things we were packed into Mrs. W's grand car and toted to Clara's show.[2] Then drinks at the Élysées Bar, and then half an hour at home, and then dinner at Clara's apartment on the Île St. Louis. Those are chic apartments on the Île St. Louis, but Clara gave me a filthy dinner and invited some terrible people to meet me—artists, who expected to exhibit in New York next winter. That's what I call a completely wasted day... But there'll be few more of such, mark my words. [. . .]

I did have to go, in fact, to Natalie Barney's last at home of the season, because I thought it would be a good chance to say good-bye to both her and Romaine Brooks. Natalie's house is the most cunning in Paris, back of the rue Jacob, with a glass enclosed room looking level on an old garden. It used to be the abode of Adrienne Le Courvreur the famous actress.[3] Natalie's party was crowded. I got there early, in time to assist in placing the four harpists who were to do Honegger's suite for harps. Then in came a pretty little girl in blue, whom Natalie introduced as the Princess Galitzin. Then everybody trooped in, with at least a hundred from New York, and the scandal and tittle-tattle were so great, that few knew exactly when the Honegger suite got played. I heard at least three shady stories that will make your baby blue eyes stare, if I remember to tell them you. They are not of course fit to pass through the mails, because they are about real people.

Albert Gallatin took me to tea Wednesday at Baron Gourgaud's. He has the most magnificent house I have yet peeped into. His wife was one of the Gebhards of New York. She's an enormous, big-boned, leopard-like creature, older of course than the Baron, and painted in wilder colors than New

1. Bernard Boutet de Monvel (1884–1949) was a highly regarded society portrait painter in the 1920s. His father was also a well-known society artist at the turn of the century.
2. For Juliana Force and Gertrude Vanderbilt Whitney, see Biographical Sketches. Flora Whitney Tower Miller (1897–1986) was Gertrude Whitney's daughter.
3. Barney moved into the house on rue Jacob in 1909. "Her house, which was at least three hundred years old, was hidden in a courtyard and popularly (but erroneously) believed to have been the home of the actress Adrienne Lecouvreur (1692–1730), a great interpreter of Racine." Meryle Secrest, *Between Me and Life: A Biography of Romaine Brooks* (Garden City, New York: Doubleday, 1974), p. 315.

York women yet dare to use. The old dowagers at the tea table had the most amazing jewels, and awfully funny faces, and I could have put in my time profitably studying *them*, but I had been really brought there to see the Baron's famous collection of Picassos and Matisses, which do look marvelous in spite of all you say against the grand old walls of the palace.

Did I tell you that Romaine Brooks lent me an electric stove during my first cold days? Joseph her chauffeur, charming person from Switzerland, brought it to me and adapted it so it would work. It did work two or three cold wet days, but the night before I went to St. Nazaire I tried it late at night, and in two minutes, bing, il sautait la plomb, and all the lights went out.[4] I was scared to death, and wrapped it up while still hot and hid it in the armoire. I had visions of people running up and down stairs, loud cries, etc., and a final row with me. But fortunately the porter fixed it up next day without saying a word, (it only affected my room) and that night we all went to Ezra Pound's concert, Josef brought me home in Romaine's car, and I smuggled the stove out to him.[5] Since then, it's been warm.

One day, when I was alone for luncheon, I went to Colombine. When finished, I was sure I saw Anita Loos in the inner room, I advanced towards her but thought, "No, that's not Anita. It's too young."[6] Twice I made towards her and twice retreated, baffled. That night, at a party on the Avenue Villars, Albert Rothbarth brought her and Anita confessed it had been she and said she hadn't seen me at all. She and Clara Thomas can both look like twelve year olds when they want to. Anita is going to shake off everybody, too, and says she is going to "parts unknown" in order to finish some work she has to do. My greatest pest, of course, is Gerald. I have a terrible time losing him. [. . .]

To Malcolm MacAdam
August 12, 1926, Callicaste, Marshallton, Pennsylvania

Dear Malc:
[. . .] As for Clara, I have no special tips, except that she should go, 1) to Vernon's on rue Royale and get you three ties, and 2) to 91 Boul. Haussman and get you a bottle of Leopold's Fluide Ideale, (for the one bottle I brought you won't last you all winter, especially if you have Sunday visitors) and

4. *Sautait la plomb,* blew the fuse.
5. Pound's opera *Le Testament de Villon* premiered at the Salle Pleyel on June 29, 1926.
6. Anita Loos (1893–1929), scenarist and humor writer, best known for *Gentlemen Prefer Blondes,* published 1925.

3) that a lot of women seemed to be crazy about Caron's perfume Nuit de Noël, which sells for 2000frs. a small flacon, and 4) that she might try getting a dress made by Yvonne Davidson, Jo Davidson's wife, and 5) that she should inveigle someone into taking her to lunch at Prunier's on Av. Victor Hugo, where she should order among other things, chocolat mousse, and thereupon become familiar with the best ice cream in the world; and 6) and 7) go to the Théâtre Marigny for *Vive La République,* and the Palais Royale for *Le Premier de ces Messieurs.*[1] Perhaps that will be enough for the first day in France.

Apparently you didn't get what I said about the franc. True, I lived on less than ever before, but then I lived differently. I paid less, than ever before, on the steamer, *but I went steerage.* The staple things the French use are cheap for us, but unfortunately we don't want the staple goods. Americans, who go to Paris, like luxuries, but the luxuries of the rue de la Paix, the rue Royale, rue Tivoli and the Grandes Boulevards are quite as high, if not more so, than those of New York. Also, hotels. Now do you get me? If Clara writes to you, she will probably write about the franc too. There are only two topics talked of in Paris, the decline of the franc and the rise of Lesbianism. I did you the honor of supposing you would prefer the first topic. You will probably have to take up Lesbianism seriously next winter, for *La Prisonnière,* the fashionable play of last spring is to be done in New York. In order to profit by the vast French interest in the subject they dramatized *La Garçone* also, just before I left. But you'll have to pursue your studies in that line unassisted, for I'm cross now. [. . .]

To Duncan Phillips
March 25, 1927, New York

Dear Mr. Phillips:

At the time I wrote of the Marins in *The Dial* I telephoned Mr. Stieglitz saying I had heard of the $6000 sale and he did not deny it[1]. . . . Later, in

1. Jo Davidson (1883–1952), known primarily as a portrait sculptor, started his career as an artist under McBride's tutelage at Educational Alliance. He was later taken up by Gertrude Vanderbilt Whitney, whom he met in Paris when both were studying at the École des Beaux-Arts. His wife Yvonne (d. 1934) was a highly regarded couturier whose steady clients included Whitney.

1. On December 2, 1926, Phillips secretly agreed to pay an unprecedented price of $6,000 for John Marin's watercolor *Back of Bear Mountain.* The details of the transaction between Phillips and Marin's dealer Alfred Stieglitz (which included a gift of

conversation, he told me practically the version you give me. Actually you paid $6000 for a Marin—but with compensations. It is as you say, a correct statement that conveys a false impression.[2] Do you wish me to give the fact in *The Dial*? I will, if you wish, but personally, I advise dropping the matter. I intended in my *Dial* comment to suggest my own distaste for the business—which is pronounced—and thought that would be apparent to my readers. I do not think that any watercolour by a living painter, however masterly, is worth $6000, and I think Marin would have been much further along in the public appreciation if such "forcing methods" had not been used for him. I have had the whole matter out with Stieglitz long-ago, but it seems to be a thing he cannot resist, and since I sincerely like him and respect his accomplishment, I have ceased to worry him. I take my artists as I find them and I suppose I must take my art promoters as I find them, also. It is particularly regrettable, to my mind, that men like you and Mr. Howald should be penalized just because it is known you are among the very few who want to buy. On the contrary artists should make a point of honour of selling to you both for less than the usual sums—just for the increased honour it gives them to be represented in your collections. The French have already understood this.

I rejoiced in your *Collection In the Making* and hope to give it a review before the season ends.[3] Could you send me a photograph of

---

two additional Marin watercolors) were almost immediately leaked by Stieglitz, who saw the sale as a victory for the general cause of American painting. Phillips seems not to have gotten angry about Stieglitz's apparent betrayal until both the *New Yorker* and McBride made dubious note of the affair, McBride writing in his *Dial* column of February 1927. Public and private letters between McBride, Stieglitz, and Phillips flew back and forth. (Stieglitz published a pamphlet quoting from their correspondence.) The affair permanently damaged the relationship between Phillips and Stieglitz, though it seems to have had little lasting effect on the Washington collector's high opinion of McBride. Elizabeth Hutton Turner, *In the American Grain: Dove, Hartley, Marin, O'Keeffe, and Stieglitz, the Stieglitz Circle at The Phillips Collection*. Washington, D.C.: The Phillips Collection, 1995.
2. Phillips's letter to McBride dated March 19, 1927, stated, in part, "Field Marshal Stieglitz manoeuvered negotiations so that I paid his record price for the Marin I liked best, receiving as compensation two others of the very finest Marin's 1925 vintage as gifts. . . . It was only the opportunity to get three A-1 water colors by this great artist at a price below their value which tempted me. . . . I realized well enough the news value of my bargain for propaganda, but, as it was in a worthy cause and on behalf of America's finest painter, I not only understood but cooperated" (The Phillips Collection Archives, Washington, D.C.).
3. *A Collection in the Making* (1926), Phillips's self-published account of the early

the new Thomas Eakins?[4] It seems to be a superb one and I do not know it.

With best wishes, and sincerely yours

To Florine Stettheimer

June, 1927 Callicaste, Marshallton, Pennsylvania

Dear Florine S.:

My respectful hommages to all the Stettheimers and my good-byes! I'm off for the summer. I did mean to drop in and *say it,* but my last two days in town were of the sort that wouldn't permit it. I suppose your sister Carrie has already been up and down every stairway in the rue de la Paix.[1] Well, she'll be able to put Bendel Brothers in the place they belong when she returns. You'll see.

I've been miserable since coming down here. Colder than I've been once during the winter! But summer will come sometime, no doubt; also the autumn, when I expect to see you and Ettie, browned and robust from your athletic exercises. Comme toujours.

PS. My bust (by Gaston Lachaise) turns out to be a combination of Mussolini and Phillip II.[2] *He* sees the heroic side of my character!!

---

stages of the building of his collection. The book also announced Phillips's commitment to building an important collection of post–World War I American art that would hang as equals next to his already significant collection of modern European masters. Phillips remained committed to collecting both European and American modernism, and the two men continued their working relationship after Stieglitz initiated a reconciliation with Phillips.

4. In 1927 Phillips acquired a portrait by Thomas Eakins (1844–1916), titled *Miss Van Buren.* Eakins owes at least some of his reputation as the greatest American painter of the nineteenth century to McBride's insightful writing on the artist; at the beginning of the twentieth century he was commonly relegated to art-historical obscurity.

1. The fashion-conscious Carrie Stettheimer traveled to Paris to buy her clothes; the rue de la Paix was the center for couture.

2. Lachaise suggested the sitting in the spring of 1927. In March 1928 McBride wrote in "McBride's Portrait by Lachaise" for *The Dial,* "When Lachaise first suggested the idea I said . . . that never in my life had a painter wished to do me, and that I was enough of an artist myself to see precisely why they didn't. . . . Lachaise insisted, looking at me with that curiously appraising glance that is so disconcerting to some people, 'there was something,' he had felt it for some time." Later in the essay he mentioned the resemblance he had noted in the letter: "Oh, very he-

To Florine Stettheimer
July 4, 1927, 118 East Kind Street, Lancaster, Pennsylvania

Dear Florine:

Notice the date? July fourth! It seems to be some day up here in Lancaster. I am staying at Charles Demuth's. . .[1] We have just had a hearty and delicious luncheon of turtle soup and champagne. It seems everybody who is anybody at all in Lancaster has turtle soup on the Fourth of July. It is a very "filling," sustaining food and at the same time has a subtle flavor. Tell Carrie, she might incorporate some of it into your daily lives, or at least on Fourth of Julys. It's time she should begin again to be 100 percent after her prolonged spree at the rue de la Paix.

Marcel's portrait stares at me out of the corner of this desk and makes your incredible news all the more startling.[2] Why didn't he then, since he likes 'em fat, marry Katherine Dreier? But Charles tells me the new one is rich, too. So perhaps it's all for the best. It seems as though we are more and more in for a fat era. All you girls will be obliged to eat rice to secure husbands, or to be in it at all.

The Demuth house is a knock-out; as you might guess. It's in the heart of town, with a narrow entrance (decorated chastely by Bobbie Locher) that opens out into bigger rooms at the back, which in turn look out on delightful gardens, in which there is a long brick terrace and many brick walks. The flowers are plentiful and many of them are family relics that have nothing to do with the fashions of the day. The house is full of quaint furniture and some amusing works of art. Among the latter are things by

---

roic. . . . Mussolini! Yes! . . . I thought of confessing that I was not, habitually, a Mussolini" (reprinted in *Flow of Art*, pp. 241, 242). Lachaise's portrait bust of McBride is now in the collection of the Museum of Modern Art, New York.

1. The Demuth family home in Lancaster was a favorite summer stopping point for McBride, who was very fond of not only Charles but also his mother. Mrs. Demuth returned the affection, leaving McBride $10,000 in her will, as well as a first edition of Joyce's *Ulysses* that had belonged to Charles, whom she outlived. McBride, a teetotaler by habit and inclination, enjoyed a lemonade wine Mrs. Demuth made each summer, often bringing a coveted bottle back to Callicaste with him, where he doled out small samples to his friends.

2. "Marcel's portrait" probably refers to a photographic portrait by Stieglitz of Duchamp that Demuth owned.

The "startling" news was that on June 7, 1927, Duchamp had entered into his first marriage, to Lydie Sarazin-Levassor, the twenty-five-year-old daughter of a wealthy automobile manufacturer. The marriage ended in divorce in January 1928.

Marin, Louis Bouché, Pascin, and Georgia O'Keeffe.[3] There are no Florine Stettheimers, which I thought odd. One would look well in my room, which is all in white, with a wall paper of small dots at regular intervals. I told Charles he'd have to have you down here but he smiled curiously and said, he didn't think you'd come.

And there's a marvelous church steeple to be seen from the garden—the finest I've seen in America. More or less baroque and foolish, but adorable. Square brick tower rises above the roof and the rest is in white wood, with four large prophets at the four corners. The tower contains great bells, which raise a frightful din on Sunday mornings at eight o'clock, but the congregational singing was charming from a distance of sixty feet. They wound up with "America" so nicely, I almost wept.

Charles sends his love to you and the admired sisters. Moi aussi. [. . .]

3. Louis Bouché (b. 1896), American painter, pupil of Richard Miller, Simon Menard, and J. P. Laurens in Paris. Bouché showed with the Valentine Gallery in New York.

CALLICASTE

Henry McBride named his house in the countryside of Pennsylvania Callicaste. According to Max Miltzlaff, Callicaste is a Gypsy word meaning "if not today, then tomorrow," and implying a sort of shiftlessness.[1] Although such an epigraph doesn't seem to suit Henry McBride's Quaker-instilled work ethic, Callicaste was his place for unwinding from his New York life by chopping wood, gardening, and, most important, reading.

Purchased in 1906 for $600, Callicaste originally housed not only McBride during the summer and early fall months but his uncle Caleb and his cousins Mary and Maria year-round. Caleb Pugh died very shortly after the move to Callicaste, but his daughters remained for thirty years. McBride's relationship with his two maiden aunts seems to have been cordial yet distant, as their understanding of his life and career could only have been superficial. The sisters could be a source of good-natured ribbing in McBride's letters, but he also appreciated them. Their cooking was good standard "Chester County" fare, and for the years they were in the house, cooking was not something McBride bothered with.

Situated on three and a half acres, at a fork in the road a mile outside of the Pennsylvania town of Marshallton, the house was built at the turn of the nineteenth century. The three-and-a-half story structure was constructed of fieldstone coated with plaster and painted white. Feeling that the house was too high to "be in good proportion," McBride added an open porch to provide a sense of visual balance. The grounds included a lawn, several impressive boxwood bushes, a vegetable garden, and flower beds. Across the road that ran behind the property was a barn, and toward the west an orchard. The house had no electricity or running water. Behind the back garden was a springhouse, the source of water for the property.

After the departure of Maria and Mary Pugh for the Hickman Home for Aged Quakers in 1936, McBride made improvements on what he finally considered his own home. Max Miltzlaff has described the interior of the house as charming and warm. Fireplaces and kerosene lamps provided

---

1. Unless otherwise noted, all quotations in this section are from Miltzlaff's unpublished notes.

13, 14 Henry McBride at Callicaste, undated. Photographer unknown.

warmth, light, and atmosphere. The beautiful flooring was framed by plaster walls with wood detail, including wainscoting and door and window recesses. The first floor had a front room, or sitting room, with a mostly unused study for McBride behind it. The colors of the rooms seem to have been highly considered, as Miltzlaff wrote: "The front room was painted a very light French gray, with a soft blue tint. In each corner were four canary yellow stripes running vertically from ceiling to floor." These more formal rooms housed many of McBride's artworks, including two drawings by Lachaise, works on paper by Marin and Demuth, and prints by Matisse, Miró, and Roualt. Underneath the front room, on the ground floor, was a cellar. At the back of the ground floor was the dining room. Its location meant it was always cool, and as a result McBride spent most of the summer months there, writing and reading. A large walk-in fireplace and a wood-burning stove kept the room warm as the seasons changed. Most of the minimal furniture throughout the house was early American, and handmade rugs covered the floors.

McBride's large bedroom on the third floor faced the road, and two smaller rooms opened to the back of the house. The bedrooms had old and apparently temperamental rope beds, "fitted for sleeping with old fashioned feather beds, wrapped in quilt covers, to serve as mattresses."

McBride relished the physical aspect of his time at Callicaste. Chopping wood, lugging water, raking leaves, and tending the gardens were all tasks McBride seems to have enjoyed. The regularity of his days in the country must have been welcome respite from his hectic city schedule. As Miltzlaff describes, "Each day Henry McBride would fix the kerosene lamps, to be ready when darkness set in. Water was fetched up from the pump in the kitchen and from the spring house. Each bedroom had an old fashioned wash stand, with bowl and water pitcher. The W.C. was down stairs in the woodshed. Henry McBride liked it that way. He lived as the farmers of the old days."

While McBride's life in Marshallton, which took up a good part of every year, is not fully described in the letters selected here, the social world of Callicaste, Marshallton, and the surrounding areas of Chester County was one in which McBride actively played the part of participant-observer. When he was younger and life in Marshallton was its most rural, McBride knew and wrote frequently about the local farmers and their families, describing everything from local feuds and gossip, to the acquisition of a newfangled razor, to the tragedy of a farming accident. Later in life, as the area surrounding Callicaste grew more genteel, some of his closest friendships were formed with his immediate neighbors, the Barrs and the Millers (see Biographical Sketches). Many of McBride's last letters were addressed to these two couples.

To Malcolm MacAdam
July 8, 1927, Callicaste, Marshallton, Pennsylvania

Dear Malc:

Just back from my Fourth of July visit to Lancaster. Had a good time—though it is more or less of an effort to get into town clothes and visit town people. Bobby and Beatrice Locher were down, visiting Bobbie's sister. There were several parties, in consequence, including a picnic, where I met the last living descendent of William Penn, a lady, whose style is about as emancipated as Muriel Draper's (Muriel is to tour the country lecturing next winter, Charles Demuth tells me).[1] George Biddle and his brother Francis were also visiting Lancaster and in the party. George wore shirts, that had zipper fastenings up the front, instead of buttons. They drink a good deal in Lancaster but I refrained. I contented myself with the amber colored wine Mrs. Demuth makes—and secured a bottle of it to fetch home for your entertainment at Labour Day. It's grand, I'll say. [. . .]

1. For Muriel Draper see Biographical Sketches.

Give my love to the family, which I hope is well. Take care of yourself and *cut out worry*. Don't get me a birthday gift. Let me get it in Philadelphia. I'll probably be late getting yours, anyway; so don't shame me into being prompt.

To Malcolm MacAdam
July 8, 1927, Callicaste

Dear Malc:

The visit to Charles Demuth was a success, I think, though I am hardly yet (three days after) recovered from it. We talked an oceanful in spite of the fact, that I thought up excuses occasionally to be alone, and Charley thought up the same for his own preservation. The house is quite delightful. It's in the heart of Lancaster, just a short distance from the station, and seems quite narrow as you go in, due to letting the street front in offices, but opens out in the rear, and above on the second floor is spacious. At the back the gardens are attractive and extensive, for the fence between the house next door (Demuth's uncle) has been knocked down. The garden near the house is mostly paved with brick, with one or two flower beds, like a Spanish patio and serves as an out door sitting room. The house is full of quaint furniture and has, of course, a number of pictures in the modern taste. My bed-room, for instance, had a particularly wild Marin, a Louis Bouché, a Georgia O'Keeffe, and shelves of literature. There was a short story by Ernest Hemingway, that was extra wild. It was called "Up in Michigan," and I can remember every word of it, and will tell it to you sometime, for, of course, it won't go through the mails.[1] There was no servant, but Mrs. Demuth, unlike my unfortunate cousins, is a wonderful housekeeper, and everything shone with a Dutch polish. They make quite a to-do in Lancaster, it seems, over the Fourth of July. People exchange gifts, explode tons of torpedoes in the street, (they nearly killed me) and everybody who is anybody has turtle soup for dinner that day. We had not only turtle soup, but champagne. Turtle soup is good but queer. The Demuths, did I ever tell you? were the original snuff makers and the first tobacconists in America, starting in 1770, and the shop still flourishes next door. It is exceedingly elegant, being more artistic than Dunhill's, or those other smart shops in London. The cousins run it. Charles disdains it, naturally, but his mother took me in when he wasn't looking. Fourth of July night, a friend motored

1. "Up in Michigan" portrayed sexual intercourse so frankly that it was difficult to publish in the United States. It was first published in Paris by Contact Editions (1923) in *Three Stories and Ten Poems*.

us over to see Lititz, to see a strange celebration, which is traditional in that odd village. They have a wonderful spring in the little pleasure park, which flows away through a canal six or eight feet wide. The women of the place make candles all through the year, especially for the Fourth, and they are placed on the intersection of wooden lattice work which is stretched across the canal—thousands and thousands of them. Also, there are some wooden swans, which float along on the current, also bearing lighted candles. There was a fine band from Reading and many spectators. The only thing to mar the festivity, was the constant series of detonations from amateur fireworks. But it seemed like Europe, the whole thing. Lititz is the place, where they speak such funny English. For instance, a girls says to another, "Is your off off?" It means "Has your vacation ended?"

I came away with a Demuth watercolor of flowers, a quart bottle of Mrs. Demuth's wine (to be saved for Labour Day), a jar of apple butter and packages of small cakes. They are very hospitable people.

By the way, when is *your* off off?

To Marianne Moore
December 30, 1927, Coffee House, New York

Dear Miss Moore:

By all means, change "pep" to vim, and replace the last phrase with an extra exclamation point. The last phrase was certainly excessive, and the exclamation says the same thing better. My excuse for "pep" was a certain something in the book that approached vulgarity, but I can't define it. It had the extra cheerfulness of modern trained nurses—the professional urbanity of clergymen—not bad things when the nurses and clergymen have had plenty of experience but rather trying when the nurses and clergymen are young.

In haste, sincerely,

To Muriel Draper
March 10, 1928, The Coffee House

Dear Muriel:

Just a line of thanks and congratulations for the Henry James. . .[1] It's wonderfully James and beautifully you. I don't believe you ever before got

1. McBride is probably referring to an excerpt from Draper's memoir *Music at Midnight,* published in 1929 (New York: Harper and Brothers), which includes a description of Henry James.

so much in print of the thing we all love in you. . . Can't you "meet" some others? It would make a swell book, with the "I meet Henry James" leading off and giving the title.

Yours, more than ever,

P.S. I think I must begin calling you "My dear child" myself—for I recollect being quite grown up when Maizie appeared, and reading her openly and with a man-of-the-world recognition.[2] You, apparently, were clandestine, just as I was clandestine, at an earlier period, with *Oliver Twist*. My parents thought *Oliver Twist* not a proper book for children.

To Georgia O'Keeffe
May 28, 1928, Callicaste, Marshallton, Pennsylvania

To Georgia O'Keeffe:[1]
It's a sample of my last-week-in-New York manners. A lady, right out of the blue, and therefore, indubitably an angel, drops manna to the value of two hundred dollars in my direction—and not a sound is heard, not a word. But the fact is I hesitated a while. I was not sure of the word on the action. It was noble and beautiful of you to do it, my dear O'Keeffe, but I wasn't sure it was noble of me to accept—and I wanted to be noble, too. I could conceive of ways of making your money go farther than that and I know only too many youngsters, who have talent and who need manna. Also, I insist I'm not really hard-up and have about all that is good for me to have. I may have complained about my affairs, but that was rather annoyance at the ingratitude of the *Sun,* than at my situation.

However, it really is your manna and it is for you to distribute, i.e., not I. That was the conclusion I came to finally. At first being in my last week, with a final article, (complicated by museum troubles) to write; packing to attend to and consultations with the *Sun;* I became frankly puzzled and had to put the letter in my desk drawer to await a cooler moment. That didn't come till Saturday. Then I decided, that it was an action typical of your usual beautiful self (but innocent . . . you and Alfred are both a pair of innocents. But of that, more anon) and it was not for me to

2. *What Maisie Knew,* Henry James's (1843–1916) novel of a young girl's loss of innocence in the face of the "modern" marriages and personal relationships that surround her, was first serialized in 1897.

1. O'Keeffe was a close friend of McBride's, leading to the conflict of interest suggested in this letter between McBride as critic and McBride as friend. McBride wrote a positive review of O'Keeffe's show at the Intimate Gallery in the *Sun* on January 14, 1928.

interfere with it. Well I'll try to live up to it, my dear, but you set a high mark.

With love and best wishes for your summer.

PS. I sail reluctantly on the Mauretania June 13.[2] Second Cabin. I'd rather stay home.

To Malcolm MacAdam
July 7, 1928, Hôtel Pérnollet,[1] Belley, France

Well Malc:

[. . .] Belley is very amusing. Absolutely provincial. The diligence at the station was the dusty, funny vehicle, that always used to figure in Guy de Maupassant's stories. The hotel is admirable but not a hint of chi-chi. No terrasse, no bay trees, nothing to indicate it is a hotel. A tiny corridor entrance from the street and a ten by ten sitting room, where I am writing this. But dinner last night was superb. The proprietor himself is the chef and very proud of his art. The dining room is immaculate (everything is) but I caught a glimpse of the kitchen and I saw it was vast, the real centre of Belley.[2] We had a thick, yellow soup with pleasant flavor, I couldn't quite dissect, some fish from a lake near-by, and Gertrude explained, they were a fish that lived sixty feet below the surface of the water. They were marvelously delicate, like the Pompano, that you get in New Orleans. Then a veal chop with string beans and potatoes of distinction. Alice is going to write down for me the receipt for the potatoes, which she has obtained from the chef.[3] Then, an interesting green cheese and some pretty peaches. (Oh, I forgot the salad.)

Gertrude and Alice were out promenading in Gertrude's funny Ford when I arrived, so I sent for hot water and had a refreshing bath and change, before they appeared. After dinner, we sauntered out on the side-

2. By 1928 the grand ocean liner *Mauretania* was twenty years old, having been launched by Britain's Cunard Steam Ship Company two months after her sister vessel, the ill-fated *Lusitania*.

1. The Pérnollet Hôtel in the south of France was a family-owned enterprise extending back five generations. Beginning in the late 1920s Stein and Toklas spent several summers at the hotel, before settling into a house in Bilignin.
2. M. Pérnollet, who cooked while his wife took care of the front of the house, is credited with coining the famous phrase "the lost generation," which Hemingway attributed to Stein. Kellner, *Gertrude Stein Companion*, p. 236.
3. In *The Alice B. Toklas Cookbook,* Toklas describes the food at the hotel as mediocre, and she did not include this recipe.

walk, and Gertrude suddenly said, "Oh, I want to show Henry the view of Mt. Blanc," and I, thinking it was something you got just up at the end of the little park, hopped into Lady Godiva along the side of Gertrude. I had no hat, overcoat nor anything. This is a mountainous region and it was dusk and getting cool. Gertrude, to my amazement, stepped on it and the car sped like mad. We went miles and miles. Lady Godiva, you must understand, is one of these old fashioned Fords, short and high in the air, with no protection from the winds, but to do her justice, she seems sure footed like a goat. We leaped from crag to crag, from mountain top to mountain top. We went 15–20 miles. I had my thoughts, naturally, and you know what they were, but I said nothing. There was no bossing Gertrude anyway. I had to take it. We got back about 9:30. The sequel is, this morning I have a cold and feel seedy. Let this be a lesson to you Malc. In fact, I blame it all on you, for I was modeling my behavior on yours. I was trying to act just as gallantly as you always act. But, henceforth, I'm through with gallantry.

Alice has just passed through the room with an avalanche of talk, the burden of which is I am to be taken somewhere in an hour. On Monday, there is to be a luncheon at some remarkable place and an English princess (that is, she is not exactly a princess, but she's something) and a consumptive English poet, who lives on one of the nearby mountain peaks, are asked to meet me.

Belley is amusing, I haven't seen it yet, but I've heard it. If anybody says anything it reverberates all over the place and the town began talking about six. But I had gone to bed at ten, so I had had enough sleep I guess. I rang for breakfast at 7:30. It proved to be cute. Very good chocolate bread and butter and some captivating plum jam. There is a rooster crowing in our backyard. There are two water closets on this floor, with enormous letters "W.C.→" painted on the corridor to guide the tourists. But perhaps I have told you enough for the present: I got the germs for this cold from Ivy Troutman. She had a cold and kissed me twice, French fashion. She is well named all right—Poison Ivy. But it required the exposure on the mountain tops to give the germs their chance.

July 10, 1928. . . The empress wasn't so much after all. Of all the queens I have met, I still prefer Queen Mary of England. This lady was the Princess of Sarawak.[4] Her exact title is the ex-Rance of Sarawak, but as she is the mother of the heir-apparent, it corresponds to dowager queen. I thought

4. Wife of Sir Charles Vyner (1872–1915), third rajah of Sarawak, and part of the British family that governed on the Malay archipelago.

she was going to be uppish at first during lunch, but it was partly her hat, which came down like a drop curtain on the side nearest me and prevented me from hearing what she said, unless she turned her back on all the others. But she livened up after a while and seemed to know as much gossip of the Latin quarter as the rest of us. She really has no "side" at all, although it is true, she objects to sulphur matches. I have some sulphur matches, which I get here in the village and when I held out one to her cigarette, she rejected it with horror and fumbled for some wax tapers of her own in her bag. She has written her memoirs, which are to appear in the fall and she wants me to review them. . . Remind me to tell you her story when I get home. It is rather odd. I happened to read of it when I came across a history of Borneo last winter.

On Saturday my letter was interrupted by the trip (via Lady Godiva) to Artamarie, thirty-five kilometers away, to a luncheon prepared by the second best chef in France. I was not sure I was up to the expedition, as I certainly had a cold and was all in from the night before. But on we sped like the wind. We had a puncture and I walked slowly along, while Gertrude re-tired Lady Godiva. So it was 1:30 before we got there and we were all so tired we were cross. But the food was really marvelous and we immediately grew good-humored. We began with écrevisses and then had a great plat, chicken and mushrooms swimming in the most perfect sauce I have ever known. Simply grand. White wine, fraises de bois, creme fraîche, and a lovely cake, the chef had baked, as an extra surprise. Then naturellement, coffee. We lunched on an outside terrasse under trees. The hotel was not chic, only the food. We afterward complimented the chef, who is an extremely sensitive person and a real artist. I drank more wine than usual and perhaps it was that, or perhaps the eucalyptus oil on my hanky, but by the time I got home my cold had vanished. As three can't squeeze into Lady Godiva, Gertrude made two trips each way, going back each time for Alice. Wasn't that heroic? You can compute for yourself four times thirty five kilometers! Would you have done as much?

Saturday we went equally far to Tenne on the Rhone, where Gertrude bought an immense sponge cake for me. Alice gave me a swell basket to tote my acquisitions in. She also gave me two cute little glass-ash-receivers and Gertrude gave me a darling group of statuary, a fisherman and wife in a little boat on a stormy sea. You won't like it perhaps.

Yesterday Gertrude motored me to Aix-les-Bains, just as soon as we got rid of the empress. It was a grand trip, too. They are here, Gertrude and Alice and I must cease. I leave this afternoon for Bourg.

To Malcolm MacAdam
July 12, 1928, Dijon

Cher Malc:

Gertrude is thorough. You must admit that. She was determined I should see everything within 50 kilometers de Belley. You remember that first night, when she took me out on the hill tops to see the view of Mt. Blanc? We didn't see it. It was too misty. Well, after three days of much autoing I thought, Tuesday morning, as my train left just after lunch, I had seen the last of Lady Godiva. But not at all. I didn't appear until eleven a-m., but I found Gertrude waiting and she said it was so clear and she couldn't have me leave without seeing Mt. Blanc and so, in we got and away we sped. Again the horizons were hazy, but Gertrude insisted that something that looked like a cloud was really Mt. Blanc and so we returned triumphantly to Alice.

However, I did enjoy the life of Belley and the being one of a family party. Those will probably be the only four days of my trip, that I shall care to remember. I spent a day at Bourg on the way to Dijon and I don't know, whether Bourg or Dijon or Paris are the most tiresome. After all, I sigh for Paris. Paris is more bearable than Dijon. Nothing to do, but sit in a cafe listening to a stupid small orchestra and smoke cigarettes till early bedtime. Last night I felt exactly the way you used to feel in Bethlehem. I had hoped to be out of Paris over the fourteenth, but I'm sure going to leave Dijon for somewhere tomorrow and it may be Paris. It is suffocatingly hot. I can't walk the street—hence letters.

To Malcolm MacAdam
July 17, 1928, Paris

c.a.:

[. . .] By the bye, please send *The Story of Ivy,* to Gertrude Stein, Hôtel Pérnollet, Belley, (Ain) France.[1] She says she adores trash and wants to know Ivy. . . Gertrude's brother Michael is to meet me at 3 p.m. at the Porte Dauphine and take me in his new house in the suburbs.[2] It is a house in the new manner. [. . .]

1. *The Story of Ivy* by Marie Adelarde Belloc Lowndes (1868–1947) was published in London by W. Heinemann, 1927; and in New York by Doubleday, 1928.
2. For Michael Stein see Biographical Sketches.

To Georgia O'Keeffe
July 19, 1927 [1928], Paris, France

To Georgia O'Keeffe:

I had one of the happiest winters of recent years, but I have paid for it with one of the unhappiest months of my life. I find I simply can't stand Paris, I hated it two years ago and when I decided I ought to come over, I fixed upon two weeks in Paris, as being enough to enable me to bluff the public with "Paris stuff," when necessary, and meant to pass the other two weeks in the country. I did go down to Belley for four delightful days with Gertrude Stein, but on my way back, touring, it became so tropical, I couldn't stand it and hastily cut the tour short and came back to Paris, which tiresome as it is, is nevertheless not quite so stupefying as towns like Dijon and Bourg. So in spite of myself, I have had a month, that seemed longer to me, I'm sure, than the unfortunate Nobile's month at the pole seemed to him.[1]

There is just nothing in Paris, that I can't get as readily at home—and the inescapable noise of the taxis, is something that puts the finishing touch to nerves already strained. Paris is still beautiful, but it is a far off beauty of another period, that has little to do with this one. Practically it is a dream background and the people, who actually strive here, have to exist without a background at all. In that, we are ever so much better off.

Gertrude wanted me to see her brother Michael's new house by Le Corbusier, and arranged for him to take me out.[2] It is out in the suburbs, beyond St. Cloud and is certainly interesting. It looks like a factory at first glance, with windows that go clear across like this . . .[3] and a facade that hides the sense of structure. The facade in fact is like a thin curtain, that is let down, for the real supports of the roof are concrete pillars, that are well inside the house. There are queer things on the roof, which I find I forget

1. Umberto Nobile (1885–1978), Italian soldier, nautical engineer, and arctic explorer. Nobile's plane crashed on an Arctic ice floe in June 1928. The Norwegian explorer Roald Amundsen, who in 1911 had discovered the South Pole, died trying to save his colleague.
2. Charles Edouard Jeanneret (1887–1965), a French architect and artist of Swiss heritage, adopted the pseudonym Le Corbusier, meaning crow, in 1920. Early in his career he was a painter who, with Amedée Ozenfant (1886–1966) was the founder of Purism. Working in the International Style, in the 1920s Le Corbusier built private homes which he called *machines à habiter,* machines to be lived in. The term is meant to imply functionalism and an admiration for the shapes and utility of machines.
3. McBride includes a drawing in the letter.

and can't draw. The interior has many pleasing, novel, clean, hygienic hospitalic effects, but they are ruined, to my mind, because the Michael Steins wouldn't part with their Louise Quinze furniture and it looks shabby and wrong. They have a lot of grand Matisses, however, which look right.[4] It is a house for America, of course, as one such bit of modernity cannot do much for Paris.

Of the new artists, I have seen three things by Miró, that I thought great.[5] He must be a half-mad person, but that is no great fault, of course, in an artist. The three pictures I thought great are not for sale. That is the latest trick in Paris. Anything with a suspicion of merit, is not for sale. It is held for the ultimate rise.

I wasn't too much alarmed by your tale of Alfred's illness and the disorders of the ménage, for I concluded long ago, that both of you depend physically upon the other and that such an arrangement is the real secret of longevity.[6] You will have scares, but they will only be scares. You will be long in hand, both.[7] [. . .]

To Gertrude Stein
May 10, 1929, Coffee House Club, New York

Dearest Gertrude:
I look with horror on the calendar. It jumps with months instead of days I do believe. Already Albert Eugene Gallatin has been in Paris two speedy

4. The Steins continued to be major supporters of Matisse, even after Leo and Gertrude Stein stopped collecting his work around 1910. Matisse believed that Sarah Stein was the most intelligent member of the family, remarking that "she knows more about my paintings than I do." *Four Americans in Paris*, p. 35.
5. By 1928 Joan Miró (1893–1983) had been painting linear forms on colorful backgrounds, the style with which he is most associated, for two years. In the first half of 1928, Miró was included in two Surrealist exhibitions in Paris. He had a one-man exhibition at the Galeries Georges Bernheim & Cie, May 1–15, 1928. McBride eventually acquired several works by Miró, and his enthusiasm for him continued for the rest of his life.
6. Stieglitz and O'Keeffe began living together in 1918, and they were married in 1929. The spring and summer of 1928 was a difficult period for the relationship. In addition to experiencing the terrifying onset of a heart condition, Stieglitz was preoccupied with Dorothy Norman, a married woman forty years his junior, with whom he had begun an affair the previous May. Beginning in 1929 O'Keeffe spent half of each year in New Mexico.
7. McBride proved to be correct; Stieglitz lived to be eighty-two and O'Keeffe ninety-nine.

months and I meant at once on his departure to beg you to send a little note to him (Morgan, Harges et Cie) permitting him to come see your pictures and yourself on some suitable late afternoon. You remember what I told you of him? He is unusually shy and stiff and has few friends but circumstances brought us together and now I really like him. He writes me he has bought Miró's *Dog Barking at the Moon* and several other pictures.[1]

The season of work is about over and in a fortnight I shall go down to the country. It is high time for I am all in and it seems to me I must lie fallow for a month or two before I even pretend to be intelligent again. We've had lots of fun and one of the pleasantest things was the hearing of your poems to the music of Virgil Thomson.[2] We roared with enjoyment but Carl Van Vechten, who sat opposite me, pulled a serious face and shook it at me reprovingly as though to say we were not taking it the right way.[3] But young Virgil Thomson really is a wonder. I never saw such self-possession in an American before. He is absolutely undefeatable by circumstances. When singing some of the opera to me he was constantly interrupted but never to his dis-ease; he would stop, shout some direction to the servant, and then resume absolutely on pitch and in time. We all pray that the opera will be given, but of course what I said in the *Dial* about your coming here was a joke.[4] Probably it wouldn't do. Our reporters would simply kill you.

1. Miró had his first American exhibition at the Museum of Living Art. In a letter dated March 22, 1929, Gallatin wrote to McBride, "The day after I arrived [March 10], I found three paintings *chez* Pierre which I at once bought [including] one of Miró's best things: *Dog Barking at the Moon*." The painting, which Miró worked on from mid-August until December 1926, is now part of the A. E. Gallatin Collection of the Philadelphia Museum of Art.
2. In February 1929 at the Stettheimer sisters' apartment at Alwyn Court, Virgil Thomson (see Biographical Sketches) sang the Stein-Thomson opera *Four Saints in Three Acts*, accompanying himself on the piano. As an encore, he sang "Le Berceau de Gertrude Stein ou Le Mystère de la rue de Fleurus" (The cradle of Gertrude Stein or mysteries in the rue de Fleurus), with words by Georges Hugnet. McBride looked back on this as one of the finest of the Stettheimer evenings. Around this time, Thomson invited Florine Stettheimer to design the costumes and sets for the production.
3. Beginning in 1913, Van Vechten and McBride were the two key American promoters of Stein's writings. Because Stein jokes abounded, Van Vechten's expression probably reflected his fear that Stein was being laughed at rather than laughed with.
4. In his April 1929 "Modern Art" column McBride wrote that American artists lived too long abroad and specifically advocated Stein's return to the United States: "If Miss Stein once gets here, believe me, she'll stay. She is too great an artist to be able to resist us." *The Flow of Art,* p. 257.

I have to write a little book about Matisse this summer, three or four thousand words—and I am embarrassed—I know so little about Matisse.[5] It would be easier to do Pablo. If you know any book about Matisse I should know, please advise me, as I shan't have to begin my essay until July. Carl tells me you actually have the house at Belley and that he thinks he is to be asked to come see you there. Both événements naturally strike me with envy. I told him that if he got the chance to lunch at Artamarre not to refuse it; but I am also resolving not to tell any more people about Belley and Artamarre for of course you don't want to be over run. (I always suspect it was the crush of visitors on the rue de Fleurus that compelled you to go south so early.)

I suppose you heard of Leo's lectures.[6] He had his difficulties, they tell me, and in one of them broke down completely. Mabel Dodge felt guiltily that she might have been to blame, for she whispered to her neighbour, just before the debacle, "Why this is all Jung," but she insisted that she only whispered it. Mabel's winter in New York had little of the former éclat. No one talked of it and nothing particularly happened in her salon. In the end she sent for "Tony" to dissipate her ennuis.

My very best love to you and Alice. (I decided it would be more legal not to type that!)

June 18, 1929, Atlantic City, New Jersey

Dearest Malc:

I begin to feel as though I, too, were deriving an easy income from the Standard Oil. Me voici installé dans une superbe chambre deluxe à double lits avec bain, electricité et toutes sortes de choses dont j'ignore employer. Aussi une fenêtre (oriel) que donne sur la plage. Aussi je ne paye rien. Je suis invité par Atlantic City pour voir l'exposition d'art. Mon tableau de Marin est dans l'exposition. Vous pouvez le voir dans le catalogue "emprunté de M. Henry McBride" et Atlantic City est très reconnaissante de M. McBride, Mr. Frank Crowninshield, Mrs. John D. Rockefeller et tous les autres qui ont aidé dans cette excellente entreprise. Je suis arrivé hier soir et un Monsieur Stern (President de quelque chose) me donnait un acceuil extraordinaire with private Scotch et ginger ale et toute de suite après un cock-tail très fort, et toute de suite après ça, un diner de vrai luxe, (consommé clair,

5. McBride's book *Matisse* was published by Knopf as part of their Modern Art series in 1930. It included a brief essay by McBride and two excerpts from earlier reviews.
6. Leo Stein; see Biographical Sketches.

lobster Paul, etc. par le meilleur chef en Amerique, M. Stern dit). En consequence de lobster Paul, ou peut lire [sic] les consummations J'ai pas
dormi très bien. Je suis résolu, maintenant de me mettre sérieusement sur
le wagon-à-l'eau.[1]

All the artists are coming down today and little Max Weber, for the first
time in his life, is going to bathe in the ocean surf and we are all going on
the sands at eleven, to see what we can see. The art reception occurs at
three and I think I will then beat it home, not staying for the dinner, that is
being given for the artists by somebody. La chaleur est épouvantable.[2] I
promenaded on the board walk last night without an overcoat. You can
figure it out from that.

Je trouve Atlantic City très chic et très Americaine, J'adore les illuminations. Il faut les voir.[3]

September 27, 1929, Callicaste, Marshallton, Pennsylvania

My Dear Georgia O'Keeffe:

Are you still down there, leaping from cliff to cliff, from mountain-top
to mountain-top?[1] It is hardly likely, but I've had no official news to the
contrary. Things have come to such a pass that the movements of Georgia
O'Keeffe are generally known, like those of Col. Lindbergh and young John
Coolidge.

I went up to Charles Demuth's on the Fourth of July (the patriotic note
is due to the Demuths—they are great on the Fourth of July for some

1. "Here I am installed in a superb deluxe room with a double bed, bath, electricity,
and all kinds of other things I don't know how to use. Also a window which gives a
view of the beach. Also I pay nothing. I am invited to Atlantic City to see the art exhibition. My painting by Marin is in the show. You can see it in the catalogue, "borrowed from Mr. Henry McBride" and Atlantic City is very thankful to Mr. McBride,
Mr. Frank Crowninshield, Mrs. John D. Rockefeller and everyone else who helped
in this excellent enterprise. I arrived last night and a certain Mr. Stern (President of
something) gave me an excellent reception with private Scotch and ginger ale, followed immediately by a very strong cocktail, and immediately after that a sumptuous dinner (clear soup, lobster Paul, etc., by the best chef in America, according to
Mr. Stern). Due to the lobster Paul, and the long list of drinks I didn't sleep very
well. I have resolved seriously to go on the water wagon."
2. "The heat is dreadful."
3. "I find Atlantic City very stylish and very American, I love the lights. You must
see them."

1. O'Keeffe had returned from her first trip to New Mexico, where she had spent
four months, in late August, heading straight for Lake George to meet Stieglitz.

reason) and as I took the train home Charles slipped the latest *New Yorker* into my hand to beguile the journey—and it did. Such things as there were about Georgia O'Keeffe in it! All of it a revelation to me! I got the idea she was a hard, managing type of female, the kind that stops at nothing, the kind that burns up her children in the kitchen stove for the sake of insurance. I got quite alarmed for Alfred. And then almost immediately there came that news that Alfred had taken to flying—had made several trips through the air to New York and back—and I had the guilty suspicion that I knew how it had all come about.[2] Alfred, I could see, had been receiving some of those inflammatory letters, and felt that he had to do something. That is why I buried my head in the sands and refused to hear any more evidence pro and con—I did not wish to be mixed up in the impending calamity.

But, really Georgia O'Keeffe, the most terrible thing you said about Taos was that down there even those who merely sat in the sun did it with energy.[3] Of course, I shouldn't blame Mabel for that, though it is true there is a mischievous streak in her, and she would not be much above poking up the fires under the niches where the lost souls perched energetically in the sunlight of Taos.

But I do sincerely hope you and John Marin are going to cool down a bit before you return to New York for the winter.[4] Otherwise its going to be damned hard on us critics.

With this provisional love to you both.

2. As noted in the September 14, 1929, issue of the *New Yorker,* Stieglitz learned to fly that summer, and O'Keeffe learned to drive.
3. McBride wrote a review in the *Sun,* "O'Keeffe in Taos" (January 8, 1930), in which he noted, "Georgia O'Keeffe went to Taos, New Mexico, to visit Mabel Dodge and spent the summer down there. Naturally something would come from such a contact as that. But not what you would think. Religion came of it. Georgia O'Keeffe got religion. What Mabel Dodge got I have not yet heard. But Georgia O'Keeffe painted a series of canvases with enormous crosses booming across ascetic landscapes" (reprinted in *Flow of Art,* p. 260.)
4. In April 1929 Marin had his first museum exhibition—at the Phillips Collection. That October he had his second solo show at the Phillips. In May 1928 Stieglitz had sold six calla lily paintings by O'Keeffe from her solo show for a record price of $25,000, generating a huge round of publicity. All O'Keeffe's travels to New York after her summer in Taos were only visits. She relocated to the Southwest, feeling that she had "used up" the subject matter that had captured her attention on the East Coast.

MCBRIDE'S YEARS AT *CREATIVE ART*

Creative Art magazine was first published in the United States in 1893 as " 'A Magazine of Fine and Applied Art' incorporating *The Studio of London*." For many years *Creative Art* was simply an American reprint of *The Studio of London*, which was problematic. Articles appeared in the United States months after their publication in Europe, and the magazine did not reflect the rapid changes of the twentieth century in the arts on the west side of the Atlantic. In its first few decades, the magazine showed a strong bias toward London and the Arts and Crafts Movement.

The brothers Albert and Charles Boni, who owned and published *Creative Art* during McBride's tenure with the magazine, were major figures in the artistic and literary life of New York City in the early twentieth century (see Biographical Sketches). In 1917 the Bonis, along with Horace Liverwright, started the highly successful Modern Library. At one point their list of publications included five Nobel Prize winners, including Faulkner, Hemingway, and T. S. Eliot. In the post–World War I period, other writers they championed included Thornton Wilder, Ford Madox Ford, Theodore Dreiser, and Leon Trotsky. In the early 1920s the partners decided to part ways, and with the toss of a coin, the Boni brothers lost their publishing house to Liverwright.

From 1923 to 1928 Boni and Boni Publishers became their imprimatur. Their Little Leather Library sold more than a million copies at Woolworth's, and the Boni name became synonymous with popularizing literature and making it accessible to a general readership. In this sense, the Boni brothers shared McBride's desire to introduce and educate the public to the virtues of the modern creative movements.

Albert took the more active role in the daily affairs of *Creative Art*. McBride characterized the elder Boni as very un-ownerlike in his kindness and courtesy. In a letter to Malcolm MacAdam (September 1, 1932, unpublished) McBride wrote, "That is why I admire Mr. Boni. He has the faculty of turning business into something human."

Under the direction of the Boni brothers, and in the years before McBride's term as editor, the scope of the magazine changed. Some idea of the intended range of the publication can be found in a sample issue of October 1927, which included articles on ship decoration, bookbinding, garden design, the modern movement in Mexico, commercial art, and such articles on artists as "Maurice Denis as a Decorative Artist." Studies of specific veins of the decorative arts often appeared, such as Japanese tobacco boxes, modern tendencies at the Staffordshire potteries, airplane design, and modern electric light fittings. The magazine also listed goings on in the major European cities; after 1929, sections on Philadelphia and New York were added.

In the late 1920s the stage designer Lee Simonson was the editor, and people who wrote for the magazine included Duncan Phillips, Walter Pach, Bernice Abbott, Osbert Sitwell, Lewis Mumford, Mabel Dodge Luhan, Holger Cahill, Fiske Kimball, Rockwell Kent, and Leo Stein.

McBride's first contribution was an essay on "Watercolours by Charles Demuth" in September 1929. Two months later McBride was listed as editor of the magazine for the first time. In his first monthly "Palette Knife" column, the new editor assured readers,

> I can safely promise an occasional outbreak though my outbreaks are far from being Simonsonian, Mr. Simonson being at heart a reformer and I not at all. I like the world far too well to wish it changed in any of its essentials. But if I work on one principle more distinctly than another it is in aiming for frankness rather than infallibility. "Being right" is lovely but it is not a condition that even a critic arrives at unaided. His chief business when confronted by a new problem is to think it out as best he may and then entrust it fearlessly to the public that in the end is the true arbiter of values. . . . When Dr. Bode got into difficulties over his attribution of a certain wax bust to Leonardo, a clever Englishman remarked warningly that "Every critic has his wax bust waiting just around the corner." That remark is as true as it is witty but after all it is nothing to stay a real critic's hand. His task is to make the public think—not to guide it in making "safe" purchases. It has been the tragedy of the art situation heretofore in America that a busy public immersed in other affairs has preferred to trust experts rather than itself.

By the January 1930 issue McBride and Albert Boni had already made changes to the magazine. An addition to the masthead was an advisory committee of fourteen that included several of McBride's friends: Bryson Burroughs, Elizabeth Luther Cary, Maud Dale, Katherine Dreier, A. E. Gallatin, Ferdinand Howald, Frank Jewett Mather, Duncan Phillips, and

15 *Portrait of Henry McBride,* 1929. Robert Chanler, oil on canvas.

Alfred Stieglitz. McBride explained the intention of the advisory committee in a note to Duncan Phillips: "I contemplate no special changes in the
magazine but hope to induce some good writers to aid us."[1]

In May 1931 McBride announced that *Creative Art* had become "an
international art magazine edited and published entirely in America. . . .
Suddenly 'everybody' seems to be willing to come in with us, and desirable

1. Unpublished letter to Duncan Phillips, November 19, 1929 (Phillips Collection,
Washington, D.C.).

writers who had been coy are now entirely amiable. . . . America is such a dominant force in the present period of the world's history that there is no occasion whatever for minimizing her efforts towards expressing herself in art and indeed it is scarcely fair, even to our European readers, to hide our light under a bushel."

During his three years at *Creative Art,* McBride brought a wide range of writers to the magazine, including many friends, from Gertrude Stein to Dudley Carpenter. In McBride's three-year tenure, Muriel Draper wrote on Mark Tobey and Robert Locher; Maud Dale wrote on Renoir; Roger Fry wrote on Matisse; and Frank Lloyd Wright wrote on "The Tyranny of the Skyscraper"; Aldous Huxley wrote some notes on decoration; Marsden Hartley wrote on the paintings of Florine Stettheimer; and a young Arshile Gorky wrote on Stuart Davis.

McBride acted as editor of the magazine until December 1932. McBride's feelings about *Creative Art* were more qualified than his respect for *The Dial,* perhaps because as editor his responsibilities and accountability were greater. McBride states his concerns in a letter of May 10, 1931: "It's not my sort of stuff, and I see I shall lose my reputation as a critic, if I don't watch out."

In addition to his fears about the rigor of the magazine, McBride also had health concerns, financial worries, and other writing obligations. As he wrote upon learning the associate editor of the magazine had quit, "There's bound to be more trouble and worry for me—and more work, which is the same thing. . . . I was on the point of walking out myself, when I received a sweet note from the *Sun* saying my salary there had been cut 10%. Although *Creative Art* is practically hell for me, I decided to try to worry along, at least the rest of the spring, just for the sake of the measly stipend."

In December 1932 Frederick Blossom, previously managing editor, became editor. In February 1933, McBride recounted to MacAdam, "Albert Boni telephoned suggesting lunch with him. Albert frankly said the idea was to try to persuade me to do some things for Creative Art, my leaving the magazine had been the greatest loss they had ever experienced."

To Gertrude Stein
November 4, 1929, *Creative Art,* New York

My Dearest, Dearest Gertrude:
You will immediately become suspicious of the double "dearests." You will say, "He wants something." But how unfair since I have no other

Gertrude whatever and certainly no other dearest Gertrude. . . It is true, I do want something—but that's a mere coincidence. I have become an editor—of a sort. I'm the present editor of the American end of *Creative Art*, the bulk of which review is put together in England and I think it would be swell (and would justify me in my new position—I'll employ pathos, tears, anything to gain my ends) if you would write me something.[1] It could be about your collection, about the beginning of it, about your "darlings" (as you used to call your artists), or about anything that we can pretend is connected with art. We pay a little; about, I believe, as the *Dial* used to pay.[2] You heard of course that the unfortunate *Dial* blew up last summer? Now I know your first impulse will be to say No—but don't say No. Don't you think it would be nice to see your name once more in an avowed art review—since you really are a maker of art history?

Personally I'm a little astonished to see my own name in another review, since the one vow I made last spring when I went home a wreck, as usual, was—that *this* winter I would simplify my life. Instead and simply because Mr. Boni, who owns this review seems to be a charming person and apparently not at all bad to work with—I agreed to double my tasks. I'm not at all sure I'll survive the attempt, but I'd think it worth the agony of the experience if I could look back, after it is all over, and say, "Well, I got Gertrude into that magazine anyway—*that* was something."

I enclose a jibe at Cocteau. It got a little mangled in the newspaper, but if you think it would amuse him, send it on. By the bye could *he* be induced to write, do you think? Are there any others that would add réclame, that you know of?

I saw the Bobby Lochers last summer down at Charles Demuth's and

1. Stein's "Genuine Creative Ability" appeared in the February 1930 issue of *Creative Art*. It begins as in reply to McBride's letter, "Could I say no to you never. *Creative Art* reminds me that the Guggenheim prize is always to be given for genuine creative ability and the scheme of study is always sent along confidentially." The article, in the form of a letter ends, "Paragraphs. How to write. Paragraphs are natural and sentences are not and if I must forget the reason why. Thanks very much I am always grateful. Gertrude Stein. Postscript. I am very busy finding out what people mean by what they say. I used to be interested in what they were. I am now interested in what they say. G.S."
2. Stein received two checks for her efforts. On January 29, 1930, McBride wrote Stein, "I wasn't quite sure what you could do in Paris with $15 . . . but Mr. Boni gave me this cheque also—for royalties—and so I am emboldened to send them both on—I think the one for royalties ought to be news for the newspapers! Gertrude Stein getting royalties. . . . But the size of the cheque needn't be mentioned" (YCAL, McBride).

they enjoyed seeing you very much. We went into it at such great length that I almost felt I had had a visit myself.

Give me love to Alice in about 50–50 proportions with yourself.

PS. I finished my Matisse essay in the greatest state of rebellion—for I am an impressionist and I had no new experience to write from. I can't sit at a desk and churn myself into a state of excitement. But it will be well illustrated. I'll send it to you.

To Malcolm MacAdam
February 8, 1930, New York, New York

Dearest Malc:

[. . .] I *did* tell about luncheon with Mrs. Pat Campbell. . .[1] Well, Mrs. Pat gave a lecture on "Beautiful Speech" and Beatrice took Basil Sidney and Mary Ellis and me.[2] Mrs. Pat looked a sight, she has such bulgy cheeks and such frowsy tresses, but she got us just the same. Basil said she performed magic. Anyway we all crowded into the dressing room afterward, to tell her, how wonderful she was. The Lytellton woman was there, too. It seems she's Mrs. Pat's pal. [. . .]

I missed seeing Carnera do his first knock-out—and now there is such a fuss over him, that the prices will go up and I suppose I won't see him at all.[3] Of course Count Vallambrosa saw him. He told us all about it at Alfred's luncheon for the Count de Prorok, the Sahara explorer (there's a traveler for you). Anna Duncan was there, too. Also Mrs. Swope and of course, Ruth. Anna Duncan wears a metal band on her teeth. She is having her mouth prepared for the movies. I like Prorok very much. He gave me a hearty invitation to visit him at this camp in mid-Sahara.

My Matisse book is out and it is terrible. I haven't had the courage to glance at it and it's been in the house four days. It's sure to be panned heavily. I don't see how I could have written so stupidly. However, it was August, when I did it, and I didn't want to write—and writing is one thing you can't do unless your heart is in it.

Last night I got a great box of oranges, apples and Maan candy from the

1. See Biographical Sketches.
2. In 1917 Campbell returned to the United States for the first time since her son's death during World War I. During that trip and several subsequent visits, she toured giving lectures on elocution and diction.
3. Primo Carnera (1906–67), an Italian-born boxer who later held the heavyweight title for a year.

Ritz Fruitier sur la part de Georgia O'Keeffe. The card said it was the only day of the year in which she could do such a thing, as my article on her show was already written (Friday) and since it hadn't appeared, the gift couldn't be called either graft or gratitude. In any case, it wouldn't be called gratitude—for I don't think Georgia will like my review.[4] I'll try and send you a copy, to see "what you think," as Ethelwynn used to say. Of course I can't eat all those oranges and as they won't keep, I gave some to Grant and to that pest of a femme-de-chambre. Have you read Lady Murasaki yet?[5]

To Malcolm MacAdam
March 7, 1930, New York

Dear Malc:

I don't seem to have much confidence in that No. 8 Bund address. At least I have not heard that you have received any letters sent there.

This is Friday—the day after Thursday—and you know what Thursdays are in my life.

Tonight I dine with Henri Matisse. He's here. Arrived unexpectedly on the Île de France, meaning to travel incognito, but was discovered by the reporters quand même.[1] The Val Dudensings are managing him and being young things are quite upset by the responsibility.[2] I've had one little chat

4. In part, McBride wrote in his review, "O'Keeffe in Taos" (New York *Sun,* January 8, 1930), "The piercingly white walls of the new rooms [Stieglitz's new gallery, An American Place, had opened December 15, 1929, with an exhibition of new work by John Marin], which so became the Marins, are not so fortunate for the O'Keeffes." McBride closed his review with the rather awkward, and not laudatory thought, "But one yearns instinctively to see this picture do its work, just as one turns occasionally at the opera to see the thought of the proffered forgiveness for too much knowledge stealing over the wrought-up Wagnerians" (reprinted in *Flow of Art,* pp. 261–62).
5. Baroness Murasaki Shikibu, an eleventh-century Japanese poet who wrote *The Tale of Genji,* translated by Arthur Waley.

1. McBride had just finished his article "Matisse in New York" for the March 8, 1930, edition of the *New York Sun,* reprinted in *Flow of Art,* pp. 266–68. This was Matisse's first visit to the United States. He arrived in New York on March 4 and found much of the city "incredible" and was particularly taken with the sky-scrapers. After seeing all the usual tourist sites (the Metropolitan, Wall Street, Harlem, and the Brooklyn Bridge), Matisse traveled by train to Chicago, then on to Los Angeles and San Francisco before departing for Tahiti.
2. Valentine Dudensing owned several galleries of modern art. In the 1930s he was one of a rare breed of dealers exhibiting modernism. Dudensing and his wife, Bibi, were close friends of McBride's.

16 Henry McBride and Henri Matisse in New York, c. 1930–33. Pierre Matisse.

with Matisse already. He's extremely simple and sans façons—a genuine, home-loving bourgeois—without any frills. He's crazy about New York—as indeed, why should he not be? They've lodged him on the thirty first floor of the Ritz Tower and he's enchanted with the view. He's going to the South Seas, and possibly around the world. If he goes to Japan, I'll give him a letter to you and you'll have to show him those geisha girls you rave so over.

On Tuesday I had luncheon with another celebrity, Thornton Wilder, author of the *Bridge of San Luis Rey.*[3] Mr. Boni is his publisher, and on Tuesday we three lunched in the public room at the Brevoort, without being noticed by anybody. He's a rather nice young man, excessively nervous, but not spoiled as yet. Mr. Boni gave him about half a bushel of press notices to look at, before he left to lecture in Chicago. I haven't read one of his three novels, and naturally during luncheon, I had to do some side stepping occasionally. The new book, *The Women of Andros*, is one of the best sellers of the day.[4] Wilder is a friend intime of Gene Tunney, and traveled through Europe with him.[5] I didn't know that till afterward—but perhaps we can have Gene for one your Tuesday luncheons some day. You'd better come home and get in on this game.

I discovered that Carl Van Vechten has one of your traits—he stands in awe of salesmen and saleswomen. It may endear him to you. You know, he doesn't come across with the promised article about Florine Stettheimer, and I met him coming out of the nut store at 57th Street and Sixth Avenue, and backed him into the shop again, in order to demand the said article.[6] I had Thornton Wilder to talk about and he had had a funny luncheon too, so we chinned for a quarter of an hour possibly. Anyway, when we finished talking and started to depart, Carl said, "Why, do you mean to say, you're not going to buy any nuts? Did you come in here to talk to me?" and he blushed fiery red for shame. I roared with laughter and said loud enough for the man to hear; "Perhaps I'll buy some nuts tomorrow." To do the man justice, he seemed perfectly indifferent as to whether I bought nuts or not.

3. The American novelist and playwright Thornton Wilder (1897–1975) later became a close friend of Gertrude Stein's after they met during her American lecture tour in 1935.
4. *The Woman of Andros* (1930) was Wilder's interpretation of Terence's *Andria*.
5. The boxer Gene Tunney (1897–1978) had retired as heavyweight champion in 1928.
6. No piece on Florine Stettheimer by Van Vechten ever appeared in *Creative Art*, though Marsden Hartley did write on her paintings in the July 1931 issue. Van Vechten's notes for the article are at the Beinecke Library.

An old friend of mine, Dudley Carpenter[7] of California, has been here, and I had strange feelings in seeing him again, for he seemed so old and changed—not changed altogether, but completely out of touch with all the things, that make up my life. I had him to lunch at the Coffee House, but we could not talk privately, and then I had him for the dress rehearsal of Sadko at the Opera, and again, we couldn't talk. I sent him a book review for *Creative Art*, which he did nicely, but then he was suddenly called back to California (going by air—at his age) and I don't suppose I shall ever see him again. Such things make you feel queer, I wonder if you and I will meet as strangers in the year 1933, if we both survive till then? I hope at any rate, that you don't develop those horizontal wrinkles on the neck. You have a morbid enthusiasm for wrinkles, but don't let it carry you too far. I don't think horizontal wrinkles at the back of the neck are distingué. [. . .]

To Malcolm MacAdam
March 21, 1930, Herald Square Hotel

Dearest Malc:

At last I've lunched with Mei Lang Fang.[1] It was Mrs. Pat, who threw the luncheon, but from some vague remarks of Beatrice Chanler, I gathered, it was Bridget Guinness, who put up the dough.[2] She could well afford to. Mrs. Pat, who sat next to me, told me that Bengie had made a million lately. I said, "You mean during these last few weeks?" and she said, "Yes" and added, "that you can always tell when Bengie's doing wonderfully in Wall Street, for then he goes about with such a shabby, demure air and

7. This is the last mention of Carpenter, who was the recipient of many of the earliest letters McBride sent from Europe.

1. In January 1931 McBride devoted a lavish photographic essay to Mei Lang-Fang, whom he described as "the Chinese actor who recently took the theatrical public of New York by Storm. . . . In China, as was the case in pre-Restoration England, women's parts are invariably played by men. Mei Lang-Fang, a leading Chinese actor in these roles, was imported to New York under arrangements aimed at the propagation of Sino-American trade-cultural relations. A number of Chinese classics were staged, and their entire freshness to the occidental mind, combined with the brilliant and almost fabulously costly dressing and Mei Lang-Fang's attractive personality and superb acting, combined to make the series a theatrical high-water mark in New York." A caption beneath a photograph of the actor dressed as a princess reads, "An amazingly beautiful figure, and though stylized to the point of fragility, the impersonation nevertheless easily takes rank among the great achievements of the theatre." *Creative Art,* January 1931, pp. 31–37.

2. Bridget and Benjamin Guinness, like Beatrice Chanler, were wealthy socialites.

during the past week he's been mousy in the extreme." Bengie didn't show up for the lunch, and I heard Bridget remark languidly that "Probably Bengie has decided to make another million."

The next day I read in the paper, that my bank, the Equitable, the Chase and a lot of other banks, had consolidated into a gigantic bank—and probably Bengie was mixed up in that deal, for he's a banker.

Well Mei Lang Fang certainly is cute. He's the next cutest person I've ever met. I thought it rather vulgar, under the circumstances, to lunch in the public room at the Ritz, with all the hoi polloi staring at us, and they did stare. Mei Lang Fang's private life, is sufficiently manly and "not what you think" (I wish you'd can that remark). He was accompanied, as usual, by Prof. Chang and another Chinaman, and all three gave the effect of highbred, cultivated men of the world. The repast began with some of those oysters, that are baked in the shell, with a cream dressing over them. They are peculiar enough, and Mrs. Pat was worried for fear Mei Lang Fang wouldn't stand for them. But he did. He looked around at us and smiled to convey the idea that he liked them. In fact he ate everything and had the usual manners, even eating asparagus exactly as we did. Beatrice had me invite Billy Bahr (Albert's friend, the dealer in Chinese antiques) as he speaks Chinese, having been born in Shanghai. Billy Bahr seized the opportunity to do a little publicity on his own and invited us all to his place to tea this afternoon, promising to show us a marvelous antique jade. His secretary had just telephoned me to be sure to come at four-fifteen, as Mei Lang Fang is always prompt.

In the evening Eugene Gallatin took me to see *Topaze,* with Frank Morgan, an excellent actor. I enjoyed it more than anything I have seen this winter, always excepting, of course, Mei Lang Fang. The play is delightful, and a great success—yet the critics were all so lukewarm about it, that I had no thought of going to see it. I liked it far better than the Theatre Guild's *Apple Cart,* to which Gallatin also took me; and the *Topaze* Company was far better than the Guild Company.

Two actors, that I have been seeing a lot of in the movies, are those two, who acted in "Is zat so?" I forget their names, but both are simply grand, and now I'm annoyed to think, I never saw them in "Is zat so?" Their slogan is "Oh, yeah?" and they say it hundreds of times in the *The Shannons of Broadway.* Another slang word, that abounds, is "O.K." Of course, you've heard "O.K." all your life, but lately the phrase is "That's okay by me," and you hear it a hundred times a day. My secretary, Mrs. Levine, is particularly fond of it. No matter what I say, she says, "That's O.K. with me."

The Japanese players, whom I saw, are not so good. In fact they're terrible. They appear to be awkward players from the provinces. It's unfortunate they came at the time of Mei Lang Fang's visit, but they shouldn't have succeeded here in any case. They were unattractive as people, their voices were disagreeable, and their costumes cheap. After the marvels of Mei Lang Fang, it was a great come-down. [. . .]

9 p.m.—Well, a good time was had by all, at Billy Bahr's. Mrs. Pat was there and Bridget Guinness, and Greenville Winthrop, and Jennie Carpenter, and Mei Lang Fang came with two learned Chinese gentlemen. Bahr showed some ancient Chinese masterpieces, that he got out of the storage vaults especially for us, and they were truly grand. Mei Lang Fang said he had seen nothing better in China. We stayed until seven o'clock, which I thought daring of Mei Lang Fang, since he had to dine and be ready to play at 8:30 pm. As I said before, we should kill him, if he stayed much longer in America, as he is entertained constantly. But fortunately his engagement ends tomorrow night. I may go to the last performance—there is sure to be a demonstration. [. . .]

To Malcolm MacAdam
April 6, 1930, Tuxedo Club, Tuxedo Park, New York

Dearest Malc:

I am just returned from the Pennsylvania Hotel, where I had an excellent oyster stew and some of those French crescent rolls, which I caused the chef to put in the oven and heat, so I'm in a fairly amiable mood for letter-writing. Also on returning, I found a letter from Duncan Phillips of the Phillips Memorial, Washington, thanking me for the little article I wrote for the Magazine they publish, and enclosing a cheque for $50.—, and giving me such extravagant praise for my writings in general, that were I a soap manufacturer, or a cigarette merchant, I should hire a full-page in the *Times* and print it in facsimile.[1] Not being either, I shall tear it up and throw it in my waste-basket, after I have answered it civilly. [. . .]

Eugene Gallatin, who sailed yesterday, insists I shall come to his Hotel in Paris, the Lancastria on the rue de Berci, for it is very smart and only sets you back 11 francs a day for sitting room, bedroom and bath. As I'm to be

1. McBride wrote an article on Henri Rousseau for the second issue of Phillips's magazine *Art and Understanding*. The letter from Phillips, dated April 4, 1930, notes the Washingtonian's belief that "in you I recognize the brilliant spokesman for the Left Wing and for the radical advance."

there such a short time, I thought I might indulge myself for once, but in the mean time Beatrice has asked me to stop with her on the Quay de Conti, and being scotch, it's likely I shall take the cheaper of these two offers. And the Val Dudensings insist I am to stay with them in Touquet, and they also say I am to stay with them at Villefranche, where they have taken Paul Morand's house for August.[2] But of course I'll be home long before then.

I went to a dinner at Beatrice's Friday night for Toscanini, but Toscanini was ill and didn't get there. Benjamin and Bridget Guinness, however honored the occasion. Say Bengie Guinness is a regular libertine. Isn't that scandalous, at his age? There was an Austrian there, who know all about jewels, and when he spoke of a certain emerald that granted the wish of any lady that held it in her hand, there was, naturally, an outcry. That little countess, whose name I always forget, was next to me at the table and she made a special fuss. I said, "Oh you'd only wish for money like the rest of us." And she said, "I would wish for something that money couldn't buy, or something, in fact, that would cost me money," I scoffed at the idea of there being any thing that money couldn't buy and so finally she confided, that if she had a wish, she would wish for a child.

Apparently she must have confided this secret desire to everybody else, for when I joined her and Bengie Guinness in front of the fireplace after dinner, I found that Bengie was acting up just like the villain in an old fashioned play, staring piercingly into her eyes, making remarks with two meanings, and alternating this with refined caveman stuff, if you get what I mean. Well, when the party broke up and the Guinnesses and the others were leaving, the countess ran over to Beatrice for protection, and when asked what was the matter, said, "Oh Benjamin Guinness has so intimidated me."

On Tuesday night Louise Delano took Beatrice, that Mme. Thompson and me to see Greta Garbo in *Anna Christie*.[3] It was at the Capitol, where it has been packing them in to beat the records. For my part, I don't like being packed in. I hate those big movie houses. We had to go stand behind the ropes, and finally the ushers seated us one by one, and in separate parts of the house. But thought Greta grand. Marie Dressler, too, was a master-

---

2. Paul Morand (1888–1976), French diplomat and writer of cosmopolitan stories and novels set in postwar Europe.

3. "The day Garbo talked," was March 14, 1930. Garbo's first, heavily accented English words to her fans were "Give me a whisky. Ginger ale on the side. And don't be stingy, baby." For Delano see Biographical Sketches.

piece, and so was that Charles Bickford, whom I always like. But it was half-past eleven before we got out, and I was nearly dead with fatigue. When they dropped me at my Hotel, Louise Delano's chauffeur said to me, "Get out this way Mr. Chanler," not that I care!

Well, you've escaped the fright of entertaining Henri Matisse, for he sailed straight to Tahiti, where he is now. But there'll be some other celebrities on your trail soon. Miguel Covarrubias and Rose are going round the world and will be in Yokohama in June.[4] I gave him your address and he said he would certainly call you up. Miguel is just a kid, you understand, but thoroughly sweet and unspoiled. You mustn't go to any expense about him, of course, but you can tip him off, where to go and perhaps show him some of the funny, low life places, that he adores. Probably by instinct, Miguel will know where the places are, for he is not an amateur traveler. He and Rose are not exactly married I believe, so you will call her whatever name he gives you. She is very handsome and just as nice as Miguel. You know Miguel's drawings in Vanity Fair, don't you? We all think him a genius.

[. . .] The town has changed a lot since you left.[5] You'd hardly know it. The Waldorf is a very deep hole in the ground, but they've already taken the braces off the plate glass windows in the neighborhood and that shows that the blasting is over and building ready to begin. By the time I get back in the Fall, doubtless it'll be higher than the Eiffel Tower. That entire block, where the Casino and Knickerbocker Theatres were, is also a deep hole in the ground. When I come out of the Opera, to saunter home, I hardly know where I am. I'm going to the Opera tonight, I think, to hear Beniamo Gigli sing "Una Furtiva Lagrima" . . . by Gosh, that reminds me. The Countess Mercati is throwing a tea this afternoon for Leopold Stowkowsky, of the Philadelphia Orchestra, and he is to tell us what art is coming to. I've got to go, because the Countess Mercati said "I'll give you your ticket then," meaning, the tickets for the performance of *The Sacre du Printemps,* for

4. Mexican-born Miguel Covarrubias was a renowned caricaturist frequently published in *Vanity Fair.* He later became an anthropologist. In his 1927 article "Covarrubias in Harlem," McBride observed, "Mr. Crowninshield probably hits it off as well as it can be hit off when he asserts that the young man 'mastered his métier solely by virtue of close observation and hard work' " (reprinted in *Flow of Art,* p. 231).

5. The years 1930 and 1931 were the heyday of Art Deco skyscraper building in New York City. In 1930 William Van Alen's Chrysler Building opened as the tallest building in the world, reaching 1,048 feet into the sky. Within a year, the 1,250-foot Empire State Building stole the honor.

which the house is already sold out, and to which all of us intend to go, coûte que coûte.[6] So, maybe, I shall have had enough excitement for today without going to hear "Una Furtiva Lagrima."

This letter is already twice as long as the article I wrote for Duncan Phillips and if he were getting it, it would cost him $85.—just think that over, kid. . . But to you—it is free gratis.

To Malcolm MacAdam
May 30, 1930, Berlin, Germany

Dearest Malc:

I flew from Malmö (Sweden) to Berlin this morning.[1] Three hours up— and believe me we were *up*. We stopped at Copenhagen airport 10 minutes, thus crossing the Baltic Sea twice. The day was beautiful, but windy and the plane was wonderfully steady until we got near Berlin, when we got a few bumps—air pockets, I suppose. But on the whole, it was steadier than a railway train, for example. I was not so scared as I expected.[2] I was a little scared, naturally, and once, when we were about three miles high and sailing well above a field of white clouds, where we could occasionally see through a chink and detect glimpses of something like blue water below, I suddenly noticed the palms of my hand to be quite moist. So I judge from that, I was a little scared, though I think I fooled the two Swedish pilots, and I certainly fooled the crowd of idlers, who sit around behind the fence at the Berlin airport watching the arrivals. I gave a great show of non-chalance for them, as I walked by on my way to the customs-house. I was the only passenger, which made it harder to bear. Also to embark in the midst of the Swedish language was confusing. The Swedes are terrible about not understanding foreigners and they simply don't try. There were

6. *Coûte que coûte,* at all costs.

1. McBride was invited to Sweden as a member of a highly social and highly publicized critic's junket to view an exposition in Stockholm. As McBride recounted in an unpublished letter, May 21, "We still continue to make the front page, however, and I begin to think publicity is very easy in Sweden. . . . I suspect my great success in the newspapers, is due to the fact, I am the oldest of the troupe—the 'Dean.'"
2. Although commercial airlines had been around since 1911, when the passenger cabin was developed, in 1930 flying was still an activity for the daring. In 1929 the instruments to successfully accomplish "blind" takeoffs and landings were developed, allowing airlines to implement much more reliable flying schedules. With no passenger fatalities in 1930, passenger airlines were the safest and quickest way to cross the Atlantic.

six people, who set out from Malmö in the bus for the air-port, including one woman, who seemed on the verge of apoplexy and who somehow made me feel brave; and when we had all weighed etc., I was suddenly shoved into the red airplane, the pilots hopped on, slammed the door and I was off—alone in the cabin—with my thoughts. The whole business of embarking, however, is novel, and full of new stuff. You will die of envy, when you see the beautiful air-plane labels they stuck on my two suit cases. I thought, when we were flying above the clouds already mentioned, that if I once got down to earth again I'd never go flying again—but the moment we landed in Berlin the whole thing seemed like a dream, as though it hadn't happened and as though it all occurred in a moment. It really seems as though there were nothing to it. Perhaps I'm air-minded. [. . .]

Sunday morning [. . .] Did I tell you of my visit to Prince Eugene, brother to the King of Sweden?[3] You know he is an artist and that was the excuse. The Royal command came the day we were slated to go yachting with the American Ambassador, but of course, I had to pass that expedition up. It was amusing for such a thorough democrat, as you know me to be, to be driving in a taxi up to a prince's house. It's a beautiful place, with a lovely garden right on the water, and the prince took me all through it and showed me all his collection. We talked for an hour, and if anything, I was the one to put him at his ease, for his English occasionally slipped. He begged me to go see the Thiel Museum, saying, it was closed, but that as president of it he would telephone and have it opened especially for me. All this was done. I liked Prince Eugene.

To Malcolm MacAdam
June 11, 1930, Hôtel Lancaster, Paris

Cher Malc:

[. . .] P.S. I see there will be no chance to do much more to this letter, so I'll add a ps and send it off. It's the Chester Dales.[1] When I went up to Maud's Sunday afternoon, she ordered tea and I decided I'd eat two brioches and call it supper—but just when we had finished, in came Chester, who was in a gay mood and insisted we should all go off to dinner at the Sporting Club on the Ave. Gabriel, where we did eat on the terrace and

3. On McBride's visit to the prince's home in Valdemarsudde, Djurgarden, Stockholm, the two played a set of tennis. No information survives as to who won the match.

1. See Biographical Sketches.

watched the fountain play and the moon coming up—and I forgot to say we had cocktails before and sauterne avec. Then Maud wanted to go and sit for a while at the Café D'Arcourt (corner of the street that leads up to the Panthéon), which was in memory of her student days, and then we went to the Dom, which was shabbier and more crowded than ever, and then we stopped to get some flowers for Helen Read, the art critic, who was an old flame of Chester's before he married Maud; and Chester picked out some yellow roses and Maud thought there ought to be some blue in the bouquet and she added some blue flowers, which made me laugh,—for they were passion flowers.[2] Chester said, "My God, why didn't you slip that news to me on the quiet," but Maud is a real sport, and she let the bouquet go, passion flowers and all.

You would adore Chester. He is the livest wire I have ever met. Like you, he's un enfant gâté and has to be noticed all the time—but he's great.[3] He has spent between $300,000 and $500,000 here in pictures this summer and naturally the art dealers, who are even more rude and rapacious than those in New York, are quite frantic. It's sickening when you go about with Chester, to see the way we are pursued. Even at the Sporting Club, a dealer popped up from somewhere, made a fuss over me and evidently wanted to be introduced. Monday we had to take Helen Read to the Sporting Club for luncheon, and that night I thought I'd have my milk-toast in my room in order to simplify matters, but Gallatin appeared and dragged me to Joseph's for milk-toast. Today Chester and Helen Read et moi to lunch at the Ritz, and afterward he took us to the Hotel Drouot to see a picture sale, and then to see the great private collection of Paul Rosenberg, the dealer.[4] Rosenberg had been high hatting everybody of late and no one gets to see his marvelous Picassos and Braques, but naturally, for the Chester Dales, all doors are opened.

That evening I bolted to the Alpes for supper, where I still maintain you get the best food in Paris (the chicken curry at the Ritz wasn't so

2. Helen Read was a New York critic who had been on the junket to Malmö.
3. *Enfant gâté,* "spoiled child."
4. Drouot remains one of the most famous auction houses of Paris. Paul Rosenberg (1882–1959) was a dealer and collector in Paris and New York. An early supporter of Picasso and Braque, Rosenberg acted as dealer in the sale in 1929 of Picasso's early masterpiece *Woman with Fan* (1905) from Gertrude Stein's collection to Mrs. W. Averell Harriman (now in the collection of the National Gallery of Art, Washington, D.C.) so that Stein and Toklas could undertake their publication venture, Plain Edition. McBride wrote about Rosenberg's collection in an article entitled "A Great Dealer's Private Collection."

much—I can make better myself), and it was well I did, for just now Gallatin rang and wanted me to dine downstairs with him. The fact is, I've got to cut out these special dinners, for my coat, this last week, has suddenly begun to grow tight, and that is one thing that helped you to get a post script to this letter—for I was dying to get to my room and get my coat off, etc.

This chaotic account of my entertainment may make you think I'm liking Paris—but I'm not. I'm really through with Paris. It bores me and so do the French. I long to be home in my own back yard. The French have still the best taste in art of all the nations—but that's the only asset of importance.

I wish I had time to tell you Gallatin's tale of how he got gypped, by the ticket agent, when he bought his tickets for Stambaul; but it's a long story. I'm trying to persuade him to make a formal complaint to the new Commissioner of Tourisme—for it has got to the point where France is the dearest and trickiest country in Europe for the traveler. American travel here has fallen off alarmingly they tell me, so I think, he'd be listened to.

To Malcolm MacAdam
June 23, 1930, Sunnycote, Rosemary Island,
Haddenham, Bucks, England

Dearest Malc:

Juliana Force sent her car down for me on Sunday morning at eleven and the two porters at Claridges Hotel, where I am stopping, on Half Moon Street, seemed quite as much impressed by its grandeur as I was.[1] I was driven in state all the way out here, seeing most of the things on the way that one can possibly see in England—quaint villages, canals, air-plane fields, churches, etc. It was an hour and a half's journey, finally ending in a village of thatched cottages with Juliana Force in the endmost one. Of course she has transformed it wonderfully, with tiled floors, amusing fire places, an electric stove and frigidaire in the kitchen, and all sorts of amazing luxuries and amazing simplicities intermixed. You have heard me before talk of Juliana's gift for finding unusual things—and this time she has

1. Force's cottage, called Cobweb, had been redecorated in the month before McBride's visit. In the spring, summer, and fall of 1930 Force was also busy with another redecorating project: the Whitney Museum was buying additional real estate on West 8th Street and preparing to open as a formal museum of modern American art.

outdone herself. I am motoring back to London this afternoon (for I want to see some Wimbledon tennis) and I shan't have seen a quarter of the diverting objects in this humble peasant's cot. As the cook was absent yesterday, it being Sunday, we drove over to Frame to a famous Inn, where we had a typically English luncheon, including gooseberry tart. Later we drove to Oxford, twelve miles away, and had tea at The Mitre and did a little sightseeing. In the evening we got supper ourselves and I enjoyed that best of all, for we had marvelous cold ham pie from Aylesbury (famous for meat pies), a fine salad of mixed greens, a new kind of coffee, which I had never heard of, called "Dandelion Coffee" and which has no caffeine, some preserved plums with thick rich cream, and ginger cake. Of course, the crockery and the table linens, are beyond anything an oriental could dream of. This morning there are eight or ten workmen here, tearing apart the salon and making it over into something else, for Juliana is mad over reconstruction. The country here is quite lovely.

But that isn't why I began this letter. I had a reason other than merely describing my travels. Alice Toklas wants some Chinese tea. She says there is no longer any tea in France fit to drink. I told her Malcolm MacAdam was in the Orient and might get her some. They both exclaimed with rapture. Both Alice and Gertrude recalled you perfectly and said they both liked you. I told Gertrude frankly, that you liked her, but you didn't like her poetry. She said that it didn't matter. Alice wants some of the real Chinese tea, the kind that the high-class merchants use for themselves and not the kind that is sold to foreigners. Also she doesn't want Oolong nor ceremonial tea. She wants the regular tea, the best Chinese use for themselves and she thinks you can inquire of some of your business friends and find it without too much trouble. I suggest you get a small amount, say ¼ lbs of some sample tea to see if she likes it, and if O.K., then you can get more later. Send, of course, to Mlle Alice Toklas, 27 rue de Fleurus, Paris, and I will re-imburse you. Remember, Alice and Gertrude both like you *very much* (that's their story anyhow). Gertrude has written another poem with me in it. I think now she'll put you in a poem, too.

To Gertrude Stein
September 11, 1930, Callicaste, Marshallton, Pennsylvania

My dearest Gertrude:
I have just been writing something—with my usual flippancy—about the "Dix Portraits" for *Creative Art*—and will send it to you when it appears,

I think, in October.[1] I enjoyed them very much particularly the Picasso, the Apollinaire and the Christian Berard. I almost wished the last had been written about me. At any rate, before I die, I'd like somebody to say in print that I liked food. Perhaps it will do for my obituary, if I get one. I always envied the remark of somebody about Walt Whitman that he was as particular about food as a high-caste Hindu. . . It was terrible to have to start writing again—especially down here where the autumn is beginning and one wants to be out doors every minute engaged in pseudo-rustic tasks. Fires, for instance. I adore burning heaps of trash in the orchard in the autumn. As soon as I finish this letter—which is going to be short in consequence—I am going to rush right out and ignite two enormous old chestnut tree stumps which have been an inconvenience for years and which at last are scheduled to disappear. But this won't interest you as much as it will Alice. By the way, I think Alice will be obliged to dip her pen in ink and begin corresponding with Malcolm and me. Just think, in all these years, I have never seen the color of her ink!!! For Malcolm has done something about the tea. I await with wildest curiosity to hear Alice's report. She must by no means be polite about it. The object is to discover tea in the orient and if the first try is not a success we will try again. It will amuse Malcolm and all of us—and of course, Alice understands that since tea costs nothing là-bas there is no occasion for her to inquire into the trifling price. That is for Malcolm or me. . . I enclose Malcolm's amusing letter. Alice is not to mind his referring to her as Alice. Malcolm has wholesome fear of both you and Alice (he suspects in spite of all my asseverations to the contrary) that you are both high-brows; and high-brows are his pet terror.

We have had a famous drought in America this summer but I haven't time to explain now, that I loved it. Day after day of sunshine and record breaking heat. I love both heat and record-breaking.

But now to the fires!

To Malcolm MacAdam
September 29, 1930, Callicaste, Marshallton, Pennsylvania

Dearest Malc:

[. . .] Keep account of your expenses in tea, for, of course, I am to pay for Alice's boisson. Alice will have a wonderful time saying to her guests, "Yes,

1. Nothing on Stein's "Dix's Portraits" appeared in *Creative Art*. In the October issue (vol. 7, no. 4, sup. pp. 42–47), McBride devoted his "Palette Knife" column to Stein, Picasso, and the death of Pascin.

this is some tea a friend of mine sent me from Mukden." You needn't wise crack about it. It is an innocent pleasure, and people, who live in the wicked city of Paris, should certainly be encouraged to go in for simple recreations.[1] [. . .]

I went to New York last week on a mild spree. Henri Matisse has come on to be a juror at the Pittsburgh show, and Frank Crowninshield threw a dinner for him at the Coffee House.[2] Never did I sit down with so many millions! It really went into the billions. There were five at least who were worth over $100,000,000 including young Harriman, whose wife has just gone in for modern art and who is opening a gallery of her own next week for fun.[3] He had been to Gertrude's, on the rue de Fleurus, and he asked me curious questions about Alice Toklas. She seems to exercise the same sort of fascination upon him that she does upon you. Also, Chester and Maud Dale were there. Maud told me she had just had an accounting with Knopf, the publisher and that $200 royalties were coming to me. That makes $700 for a punk book that I cannot read myself. Chester and Maud (they both now call me Henry) fetched me down to the Herald Square in their car, after dinner—and Maud actually kissed me good-bye. I fancied that Chester looked surprised and possibly I, too, looked so. But Maud loves me because she has been able to do me a good turn. Do you understand the psychology?

I liked the paper bag the Chinese silk came in. Do you suppose you can get me 25 similar one-pound bags, with ads on them, for my grapes next year? It would be grand to put Japanese bags on our grapes. I should certainly be one up on Alice then. Incidentally, our grapes are grand this year. The drought helped them. [. . .]

1. When the tea arrived, Toklas considered it subpar, as was a subsequent shipment. The good-natured correspondence soon degenerated, as MacAdam grew angry over what he considered Toklas's ingratitude toward his efforts (letters in the Stein/Toklas collection at YCAL).
2. On September 14 Matisse sailed for his second trip to the United States to serve on the award jury for the twenty-ninth annual International Exposition of Paintings at the Carnegie Institute. The jury voted to give the first-prize medal to Picasso. During this United States trip Matisse traveled to Merion, Pennsylvania, where his patron Albert Barnes commissioned him to paint a mural for the central gallery of his museum. McBride wrote about the Frenchman's trip in the *Sun* (March 8, 1930) and *Creative Art* (December 1931), quoting Matisse's impressions of New York extensively.
3. Marie Harriman, owner of the Harriman Gallery at 61–63 East 57th Street.

To Malcolm MacAdam
February 27, 1931, The Coffee House, New York

To Malcolm MacAdam:

The two packages of tea have just arrived, after, apparently, some rough traveling. The pasteboard box was broken, the two tins squeezed so that the lids had been forced off, and some of the tea leaked. This is not ungratitude on my part, I have to tell you so you can prepare against the vicissitudes of postal service. I am grateful and impressed just the same. I intend to give one of the tins of tea to Mme. Gaston Lachaise, with whom I dine next week. The other I intend to try myself, down home; though there is no use wasting any of it on the Misses Pugh. They gave themselves away last summer, by not liking that tea that Alice Toklas raved about. It takes a "high class, intellectual-tasting" individual to get it. . . There was another package of tea, that arrived a fortnight ago and which I immediately re-sent to Gertrude and Alice—but they have not acknowledged it yet. . . Bibi Dudensing says "it must be nice to have a friend in China sending you things" and I tell her it is. . . Did that tea really cost $1.50 a lb.? If so, I think it's a sin. Just the same, send me a truthful bill of what I owe you.

I am sending you two books. One of them called *Look Homeward Angel,* is a lend, and you can return it any time next summer.[1] The other, in French, *Molinoff* is very amusing, and you can keep it. You will think I send *Look Homeward Angel* on account of the title, but the truth is, it is very much read by the young intellectuals. Betty Burroughs, whom I met at a tea-party, just had time to whisper to me to get it, and I did so. It is amazingly clever, but formless. I lost interest half-way in the book, but there are some powerful scenes, I admit. You will think it vulgar. You are so refined. But you will see by Carl Van Vechten's book, that refinement is not so much the thing, as it used to be.[2] [. . .]

To Malcolm MacAdam
May 10, 1931, Herald Square Hotel, New York, New York

Dear Malc:

Yesterday, as I was paying for my lunch, Mrs. Barclay said, "Going to the parade?" and I said, "What parade?" and she said, "Mayor Walker is march-

1. Thomas Wolfe's (1900–1938) first novel was published in 1929.
2. Van Vechten's *Parties: Scenes from Contemporary New York Life* was published by Alfred A. Knopf in 1930.

ing up Fifth Avenue at the head of all the police." As I have always been pre-disposed to Jimmy Walker, I took the hint and sauntered down the Ave-nue.[1] When I got to 50th Street, I saw Cardinal Hayes and two attending priests sitting out in State on the Cathedral steps, in full blaze of the sun, which was hot.[2] So I decided to wait there. In a moment along came Jimmy, looking very swell in a topper and morning coat, with six or eight officials similarly attired. The people cheered and Jimmy doffed his topper and looked hot—he had walked from City Hall. Seeing Cardinal Hayes, Jimmy left the ranks and darted over to him, making a profound obeisance and kissing the amethyst ring on the Cardinal's hand. Somehow it looked cute and affecting. I'm not so pious, as you know, but away inside there must be a relic of former piety, for I actually felt a little troublesome stab in the heart at the moment. Don't you think it's odd? But everybody cheered, so others must have felt the stab, too. Jimmy certainly knows that right thing to do. Anybody else would have contented themselves with a salute, but Jimmy is spontaneous and natural. I said all this to Grant, when I came home, and he agreed with me, that Mayor Walker is all right. "He's a regular fellow," said Grant. Coming from Grant, you'll have to take it. If it were I alone, you'd say it was high-brow stuff. [. . .]

I've told you before that I'm not happy entirely at *Creative Art,* and now that we get out the entire magazine, it's an extra tax.[3] I haven't the time to do it properly; and I'm not in sympathy with the way Mr. Boni wishes it run. He loses on it, and is eager to do sensational stuff and attract free pub-licity. I don't blame him for that, but it's not my sort of stuff, and I see I shall lose my reputation as a critic, if I don't watch out. Next fall I may resign. Then, too, and this is where joke comes in, there have been efforts to join the *Post* and the *Sun.* It is the *Post* that wants to buy.[4] The *Post* has no circula-

1. James John Walker (1881–1946), mayor of New York 1925–32.
2. John Patrick Joseph Hayes (1867–1938) became cardinal in 1924.
3. In 1931 *Creative Art* became fully independent of its long-standing association with *The Studio* of London. *Creative Art's* title page no longer proclaimed, "Incor-porating 'The Studio' of London."
4. The beginning of the end of New York's great newspaper era was at hand. As McBride wrote to Malcolm on February 27, 1931, "*The World* passed out this morn-ing. It's a great sensation. Sold to the *Evening Telegram* and will be an evening paper hereafter. It's a blow for us intellectuals. *The World* was really the only paper we had. It was the only paper, whose editorials I could glance at. What shall I read in the mornings? The 'cold,' 'impersonal' *Times,* or the sticky *Tribune?* It's a sad prospect, and incidentally, it's going to make severe rivalry for The *Sun.* Not that I care."

tion and loses money, but the owner is rich. The *Sun* is paying and therefore puts a high price on itself. So far the deal is off—but if it should go through, I might not be transferred to the *Post*. One never knows. So you see?

I got to see Noel Coward and Gertrude Lawrence in *Private Lives* at last.[5] They are great. I wished for you, for you would simply have eaten it. I haven't seen an audience laugh so much in several years. It reminded me of the Oscar Wilde things, though it is not, I dare say, literature. It is better theatre then the Wilde Plays, more actable; but it is not so quotable. After this I shall make it a point to see all Noel Coward's plays. [. . .]

I have just finished my essay for the catalogue of the great Matisse show in Paris.[6] It has agonized me for two weeks, but thank heavens it is finished. The principal critics of each country contribute an essay about Matisse—hence you see the flattery involved. [. . .]

To Malcolm MacAdam
May 22, 1931, Herald Square Hotel, New York, New York

Dear Malc:
I've just got my orders to sail on the Île de France, June 5th.[1] Isn't it tiresome? I had hoped to avoid it, as the one thing necessary for me at present is a little bit of quiet—and Paris isn't quiet. It's the Dales, of course. You see there is a big Matisse exhibition at the Georges Petit Galleries, for which I have written a catalogue-preface, and the Dales are mixed up in it and insist on having their friends with them. Helen Read, of the *Brooklyn Eagle,* who is crazy to go to Paris and couldn't go unless assisted, is the one who urges the Dales on; and as the Dales have become the head of the French Institute, they use that pull to have the French Government invite us over.[2] There are just four invitees; Helen Read, Margaret Breuning, Jewell

5. *Private Lives,* Noël Coward's exploration of the British high life between the wars, opened in London on September 24, 1930, with Gertrude Lawrence and Laurence Olivier. The play moved to Broadway in 1931.
6. A retrospective exhibition, the second of four for Matisse in 1930–31, was held in Paris, June 16–July 25, at the George Petit gallery. The exhibition of 141 paintings, many of them from the Nice period, was the artist's first major show in Paris since 1910.

1. McBride and several colleagues from American newspapers were invited by the French government to review the Paris Colonial Exposition.
2. In spring 1931 McBride wrote in his "Palette Knife": "A new public art gallery has come to town. It occupies the top floor of the French Institute. It was presented to

of the *Times,* et moi. Some of those not invited are sure to make remarks—but one of them could have my place, if it could be decently managed. There is no chance of your hitting me with a letter in Paris, as this notice it too sudden. My program is this; Sail June 5th, ten days in Paris, ten days in London, returning July 2 on the Île de France. I may get to see a tennis match in London, and I may get out to Juliana Force's cottage near Oxford; but all the rest will be boredom. There are to be several big parties in Paris, but as I can't drink and can't stay up late at night, I look forward to them with fear. The real excuse for the trip is the French Colonial Exhibition, and I presume we'll have to write it up, which won't add to the gaiety of the expedition. It's a little bit like your going to see a Japanese temple and putting in most of your day "taking stock." Consequently I know I have your sympathy for all this. [. . .]

To Gertrude Stein
Wednesday June, 1931, Hôtel Roblin, Paris, France

My dearest Gertrude:

I am broken hearted not to see you and Alice. It is ridiculous to come to France and return sans vous nouvelles. I came unexpectedly for ten days only to see the Matisse show and the Colonial affair and depart for London next Tuesday and for the States on July 2. The newspapers interviewed me and so let loose a million old friends who descended upon me with invitations, which I accepted until I suddenly got cross and found I'd have to chuck most of them; for the fact is I seem to be somebody's guest here in Paris, the French Government or the French Steamship Line, I don't know which; and I am put up at this measly hotel and am expected to write at least two articles for the *Sun,* and I don't feel equal to writing a line.[1]

I saw Picasso last night at the Matisse vernissage and again this afternoon at his studio. He tells me he is going to see you soon and I charged him to give you and Alice my love, and probably he will do so. He is in excellent spirits and has some marvelous pictures in his studio. Always the last one seems to be the greatest.

---

that institute by Mr. Chester Dale, and Mrs. Dale has agreed to direct it for a term of three years. Consequently it is generally spoken of as the 'Dale Gallery,' though that may not be its official title" (vol. 7, supplemental page 78).

1. The article of which McBride complained was "Leading U.S. Critics Arrive for Matisse Show Opening: Henry McBride of *Sun,* Mrs. Anderson of *Post,* and Mrs. Read of Brooklyn *Eagle* in Paris for Great Art Event," *Herald,* Paris, June 13, 1931.

Matisse's vernissage was very mondaine.[2] All sorts of picturesque specimens. I had dinner with Matisse preceding the party and he was most amiable and kind—as usual.[3] They say in America he is getting 6,000,000 francs for his Dr. Barnes decoration.[4] Even allowing for exaggerations he seems to be getting well paid.

In the pell-mell on Pablo's table I noticed the blue covers of *Lucy Church Amiably* and when I pointed it out Pablo smiled and said, "Ah, oui, chère Gertrude."[5] My address in London is Clarges Hotel, Half Moon Street. Don't empty any vials of wrath on me for not coming south—I feel sufficiently convicted of sin as it is.

With love to you both.

To Ettie Stettheimer
June 1931, Paris, France

Dear Ettie:
You never write to me—but that's no reason why I shouldn't write to you, is it? But perhaps I should not write too much until I find out.

Anyway on the present occasion I merely wish to inform you—and possibly the entire Stettheimer family, through you—that the Virgil Thomson concert was not so hot as it might have been. "This is a serious concert," the 'auteur' said to me in the lobby as I went in, and it proved to be almost too serious. Just the same the entire audience laughed, when the Oraison Funèbre from Bossuet was sung. Such phrases as "C'est inutile à dire que," sound odd in musique . . . almost as odd as the Gertrude Stein opera. The 'auteur' told me that the row occurred when Georges Hugnet's poem with a translation by Gertrude appeared, the translation being in second place and in smaller type—an indignity Gertrude could not support. The auteur being a friend of Georges Hugnet, received a visiting card

2. In his October 1931 "Palette Knife," McBride wrote of the exhibition, "The Matisse affair was undoubtedly an apotheosis although all connected with it shunned that word. . . . In the days to come I think Matisse will be considered the most important link between the extreme realists and the painters of the abstract." *Creative Art,* vol. 9, pp. 269–70.
3. McBride wrote that after the dinner Matisse fled and did not attend the general opening of his show (p. 269).
4. See Biographical Sketches.
5. *Lucy Church Amiably* [A Novel of Romantic Beauty and Nature and Which Looks Like an Engraving]. Published January 5, 1931, by Plain Edition.

shortly after saying, "Miss Gertrude Stein does not desire to continue the acquaintance with Mr. Virgil Thomson."[1]

Such is life in Paris. [. . .]

To Malcolm MacAdam
August 25, 1931, Callicaste, Marshallton, Pennsylvania

Dear Malc:

[. . .] I thought I'd do some writing during my visit to the Dales, but of course I didn't. I wrote you from there, didn't I? If so, I must have told you of the growing cult for nudity that prevails in fashionable circles. I don't practice it but I like to see it practiced by others. By the time you return we'll be quite Greek; so look at your waist line, mon brave. From my window I looked into the tennis court of the Mitchells (President of City Bank) and noticed the men playing in short trunks and almost no bathing shirts. The idea was that the sea-bathing would occur afterwards—but ladies were present. As for the Dales, I know almost everything about Maud and quite everything about Chester. I have not only seen Chester in the all-together, but one evening, when I thought my nose had too much sunburn, I knocked on his door in search of talcum powder and when Chester's voice said, "That you Henry," I pushed in only to find Chester completely nude and seated on the crapping machine in his bathroom and the only light focused fully on the pose. To do Chester justice he was not in the least abashed. Chester never is abashed about anything. Then, too, on the beach, the men only wear trunks; no shirts at all. When the Dales took me to lunch at the fashionable Beach Club, most of the men lunched in their bathing suits. So the famous mixed bathing of Japan has got very little on us. [. . .]

Another thing that will astonish you on your return, will be the unemployment. No doubt the "depression" will continue another year and you will see it in force. You must have read of it till you're sick of it—but it startles you the more, when you actually see the able bodied men, who ask you for jobs and who talk threateningly about what is going to happen to the rich soon, if something isn't done for the poor. Practically all of them are socialists for though none of them admit they'd like to live in Russian,

1. Stein's break with Hugnet occurred in December 1930, followed by her break with Thomson the next month. Stein published her version of Hugnet's work *Enfances* under the title *Before the Flowers of Friendship Faded Friendship Faded* in 1931 (Plain Edition, 120 copies). Stein's piece also appeared under the title "Poem Pritten on the Pfances of George Hugnet" in *Pagany,* vol. 2, no. 1, Winter 1931.

they all read the Soviet propaganda and base their complaints on its teachings. [. . .]

To Malcolm MacAdam
October 8, 1931, Pittsburgh Athletic Association,
Pittsburgh, Pennsylvania

Dear Malc:

[. . .] I have now seen all the pictures and have had my formal luncheon with Homer St. Gaudens and intend to spend the evening quietly in my room writing—this letter being part of it.[1] [. . .]

I thought the photo of you and the scared deer showed you to be tired, to be under strain. Carson, your companion looked debonair and carefree by comparison. Now you must learn not to strain. You are homesick and fed up with your work I know. I know too that you dream of retiring, with fortune made to a life of ease. Such dreams seldom come true. I mean, that the person who strains his nerves to the breaking point, to achieve fortune is not in a condition to enjoy fortune. It is much wiser, in my opinion, for you to concentrate on learning how to protect your health, while keeping on working. In fact, I don't believe much in retiring. All those I have seen attempt it, collapse utterly just because they no longer feel themselves part of the machinery of the world. Of course, at a certain age, and you have reached it—somebody has to tell you—it is necessary to go slow. But it is equally necessary to have a job—just for ones peace of mind. Being a gentleman of leisure is not a part of the modern system. It's not being done. But the main part of this diatribe is for you to learn to take your work easily. Give up the idea of trying to audit twice as well as your predecessor. That's all foolishness—in your case at least. You can answer this argument only by sending me another photo in which you look just as spry as Carson.

As for my own photos, I'll try to get you one. My secretary Mrs. Levine wrote me that Frank Crowninshield had me in Vanity Fair again "minus several chins," which I thought was not a tactful comment for a secretary to make. But I don't see it. Alfred Stieglitz has promised to photo me, and I'll hold him to it. I always forget to tell you, that you have no less a person

1. McBride was on his regular visit to Pittsburgh, this one to review the thirtieth annual International Exhibition of Painting, organized by the museum's director, Homer St. Gaudens. The show ran October 15–December 6, 1931, and the prize winners were McBride's friend Raoul Dufy (1877–1953), and Yasuo Kuniyoshi (1893–1953).

than Mrs. John D. Rockefeller as a rival purchaser of my Peggy Bacon caricature. You know it is life-size and in pastel, and when I went to the gallery they told me Mrs. R. had wished to buy it and has been turned down as the gallery wished to sell the set of four caricatures to the Whitney Museum. I now hear that the museum has said no to them. Perhaps I can still get it for you, but the price was $250.—you certainly couldn't retire if you squandered your money that way. Peggy might sell it to me for $100.— but I think you had better wait and see if my photo won't content you just as well. [. . .]

To Malcolm MacAdam
October 30, 1931, Herald Square Hotel, New York, New York

Dear Malc:

[. . .] I've called off the dinner tonight with Florine Stettheimer, which was disappointing, as Phil Moeller is to be there and it would be fun to hear what he would say about *Mourning Becomes Electra*, which he directed.[1] It really is a powerful play and wonderfully well acted by Nazimova and Alice Brady, and also by my old friend Thomas Chalmers; but the play is not quite the masterpiece the papers would have you think.[2] Poor Eugene O'Neill is no more the deep thinker than ever he was, but is a shade deeper than the ordinary citizen so the ordinary citizen thinks him measurelessly deep. In the last of the three plays, O'Neill doesn't quite know where he is at, but the audience has been so stirred by the tremendous second play, that it falls for everything finally. . . I suppose there hasn't been so impressive a success in years, but this is partly because good plays are scarce. There is no other that people tell you must go see. [. . .]

. . . Marie Sterner is married—to Bernard Lintott—I suppose you heard. I said over the telephone, "How do you like married life?" and Marie replied,

1. Phillip Moeller (1880–1958) was a playwright and director. A founder of the Washington Square Players, a member of the board of the Guild Theatre, Moeller had staged George Bernard Shaw's *Saint Joan* and worked with Eugene O'Neill (1888–1953) as director on *Strange Interlude* (1928). O'Neill's *Mourning Becomes Electra* opened in New York on October 27, 1931.
2. One of the last performances by Alla Nazimova (1879–1945), a Russian actress who immigrated to the United States in 1906 and was a favorite of Henrik Ibsen's. O'Neill later said of the lead actresses, "Alice Brady and Alla Nazimova gave wonderful performances in *Mourning Becomes Electra,* but they did not carry out my conception at all. I saw a different play from the one I thought I had written." Gelb and Gelb, *O'Neill,* p. 748.

"Why, do you know Barney has greatly improved, I'm actually beginning to like him," which shows you the way married people talk these days. Beatrice Locher has been spending the week-end with the Eugene O'Neills and has all the latest dope about Eugene and Carlotta, which in turn gives Beatrice a secure position in society, for really, say what you like, there is a great deal of general curiosity about those two.[3] John Anderson is frantic in his admiration of the new *Electra*. I asked him if there were any bon mots about it. At first he frowned and said it wasn't the sort of play about which people joked, but finally he confessed, that he had heard some one say, that "The Greeks had ten thousand words for it." The play is a bit long, long.[4] Gosh, I thought I'd have to be taken home in an ambulance. But high art has to be paid for, don't you think? [. . .]

To Gertrude Stein
November 24, 1931, *Creative Art,* New York

Dear Gertrude:

I am going to use your broadside—it seems like a broadside—in *Creative Art*—but the pay, unfortunately is not at all on the scale used by your rich European editors.[1] Europeans do not seem to realize that gold no longer drops from the clouds in America. As a matter of fact we have *all* had to take in our sails—and the going is not as it used to be. . . I suppose you heard of the Knoblauch misfortune? I only heard of it last week and I have been crushed ever since. Everything has been swept away in Charley's failure and they have nothing left! It seems incredible a disaster could be so complete. . . I, too, in a minor way, know what the word "depression" means, but as I never did touch the heights of glory my retrogression is not important.[2]

3. Carlotta Monterey had been three times married and divorced—her third husband, Ralph Barton, was a philandering caricaturist for the *New Yorker*—and O'Neill had been twice married. Their highly romantic love affair and marriage captivated society and the press. In May 1931 Barton killed himself, leaving a highly publicized note lamenting unrequited love for his ex-wife, and the O'Neills figured prominently in the newspaper stories about the incident.
4. During its general run, the trilogy began at five P.M. and was not over until almost midnight.

1. Stein's "Thoughts on an American Contemporary Feeling" appeared in the February 1932 issue of *Creative Art*.
2. Stein would have been interested in the fortunes of May Knoblauch (née Bookstaver) and her husband because the women had had a romantic relationship 1901–3, a relationship portrayed in Stein's first novel, *Q.E.D.*

Oddly enough, I'm just dashing off a note to your friend Carl. He never inscribed my *Parties,* and when I reminded him of it, he wrote to ask me to lunch and to bring along the book, but unfortunately I had asked Bignou, the Paris dealer, to lunch with me the day Carl fixed.[3] Carl is mad over flying. He has given up drink completely and taken to aviation. He flies somewhere every weekend. Fania is acting again, and with success.

Love to Alice and yourself.

To Malcolm MacAdam
November 28, 1931, Herald Square Hotel, New York

Dearest Malc:

Well, Malc, I saw Primo knock out Campolo last night. It set me back $5.25. I don't particularly regret the outlay, though I was annoyed as usual by the kind of seat I got. The fellow told me I was in the arena just opposite the ring but I found myself at the extreme end next to the entrance, with late-comers blocking me from sight of the two earlier Matches. I got gypped in the same fashion at the Baer-Schaaf fight, if you remember. Why must the entire outfit in charge of these fights be crooks? The usher made a man called "Eddie" get up from his seat, saying: "Sit over there Eddie, I'll take care of you later"; and six noisy customers who sat back of me, were later shifted into a box by this same usher—for a consideration, of course. Now, do you think that's nice Malc?

I've been reading the newspaper accounts of the fight this morning and also with my usual indignation. All these writers from the beginning, and without seeing him box, have been hailing Carnera as a bum and a fake; and now they hate to admit what the public knows well enough, that he is an extraordinary apparition in the prize-ring. They gave themselves away a little by their elation over Sharkey's defeat of Carnera, and by claiming that because of the victory Sharkey really was a great fighter. Well, the fact is a man has got to be a great fighter to beat Carnera, and if Carnera were always to fight as he did last night, nobody could beat him.[1] It was true that he gets up slowly from his seat. He doesn't spring from his corner like a wild-cat, as they say Dempsey used to do, but once on his feet, he seems to be limber enough and although the scrap was fast and furious while it lasted, he never once seemed out of position. In fact, he had considerable

3. Carl Van Vechten, *Parties: Scenes from Contemporary New York Life* (Knopf, 1930).

1. Jack Sharkey (1902–94) later held the heavyweight crown for a year, until Carnera knocked him out in a June 1932 title bout.

style. What deceives critics is the calmness of his demeanor. He never betrays excitement in his face, and I was a little amused once, when in close embrace with Campolo, he calmly turned his head to the referee as though saying, "Do you stand for this sort of thing?" and apparently getting no answer, he went on dutifully slugging the unfortunate Campolo. He's handsome, too, in a way. From my distance, he distinctly had a waist—though he's not exactly an artist's model. The audience screamed with excitement during every second of the match and most of them stood on their feet— yet that idiot Muldoon vetoes the Carnera matches on the plea that people don't get their money's worth.

Sunday, a.m. I have read the Sunday *Tribune* and washed up the breakfast dishes. Yes, I am housekeeping again. When the hotel was made over they put in extra electric plugs along the walls, for radio sets, or whatnot, I got an electric stove at Macy's and the material to make a breakfast and tried it out not unsuccessfully. But I am scared to death of electricity. I had the devil's own time getting my crumpets toasted. Of course, I'll only do it on Sunday—and perhaps not then after the novelty wears off. [. . .]

To Malcolm MacAdam
December 9, 1931, Herald Square Hotel, New York, New York

Dearest Malc:

I have time for a short note, and think I had better write it or else you won't even know you got a Christmas present when you get it, for I had to order *Sanctuary* and *Memoirs of a Polyglot* over the phone, and you would probably think they came from the Literary Guild.[2] I had not read *Sanctuary,* but it is talked about by the young crowd who read Hemingway, etc., and in ordering one for you, I ordered one for myself also—and when I dipped into it (I've read several chapters) I thought it heavy and dull—so we may as well call the *Polyglot* your real present. It at least is not dull. I've laughed over it all week. It may be more amusing to me, than to you, as I seem to know so many people in the book. The little chapter about Cecil Beaton is a scream to those who know Cecil (Cecil is here now. I met him yesterday at Marie Harriman's. As you are interested in fashions I may tell you, that Cecil wore a brown suit, with a white shirt and a cravat of the

2. William Gerhardie (b. 1895), *Memoirs of a Polyglot* (London: Duckworth, 1931). In a letter dated January 1, 1932, McBride wrote MacAdam that he had finished William Faulkner's *Sanctuary* "after all. At first I thought I never could [. . .] but it ends better than it begins" (YCAL, McBride).

same woolen material as his suit).[3] And then there was the chapter about poor Bridget Guinness. I dined with Mrs. Pat Campbell last night at Mrs. Finley Thomas' and Mrs. Pat told me that Bridget left her 500 pounds a year in her will, "And how much a year are my poor little pounds now?" asked she; for Mrs. Pat is always pulling a long face and looking on the dark side of things. However, it's a great relief to know that Mrs. Pat has something, for she has been in a desperate state these several years past, and all the great ladies of fashion have done nothing but agonize over her. Of course they gave dinner parties for her, too. As Mrs. Campbell is a lady of large gestures, the 500 pounds will only occasionally alleviate her miseries. There was an English actor there, whose name I didn't catch—a nice fellow—and who was an old friend of Mrs. C.'s for he said, on entering, "Darling Stella" and gave her a kiss. After dinner we were sitting together and Mrs. Pat noticed his rather showy silver rimmed monocle and two handsome finger rings, so she said; "Why you must be rich." The young man smiled amiably and said, "No, but I am loved." No special explanation vouchsafed. [. . .]

Affectionately (you say you want affection, so I'm saying "affection" instead of the usual love).

To Malcolm MacAdam
February 15, 1932, Herald Square Hotel, New York, New York

Dear Malc:

Marie Harriman gave me her box at the opera, and I took Maud and Chester Dale, Mrs. Finley Thomas, Mrs. Pat Campbell and Henry Schnackenberg (the later being asked for his good looks). The Opera was *Gioconda*. Of course it might have been *La Juive*. It generally is when people give you a box at the opera. *La Juive* is the world's worst, though *Gioconda* is a close second. Maud took an instant dislike to Mrs. Pat Campbell, in spite of the fact, that Mrs. Pat made a great fuss over Maud's good looks. Mrs. Pat expressed a wish to see the Dale collection, but Maud told Mrs. Thomas afterwards, that no power on earth could make her show her pictures to that woman. Mrs. Thomas was thrilled. Nothing enchants a mondainite like a row between celebrities, and so, in consequence, my little box party has a chance to become historical.

3. Sir Cecil Beaton (1904–80) British photographer, writer, stage designer, wit, and socialite, known for his photographs for *Vogue*.

To Malcolm MacAdam
March 12, 1932, Herald Square Hotel, New York, New York

Dear Malc:

[. . .] Although slightly ship-wrecked this morning, I think I ought to add a post-script, to my letter of yesterday, to say that Chester did give me a thrilling evening last night. Chester was entertaining a beautiful young lady with cocktails when I arrived (Maud is in Europe) and had imbibed two, I noticed. He suggested dining at a wonderful speak-easy he had lately discovered, instead of dining at home, and I was loath if I could be excused drinking. So we took the young lady home in the grand Belgian car and proceeded to Owney Madden's.[1] Yes, the speak-easy was run by the famous gun-man, Mr. Madden. You remember my telling you about him last year, before he got into the papers? He's now in the newspapers all right. The speak-easy is at 35 West 53rd Street, the former home of Ogden Mills, therefore un palais.[2] It was the blackest thing you ever saw, outside, and it was fun getting in. IT IS VERY HARD TO GET IN, Chester says, but naturally we got in. The bar was on the second floor at the head of the stairs and was very solid, permanent looking and imposing. The people sitting on the stools were extraordinary. My eyes popped out of my head to see them. Right next to me was Georges Carpentier, looking very handsome, and with him a famous aviator with his arm in a sling, and all the people were like that, the ladies being especially unusual.[3] I took one cocktail, which was excellent and Chester took several and straight-away got lit up. The Maître d'Hôtel came for our dinner order and I saw he was the higher class kind of Maître d'Hôtel, the kind, that years ago would have been at Sherry's or Delmonico's. The prices were terrible. Any item was $2.—and up. We chose caviar, sweetbreads sous cloches, etc. salads, and a bottle of Chablis for Chester. Horribly expensive, but Chester said, What the Hell, you don't mind paying, when the food is superb, and the food was superb. Owney Madden came along and I was introduced and shook hands and had a little chat, and Chester leaned over and passed a few remarks with Georges Carpentier, who was amiable. There was also a lady named Alice with whom Chester was demonstrative and who was he said, one of the aristocratic neighbors at Southampton.

1. Also operator of the Cotton Club.
2. Darius Ogden Mills (1825–1910), American financier and philanthropist and benefactor of the Metropolitan Museum.
3. The French boxer Georges Carpentier (1894–1975) was knocked out by Jack Dempsey in a world heavyweight title bout in 1921, the first fight to bring one million dollars in gate receipts.

Then we went to the dining hall, which was entirely in Blood-red, walls, floors and ceiling, with stripes of ornamental silver here and there to set it off. Very correct and impressive for a speak-easy I thought. Chester by this time was quite maudlin and was telling me how these other girls were nothing at all and how, after twenty years, he was more in love with Maud than ever. I saw Chester tip the Maître d'Hôtel four dollars and several more to the actual waiter, and tips besides to several other facototi, including the gunman, Richard, who walked up and down outside on the trottoir. It was nine-thirty before we got to the Garden, and we entered the private door and went up to the Club, where we left our coats, and saw a bunch of other millionaires. Chester said, "I'll bet you $100 on Ran, ringside odds" and a Mr. Hayden said yes indifferently. Chester tried to bet some more, but nobody seemed to listen to him. Down at the ringside (it's nice to sit right down in front) he laid another $100 with a tough guy, Chester said was a bootlegger, but the moment I laid eyes on Battalino, I recognized to my horror that Chester's $200 were sunk. Heavens that Battalino is good, I never saw such an exciting fight. I am at last converted to welter-weights. Battalino clapped both mitts to his jaws and Ran couldn't touch him, and at the same time Battalino kept pressing his head against Ran's stomach, so that Ran never was in a position to strike. Battalino has a wonderful defense and at the same time hits out like a snake. But you read all that in the papers. Mayor Walker was there, and we all stood and said a prayer for the return of the Lindbergh baby. After the fight Chester got Grantland Rice and me and led us to the Firehouse at Lexington and 50th Street, of which he is a member, and we chinned with the Chief till 11:30, when an alarm sounded, and Chester slid down the pole with the rest of the firemen and went to the fire, and Grantland Rice and I escaped to our homes.

This morning Chester called me up to see if he had misbehaved too much and to apologize, but I assured him there was nothing noticeable and that I had had the time of my life, which was true.

To Malcolm MacAdam
April 17, 1932, Herald Square Hotel, New York

Dearest Malc:

What do you think? I've just got a real, autographed letter from Frank Sullivan, HIMSELF.[1] In a review of Louis Bouché I said that Louis had quit being a wit and I didn't blame him, adding: "And besides, wits as every-

---

1. The American humorist Frank Sullivan (1892–1976) published several books including *Broccoli and Old Lace* (1931).

body knows, lead a dog's life. The private lives, they tell me, of such people as Frank Sullivan, Alex Woollcott and Ogden Nash are harassing in the extreme."[2] And this is the way Frank Sullivan comes back: "Dear Henry McBride: I don't know about Woollcott or Nash, but my private life isn't harassing any more, since they harassed the *Morning World* out of Park Row. I could stand a little harassing, I sometimes feel, if the harasser knew his business. They had some damn good harassers on the old *World*. I hope Keats Speed or Ed. Bartnett harasses you occasionally, as there is nothing like harassing for promoting metabolism, increasing the red corpuscles and stimulating the ductless glands. Sincerely, Frank Sullivan."

Don't you think it's cute? I am immensely set up to even think he noticed me. I never dreamed he glanced at my column; and probably he doesn't; probably someone called his attention to it. But anyway, now you'll like him better, I think. [. . .]

To Malcolm MacAdam
June 5, 1932, Herald Square Hotel, New York, New York

Dear Malc:

[. . .] I get up to the Coffee House for luncheons every day, taking the elevated to 42d Street, for I can't even walk that distance. Royal was very sweet to me yesterday. He divined something was wrong and came and sat beside me and even pretended he had something of the same symptoms. He took down my country address and said he would write me after I got down there, as he wanted to know how I got along. At four I went up to Florine's to see the unveiling of her new picture, *Cathedrals of Fifth Avenue,* which Carl Van Vechten, Muriel Draper, Max Ewing, Ettie and I admired very much.[1] Then I came home and read the evening newspaper until time to sup at Schrafft's, then more newspapers, solitaire and newspaper until I went to bed. [. . .]

The newspapers are not much help to me. Each day the headlines are more astonishing and disturbing. The riots of men, who demand the bonus, suggest what we are coming to. It is every man for himself apparently.

2. Alexander Woollcott (1887–1943), American journalist, writer, and radio broadcaster whose books included *Shouts and Murmurs* (1923) and *While Rome Burns* (1934), and Ogden Nash (1902–71), American humorist whose publications included *Hard Lines* (1931), *The Primrose Path* (1935), and *Good Intentions* (1942).

1. Florine Stettheimer, who showed her work in a solo exhibition only once in her lifetime, traditionally unveiled her paintings at parties held in her studio at the Beaux Arts building. She typically invited the people who appeared in the work. Barbara Bloemink dates the painting to 1931.

They don't care what becomes of the country, if they only get their bonus. Muriel Draper, who lives for mental excitement, professes to be enchanted with the situation. She thinks that future ages will look back on this period as a great moment in history. Not being that quick witted, I couldn't retort, or I should have said that future ages, as a rule are only interested in great achievements, and that the real interest will center on our period of inflation, when we built the great skyscrapers, etc., and they won't care much for the collapse. Any period can collapse, but not every period can have an inflation. See? But I couldn't think to say that to Muriel. [. . .]

I feel horribly lonely and discouraged and I do some bitter thinking once in a while. However, we all have to take our turn at this sort of thing.

To Georgia O'Keeffe
July 11, 1932, Callicaste, Marshallton, Pennsylvania

Dear Georgia O'Keeffe:

When I discovered how tiresomely medical my letter to Alfred was getting to be I cut it short.[1] Let him regard it not as a letter but as a consultation and he can puzzle out a diagnosis for me if it amuses him. I thought to state my experience in a few dry, plain words, but to my horror I found the symptoms filling an entire letter—and I assure you I left out half of them! For you I shall not be so medical.

As my letter writing is scarcely up to par it would have been better for me to have talked my thanks to you for the Shaw-Terry letters which I though immensely entertaining and which tided me over my last three unfortunate weeks in New York.[2] That is to say I liked the first half of them immensely. Towards the end they faded out. "All men kill the thing they love" and when Shaw finally won his point and got Ellen to acting in *his* plays, then he had little more use for her. . . In fact the whole thing is not so much a romantic episode as a business interlude. It is an illustration of the way certain types of writers put themselves over. Not but that Shaw really liked Ellen. All business men truly love the people with whom they can do good business. Did you ever go down to Wall Street in the noon hour? You would be amazed at the way the brokers go about with their arms around each other, like schoolgirls. You might think Wall Street the capital of the

1. McBride wrote Stieglitz a long letter on July 9, going into some detail about his maladies of the spring and early summer, which led eventually to the removal of his teeth.
2. *Ellen Terry and Bernard Shaw: A Correspondence* was published in 1931.

Country of Comradeship that Walt Whitman dreamed of; only you'd find later on that affection in Wall Street is a day-by-day experience. It seldom lasts as long as the Shaw-Terry affair. . . But I liked the shop-talk of the theatre, although I don't think Shaw profound. He is only clever. The theatre was an early passion with me and I still think I could have written more easily about it than about art; and more constructively. One can do something with the theatre, still, simply because so many people follow it.

I pass most of my day in reading, being forbidden exercise. I have a fairly sizable collection of books, and my memory is so faint that each summer I can go through my library as though for the first time. I am just now reading the Heine memoirs over again, and marveling at the instinct that man had for getting along. He knew as much in a minute as Shaw knew in a year. . . "The second part of my *Travel Pictures* will be most wonderful and interesting book to appear in these times." "I have attempted pure humour in an autobiographical fragment. So far, I have shown only wit, irony, caprice, but never pure jolly humour." "The first part is in splendid epigrams even more original and magnificent than the earlier ones. . ." etc. Now Georgia, I ask you, what would you think if I were to suddenly launch forth into statements like those in regard to my writings? However, it must be conceded, that in Heine's case it was no lie.

I have read the entire Encyclopedia Brittanica; the DeGoncourt Journals; Memoirs of John MacDonald, the 18th century valet; the Froude life of Carlyle; *Dr. Jekyll and Mr. Hyde;* Thoreau's *Walden; Summer on the Lakes* by Margaret Fuller; *Biography of Samuel Butler;* Hazlitt's *Table Talk;* and many more. Rather hap-hazard reading.

I am glad you are back at Lake George. There may be less drama than at Taos but there certainly is just as much nature.

With love to you both,

To Florine Stettheimer
July 16, 1932, Callicaste, Marshallton, Pennsylvania

Dear Florine:
[. . .] Yesterday in the midst of the hot afternoon I chanced upon an enterprise that assumed vast proportions and had to be abandoned. This was the job of assorting my old letters. One result of living in a house thirty years is that trash of all sorts accumulates and though trash is a hard word for my old letters, it is as near to the right one as legal is to honour. I had evidently tried to assemble these old letters once before for some of them

were tied in bundles and it certainly gives one curious feelings to re-read letters from a once ardent friend from whom one has not heard for, say, twenty years. I even found letters that I once thought worth preserving signed by names I could not now place! The most amusing ones by far (I know they'd amuse you) are those from artists in response to my newspaper work. I was astonished I had so many piquant ones. Especially the ones who retaliate are entertaining. There is one so unusual I must copy it off some day and send it to you. It is anonymous but evidently by some one who knew me well for the burning accusations have a good deal of truth. I think they'd make a readable book. I dived into these letters out of an impulse that was parsimonious rather than sentimental, for it occurred to me that I had many letters from celebrated persons and it would be well to assemble them. I find, however, that my correspondence does not include many world celebrities, unless you include Gertrude Stein among such. But I have some from James Stephens, the Irish poet, and of course, from all the American artists "du jour." Don't you think they'd make a book? But I dare say one has no "legal" right to publish letters from other people. One has command only over one's own.

In spite of my seclusion here adventures look in upon me occasionally. One of these seems to me to be in your line, for ever since your Asbury Park picture, I've known you to be a connoisseur of negraic distinctions.[1] A colored youth, one day lately, rode up on his bicycle, in the state that you artists call "the altogether," and asked for work. I wanted the lawn mowed and the hedge-rows cleaned, so I said yes. The youth, who seemed quite unabashed by the scarcity of his attire (the Biblical loin-cloth!) was extraordinarily handsome; so much so, that even my aged cousin Maria Pugh comments on it, and she unlike you, has never been subjected to the Carl van Vechten influence.[2] So George, that is his name, has been looking in on us at intervals ever since, and indeed, is outside now engaged in clearing away a mass of poison-vine. After George's third appearance here, the village papers contained the startling news of a murder in the neighboring West Chester of one colored man by another, and the nom-de-famille was the same as George's. I have just been asking George if the murderer was possibly a relative, and George, in a cold, disinterested voice has just replied, "My brother."

1. Stettheimer's painting *Asbury Park South* (1920, Collection Fisk University) is dominated by African-American figures.
2. Van Vechten was known for his support of African-American culture and his sexual attraction to African-American men.

That makes two of my friends involved in murder cases, for I see that Blanche Yurka was in the young millionaire Reynolds's house the night he got bumped off.[3] Poor Blanche! What emotions she must have undergone. But she will probably play *Electra* all the better now. I almost wished myself back in New York just to see how the tabloids were handling that case. It was pure tabloid; and, of course, here in the country the only thing we don't have is a tabloid. [. . .]

To Malcolm MacAdam
October 14, 1932, Herald Square Hotel, New York

Dearest Malc:
[. . .] P.S. Tuesday—October 18th. . . I had so nice a weekend, that I have not got over it yet. Everybody has been petting me—and I find that was what I was needing. Royal Cortissoz was quite wonderful at the Coffee House on Saturday, forsaking some social lights, such as Chatfield Taylor, etc., to make an uproar over me, and coming back to the theme over and over again. He did put me such a glow that I still feel it. Today I got the letter Royal wrote me down in the country inquiring after me, and it is so sympathetic that I may copy it off as a model for you to adopt.[1]

Then Sunday I went out to Flushing and Bryson and his wife were there as well as Bett's new baby. It is called "Caleb." Try to laugh that off. [. . .] We had a very good time, and Bryson and Louise fetched me back to town through the rain in their car, Louise driving. Fancy Bryson having a car, anyway. It shows what marriage does for one, don't you think?

3. The actress Libby Holman was accused of murdering her husband Smith Reynolds, an heir to the R. J. R. Reynolds tobacco fortune, at his North Carolina estate Reynolda. The actress Blanche Yurka, a teetotaler amongst the big drinkers that night, was considered a key witness to the events.

1. The letter reads:
"Dear Henry: I am surely a dog of a paleface. When we last met I promised to write and then in the usual fashion of the man on holiday I failed to do so. I am sorry, too, to hear, vaguely, that you are not well. I wondered about you when I missed your winged words in the *Sun* and *Creative Art*. How are you, mio caro? Tell me, and be sure to send me good news. I hope it is only some passing bother that keeps you at home.
"Perhaps you are not missing such a lot these immediate weeks. But I do hope that it won't be long before you are back at your post and that I may soon see you strolling into the Coffee House looking all well and set up. Meanwhile, I want to know all about it. With all the sympathy in the world, I am, Affectionately yours, Royal"

And yesterday the Whitney Museum opened and Juliana Force threw a luncheon for the critics, etc., and I got some more petting. Jo Davidson was there. Juliana brought me back from London a monstrous bottle of Floris "Honeysuckle," enough for a lifetime—for my lifetime surely. And after lunching I walked up to Mr. Boni's. He was as sweet as usual and proffered me the editorship again and when I refused took me in and introduced me to my successor, a Dr. Blossom. They have asked Elizabeth Luther Cary of the *Times,* to write a tribute to me for the December number.[2] That ought to make enjoyable reading for you.

Well by all accounts, you are in for a lively visit in Mukden. You'll go about armed.

To Malcolm MacAdam
November 4, 1932, Herald Square Hotel, New York

Dear Malc:

You say I still have my sense of humour. [. . .]

Of course, if one didn't have a sense of humour to begin with one would shortly acquire it with false teeth. The most appalling contretemps that has yet occurred to me, happened, as it naturally would, in the presence of Eugene Gallatin. Gallatin had asked me to dine with him at the Union Club, and the Union Club, as you must remember, is the holy of holies in New York. It is a place where eccentricities are not tolerated. One conforms. One does precisely what everybody else does. Well, I arrived on the dot of eight and we went up to the dining room where the oysters were already awaiting us. They looked remarkably appetizing. Those large ones, you know; and the array of condiments pleased me, too. I know fairly well by this time, what I can do and what I can't do in the way of food, but somehow it never occurred to me about oysters, for of course I had not practiced on them down home. Well, the large, delicious oysters simply would not go down my throat. Fortunately Eugene was embarked upon a long story. I struggled and struggled and finally without a word of apology, for I was speechless, I arose, left the room, and found a dark corridor, where I could remove the cursed "plate," swallow the oyster, and slightly recover my sang-froid. I made no explanation whatever to Eugene. He imagined I had swallowed something "the wrong way," and I let it go at that. I had

2. "Henry McBride," by Elisabeth Luther Cary, appeared in *Creative Art,* December 1932, pp. 281–84.

indeed swallowed something the wrong way. But I shall never commit that particular crime again. [. . .]

To Malcolm MacAdam
November 25, 1932, Herald Square Hotel, New York

Dear Malc:

I suppose when you open one of my letters you say to yourself, "What now." [. . .] But I have another tragedy to tell. Poor Nichol is dying.[1] On Wednesday, Bignou the Parisian art-dealer, was giving a dinner at the Ritz Tower for the Chester Dales, and certain of the critics. I was trying to finish up my page in advance, in order to go to the dinner with a clear conscience, when at 5:30 p.m. the telephone rang and a voice said that Mr. Nichol was dying at the Presbyterian Hospital and had expressed a wish to see me. The Hospital I found was at 168th Street—one hour to go and one hour to return as you know. Well, there was the necessity to call off the dinner, and also the necessity to finish my page, for in the newspaper world you go on with your work, if the heavens fall. My article, already half-done, had a light flippant tone—and so I went on being light and flippant, as the clowns in the circus do in similar circumstances. I got to the hospital about 8 p.m. Nichol was past speaking and I was told by the nurse not to speak. He seemed to know me and gave me a hand-clasp, but the mark of death was plainly on him and I stood there like one petrified. It is curious, but I simply cannot take in the thought of death. My mind rejects it just as the stomach rejects unwelcome matter. I say that I am ready for my own death and that I do not care, but I cannot believe that my friends die. The only one whose death left a real vacancy in my life was Edith Burroughs, but at the time of her death, I was not emotionalized. I read what the great writers say about death and most of it seems false—the conscious play-acting of artists. So, after five minutes of anger—anger at the condition of Nichol and anger at myself for being so unfeeling about it—I slunk away. How horrible a hospital is—quite as horrible as death itself. Particularly one of those swell modern hospitals, with its shiny hygiene and complete indifference to tragedy . . . then I shook off these thoughts and made the long journey back in the Subway, leaving Nichol to die alone. What I said the other day

1. Letter to Malcolm of November 4 notes, "At the museum, asking for Nichol, they said, 'Didn't you know he had a stroke and is in the hospital?' I went to see him Sunday, for he has returned home, but he was in a deplorable and almost helpless state. Evidently all the signs are wrong."

about dying surrounded by weeping mourners was all nonsense.[2] The elephant, the gentleman of beasts, always goes off to die in solitude, they say. That's why they say, I presume, he's a gentleman.

But, assez, assez, don't you think? I swear I'll write you a cheerful letter next time, if I have to fill it with lies from end to end.

To Malcolm MacAdam
December 10, 1932, Herald Square Hotel, New York

Dear Malc:

[. . .] I went last night into the wilds of Brooklyn to see a boxing match. Chester Matan was the attraction. You remember my admiration for him, as a spectacle? I used to think that Gaston Lachaise should do a bronze of him, or that some one should paint him—but that's all more or less off now, for Chester is a dub. Or, as you would say, he's dumb. He's as handsome as ever physically, but he is so slow and unthinking, that he is a bore to watch. [. . .] The event of the evening occurred, when a man who was certainly fifty years old, stood up and called over to me: "Say, Pop, would you mind moving over a couple of seats? Thanks."

I go this afternoon to the Opera to hear Tibbett do *Simon Bocconegra* and I expect to have a seat. I dropped in the other night to hear Lily Pons do the mad scene from *Lucia.* [. . .] Incidentally, Lily Pons is not so hot. Anything more ridiculous, than that mad scene, could not be imagined. Lily did get off her thin, penetrating and exactly correct coloratura with her usual success, all the while clasping her blond wig, as though her main consideration was to keep it on. Melba is the only singer I ever heard who put real madness into that aria—and she didn't act it, she merely sang it. But the thing is absurd, and the chorus, heavily and shabbily upholstered, is—to die. Here and there one or two of them, pretended mild surprise when Lily Pons went mad but most of them just waited till it was over—which is what I did—and then beat it.

P.S. I have been heavily social this week. Mrs. Harry Payne Whitney asked me in to hear her protégée, Miss Bannon, play, on Monday after-

2. On November 19, 1932, McBride wrote, "I am really petted a good deal, which makes me think that when I do die, I'll get a lot more out of it, if I manage to die here in New York. I felt that, too, when down in the country, for I have always been such a recluse down there, that I have practically no help from friends, and believe me when on your death bed it's a great help to see a lot of mourners weeping around. It distracts your attention from the main facts" (YCAL, McBride).

noon, and it turned out to be très intime. There were about twenty there, and most of them members of the family, including Count Széchenyi, "Sonny" Whitney, and my especial favorite, Flora Whitney.[1] The only arty person, besides myself, was Jo Davidson, for the Delanos have grown up with Mrs. Whitney and did not win her affection through architecture. Miss Bannon played very well, in the upstairs salon of the palais. I went home with the Delanos, to dine with them, and go to the first night of Eve le Galliene's *Alice in Wonderland*. In spite of the fact that the Delanos, from my point of view, are rich themselves, it is quite evident that they look with awe on Gertrude Whitney's position in the world and regard her invitations as royal commands. They are not themselves aware of this. It's not snobbery, it's just that "plus fort qui moi" respect that Americans have for power. I suspect on the other hand, that Gertrude herself would cut "society" absolutely, if she quite dared. She apparently yearns to have real relationships with people and seldom accomplishes it. [. . .]

To Malcolm MacAdam
December 27, 1932, Herald Square Hotel, New York

Dear Malc:

I had a fair Christmas—as Christmases go. [. . .] After the Dudensing dinner I went over to the Stettheimers', where Virgil Thomson was to sing some of his opera, composed to a long poem by Gertrude Stein. It was to die, of course: especially as Virgil had a cold and all his top notes cracked. He has had a row with Gertrude, and he sang also a satirical song, entitled "La Mystere de la rue de Fleurus," which was also to die. He says the Stein-Thomson opera really is to be given next year.[1] Then last night, the John Andersons asked me over to six o'clock dinner and Constance Collier and Glen Anders were there, too.[2] Dinner was at six, because we all had to be at our various theatres at eight. John and I were going to Walter Hampden's

---

1. Cornelius Vanderbilt ("Sonny") Whitney (1899–1992), Gertrude Vanderbilt Whitney's son. Count László Széchenyi (1879–1938), member of a distinguished Hungarian family, was a diplomat who married Gladys Moore Vanderbilt, daughter of Cornelius Vanderbilt. He was Hungarian minister to the United States, 1922–33, and to Great Britain, 1933–35.

1. In January 1931 Stein had excommunicated Thomson, and it was only *Four Saints* which renewed communication between them.

2. Constance Collier (née Hardie, 1880–1955), English actress; Glen Anders (b. 1879), actor who appeared in Orson Welles's *The Lady from Shanghai* and was well known for his role as Cyrano de Bergerac.

Cyrano. Walter Hampden really is, as Alex Woollcott said, a mere "Ham"; but the play itself is grand and almost fool-proof, so it wasn't such a bad evening. You would adore Constance Collier. Of course you do already. But she has that same death-bed voice in private life and you almost feel as though you ought to pay admission, just to see her sitting on the sofa. This time, however, I sat with her on the sofa. Glen Anders is nice, too. Remarkably handsome and very affectionate. Always putting his arms around people. Even I came in for a hug, when I said something that pleased him. But at dinner, there was a long stretch, that was very embarrassing for the hostess, Margot Anderson, for Margot knows I have false teeth and suddenly something started Constance Collier to telling stories of mishaps of English actors, with their false sets of teeth, and it went on and on, screamingly funny, all of us perishing with laughter, except poor Margot, who made frantic efforts to change the subject of conversation in order to spare my feelings, which, however, were not hurt in the least. I felt that Constance didn't know the half of it. [. . .]

To Malcolm MacAdam
January 22, 1933, Herald Square Hotel, New York

Dear Malc:

[. . .] Nothing momentous has occurred to me lately. I survived the cold which I shared in contagion with all the other New Yorkers, by staying in one week. For the first time in twenty years I didn't write my page. That Saturday night my phone rang eight or ten times, so that I began to feel quite like a public character. The afternoon I first ventured out, Royal Cortissoz called at the hotel for me, leaving a card with a corner bent, according to the old fashioned laws of etiquette, and saying "love and sympathy." It was nice of Royal, and when I went up next day to lunch at the Coffee House and confer with Frank Crowninshield about an article for *Vanity Fair,* I got what was for me an ovation. It's not that I am popular socially, for I'm not, but it was a case of esprit de corps. All the writing people have a peculiar interest in the doings of all the others, especially when there is a suggestion of "dropping out." Just the same, I enjoyed being petted. After saying yes, I would write an article for Frank, I thought it over and then said, No. I don't seem to be able to write for *Vanity Fair.* It's too fluffy for me. [. . .]

I have seen Lawrence Tibbett twice in *Emperor Jones*.[1] Lawrence is magnificent, but it is no opera. The composer was afraid to interfere with the play, and so he didn't. Once in a while you hear a little tinkle in the orchestra pit, but you pay no attention to it. Lawrence has to make up all over, as in the course of the play he loses all his clothes. We never saw, at the Opera, such a display of flesh before. Chaliapin once stripped to the waist for *Mephisto,* but Lawrence practically does the all together.[2] You never saw such an infinitesimal loin-cloth. It was rather sensational to see Lawrence taking the curtain calls in a state of nature. It seemed like Paris. However, Lawrence, you have to hand it to him, is as affective physically as he is vocally. Vocally, he is now the best male singer in the world. I forgot to say that Lawrence turns himself into a café au lait coon. I feel like writing him to tell him to go completely black. It would be more aesthetic. [. . .]

To Malcolm MacAdam
February 11, 1933, Herald Square Hotel, New York

Dear Malc:

I've just had a post-card from Carlo Van Vechten to say that my photos are "magnificent, in the Thomas Eakins tradition." I'll believe it when I see them. I explained to Carl that there were no photographs of me in existence, and for a good reason, because I was camera shy. I always blink or do something at the fatal moment. I went up to Carl's last week by appointment at 9 p.m. Was sandwiched in between appointments with Escudero, the Spanish dancer, and Pauline Lord, who was to come at 11 p.m. Carl had all sorts of contraptions. It was my idea of Hollywood, and I was so diverted by the various lights, etc., and Carl's remarks, that finally I was aware, that I was actually being natural. Carl caught on too and started to click the machine, but quick as he was I was still quicker—and stuck out my tongue. Carl was annoyed. However, he shot me about eight times in all, and in any case, the backgrounds ought to be good, for we were in Carl's picturesque

1. In 1930 the composer Louis Gruenberg began working on an operatic interpretation of Eugene O'Neill's 1921 play *The Emperor Jones.* O'Neill approved of Gruenberg's efforts as composer and librettist, and the opera opened at the Metropolitan in New York in January 1933. Lawrence Tibbett (1896–1960) played the title role in blackface.
2. Feodor Ivanovitch Chaliapin (or Shalyapin) (1873–1938), Russian-born operatic basso.

17 Henry McBride, February 1933. Carl Van Vechten.

library. . . But you must have seen that atrocity of me in *Creative Art* by this time. Elizabeth Cary's article was grand—but the photo was terrible.[1] [. . .]

I am sending you some of my recent art pages, including the one about the Whitney Museum, which raised a big row. Juliana Force was annoyed, and I am going down this afternoon to see if I can make up. She is in another scrape with Benton, who did some murals for her, and now says he wasn't paid enough and threatens to bring suit.[2] In such an event I am on her side. I have just been in court—testifying for Clag Wilson, who sued a rich lady, because she would not pay for murals painted to order for her tennis court. I merely testified, that the finished paintings were better then the sketches that she had accepted. Clag won the case—but I hope I don't have to testify again. It's harrowing—much more harrowing than your visit to Mei Lang Fen's theatre in Peking. [. . .]

P.S. Juliana and I "made up." We made up, but we don't agree. I still think a mistake was made in spending all that money for poorish pictures—and she insists it was justified.[3] [. . .] In the evening I joined her in Mrs. Whitney's box at the opera to hear the last *Emperor Jones* for this year. That made the fourth *Emperor Jones* for me. I get a great thrill out of Lawrence Tibbett's success. I love to see the house get petrified into silence as he sings the "Standing in the Need of Prayer," practically nude, and the full mechanic of his enormous lungs on display. His voice has become magnificent. It always was good—now it is the best man's voice in the world. [. . .]

To Gertrude Stein
February 17, 1933, *The Sun,* New York

Dear Gertrude:
    A young friend of mine, George Morris, asked for a letter of introduction to you, and so I gave it to him.[1] Doubtless he'll present it soon as he is eager

---

1. The photograph that illustrated Cary's December 1932 article was taken by Martin Voe.

2. "Thomas Benton's Murals at the Whitney Museum," *New York Sun,* December 10, 1932, reprinted in *Flow of Art,* pp. 295–97.

3. The first Biennial Exhibition of Contemporary American Paintings was held in 1932. Prizes were not awarded, but Force and Whitney set aside twenty thousand dollars to make purchases from the exhibition.

1. George L. K. Morris (1906–75), a wealthy patron of the arts and, briefly, a painter whose output became highly respected after his death.

to enroll himself among your disciples. . . . He is what you call a "fils de famille"—he has ancient lineage and, I believe, some money. He buys modern paintings occasionally from artists who sell but seldom—and he is a patron of Gaston Lachaise, whom we think our best sculptor. Be as nice to him as you can, though of course I know you are overrun with these petitioners for friendship.

You've probably been wondering about my long silence. I've been ill. It's mostly old age, for the doctors don't say definitely that it is anything else. But last spring I thought I was destined for an immediate ascension to the realms above, and went through several physical agonies, but in spite of all that I continue to write for the *Sun* on Saturdays. I gave up *Creative Art* last year, to my regret, for it was just getting to be something at last, and the right people were beginning to be willing to write for it. You've no idea what snobs writers are, and how afraid they are to be mixed up in the wrong circles—as though *Hamlet* were not *Hamlet* if printed in a newspaper—but probably you do know. Then, too, *Creative Art* began to be so slow in paying my unfortunate contributors. (Were you ever paid, par example?) And that was harassing. All the reviews are in desperate circumstances, and of those devoted to art, *Creative Art* is the only one left. But I couldn't cope with that situation, and am only writing for the *Sun* to beguile myself. I enclose something of last week about Muriel Draper's "America Deserta" which aroused a mild storm.[2] Like most things I write it is thought to be an "attack"—whereas really it was an act of friendship—to call attention to Muriel's book. But Muriel has not written a note of thanks!

Love to you and Alice.

To Malcolm MacAdam
February 28, 1933, Herald Square Hotel, New York

Dearest Malc:

Yesterday I had one of those particularly flattering days, that sometimes happen, and all the more surprising and pleasant, because preceded by three days of complete depression. [. . .] On Monday I was free enough from my cold to venture down to the Whitney Museum, to see a private view and talk shop with the other critics. Then began my flattering experi-

2. "America Deserta" was Muriel Draper's long abstract manuscript about the state of America in the Depression; not published in its entirety, the manuscript is in the Muriel Draper papers at the Beinecke Library.

ences already mentioned. Ralph Flint had telephoned to suggest lunch, after the private view, and then Albert Boni telephoned suggesting lunch with him. Albert frankly said the idea was to try to persuade me to do some things for *Creative Art,* that my leaving the magazine had been the greatest loss they had ever experienced, etc. etc., I mentioned my date with Ralph and Albert said, "bring him along"; so Ralph came in for all the flattering offers that Boni made to me. Of course, a compliment is doubly effective, when you know others hear it. . . Then we went to Mrs. Halpert's Gallery, and Mrs. H. told me that the great Albert Barnes of Philadelphia (millionaire art collector) has been in and had spoken most feelingly of me, and what a shame it was, that I was so badly paid by the newspapers, for which I had worked so long, etc., and had asked to be remembered to me.[1] This was a surprise, because I had always thought him my bitterest enemy. The last I had heard from him years ago when he threatened to come over from Philadelphia with a gang of roughs and have me horse-whipped for saying Glackens (one of his pet artists) was a poor imitator of Renoir. . .[2] Then in the next Gallery the dealer, still with Ralph listening in, implored me to consider writing an article about John Kane, of Pittsburgh.[3] When I got home, the phone rang, and John Urban wanted me to speak for ten minutes over the radio on the subject of his work at the Architectural League. I refused with thanks, and then the phone rang again, and Mrs. Walton Martin suggested dinner next Sunday and a musicale after at the Coffee House Club; and added that she had seen Clarence Day, author of *God and My Father,* and told him of my admiration for the book, and had arranged to take me to see him some day soon. Altogether quite a day, don't you think? Especially for an invalid.

[. . .] I've been photographed again. This time by Pierre Matisse.[4] He took me to the Metropolitan Museum and I posed before Greek statues, Egyptian vases and modern French pictures. Only one of Carl Van Vechten's turned out to be good. I'll send you it.

1. Edith Gregor Halpert founded the influential Downtown Gallery in 1926, where she showed Stuart Davis, Alexander Brook, Yasuo Kuniyoshi, Charles Sheeler, and William Zorach, among others who got their start at the Whitney Studio.
2. "And the clever Mr. Glackens, who paints so like Renoir that he will be regarded as a mere trouble maker for Renoir enthusiasts fifty years hence." "The Growth of Cubism," *New York Sun,* February 8, 1914, reprinted in *Flow of Art,* p. 55.
3. McBride did write "John Kane's Memorial Exhibition," a review in the *New York Sun,* February 2, 1935, reprinted in *Flow of Art.*
4. See Biographical Sketches.

18 Henry McBride at the Metropolitan Museum, February 1933. Pierre Matisse.

To Malcolm MacAdam
March 26, 1933, *The Sun*, New York

Dear Malc:

I got through the "historic week," as the newspapers call it, as composedly as the lady whose diary Dorothy Parker gives us in this week's *New Yorker*. I had $30.—in my pocket, that morning that we read in the newspapers, that the banks had closed indefinitely and I had dinner invitations for most of the nights, so I had nothing to pay for, except for an occasional lunch and when the banks did re-open, I had most of my wad intact.[1] So that was that. But the way people went on—and the way the newspapers went on, was a caution. It gave it pretty definitely away that our beloved countrymen know nothing but money, and, when you take money away from them, you have nothing left. Since the banks have reopened Roosevelt has become a God. I have never seen anything like it, for though certain European nations did look on Wilson for a time as a God, the home folk didn't by any means. This time, it's unanimous. As I'm more suspicious of Gods than of plain human beings, I'm afraid our hero is due for a tumble. To do him justice, Roosevelt, himself, seems confident and unafraid.

1. Franklin Delano Roosevelt was sworn in as president in March 1933 and one of his first acts was to call a weeklong "bank holiday" to prevent panic withdrawals. Roosevelt's action restored confidence in the banking system.

[. . .] I had a letter from Gertrude Stein the other day and she was very cheerful and told me to keep an eye on the *Atlantic Monthly*. The same night at Mrs. Finley Thomas', there was a lady from Boston who told me that the editor of the *Atlantic Monthly* had accepted *An Autobiography of Alice Toklas* and was so enchanted by it, that he sat up all night reading it. There was the insinuation, however, that Gertrude had really written it.[2] [. . .]

The sensation of the winter, though, is, Mabel Dodge's new book, *Intimate Memories*. Lord, what a book that is. Mabel tells everything; but only up to her 18th year. I should think it would completely up-end Buffalo, where her early years were passed. Dare I send it to you, I wonder? It would completely disillusion you. I must confess, it even told me things about servant girls, I never knew before. Perhaps I'll send it to you for your birthday, and perhaps, with all this warning, you won't be shocked.

We've just had another 10% cut on *The Sun*. My pittance is now down so low it can scarcely be cut again, not with the naked eye at least. Even so, I don't economize at all, and take taxis with greater frequency than I did ever before. There seems to be no sense in saving money to have it diminish in value constantly. [. . .]

To Malcolm MacAdam
April 14, 1933, Herald Square Hotel, New York

Dear Malc:

I am so far behind in my personal news, that I hesitate to begin. Probably because it is trifling, anyhow. I suppose you'll be interested in the fact that I dined with your friend Nelson Rockefeller last week.[1] As you say, he's

2. *The Autobiography of Alice B. Toklas* was serialized in the *Atlantic* for four months, beginning in May 1933, prior to publication the same year by Harcourt Brace. The book proved to be Stein's first financial success. In addition to buying a new eight-cylinder Ford, she also bought her poodle Basket a custom-made coat from Hermès, as well as two new studded collars from the proceeds.

1. In May 1933 Nelson Rockefeller (1908–79) entered the fray of politics and modern art. As director of Rockefeller Center he commissioned Diego Rivera to paint murals. In addition to a portrait of Nelson's father, John D. Rockefeller, in the painting called *Man at the Crossroads*, Rivera included a likeness of V. I. Lenin, which Rockefeller asked to have removed. In a letter to the *New York Times*, Rivera declined the request, stating in part, "I am sure that the class of people who is capable of being offended by the portrait of a deceased great man would feel offended . . . by the entire conception of my painting" (May 6, 1933). Rockefeller canceled the proj-

quite nice; unspoiled, simple, good-looking and intelligent. I mentioned you and he smiled and murmured something complimentary. The dinner was at the house of young Mr. Matthews, a friend of the Rockefellers, and concerned a new building in Radio City, to be devoted to the arts, and Juliana Force, Robert MacBeth and Mrs. Halpert and I were asked for our opinions.[2] We were also put upon the advisory committee for the enterprise. Radio City, of course, is one of the things that will make you blink on your return, for in addition to being stupendously ugly, it is stupendously big and—most people think—stupendously unpractical. People wonder how the clever John D. Rockefeller ever got inveigled into it, and pessimists say it may even wreck his vast fortune eventually. In the meantime people crowd into the Radio City Music Hall and it is difficult to get a seat for "Cavalcade." I told you, I think, that a scientific economist, that I met at dinner somewhere, said the wisest thing to do would be to scrap immediately the enormous Radio City building, although it is not finished yet and there are fourteen millions in mortgages on it. Such is the sort of wild talk you hear these days.

The panic of the week, however, has been over Bernard Shaw.[3] Tired as I have been of him for these dozen years past, he never the less seems so much more clever than the stupid newspaper commentators that I almost incline to take him on again. His speech, I thought, was quite good; better at least, than any speech by anyone else this winter. I thought it good only from his point of view, however, for I exactly disagree with his premises. I think that democracy is not a failure, but an extraordinary success and I think capitalism is far from being a failure, though it is having a bad quarter of an hour. These reformers think a perfect state is possible, which makes me think they don't understand humanity. I won't write you an essay—I charge for those—but I'll venture the thought, that even with millions of unemployed in this country, the proportion of people who are reasonably comfortable is greater then in any other country in any period of the world's history. We are horrified, because we have a few poor people

---

ect and eventually destroyed the work of art. In the *Sun* on May 13, 1933, McBride suggested in an article called "Diego Rivera and The Radio City Scandal" that the first error was in selecting Rivera for the commission and the second was in suppressing the murals.

2. Robert MacBeth owned a gallery at 450 Fifth Avenue that specialized in modern American painting and sponsored the first show of The Eight in 1908.

3. In the early 1930s Shaw spent time in the Soviet Union and wrote and spoke extensively about his firsthand experience of the communist system.

with us—but when, except during the short time of unnatural inflation, have we not had poor people with us? But George said his say discreetly, and rather stylishly. Of course he didn't say anything to me, particularly. George specializes in teaching the totally uneducated, and the "masses" all rose to him, as usual.

My Jewish friends are up in the air, naturally, about Hitler. It does seem a foolish move on the part of the Germans. None of us get it. There is extraordinary unity in condemning them, just as in the war days. One can understand their hysteria over the injustice of the Versailles treaty—but this sort of thing is like running amuck, only possible to desperadoes, who want to commit suicide anyhow. Albert Boni says the other European governments are only waiting for an excuse to sail in and dismember Germany completely. And that is a sad outlook. . . At the same time we have our jokes. Our crowd was amused to hear the other day that Katherine Dreier has announced herself a Hitlerite. This is sure to lead to comedy. [. . .]

To Malcolm MacAdam
May 7, 1933, Herald Square Hotel, New York

Dear Malc:
   [. . .] Everybody talks finance incessantly and of course, ignorantly. What do we know about it? Yet we go on talking. Several things are fairly clear; such as, that people like myself and yourself, who have economized for old age, are not going to profit much with our savings. The deflation appears to help business men and penalizes people who live on incomes. But can you do anything about it? But I practice what I preach to you, and do not worry. I ignore finance as much as possible, just as I ignore the mutilations the dentist did to my mouth last summer (I have never yet looked at the alterations in the mirror). I used to, like you, take a mild pleasure on January 1st in totting up my funds and noting down the increase but this year, I never bothered to figure it out, and when March 15 came around and I had to file some sort of an income report, I was embarrassed, and hastily ran around to the banks and got the totals regulated and then made my pitiful confession to the government. But it really sounds too sad as I tell it. Really and truly, I don't seem to give a hang. In the meantime, tales of woe come in every direction, and there is no sign of a rainbow. The country now realizes, what inside people knew last year— that the country is practically bankrupt. This doesn't imply that capitalism is a failure, to my mind. It suggests rather that the country has not been

run on a business basis. We appear to be taking on the entire cost of the European war, and I look on the "conversations" with European statesmen with cynicism, for as in the past, if we have anything to do with Europe at all, we pay. They are too cute for us. If Roosevelt puts over anything on the French, then he really will be the smart man that the populace thinks him. At present, he is rated higher than George Washington. I rather like him myself—but my own little dream, is to put up the bars, keep everyone away, make this a hermit nation—and live on the stuff we produce. To my amazement, I read in the *Tribune* this morning a headline saying some deep European thinker had declared "all foreign commerce to be obsolete." But what nonsense this chatter is. However, it's a sample of what you hear everywhere.

I sent you Gertrude's *Autobiography* in the *Atlantic*. Yesterday I got a cheerful note from her, on swell new stationary, saying she has a new car, and a new valet de chambre on the strength of it, and asking me to come over and see both. She also hinted I'm mentioned in the *Autobiography*. She didn't say whether you were or not. Perhaps the tea episode got edited out. The strong language you used made it unfit for the general reader. [. . .]

To Malcolm MacAdam
May 26, 1933, Herald Square Hotel, New York

Dear Malc:

[. . .] Henri Matisse was here this week, and I felt flattered to be asked by his son Pierre to lunch with him and papa.[1] We fed at the L'Aiglon and Matisse asked me why one only saw ladies in American restaurants. I didn't know how to answer him, but finally said, I thought men lunched at their clubs. Afterward I decided I should have said at lunch-counters. It was a severe ordeal as Matisse speaks no English, but on the other hand he is the type of Frenchman, who understands my kind of French. I was further flattered to get from him yesterday a deluxe volume of his drawings, with an affectionate "dedicace" on the fly-leaf, and a note as well.[2] I had to write my thanks in French, too, which I did tremblingly. At my request, Matisse

1. Matisse sailed from New York for Nice on May 25, after arriving in New York on May 11. On the trip he transported his long awaited mural *The Dance* to the Barnes Collection. The mural was installed in Merion on May 15.
2. Probably the Albert Skira publication *Poésies de Stéphane Mallarmé*, for which Matisse prepared twenty-nine etchings. Published in October 1932, it was Matisse's first illustrated book.

submitted to being photographed by Carl Van Vechten and Carl is much indebted to me. I send you one he took of me. Remember, it is not a common photograph. It is a Carl Van Vechten. I'm also sending the second installment of Gertrude's memoirs in the Atlantic. I had a note from her some time ago in which she said I was mentioned in it somewhere. Carl scared me, by saying in a letter to him she had said: "Tell Henry not to worry. He will get his tea." What on earth do you suppose she meant by that? Do you suppose—but I refuse to suppose. [. . .]

Did you hear the story of Straus, president of R. H. Macy's, who is ambassador of France? They say he said, on arrival: "Galerie Lafayette we are here," and the French, who were much touched by this, replied: "Macy beaucoup." [. . .]

To Mabel Luhan
June 8, 1933, Callicaste

Dear Mabel Luhan:

Just because I made some light and frivolous remarks about *Intimate Memories* in my Academy review in the N.Y. *Sun* (I am invariably frivolous in my Academy reviews), I think I ought to tell you that I am far from regarding *Intimate Memories* as a light contribution to modern knowledge.[1] On the contrary, I think you've immortalized yourself. No one, it seems to me, who once reads it, will ever forget certain stabbingly clear episodes in it, nor, for that matter the sure progress of the picture as a whole. I was, I must confess, surprised. Even after *Lorenzo in Taos* I was surprised.[2] *Lorenzo* will live too, but I thought that might have been written under propulsion from Lawrence. No one can say that of the *Memories*. They are undeniably, and all over, you.

So I write to say Hail and Farewell. When my friends become too famous I have to say Good-bye. Being destined to permanent obscurity myself, I blink and feel ill at ease in the presence of those who blaze with a great

1. McBride had read a draft manuscript of the third volume of Luhan's memoir, which Harcourt, Brace published in 1936 as *Movers and Shakers*. The preceding volumes were *Intimate Mémoires* and *European Experiences* (both 1933). *Movers and Shakers* presents one of the fullest and most vivid pictures of New York (and especially Greenwich Village bohemia) from 1913 to 1917. *Edge of the Taos Desert* was published in book form by Harcourt Brace in 1937.
2. Mabel Dodge Luhan helped support the English novelist D. H. Lawrence (1885–1930) during the three years he spent in Taos. Her first published book, *Lorenzo in Taos* (Knopf, 1932), was about Lawrence.

light. And what a light you have ignited down there in Taos! Really I don't think so many good books have come out of such a small place since the Lake Poets hovered around Wordsworth at Grasmere. . . I have just finished Brett's and that, of course, will not be the last.[3] Witter Bynner surely, will do one, and "Spud" and Clarence, when he becomes an old man will probably recollect a few things, too. . .[4] I will read them all. . . Brett surprised me even more than you did for after all, I expected something from you. . . But Brett! Hers is the perfect "Curate and Spinster" episode for all time. And how extraordinarily she vindicates you and Frieda. You must know, of course, that certain of the English blamed you for "using" Lawrence, and in the Huxley Letters that was an evident wish to suppress you—but Brett herself is English and makes it only too plain that she was responsible for at least 60% of Lawrence's spiritual difficulties in Taos. She was so insufferably self-sacrificial and at the same time so incapable of the supreme sacrifice of going away and leaving the Lawrences to fight their little fights in peace. She had to be told to go. I wonder Frieda didn't massacre her. . . With it all, Lawrence is very clear in her book, too.

I am become aged and infirm and am not long for this world but I have enjoyed all my life so far and particularly your recent contributions to it—so merci beaucoup [. . .]

To Mabel Luhan
June 28, 1933, Callicaste, Marshallton, Pennsylvania

Dear Mabel Luhan:
You get better and better. Each volume improves upon the one before it. There is no padding to it, nothing to be discarded. The remarkable part is that the backgrounds and the lesser personages (such as Drs. Brill, Jelliffe and Bernhard, Isadora and Johnny the chauffeur) are as vital and indispensable as the hero and heroine—you and Maurice.[1] It seems to me that

3. Lady Dorothy Eugenie Brett, friend of Katherine Mansfield, D. H. Lawrence, and Mabel Dodge Luhan. Daughter of the Second Viscount Escher Brett, Brett studied art at the Slade School in London and associated with the Bloomsbury group, settling in New Mexico after 1925. Her book, *Lawrence and Brett: A Friendship,* was published by Lippincott in 1933.
4. Witter Bynner, a wealthy dramatist, poet, and translator of Chinese, lived in Taos, as did his lover Willard "Spud" Johnson, who worked as Mabel's assistant, and started a local literary magazine called *Laughing Horse.*
1. A. A. Brill, Smith Ely Jelliffe, and Bernard Sachs were early psychoanalysts in New

you have cooked the old-fashioned type of romance permanently. Henceforth we will have the Vol. 4 type of romance or do without—for, somehow, I think it a romance rather than autobiography. I began reading with empressement the very first page and never had a dull moment anywhere—which is more than I can say for the novels of your great god D.H.L. D.H.L. never finished anything satisfactorily to me. In spite of all his vividness and undeniable genius he never solved the puzzles he propounded. You do.

What a pity it cannot be published instantly. Eventually it must be. I was not in the least bothered by your celebrated frankness; was, in fact, scarcely aware of it. If I can pass unscathed through the fires as Ralph and Carl and all the others have, who have read it, why cannot it be safe reading for all the rest of the fairly educated public? As to Maurice, it cannot hurt his feelings. In fact, he'll feel vastly flattered to find himself such a Don Juan. Didn't you really flatter Maurice just a teeny bit in order to justify yourself in the eyes of your lady friends? Your lady friends may understand the psychology of your final descent into marriage but none of your men readers will. If *I* had been writing the novel I think I should have based your qualms upon fears of what John and Bobby might have thought—and discarded the unimportant Agnes Pelton completely.[2] However, your version is, of course, more like life. The compelling motives really come from inside and frequently just a breath stirs to action.

Your Maurice is to the life. I see him in your book just as I saw him in the flesh—furtive glances, agonized mouth et al—though I am surprised you found him handsome. He always looked to be anticipating the tragedy that has now come upon him—for the world, at last, has found out that he is not an artist.

York, and each worked as Luhan's therapist. Brill was a prominent early psychoanalyst, and when he spoke at Mabel Dodge's Evening in 1913, he introduced to Greenwich Village many of the ideas of psychoanalysis, then known as Freudism. Jelliffe was Dodge's psychoanalyst around 1916 and 1917. Sachs was a neurologist Dodge consulted in 1912. Isadora Duncan was the pioneering dancer who espoused freedom of movement, and Johnny was Dodge's chauffeur.

The artist Maurice Sterne (1878–1957) began a romantic relationship with Mabel Dodge in 1915, married her in 1917; they separated a year later and divorced in 1922.

2. Agnes Pelton (1881–1961), American painter. John Reed (1887–1920), the author of *Ten Days that Shook the World,* was Mabel Dodge's lover from 1913 to 1914. Robert Edmond Jones (1887–1954) was an innovative set designer and a close friend of Mabel Dodge's.

I pray the Lord I may be permitted to see the other volumes. As I said before, I am spoiled for other reading. Thank Ralph for his good offices in regard to this one; and of course, thank yourself mille fois. [. . .]

To Alfred Stieglitz
July 21, 1933, Callicaste

Dear Alfred:

[. . .] It's not the news of the London Conference that keeps me going, so much as the tennis news from that city. I enjoyed the Wimbledon tournament so much that even at this late date I actually think of writing a tennis article to tell some of those boys where to get off. The London Conference, Walter Lippmann says, was a failure—but at any rate it showed up France, and that I think was the actual object. What a funny job Lippmann has created for himself![1] And how seldom he permits himself to be frank, although frankness is his avowed specialty! The fact is, of course, that diplomacy cannot be frank. The moment it becomes frank it ceases to be diplomacy. The most encouraging point in *our* diplomacy is that at least we are being resolute to Europe: although the college men who help Roosevelt do bow the knee too much to Keynes and the other British economists. Why we should always be such wax in the hands of the English I cannot quite see. We need an American Nietszche to teach us to be "hard."

Everything that you and others tell me about Georgia indicate nerves—and for nerves there is nothing but rest and mild distraction.[2] Nerves, though, are not immediately fatal. If you read the life of Carlyle you'll find these prostrations occurring early, and then plenty of recoveries for more work—and then ultimately a long life. It seems to be these brokers and bankers who refuse to rest, that snap completely. I saw Matisse and in fact lunched pleasantly with him and Pierre. He looks amazingly well. He sent me a handsome volume of drawings and since his return to Nice I've had a pleasant message from him. He is quite confident of the success of the

1. Walter Lippmann (1889–1974), an economic and foreign policy expert, adviser to presidents, and writer of a syndicated column in which he denounced Roosevelt's New Deal.
2. O'Keeffe suffered a nervous breakdown in the fall of 1932 and stopped painting for a year in the wake of crises both professional and personal. Professionally O'Keeffe found herself under fire because Stieglitz disapproved of her participation in a mural exhibition project curated by Lincoln Kirstein at the Museum of Modern Art. Personally, Stieglitz's affair with his assistant Dorothy Norman had a severe effect on O'Keeffe's confidence and mental well-being.

Barnes decorations! Carl Van Vechten photographed Matisse and did it well. Matisse, by the way, was furious at Gertrude Stein's revelations in the *Atlantic*. He says it is mauvais goût.[3] But people read it in spite of that. The great American public is not wholly averse to mauvais goût—as you may have discovered. . . Write me again. Il me faut les distractions! And give my very best to Georgia.

To Carl Van Vechten
September 11, 1933, Callicaste

Dear Carl:
THEY SAY you have to join in a class and listen to lectures by Mr. Barnes and one of his lady assistants before you are allowed to see the pictures. Otherwise, of course, you wouldn't understand them. . . They say it's terrible; worse than all the tests the unfortunate singers of *The Magic Flute* have to undergo! But they also say that Dr. Barnes intends to relent for one moment in order to let the riff-raff of critics see the Matisse decor. Perhaps in that case you could demean yourself as a critic and go along. . . I am not in Dr. Barnes' favor. Indeed he once expressed himself as desirous of having me horse whipped.[1] The only person I recall who was in favor, at last accounts, was Dorothy Brett, but that was sometime ago and no one stays in favor long at a time. It is all very hazardous and uncertain. If I hear of anything propitious I'll let you know.

I have not yet seen the *Autobiography;* or only that part that appeared in the *Atlantic*. I have sent on for a copy and await it impatiently. The reviews are swell. I half begrudge handing Gertrude over to the general public in this fashion but as Louis Bromfield says, Gertrude herself has always wished to sample all the various kinds of success. I want to see your *Three*

3. *Mauvais goût*, in bad taste. Writing about *The Autobiography of Alice B. Toklas*, Matisse contributed to "Testimony Against Gertrude Stein," a special 1935 issue of *Transition*.

1. "When the memorial show to William Glackens occurred at the Whitney Museum I gave an adverse report of it in the *New York Sun*. . . . The group of painters most closely united to the Whitney Museum, all of whom adored Glackens, for it seems he really was an adorable person, decided not to like me for a while and, furthermore, the news came to me, from that source, that the great Dr. Barnes of Philadelphia was also much annoyed. The specific message said that he was actually preparing two heavyweight boxers (one would have been enough) to come over to New York to give me a horse-whipping." "Dr. Barnes R.I.P.," reprinted in *Flow of Art*, pp. 433–38.

Lives instantly, so if it comes out before Oct. 5 (when I come up to town) do please send it down here.[2]

The pineapples were delicious—cooked!

Your greatly indebted

To Gertrude Stein
October 27, 1933, Herald Square Hotel, New York

Dearest Gertrude:

I suppose you thought me dead! I almost had the thought myself last summer and for that reason delayed writing. I wasn't quite sure that you cared for death-bed letters! But the country-side, where I live in summer is so remote and peaceful and slow that time itself is almost destroyed and so the death-bed scene got to be quite as interminable as King Charles', and à la fin, and slightly bored by ineffectual invalidism, I came up to town and started to work. . . Everyone now tells me I look wonderfully and when I attempt to detail a few of my symptoms I only get amused listeners. . . So I've quit dying, for the moment.

The autumn is no time to die, in America, anyway. The country is un-believably beautiful. Thanks to the very rainy summer the leaves on the trees are still green and intact and only here and there do you get a bit of red to suggest that eventually the winter may come. Usually by the time I come up to New York things are bleak and bare. So we still had the flowers in the garden, and though they had had so little attention that they were almost on the status of weeds, they never-the-less made swell bouquets. Those last weeks of summer in Pennsylvania are always the best of my vacance, and thinking to squeeze still another one from the lap of Fate, I thought I could make my first *Sun* page out of gleanings from your *Auto-biography,* and do it down there. But would you believe it, the bright young publicity agent for Harcourt Brace refused me a copy, saying they already had had a review of the book in the *Sun,* and apparently didn't care for another. . . By the time I finally secured the book, I had to be in New York, and I actually wrote something about it and you before I found time to read it. Isn't that American journalism for you? But it explains the thinness of my article.

It was apparent, with the very first chapter in the *Atlantic* that the book

2. *Three Lives* was republished by Random House, with an introduction by Van Vechten.

was doomed to be a best seller.[1] (Doomed, is my word for it, not yours. I don't like giving you up to the general public and sharing you and Alice with about a million others). The most unlikely people came to me with praises on their lips, such as Mr. Everett, the book-selling dealer in Early Americana, who rather wanted to secure the rights. An individual not so highly pleased however, was the great Henri Matisse, with whom I lunched about that time. His son Pierre had translated the story of the omelette to him and he didn't like it at all. He told me a long tale of refutation, which I didn't rightly understand, for it didn't seem to refute. He has become, or perhaps always was highly conventional and does not indulge in humor. I tried to tell him that the recital of your frank and jovial relationship to artists would be a bonne réclame in America, but he shuddered. He would prefer, it seems, to be spoken of sepulchrally, as though he were Poussin and you were Bossuet.[2] Well, there are all sorts of ways of taking the world, and all sorts of attitudes towards fame.

I flew down to Pittsburgh to see the International and flew back; liking the air voyage more than the show. I'll send you my account of it, and perhaps you can induce some Frenchman to read my animadversions against the French section. It's silly of the French to permit themselves to be so mis-handled at Pittsburgh and about time they wake up to the opportunities they have there.

Love to you and Alice,

P.S. When I finally did the read the book I thought it too short. I had the same feeling that I have so often when walking down the Boulevard Raspail after an evening in the rue de Fleurus—that we had not threshed half the wheat I had intended.

1. The first printing of *The Autobiography of Alice B. Toklas* sold out nine days before publication and quickly ran through four printings. The Literary Guild offered the book as one of its selections, it appeared on the best-seller lists, and was featured on the cover of *Time* magazine. Stein received $8,495 in American royalties alone.
2. Nicolas Poussin (c. 1593–1665), French painter and draftsman who spent many years in Italy and was the primary formulator of the French classical tradition. The influence of the Venetian masters of the sixteenth century is pronounced in his late style. Jacques-Bénigne Bossuet (1627–1704), bishop, orator, and author who defended the rights of the French church against the Pope and the influence of Rome.

MCBRIDE AND *FOUR SAINTS IN THREE ACTS*

The series of articles for which McBride probably received the most attention was not art criticism but articles about the opera *Four Saints in Three
Acts*. Progress on this epochal work can be followed in McBride's letters, beginning with his first hearing it in 1929, sung by Virgil Thomson at a Stettheimer party, and culminating in its 1934 production at the Wadsworth
Atheneum in Hartford, Connecticut. Gertrude Stein wrote the libretto in
1927, and Virgil Thomson set her words to music in 1927–28. Florine Stettheimer designed its fantastic sets and costumes, John Houseman made his
debut as theater director, and Frederick Ashton sailed from London to choreograph dancers whom he recruited from Harlem's Savoy Ballroom. The
all-black cast of singers, a first, was selected from Harlem church choirs and
vaudeville. Chick Austin, director of the Wadsworth Atheneum, produced
the opera to christen the first architecturally modern wing in an American
museum on February 8, 1934. Twelve nights later it moved to Broadway,
where its six-week run made it the longest-running opera on Broadway. (Its
record was broken the following year by *Porgy and Bess*.) The opera became a
touchstone for a generation, a triumph of the avant-garde in both the
popular culture represented by Broadway and the institutional culture represented by the Wadsworth Atheneum, America's oldest public museum.

McBride's invaluable perspective on the preparation of *Four Saints in
Three Acts* reflected his closeness to several key participants, especially Stein
and Stettheimer. The opera received more press attention than any cultural
event of the previous decade, but it was McBride who wrote about it at the
greatest length and with more inside knowledge than any other critic.

To Malcolm MacAdam
January 12, 1934, *Creative Art,* New York

Dearest Malc:

[. . .] Then the Stettheimers gave a wonderful party. You must know "our
set" is all agog about the Gertrude Stein–Virgil Thomson opera which is to

be done at Hartford on February 8th, and as Florine is deeply involved (Doing the sets and costumes) she had all the opera people except the cast (I'll explain that later) at the party. We talked of nothing but the opera, but Virgil himself is so wrecked by the arduousness of the enterprise that he is practically speechless, and in ordinary times he is anything but. In fact he is famous for speed in conversation, as well as for Music. The cast is composed of Negroes who, I believe, are to wear white faces. They were chosen for the natural beauty of their voices, Gertrude's words being so wonderful that every care is being taken to have them pronounced exquisitely. But Florine had been to a rehearsal and she was slightly aghast at their looks. She whispered to me; "I wondered what they'd look like in my costumes." But the ex-Duchesse de Clermont-Tonnerre, who has seen Florine's models for the sets, says they are wonderful, and she ought to know as she has had great experiences in Paris. I met the ex-Duchesse at Muriel Draper's New Year's Eve Party.[1] I had never been to Muriel's before although, as you know, I adore Muriel. But I never had had the courage. This year, somehow, I went. The house is extraordinary. You know Muriel lacks funds and gets along on nothing at all. The house is almost in a state of ruin, and whilst I was chatting with the ex-Duchesse de Clermont-Tonnerre something hit me on the shoulder and I looked up to see several great yawning holes in the ceiling. It was a bit of the plaster that had hit me. The condition of the ceiling seemed quite menacing, so I left the ex-Duchesse to her fate and joined Blanche Yurka over in a corner, where the walls seemed more secure. Blanche was in great form and we had an amusing talk but I never thought to ask her about the Reynolds murder. I suppose I shall have to take Blanche to lunch someday if I am ever to get the facts of the affair.

At Philip Johnson's for tea, yesterday, I met your friends the Nelson Rockefellers.[2] Young Nelson is really a nice lad. We appear to be getting acquainted. They are giving a midnight party next week at the Modern Museum for the Theatre exhibition—and it probably will be fun.[3]

1. Muriel Draper was traditionally "at home after eleven" on New Year's Eve, and a large and distinguished international crowd appeared; her gatherings were the essence of high bohemia.
2. Philip Cortelyou Johnson (b. 1906) did not become an architect until the 1940s, but he had already made an impact through the exhibition of modern architecture he organized with Henry-Russell Hitchcock, which opened at the Museum of Modern Art on February 9, 1932. Nelson Rockefeller became associated with Philip Johnson because they were both members of the museum's Junior Advisory Council; Nelson's mother Abigail Rockefeller had been the key organizer of the museum.
3. "Interaction: Exhibition of Theater Art."

To Malcolm MacAdam
February 2, 1934, Herald Square Hotel, New York

Dearest Malc:

Your steamer letter from Aden, Jan 1, reached me Feb 1—one month in transit. Apparently, in India, you are going to be far away. . . Seeing me with letters in my hand, Grant said, though the car was full of passengers, "Had any letters from dat gemman yet?" and when I answered, "Here is one now," Grant replied, "When you write to him give him my kindest regards," and all the passengers stared solemnly, as Americans always do, when brought face to face with mystery.

[. . .] What have I been doing that would amuse you? I went to the Ballet Russe and liked it for one thing. I went standee, and then got ashamed as the standee place was conspicuous, and sauntered out into the lobby to bump into John Becker and his little cousin Benjamin Ehrich, age 7, who was seeing his first ballet.[1] John was horrified to learn I had no seat and insisted I should take his for one ballet at least, and in spite of protests it ended in my doing so; and in fact it ended in my sitting for the entire evening, since John and Aaron Copland (the composer) knew the management and had seats ad lib. It was fun sitting with little Benjamin, and still more fun later on, going back stage to call on Baronova, the ballerina. She is only 16 and closely chaperoned by her mama. Louis Galantière, the playwright, whom I met at the Stettheimers' and like quite well, pounced on her the moment she appeared and said, "Voulez-vous sortir avec nous, mademoiselle—pour prendre quelque chose?" and as mademoiselle knew very well she shouldn't do that, she said, "No, Monsieur" and turned her back on him and conversed with little Benjamin, John and me. Louis Galantière, whom I never thought of as especially Jewish, instantly became Jewish, and stood back of us all the time we talked, biting his thumb, and looking frustrated and like a villain.[2]

I went back stage again on Tuesday night to call on Horowitz, the pian-

1. Educated at Andover and Harvard, John Becker exhibited photography and modern painting at his gallery at 520 Madison Avenue from 1929 to 1933.
2. McBride's anti-Semitic comments reflect the growing threat he perceived from political and economic changes in the world during the 1930s and 1940s. Anti-Semitic comments became more frequent and virulent over the course of the period from the Depression to World War II. McBride reacts strongly against the rise in popularity of communism and socialism after the Depression, particularly among his social circle. An increasingly staunch conservative, McBride dismissed both political positions as dangerous and naive. As World War II approached, McBride's anti-Semitic feelings also reflected his lifelong pro-German sympathies.

ist.[3] It happened this way. I went alone to the concert, dressed shabbily, sat in the balcony and hoped to escape observation. Would you believe it, when I stood up for the intermission, who should I find, two rows behind me, but Louie Delano and Mrs. Harry Payne Whitney. I said, "Are you hiding up here?" and Louie Delano said, "We are not. She is my guest, and I couldn't afford the expensive seats downstairs, and we like it very much up here." The poor things had walked up, too, not knowing there was a lift at Carnegie. The concert was swell, naturally, and afterwards, Louie dragged us backstage to call on the genius, and after that, Mrs. Whitney drove us each home in her magnifique Rolls-Royce.

There was a tea party next day at the Whitney palazzo, and so we all met again. Only twenty people; I begin to like Mrs. Whitney more and more. My presence at her parties has nothing to do with my criticisms, since I have been giving bad ones to the Whitney Museum of late.

Next week we go to Hartford for the world premiere of the Gertrude Stein, Florine Stettheimer, Virgil Thomson opera. We've been having fits of excitement for a month past, as you can imagine. I dined at the Stetts' last night, supposedly with the Gaston Lachaises but Lachaise had a cold and did not come. Instead we had Georgia O'Keeffe and Ralph Flint.[4] Carl Van Vechten, Fania and Florine and I had visited the Lachaise studio Sunday afternoon, and it seems Fania was shocked at what she saw. Her vivid description of Lachaise's new effort, *La Creation,* completely upset a dinner party they had all attended the night before.[5] In fact, I think *La Creation* would upset you, too, so I think I had better say no more about it. When I tried to justify Lachaise a little bit last night, Ettie looked at me, much impressed against her will, and said, "You are wonderful."

[. . .] I wore my new smoking last night for the first time. I got $125.—for testifying in the Claggett Wilson law suit and blew it all in at Brooks for the new smoking, which I urgently needed.

To Malcolm MacAdam
February 16, 1934, Herald Square Hotel, New York

Dearest Malc:

We are still so dizzy from Gertrude's and Virgil's and Florine's opera, that we cannot think straight. I had the most difficult time yesterday getting

---

3. Vladimir Horowitz (1904–89) fled the Soviet Union in 1925 and debuted in the United States with the New York Philharmonic in 1928.
4. A Stieglitz protégé, Ralph Flint was a critic for *Artnews.*
5. Lachaise's most explicit of his explicit work, *La Creation* was a sculptural exploration of the female genitalia.

my page done ever. In spite of the fact that I had occasion to review a new heroic statue of Babe Ruth I could scarcely concentrate on the theme. I went into Julien Levy's gallery two days ago and Julien almost hugged me he was so glad to see me and he said he found he didn't care to talk anymore except to those who had seen the opera at Hartford.[1] And we're all that way about it (say what you like in rebuttal). Cecil Beaton gave a cocktail-tea in his gorgeous suite on the 40th floor of the Waldorf and I went too early. I went at 5:45. One shouldn't really go until an hour later to be in good form, but anyway I blundered and found Cecil seated at a tea-table with five of the most gilt-edged youths I have ever laid eyes on. They were excessively superior and two of them had Oxford accents. But Cecil instantly asked me about the opera and my modest and restrained and unexaggerated account of what I had seen and heard, reduced the Oxford accents to nothingness. As we say in America—"I put it all over them." Promptly at 6:45 le monde arrived—and quelle monde! Cecil only knows sensational people, or at least only has sensational people at his parties. Everybody makes a point of sitting, so that they may see the entrances and the old-timers make a point of making entrances. There was the usual percentage of cinema celebrities. I was slightly shocked at Edmund Lowe's salt-and-pepper hair. I had thought him young and vigorous. And he has three chins! And Maxine Elliot.[2] Mon dieu! Could you believe it, if I told you, that she tips the beam at about 300 lbs? Nevertheless we had a most amusing talk—slamming Mrs. Pat Campbell most of the time. The young lady who had the most success, however, did it with a new hat, that threw a scared silence upon all the conversationalists. It was a simple black affair, fitting the skull tightly and with two large black lobes flaring up, to be pinned down exactly in the middle of the fore-head, a la Mary Queen of Scots. The young lady seemed to be a person of wealth and she told me afterward that a representative of one of the great fashion emporiums has offered her $5000.—for the model of her hat the first time she appeared in it. She told me languidly, that she refused.

I am caught in a tangle of engagements, and am again not well. I go to the Stetts' tonight, and did think of telephoning to call it off, but it takes more courage to do that than to go to the dinner. I have dates tomorrow and Sunday, and then Tuesday comes the New York debut of Gertrude's

1. For Julien Levy see Biographical Sketches.
2. Real name Jesse Demot (1871–1940), American actress and manager of Maxine Elliot's Theatre, New York.

opera. I am to sit in a box with Florine.[3] In addition the management sent me very good seats which I forwarded to Mme. Delano. Apparently there is going to be a terrific crush. The publicity has been voluminous. Of course, the wits have been busy. Frank Sullivan, no doubt, will have the time of his life. The *New Yorker* was already very funny about it this morning.[4] If I enclose John Anderson's effort, will you send it back to me? I think of collecting the reviews. My own, which I sent you, has had a "succes fou." I have had countless messages of congratulation, even from distant places; all of which goes to show the interest that has been aroused in Gertrude. [. . .]

To Malcolm MacAdam
February 25, 1934, Herald Square Hotel, New York

Dearest Malc:

I suppose I ought to tell you something about the début of "our" opera but there has been such an incessant amount of talk ever since, that the mere amount of talk makes it seem as though it all happened long ago. It happened last Tuesday, and you must have read Lawrence Gilman's account in your *Tribune*, though Olin Downes in the *Times* was more intelligent. The papers have been full of it, arguing pro and con, but none gave a worthy account of the first night audience, which was remarkable. All the notable people in town were there, and the ladies, as you can imagine, were attired sensationally. I sat in a box with Virgil and Florine and Carrie Stettheimer, and gave the two grand seats they sent me to Mme. Delano. We had so much "business" of our own to attend to, that I didn't get out into the lobbies for the entrè actes, but I'm told the doings there were striking. Frank Crowninshield was in a neighboring box and came over to me, saying: "Do please introduce me to Miss Stettheimer" and I did that and to Virgil, too. Frank sat with us for the second act, and I could hear him saying, "Lovely, Lovely," to himself, as each new little thing came along. The reception by the house was almost instantaneous. For the first five minutes they laughed at some of Gertrude's words but soon they were gasping in admiration at Florine's marvelous color arrangements and Virgil's really adorable music. The tumult of applause, at the curtains was almost

3. *Four Saints in Three Acts* opened at the Forty-Fourth Street Theatre on February 20, 1934. In the Stettheimers' box sat McBride, Virgil Thomson, and Florine and Carrie Stettheimer; Ettie Stettheimer cabled that she couldn't attend because she was swelling with asthma.
4. Unsigned "Talk of the Town" segment entitled "I'm Sorry, I'm Sorry," *New Yorker*, February 17, 1934, p. 12.

riotous—and it was real (in contrast to the applause for *Merry Mount* at the Metropolitan, which was all claque).

I was surprised to see how cool Virgil and Florine were. I never sat with a composer before, as his opera was being produced for the first time, and I don't believe any composer ever before, went through the ordeal so easily. Though, of course, to Virgil, it wasn't an ordeal. He is the most unfussed person I have ever met. After the final curtain, we went back stage to thank the artists and I had the pleasure of a chat both with Ignatius (who is swell) and St. Theresa No. 1 (who is a great singing actress, but over sentimental in private life).[1] Then most of the audience went to a party at the Julien Levy's—a terrific crush—but I got home by one o'clock, though not to sleep. I passed a nuit blanche—the excitement had been too much. [. . .]

My article about the Hartford premiere of *Four Saints* brought me numerous letters of praise, and many people tell me, it is the best thing I have ever done.[2] No newspaper critic, naturally, has been up to Gertrude's prose—and all try to be funny but merely show up their own inadequacy. I refuse to "explain," myself, for I think, that if they cannot understand what cubism is in prose, after twenty years of cubism in painting, then they had better remain dumb. But I can tell you privately, that the libretto is not nonsense and has a vast amount of the spirit of St. Theresa in it. I should like to go two or three times more to see it.

To Malcolm MacAdam
March 18, 1934, *The Sun,* New York

Dearest Malc:

Today is a bright sun-shiny Sunday, rather warm, but with life in the air and that is why I feel rather well, I suppose, in spite of some indiscretions yesterday. Yesterday was warm, too, but heavy, and I felt like ——, but I insisted on going up to see Stoeffen beat Mangin in the tennis matches, in spite of being booked for the final performance of *Four Saints,* and a party at the Julien Levy's, with Chick Austin doing "magic at midnight."[1]

---

1. St. Ignatius was performed by Edward Matthews and St. Theresa No. 1 was performed by Beatrice Robinson Wayne.
2. " 'Four Saints in Three Acts' in Hartford." Reprinted in *Flow of Art,* p. 311.

1. Arthur Everett ("Chick") Austin Jr. (1900–1957) arrived at Harvard in 1921, and departed in 1927 to become the acting director of the Wadsworth Atheneum, where he continued until 1944. A hands-on painter, curator, architect, museum director, actor, and stage designer, Austin was an incomparable impresario of mod-

The match was not as good as it sounds in *The Tribune* this morning for both boys are the "killer" type, and wish to smash each ball for a kill, and never think of playing the other man out of position. [. . .] When I left the games I felt scarcely able to toddle to the subway, and when I got home I lay down until supper time. In spite of that, it was again an effort to get into smoking for the opera, but I did manage it, and in spite of my fatigue, did enjoy *Four Saints* more than ever. It was a wonderful performance, and the packed audience cheered and cheered at the end, and refused to leave, until the manager came out and said they hoped to resume the run in two weeks—but I doubt if they do. Lots of us went back stage to say good-bye to the players and it was rather affecting. The crush to get in to see St. Ignatius' dressing room was exactly like the crushes at Carnegie to get to see Horowitz, after one of his recitals. A colored fellow at the door, who was letting them in, six at a time, recognized me and called me by name, and I asked him if he were in the play. He said: "No, I am Mr. Matthews' secretary,"—Mr. Matthews being the lad, you may remember, who sings St. Ignatius. He truly is a great artist. Last Sunday night, the colored cast gave a party at a club in Harlem for those who had been kind to them, and I went for a half hour and had amusing chats with St. Theresa and St. Ignatius. Needless to say, the colored people present were terrifically intellectual and fashionable. St. Ignatius, for instance, speaks German and French better than you and I do. At the theatre last night the excited talk in the lobbies between the acts was just as it was the first night. "Everybody" was there.

The party at the Julien Levys' was fun, and Chick Austin is a really clever magician, besides being a dear.[2] Again, "everybody" was there, but I beat it at quarter to two, and gave myself up for lost when I saw what time it was. However, here I am this morning feeling rather well. Is it not queer? [. . .] Oddly, just as I was sallying to the *Four Saints* last night, I got a letter from Gertrude, sentimentally grateful for my review of the Hartford premiere. Well, it's all over, and you will never believe it was grand, but it was.

---

ernism. A highlight of his career was the simultaneous premiere in 1934 of *Four Saints in Three Acts*, the first American Picasso retrospective, and the opening of the first architecturally modern museum interior, the Avery Wing of the Wadsworth Atheneum. Austin performed magic under the name of Osram, Man of Multiple Mysteries.

Four Saints in Three Acts closed on March 17 at the Forty-Fourth Street Theatre but reopened at the Empire Theatre on April 2, closing finally on April 14. By this time it had set the record as the longest-running opera on Broadway.

2. On that evening Austin performed a trick that involved a balloon that was really a condom.

To Gertrude Stein
March 20, 1934, Herald Square Hotel, New York

My dearest Gertrude;

Well, the *Four Saints* is finished, temporarily they say, but I fear permanently, and we are all somewhat depressed. I am depressed to think of all those who did not see it, including yourself—for positively you can have had no conception of the way it visualized itself for us. When we went up to Hartford for the premiere we were expecting some kind of a good time, naturally, but we were totally unprepared for the unearthly beauty that the first curtain disclosed and which mounted and mounted as the thing went on and finally left all of the hard-boiled and worldly connoisseurs in tears at the end. I saw it four times in all and last Saturday's final performance was the finest of all. It has been years since I have cared to see anything in the theatre twice, but honestly I wanted to attend the *Four Saints* constantly; and sorry as I am for your having missed it entirely I am also sorry that I only saw it four times.[1] It now ranks with the two or three exalted experiences I have had, with Mei Lang Fang and the Mme. Sadda Yaccoi of years ago. The fact of the matter is that everybody connected with the presentation caught an inspiration, all of them had to create and all of them did—so that the word miracle is the only one that describes what happened. Even now, thinking it over in cold blood, I can't conceive how Virgil dared to do what he did; how he managed to sweep the refrains and repetitions along so beautifully, and how he came out so pointedly with the phrases that established the atmosphere, such as the "Authority for it," "Saint Settlement aroused by the recall of Amsterdam," etc. You must not think this the sentimental moonings of a friend. The incessant inventions in choreography supplied by Freddy Ashton seemed like some baroque dream of the eighteenth century (only far more finished and perfect than the eighteenth century itself could have dreamed of) and Florine Stettheimer's costumes and sets and the Feder lights that were flung upon them, were simply unbelievable.[2] Unite all this to the exotic effect of the

1. Stein finally saw the opera on November 7, 1934, in its Chicago production at the Auditorium Building.
2. Sir Frederick Ashton (1904–88) was at an early point in his career as a choreographer when Thomson enlisted him to choreograph the opera. He designed movements for his amateur dancers that did not require formal ballet training. Stettheimer's sets were probably the first in America designed by an artist rather

beautiful Negro performers and their incredibly fine voices—and even then you haven't got the whole of it.[3] It is, indeed, indescribable. . . With all this, the regular music critics (who know nothing of painting) did not "get" it; and quite a few people who were bowled over by the performance tried to repudiate their emotional collapse afterward, and keep ringing my telephone to "explain" it to them. "What is the real meaning underneath, for clearly it must mean something?" they ask. All this is tiresome. After twenty years of cubism and abstract art, it seems that these unfortunate people have not yet heard of it. I loathe explaining any work of art, and always insist that any work of art that can be "explained" is worthless; yet nevertheless, I suppose I must at least bully some of these people into reasonableness. What I really feel is, that people who do not feel greatness in the best things of Picasso and Braque (now being shown here by Paul Rosenberg) do not know what painting is; and those who do not see poetry in your *Four Saints* do not know what poetry is.

But I mustn't tire you with shop talk. When I see you, if I do this summer, I can tell you why the run of the play was so short. The commercial management were not up to it.[4] They hadn't the faintest idea of what it was all about. Even so, the event has upset New York as nothing else has this winter. I thought last autumn the *Autobiography* made such a terrific success that I was finished with you and that I would have no further occasion to write about you (for all the population seemed delighted to have established contact with Gertrude Stein) but this confusion about the *Four Saints* shows me there is still some work to be done by somebody. Did Carl send you one of his photographs of your name in electric lights on Broadway? It seems to me that ought to content you with fame. Love to Alice. Love to you. . . Perhaps I'll be coming over, in spite of the dear francs.

---

than a stage designer. She used unconventional materials, including a cellophane cyclorama. Abe Feder pioneered lighting design on the American stage and became known as the dean of lighting designers.

3. Thomson decided to use a cast that consisted entirely of African Americans, for he believed their musical diction superior to white singers. This was the first instance in which black performers were used on stage in a production that was not about Negro life.

4. There were plans for Harry Moses's production to travel to London, Philadelphia, and elsewhere, but only the Chicago production came to fruition.

To Malcolm MacAdam
April 7, 1934, *The Sun* Hotel, New York

Dearest Malc:

[. . .] Do you recall Jean Lurçat, the French painter?[1] You thought him the distinguished individual at the Whitney Museum party, do you remember? Well, he really is a distinguished artist, and a rare character, but he managed to scare me yesterday. He had asked me to his flat to give me a costly book about Picasso's etchings which had been sent to me in his care, and in the course of talk I learned he was violently communistic. He is a gentleman and has the reserve of a gentleman but I could see the passion that lay underneath his arguments and I got quite frightened at this picture of the seething intellectual rebellion, that is taking place in France and in fact, in all Europe. I said, at first, that it was "un jeu intellectuelle" (we spoke French) and he retorted "You call it un jeu intellectuelle but I was proscribed by the government during the war and at one time was under sentence of death, etc." He then went on to tell of his association with André Gide (he pulled a letter from Gide from his pocket and it thrilled me, too, to see a letter from such a celebrity), and how Gide and a number of artists that I know had quit all artistic work and had taken up manual labor instead, against the dawn of the revolution.[2] I won't bother you with the details, but he succeeded in making me feel the general terror that is now spread over Europe. He said, for one thing, that the French government doesn't dare to arm as it would like, because it isn't certain which way its own troops would go in case of war. . . Of course, all the old American ladies are in the same state of panic, but as a rule I pay no attention to the talk, I refuse to worry in any personal way and in reality my only fear of communism is the boredom of it. It would simply be terrible to have to begin calling you "Comrade," for instance. I definitely won't say comrade until they point the guns at me.

However, at Marie Harriman's cocktail party yesterday, I had the pleasure of meeting Comrade Harpo Marx. He's real cute. I like him much

1. Jean Lurçat (1892–1966) was a School of Paris painter with a particular interest in tapestry designs, who made designs for Aubusson and Gobelin. He showed his paintings with Bignou.
2. The French novelist and iconoclast André Gide's (1869–1951) work was celebrated and lambasted by critics. A strikingly honest intellectual who believed in the importance of satisfying both the mind and the flesh, Gide was the author of more than eighty works and had a profound influence on the course of twentieth-century French literature. He was awarded the Nobel Prize for literature in 1947.

better in private life than on stage. I was introduced and gave him only a casual nod, for, as you can imagine, the name Marx meant nothing to me and besides I was wishing to talk to Walt Kuhn, who had his overcoat on and appeared to be leaving.[3] But my nonchalance was not excelled by that of Mr. Marx, who, on being reminded by Marie Harriman; "You know who Mr. McBride is don't you?" and heard him murmur something about "Always get my theatre tickets from him." But afterwards had a trifling more extended conversation and I liked him. He has charm.

The "dam-fool" opera as you call it, was revived Monday night with great éclat, and was almost as wonderful as ever but not quite. Florine, as you can guess, is now quite up-stage with all the flattery she has been getting, and in the absence of Freddy Ashton who has gone back to London, changed and recostumed the last act, and considerably spoiled it. It's about 40 percent less than it was. Those seeing it for the first time are enchanted, but we old-timers regretted the change. If they take it to London, as they say they will, I'm going to insist that they return to Freddy Ashton's better version.[4]

Did I tell you about the party Walt Kuhn gave me in his studio, with all his acrobat models present? I wonder?

To Malcolm MacAdam
April 20, 1934, Herald Square Hotel, New York

Dearest Malc:

I was all set to write you, in a gay mood, about my luncheon, just now, with Beatrice Chanler (she has come back)—when something crushing occurred. An unfortunate unknown artist who has been calling me on the phone imploring my assistance to make him famous, stopped in at the hotel, insisting that I give him at least five minutes of advice. Well, it was the usual thing. The poor man, somewhat elderly, painfully scrubbed and made neat for the ordeal, had a nice face and a sensitive nature, and had probably been egged on to this unusual interview by "the wife," and he

3. Walt Kuhn (1880–1949), a member of The Eight, was one of the staunchest advocates of the Armory Show. The show was a turning point in his career, as his focus changed from cartoon and magazine illustration to fine art. His professed goal was to interest the "buck eye," or the general population that had a healthy suspicion of modern art. Among Kuhn's most endearing subjects were acrobats and clowns from the circus.
4. Charles Cochran expressed interest in taking the opera to London, but it did not happen.

showed me a photo of a portrait in the Independent Show and begged me to just mention it in the paper. When I told him my article was already written and in type he became greatly distressed, and when I went on to tell him, as delicately as I could, the difference between his work and that of, say, Sargent, he collapsed still more. But what can you say to such people? I get dozens of letters, some of them clever, some of them illiterate, asking advice and help—and most of them I can't even answer.

Well, after the sad face of that old artist tottering away, I scarcely feel I have the right to go back and dilate about the soft shell crabs we had at Beatrice Chanler's luncheon. [. . .] I forgot to tell you about Emmy Winthrop's hard luck. She apologized for the lack of flowers in her drawing room and said that she had had to let her summer place in Syosset. I said, "I hope not for the usual reason," and Emmy gave me a nod and said, "It was for the usual reason."

On Wednesday afternoon I had a thrilling experience at which you will scoff. The young colored man, who sang St. Chavez in the opera called to see me and ask my advice. He is up in the air since *Four Saints* quit, naturally, and he wanted me to think of him, if I heard of any jobs going loose. He is a remarkably handsome fellow, highly educated (a year in Paris) and has quite fine ideas. His opinions on *Four Saints* would put you to shame. He quite understood all the psychoanalytical stuff connected with it. He stayed an hour and said he would like to come see me again sometime. I haven't the cult for negroes but these superior types like Roland Hayes, St. Chavez and the woman, who sings St. Theresa, quite win my sympathy. It's remarkable how they keep their sweetness of character in the face of the restrictions they meet—and of which we know nothing.

The Stettheimers are giving a grand dinner tonight. Cecil Beaton is to be there and that will be fun. Carrie and Ettie came back from the South, just in time to see the last performance of the opera. I sauntered in about 10 p.m. to say good-bye to the best of all operas and was surprised to see all three sisters in a box.[1] The house was packed and it didn't look like "paper," either. They talk of putting it on for three weeks at the Chicago Fair—but I dare say they won't.[2] What I should like, would be to do it in the films. Then you would have to go. And you would just love it. . . But I could

1. One of the tacit rules of the Stettheimer household was that one of the sisters would remain home with their mother, and this is the first recorded time all three sisters went out on the same evening.
2. They didn't.

scarcely bear to see it again unless they had the same cast. When you've once seen a thing in perfection, you hate to have it changed.

To Malcolm MacAdam
June 3, 1934, Hotel Blackstone, Chicago

Dearest Malc:

I am already acting true to form—you would say. In fact if you were here you'd be so annoyed we wouldn't be speaking by this time—and that being the case I don't see why I'm writing to you—only if I don't, of course, you won't know why you're mad at me. Well I arrived cross and tired from the trip in the "air-conditioned" train (the worst invention of civilization) and asked for a quiet room at the minimum rate. When I got it I wasn't much pleased, as it turned out to be air-conditioned, too, but the real unpleasant-ness was the constant hubbub from my neighbors, constant loud voices, telephone, etc. So I spoke up to the clerk a while ago saying I'd have to have another room (it seemed it was a bunch of Chicago politicians putting over a new deal) and to propitiate the complainer he gave me a much better one and two stories higher up.

My private opinion is that it is the air-conditioning that causes the terrible amoebic dysentery you hear so much about back east. Everybody there is thoroughly scared of Chicago and indeed you do hear of lots of cases. Lord Duveen is the only one so far, who had had it and got over it easily.[1] Some of the others die, and some have operations, etc. But here in Chicago, they pretend not to have heard of it. Ettie Stettheimer made me promise to drink bottled water and eat only cooked things—but que volez vous, Chicago is not Europe and they don't have bottled waters and I already ate a cantaloupe, before I thought. But if I get it, I'll blame it, as I said, on the damp icy air, that is forced into your rooms. The curious part, on the train, is the stuffiness once you get into your berth, for all the windows are doubly shut and when the curtains are down, the berth be-comes an oven. When we stopped at Ft. Wayne, I got out, as I said, to the porters, "to get warm," and all the porters immediately joined in and said they hated it. One old colored porter said to me "Don't they have air-conditioning in England, sir?" He took me to be English, I suppose,

1. Joseph Duveen (1869–1939), a dealer in art and antiquities, became Lord Duveen of Millbank late in his career. Duveen helped Henry Clay Frick, John D. Rockefeller, and Andrew Mellon amass their collections. Duveen's highly readable and subjec-tive memoir, *Art Treasures and Intrigue,* was published in 1935.

because he couldn't imagine a docile American having enough nerve to complain of a new invention.

Did I tell you why I am here? There is a Grand Century of Progress Show at the Art Institute and I am invited out and allowed $150.—for expenses. But I think I will take more. Already I am alarmed at the thinness of my pocketbook. And it didn't help when I had to pay for Thérèse Bonney's lunch. When I arrived in the lobby, there were loud shrieks of "Oh Henry" and there upon Thérèse appeared and as she was leaving in an hour for New York we lunched, as I thought in my innocence, Dutch; but it proved sadly un-Dutch. Tired as I was, I toddled over to the Institute after I got rid of Thérèse, saw the pictures, which really are fine—all except the ones by the living boys. I was too tired to go out to the Fair that evening, as I should have done were I younger, as I'll probably have to write my stuff for *The Sun* tomorrow, without the advantage of throwing in casual allusions to the Fair. In a minute I'm going to soak myself in warm water and go to bed—hoping to be slightly spryer demain. Oh, I forgot to tell you what happened just now. After dinner, I sat all alone in the foyer of the hotel and all at once a nice looking young man appeared and said, "May I speak to you a moment?" and I said "yes." He thereupon proceeded to asked me about my glasses, and in the end produced a nickeled case, like a lip-stick holding a paste, which if rubbed on the glasses in the morning keeps them free from dust and moisture all day. Price 50 cents. I said, "Nothing doing." Finally he threw the instrument into my chair, and said "Well, I could have it for a quarter." This conversation lasted so long and was so full of unexpected turns, that I hadn't the heart to throw the lip stick at him, so I gave him a quarter. Then I promptly came upstairs, before I had more goldbricks sold to me. They do seem to be very enterprising here in Chicago.

Monday. . . Have been around the picture show again, less tired than yesterday and had pleasant chats with the officials and lunched with Dr. Harshe at the famous club, The Cliff Dwellers. Thought to sally out to the Fair, but there's a big black cloud and it smells like rain. Dr. Harshe is very annoyed at Lord Duveen. He says Duveen blackballed the show and tried to persuade people not to lend their masterpieces to it, just because he got the amoebia last year. Isn't that Lord Duveen all over. He's a trouble maker. [. . .]

Wednesday [. . .] Did I tell you Virgil Thomson's scheme for next year? You know they are starting a ballet school in New York and the suggestion now is to do a ballet-opera on the Uncle Tom's Cabin motif, with Eliza escaping across the ice on points.[2] (Do you know what points are? Points are the ballet-girls toes, See?) Virgil is attracted by the notion.

Alice Fourmier, with whom I had tea at the Arts Club this afternoon, told me that the *Four Saints* is positively booked for two weeks in Chicago next November.[3] In that case Virgil probably won't wish to bother with Uncle Tom, the *Four Saints* being enough responsibility for one thing. [. . .]

To Malcolm MacAdam
October 12, 1934, Herald Square Hotel, New York

Dear Malc:

I came to town Monday, arriving at six o'clock, and to show you the difference, between unpacking and packing (which is arduous and time consuming) I had all my little necessities installed in the places where they belong, and my big wardrobe trunk shoved out of sight into the closet, by seven; when I went over to Schrafft's for a bite to eat. Schrafft's, of course, is the same, and there seemed to be a reason why each particular item on the menu wasn't suitable to the occasion. Getting over there was comparatively simple. I never did find crossings at Thirty-Fourth Street so difficult as you used to make out. But the old newspaper man at Sak's corner had lost all his pep. "What's the matter with you, you look thin?" I cried, and with a wan smile, he replied, "I ain't been well." I always laugh, too, when I tell people about my ailments. What the psychology of that is I don't know. [. . .]

Just now Ettie Stettheimer phoned to say she had stopped in the hotel lobby to inquire if I would come to dinner tonight, (she was on her way to Macy's) and I said, "Why not take the lift up to the sitting-room and I'll come down," and Ettie very daringly did. She said she was the only member of the family who would do such a thing, and tonight at dinner we shall both be chided, no doubt, by Carrie and Florine. Virgil Thomson and Ralph Flint are to be there. Virgil is doing the music for a version of *Medea*, to be done with Negro singers and with a décor by Chick Austin, the director of the Hartford Museum, where *Four Saints* had its premiere last year.[1]

2. The plan to do a ballet based on *Uncle Tom's Cabin* was not realized.

3. The Arts Club was a center of modernist activity in Chicago, including exhibitions and a lecture by Gertrude Stein.

1. The Harlem Renaissance poet Countee Cullen adapted the play, but it was not produced.

That will no doubt be our excitement this year. Gertrude, of course, is coming over and will lecture at some of the colleges, but not in New York. Gertrude doesn't care to be bousculer by the New York mob—and she is quite right about it. I have not written to her all summer. There is such a crush of people writing about her à tout propos, that I feel inclined to keep off. In the *New Yorker* this week, there is again a lot of stuff about her, and about Alice,—and most of it is wrong.

I take the sleeper tonight for Pittsburgh so I shall leave the Stettheimer dinner early. [. . .]

To Malcolm MacAdam
October 20, 1934, Herald Square Hotel, New York[1]

Dear Malc:

I've just had Alice on the phone. It's Saturday mind you, and they arrived Wednesday. But I thought I'd wait till the first rush of reporters was over. But last night, at the Stettheimers, they were trying to psycho-analyze why I had not hooked up with Gertrude—"If you really cared, of course. . ." and that sort of thing. So this morning I called up to end the scandal. A long wait. The phone was busy. Naturally. Then Alice's voice, finally, clicking at the rate of ninety miles a minute. Would Alice and Gertrude lunch with me today? Can't we postpone that? Gertrude has been so tired, that I'm trying to keep her flat on her back a proportion of the day. She's in a hot bath at this moment and I don't dare call her to the phone. Enchanting to hear your voice. Can't we call you up later this afternoon? Do you know the first astonishment, that Gertrude and I have had is to find New York so quiet. Yes, so I have just heard. They are giving the news-reel interview with Gertrude at the Embassy.[2] I must take her to see that. Very well, I'll call you up later this afternoon.

I am sending you a slight helping of the publicity. It was one occasion, I think, when you would have enjoyed being a reporter. You could have vented some of your totally uncalled for animosity against Alice. As it was, she got off very well. One of the ruffians spoke of her as "twittering" in the background, but for the most part, they liked her evidently. I was most amused by that reporter, who studied Gertrude's silhouette and remarked,

1. This misdated letter could not have been written on Saturday, October 20, because Stein and Toklas arrived in New York on Wednesday, October 24.
2. This Pathé newsreel of Stein and Toklas was shot on the evening of October 24, 1934.

"Apparently she likes her groceries." They do think up odd uses of words, don't they? [. . .]

Friday, November 2, 1934—I saw Gertrude at last on Tuesday night at Mrs. John Alexander's, where she tried her lecture on "the dog"—the dog consists of forty-five carefully chosen listeners. She looked grand, ruddy, animated, and herself. Her dress had great style and when I asked her where she got it, she looked all around to see if anyone were listening, pulled my head down, and whispered that she had had it made in Belley. Her greeting to me was more than affectionate. In fact I got kissed on both cheeks to the edification of Frank Crowninshield, who was standing by. This seems to be a great year for kissing. I told you I think, about kissing Beatrice Chanler last year on her arrival, and we kiss just at ordinary dinner parties. And of course Maud Dale and I have been on oscillatory terms for years, and when I went to the Askews' "cocktail" Sunday evening, Constance joined the ranks of those who now kiss me.[3] This you won't mistake for bragging. I merely indicate a trend in fashion—like the saying "darling" a few years ago. To be kissed publicly promotes you to the inner circle. When a carefully rouged lady risks the maquillage in this fashion, then the other people present understand definitely that you are there. So it was at least at the Askews. But it can be carried too far, of course. When, after dining at a Japanese Restaurant, the Askews and Russell Hitchcock and I called on Virgil Thomson, the good-byes were kisses—all except mine.[4] Constance and Kirk kissed Virgil, and Russell Hitchcock kissed Virgil—but I contented myself with a correct coup de main. Of course, if kissing gets general, as it probably will by next year—I'll be off the whole thing, I'll kiss no one. It's not hygienic anyway, the doctors say.

Four Saints opens in Chicago a week from Wednesday. Gertrude, Alice and Carl Van Vechten are flying out for the premiere. I wish I were. . . I have a date with Gertrude and Alice for luncheon the following Saturday, as they fly back immediately. It will be fun to hear Gertrude's verdict on the affair. Of course, as you can imagine, Florine and Virgil are both slightly miffed at the way Gertrude "Hogs" the publicity. But que voulez-vous? It's

3. The Askews (see Biographical Sketches) stopped their social gatherings around the beginning of World War II.
4. Henry-Russell Hitchcock (1903–87) was the co-curator (with Philip Johnson) of the Museum of Modern Art's epochal 1932 exhibition "The International Style." An important figure in the Harvard modernist circle, Hitchcock taught at many prominent institutions, and became the acknowledged dean of American architectural history in the United States.

the way of the world. Today again Gertrude makes the front page of the *Tribune,* with her lecture.

To Malcolm MacAdam
November 16, 1934, Herald Square Hotel, New York

Dear Malc:

Willie Ivins, of the Museum, has just called me up to tell me that Bryson Burroughs died this morning.[1] Willie used the expression "passed out"— but before he could finish telling me his voice broke and he had to hang up the phone. Willie and I were among Bryson's oldest friends. We saw him all the time at the Museum, but of late, due to old age, and Bryson's marriage, and Bett's re-marriage, I have not been seeing him often. It amazes me to think I survive him. I was up at the Museum a fortnight ago and saw Louise, who told me Bryson was off duty and that doctors said it was a peculiar form of tuberculosis, but she seemed so cheerful, that I was not alarmed. [. . .] I've not had much to do with death. The first to make a difference was Edith Burroughs (Bryson's first wife). The second was Laurence Reamer and a third was Mildred Aldrich. I found out, what other people have told me, that a large part of yourself dies with a friend.

Gertrude and Alice lunched with me last Saturday. I took them to the Coq Rouge, but it was not especially nice. Both Gertrude and Alice were in good form and were not annoyed by the interruptions. Three times, total strangers came over to us and greeted Gertrude profusively. One lady said her son was one of three seniors at Harvard to be asked to the banquet, that is to be given Gertrude at Cambridge, and she hoped Gertrude would speak to him, if she got the chance. Her name, she said, was Mrs. Trout. Gertrude said, amiably, that she would be sure to tell the young man, that she had met his mother. Afterward, we walked down Madison Avenue and Alice was enchanted with the shop windows. I explained it was the rue de St. Honoré of New York. We even went into Charles' grocery shop and Alice bought some bran biscuits. Everybody stared at us on the street and seemed to know my companions. Gertrude thoroughly enjoys the success she is having. She said several times: "Isn't it wonderful Henry? Isn't it wonderful?" and of course, it is. Her publicity equals Lindbergh's, almost, and she'll be considerably richer, because of it. Carl throws a party for her Sun-

1. William Ivins, curator of drawings at the Metropolitan, was Burroughs's colleague and friend.

day night, which is sure to be fun. I'm hoping St. Theresa and St. Ignatius will be there. From Gertrude's account I judge *Four Saints* were not so well given in Chicago. The Auditorium is vast and seats 5000. Gertrude said she couldn't hear half of it. I knew that would be the trouble. [. . .]

To Malcolm MacAdam
December 28, 1934, Herald Square Hotel, New York

Dearest Malc:

[. . .] So now for the parties. The most thrilling one occurred last Sunday night and indeed it was one of the most astonishing experiences I have had in years. Jessica Shewan, who paid for Queena Maria's musical education, and has clung to her ever since, asked me to supper and to hear Queena do a broadcast. Now I have a radio and am a radio fan (more or less) but it seems that I didn't know the half of it. I suppose you are better informed as you read every printed word in the newspapers. Well, anyway, I began to be astonished when they told me there would be an audience of 1700 at the broadcast, for I had supposed, in my innocence, that it was all done in a glass cage, but on the contrary, the crowds going in, at Radio City, resembled crowds at the opera. They were doing *Hänsel and Gretel* for the first time on the air, and the big stage and its equipment, were so different from anything I had expected that I thought I must be dreaming. The hall itself was big, with a balcony, and in one wall there was a large glass window behind which some men were to listen in and wave occasional directions to the actors. The large platform was open and unprotected from the audience, but there was a large curtain at the rear, the only concession to the eye. All the rest was hard-boiled and strictly radio. The philharmonic orchestra played better than the Metropolitan Opera, and the singers included Queena and Miss Fleischer and Miss Manski as the witch, but they had a double set of players who sat in front and did all the spoken parts, and there was a young man for the mechanical effects. It may interest you to know that when they threw the old witch into the oven, the flames were simulated by the young man's crunching some cellophane paper in his hands. The fellow who did the announcing, advising us all at frequent intervals to drink Chase and Sanbourn's dated coffee, was remarkably handsome in the laughable way, and Jessica says he is the next best announcer in the world to Graham MacNamee. Jessica knows all the inside stuff. [. . .]

To Malcolm MacAdam
February 1, 1935, Herald Square Hotel, New York

Dear Malc:

I've turned the Pro Arte Quartet off the air so that I might write to you. And they were doing Beethoven's first quartet, too. I wonder if you would do as much. I doubt it. This is Friday afternoon, which corresponds to your old Sunday of rest and diversion. I woke up a wreck this morning, after yesterday's struggle with my page, but loafing in my room all morning and eating a capital lunch at the Barclay (potage, fried smelts, lemon pie et café), restored my morale, if that's what you would call it. And so this afternoon continuing to loaf in my room, playing solitaire and listening to the radio, suddenly and quite reasonably a distinct feeling of bien-être stole over me. I wonder what it is that does that to you? Agreeable feelings up and down the spine, and all through you, much, I image, the kind a cat gets, when you stroke her back on a frosty day. So I listened on and on to the nonsense of the radio, afraid to break the spell. I heard "Walking in the Winter Wonderland" by a sentimental tenor (you can't listen in long without hearing that one) and "Pop Goes Your Heart" (that's terrible), some orchestra selections from *Anything Goes* and then a young lady named Miss Wilson gave a lecture on "Charm," (it seems she's an authority on it—so the announcer said, anyway) and she mentioned the ten most charming people in the world and you weren't on the list, and the ten most charming native Americans and you weren't on that list either. Perhaps she thinks you have been out of the country so long, that you have become a foreigner, or perhaps she just thinks you have slipped. Then we got the Pro Arte Quartet, coming on the air from Washington, and they were pretty good, too, but when we got well into the second movement, I decided, that if I were going to write to you I'd better start. So off the Pro Arte Quartet went. You just turn the button and out they go. It's as simple as that. Oh I forgot to tell you that Miss Wilson had Alex Woollcott on her list. I suppose that won't console you any.

Beatrice Chanler threw a rather large dinner party Saturday, forty convives, and getting Willie, Jr., to foot the bills. It was amusing to the psychoanalysts present, of whom there was at least one. I think you've gathered by this time that Beatrice is desperately poor. The late Willie, Sr. cut her off with a mere $600.—a month and of course Beatrice wouldn't know how to get along on that. She is as generous as a sailor and simply throws money away, when she has it, and I suppose it was because of that that her husband left it all to the two boys, Willie Jr. and Ashley. [. . .] Prince and Princess Obolensky were among the diners. Beatrice always likes a few titles at her parties. The prince, it seems gave a dinner a few nights ago, which he cooked himself, Russian style. I asked him how he learned and he said, "Oh I grew up between the stables and kitchen." He in fact looked not unlike the chefs in the cheaper restaurants, and the princess, for her part, resembled a dame au comptoir. She appeared to be corseted, and her décolletage spread out over her squeezed in gown with an amplitude, that quite outclassed Mme. Lachaise's.

Wednesday Marie Harriman gave me her box at the opera. [. . .] It's unfortunate, after such a favor that I had to slam the show in Marie Harriman's gallery this week, the show by your friend Noguchi.[1] His stuff is very clever, but not important. The Lachaise sculpture at the Modern Museum is the sensation of the week, I'll send you my review.

To Malcolm MacAdam
March 18, 1935, Herald Square Hotel, New York

Dear Malc:

I read the *Tribune* with interest on Saturday. There were four topics for me. There was the tennis—for I have seen Bell and Mangin playing in the afternoon, and the reviews of Alex MacLeish's poetic play *Panic,* to which I went with the others of Mr. Ralph Willis' swank dinner party, and the boxing match of Carnera and Impelletière which I had to give up in order to go to the dinner, and finally the precious message, which Gertrude gives to the world each Saturday.[1] It's perfectly true what she says, that the American colleges stamp indelible imprints upon their unfortunate pupils, and what a pity it is that the word Syracuse is written all over some of them. And you needn't tell Gertrude to go to hell just because she said that. She's telling the truth, remember.

1. Isamu Noguchi (1904–88) a Japanese-American sculptor who began work as an academic but in 1927 went to Paris, sought out the modern master Brancusi, and became his studio assistant. Back in New York in 1929 Noguchi exhibited his modern work but was forced to return to representational portraiture to support himself. In 1930 he traveled to China and Japan and was influenced by, among other things, ancient Japanese ceramics. Beginning in the 1950s, with the rise of formalism, Noguchi's abstractions became highly influential.

1. *Panic* by Archibald MacLeish (1892–1982) was the opening production of John Houseman and Nathan Zatkin's Phoenix Theatre, its direction shared by Martha Graham and James Light. Beginning March 9, 1935, six articles by Stein were published in the *New York Herald Tribune.*

I got to the Ellis dinner through Beatrice Chanler. Mrs. Ellis is Alice Garrett's sister and lives in River House, the palatial apartment house on the East River Bank. *Panic,* as you saw in the paper, was on for only three performances, and Friday night's performance was for the haute monde, apparently, at $5.—per. We were all in white ties and tails, and the play was a jittery account of the collapse of the bankers, with the assaults of the populace, and the one that was clearly intended as Morgan, committing suicide in the end. It was terrible, but we had just had to sit there and take it. And in addition it was a bad play. I at last have given up. I'm licked. I tell everybody that I'm going to Russia and take out my papers there, for this country is doomed, and as the Soviet is ten years ahead of us, will be at least ten years ahead of the game, such as it is, over there. So comrade, I advise you to do the like. No use dreaming of retiring on an income, as by next year there won't be such things as income. The unfortunate capitalists have no spokesman with enchanting programs for the populace. They only preach common sense, which, of course, isn't enchanting. Father Coughlin tells millions over the air, in the most passionate accents imaginable, that the worst of the idlers is entitled to $200.—a month for doing nothing, and that the dastardly bankers have got it give it to them.[2] That is a pleasant doctrine for the idlers and naturally they are all for it. Father Coughlin doesn't tell them that the laying of this golden egg will kill the goose that lays it—that would be asking them to think ahead and thinking ahead is as unpleasant as work. Seriously, the situation is out of hand. Nothing is ever done to prevent situations such as this from developing, nothing in the way of entertainment for the mobs has been engineered since the Civil War, and if they are not distracted they end up taking the job of self-distraction over for themselves. You should see the mobs on Union Square these days. In the midst of jangling street-car bells and other noises the speakers shout themselves red in the face and the thousands listen rapturously. It's perfectly plain they are incapable of ruling anybody, not even themselves, and why were these nit-wits allowed to begin thinking they could govern better than those trained for the job? But it's too late now. There were some well written lines in *Panic* that the communist will quote with glee. Something like this: "We're on the conquering flood. We're on the upgrade. History is with us—" and it is a fact, that the so-

---

2. Father Charles Coughlin (1891–1979), the Canadian-American Catholic priest best remembered as a rabid right-wing radical radio personality, first came to prominence as a voice for "social justice," prompting some critics—including McBride—to decry his supposed socialist tendencies.

called educated classes are completely bewildered and demoralized. But the look on the faces of the young Communists in Union Square is different. They are like conquerors. They seem to think the main battle is won—nothing but the trifling details.

You see that Morgan sold his art collection, did you not?[3] And they say he is going to live in England. . . Mais moi, je crois que Russie est mieux. Plus practique. Muriel Draper is already there and Billi Bullet, our ambassador, is a friend of mine. I won't like it but it's the best thing for me, at my age.

Postscript. Tuesday. . . My letter was held over, and re-reading it, it sounds stagy—like the kind of stuff I write in the newspaper. I suppose it's no wonder I have the habit, after twenty years of nothing but. [. . .]

One of the odd features of Clara's painting job is that Ralph Flint is now one of the assistant painters, and even lives in a room in the studio building, which is really Bob Chanler's abandoned old house.[4] Ralph's story is remarkable. You may remember that he used to be an art critic, but got fired almost two years ago. Ralph always lived up to what income he had, and consequently was instantly in the gutter, when the collapse came. He stayed at the Hotel Montclair and was very social and kept on going to week-end parties and boxes at the opera, though without a cent. His spirits were wonderful and he was the life of the party when he got to it. This was because—here's the queer part—he is a Christian Scientist. It seems that that religion applies to money, as well as health, and Ralph was convinced the Lord would provide. Well, I must say the Lord hasn't done so much, and it would have killed me long since to have gone through what Ralph has gone through, but he still has faith. And still goes to the opera and dinners. At the Julien Levy party the other night, after the American Ballet opening, Ralph left just as I did, and as it was a balmy, pre-spring night, I said let's walk a bit, knowing that Ralph was going to walk home anyway. We finally got to the theater district, where we made a sensation with out top hats, white scarves, etc. Girls ogled us, people stared and finally, as we were saying good-bye on the corner, a beggar approached with a whining

3. John Pierpont Morgan, Jr. (1867–1943) succeeded his father John Pierpont Morgan (1837–1913) as head of J. P. Morgan and Co. and dispersed parts of his father's enormous holdings of art and rare books, including a gift of about seven thousand objects to the Metropolitan Museum of Art.
4. The artist Clara Thomas was commissioned by the Elizabeth Arden salon to paint a series of mural panels. Robert W. Chanler (1872–1930), a.k.a. "Sheriff" Bob Chanler, was a successful decorative artist and mural painter, also renowned for giving flamboyant bohemian, drunken parties.

request. Ralph drew himself up, and said with an air of solemn sincerity that the beggar recognized: "You may not believe it, but I haven't a cent to give you and I have gone without breakfast and luncheon." He didn't add that he had dined luxuriously with Emmy Winthrop and heard *Meistersinger* that evening in a parterre box before going to the Levy's. But the beggar, recognizing a worse case then his own, slunk away, visibly impressed. . . Such is the life in the big city.

To Malcolm MacAdam
May 1, 1935, Herald Square Hotel, New York

Dear Malc:

When the time comes, for your grand reconciliation with Gertrude and Alice, I think I'll stage it at the Algonquin; there is such an eager audience there. I got the impression that all the eyes in the salle à manger were focused on Gertrude, Alice, and me yesterday. I'm not much fussed by such things, but I did feel that the barrage of glances was unusual. You see the Algonquin is the head quarters for the celebrities in New York and Gertrude has been the chief celebrity this winter and all the emotional think they have to touch the hem of her robe, or something. So there was the constant interruption of people coming up to say a word, and the reporters held at bay in the outer rooms, and Frank Case, the proprietor, hovering about to see there were no contretemps. You might have picked up some ideas as to ordering luncheon from Alice. Alice wanted oysters on the half-shell, as it was the last day of April, and discussion with the maître d'hôtel, who finally persuaded her to take clams instead, would have been a model for you. I had chosen a plat of broiled lamb kidney and spinach, and Alice called the maître d'hôtel back, after I had said something to her about the épinards velouté that we used to have in childhood, and insisted that the spinach must be creamed with sliced hard eggs on top, and, as our food was a long time coming to us I think the entire establishment must have halted in order to make the spinach velouté especially for me. The maître d'hôtel and all the servants apparently have had orders to indulge Gertrude and Alice in their slightest wishes. But I did think the maître d'hôtel was going to lose his grip upon himself, at one moment, before the idea of the spinach was made clear.

Well, the two girls have had a lovely time, and are sailing home Saturday. I'm going down to see them off. Gertrude has practically settled it, that when I come down to visit them at Billignin next summer, then I am to fly down to Geneva, where they will meet me. It is only 1½ hours away, it seems, and the Geneva airport is quite O.K. Gertrude flew from Los Angeles to Chicago and thought both the Sierras and the Rockies superb as seen from above. She didn't care much for California, but liked Charlie Chaplin. She says he is quite a talker. She ought to know as she has met many of them. . . After I left I realized we had gossiped for two hours and never once touched the subject of communism. Gertrude is not easy to panic. She stays firm, and that's why she is so satisfactory to know.

At Elizabeth Thomas's fashionable dinner Sunday night we talked communism all right. It used to be considered a breach of etiquette to talk politics at dinner, but that rule is obsolete. Mrs. Ernesto Fabbri, a great swell, who sat next to me, actually confided, that she thought great fortunes were wrong. The great swells, in fact, seem to feel, that they are completely licked. I told Mrs. Fabbri that I certainly didn't want a great fortune myself, but that I liked knowing people who had them. [. . .]

Friday, May 17, 1935. . . I half hate to tell you what happened the other night, while *Waiting for Lefty*.[1] That's the communist play you remember, and young Joseph Alsop, who writes so nicely in the *Tribune,* and seems to be a pet, made such a fuss about it, that Louie Delano decided we ought to see it.[2] I knew in advance it would be harrowing but to tell the truth, it shattered my morale completely—not so much the play, as the audience, the cruel, relentless new people from the lower East Side, nicely enough dressed and evidently prosperous enough, but bitter with determination to shipwreck a society that they think is holding out something on them, and not realizing in their stupidity that when they have wrecked society they will be more out than ever. The rapt way they received the two plays (which should have been stopped by the police, in my opinion, since the burlesque showing up of Hitler in the first one, was almost enough to start riots in the streets) and the way they cheered the points, were enough to curdle your blood. Louie Delano took it lightly and was not much concerned—but she doesn't know what's going on. However, she added to my fright by defending Pierpont Morgan from the slanders of the actors, and

1. *Waiting for Lefty,* a one-act plea for unionism that was the first success for the playwright Clifford Odets (1906–63), was staged on Broadway with another Odets one-act play, *Till the Day I Die,* about the underground anti-Nazi movement in Germany.
2. Joseph Alsop, Jr. (1910–89), the anti-Communist columnist for the *New York Herald Tribune* and good friend to Franklin D. Roosevelt, was a fan of *Four Saints in Three Acts.*

saying he was a dear, sweet thing, who had to carry on the bank, because his father left it to him, and that in reality he was sick of it and was counting the days till he could give it up and retire to his small garden in England. In other words, Jack Morgan is licked—like all the rest of us. . . I may add that the acting of these two frightful plays was superb. [. . .]

To Malcolm MacAdam
May 26, 1935, Herald Square Hotel, New York

Dear Malc:

I turned in my last page Thursday and since then have done nothing in the way of packing up—have just loafed. Apparently I am not going abroad, as nothing further has been said about an invitation from the French Government, and I don't seem willing to afford it, myself. Thanks to our communist system my income has been so reduced that I should have to dip into my capital in order to make the trip, and I still cling to my old-fashioned capitalistic notions and hate to do that. However, I may, I have no positive plans.

I am sending you one or two of my "pages" with yesterday's *Post,* which included Marguerite Zorach's picture of *Eva Gautier and Henry McBride* (at the Rossin musicale), which you may like to add to your collection.[1] Mrs. Z. did it, of course, as a bid to get some publicity, and it is hopelessly stupid, but we all amiably noticed it. I said some supposedly funny remarks which I now blush to think of, something about my being a regular Clark Gable in the picture, but after I sent down my copy I thought of what I really should have said. I should have said that the title ought to have been "You and the Night and the Music"—which would have flabbergasted Eva. Do you know that song? Thanks to the radio I am absolutely au courant with all the popular songs of the day and could even sing them for you if you were here, and if you would call it singing. I am amused to note that in spite of our instantaneousness of action the west is still behind the east, and I when I tune on a concert in San Francisco, I am horrified to hear them singing with gusto "The Isle of Capri" which we dropped months ago. Our own favorites at present: "Love me Tonight" and "She was a Latin from Manhattan," and the "Lullaby of Broadway" still persists.

1. Marguerite Thompson Zorach (1887–1968), born in Fresno, California, arrived in Paris in 1908 to study at the École des Beaux-Arts. She soon turned her interests to modern art. A frequent visitor at the Stein salon, the highly social Zorach returned to New York in 1912 and married the painter William Zorach (1887–1966), who was soon to become an important sculptor.

I have had another portrait done of me and in a way that will astonish you—nothing less than a musical portrait by Virgil Thomson. I had to sit for it.[2] Virgil gave me a detective story to read, one of those Jimmy Dale things, and I read and he scribbled notes and in an hour and a half it was finished. I think it's pretty good. Virgil cribbed the idea from Florine's portrait and the last part of the composition—this will slay you—he has me on a tennis court dashing hither and yon, but winding up with a big smash. Evidently I won the game. I'll see if I can get a copy of it made to send you. Your interpretation of the piece would be worth hearing. Virgil has done about ten of us and says he will do them in concert next winter. He has put Ettie Stettheimer into polka time. It amuses the rest of us but I don't think Ettie will be amused. As to mine, when Virgil explained about the tennis match, I said it sounded to me as though I were being chased by an angry artist. Virgil laughed and said, "Well, it could be that, too." [. . .]

To Malcolm MacAdam
November 3, 1935, Herald Square Hotel, New York

Dearest Malc:

[. . .] As for my health—you'd have no patience with it. That is, you wouldn't believe it—any more than you'll believe this letter. When I meet some one they say, "How well you look, etc.," but if I walk three short city blocks I'm tired and have to rest. My writing doesn't go at all. I got lots of praise for my memorial to Lachaise, but I was deeply attached to Lachaise and his work and his un-called-for death so shocked me, that I embarrassed to be praised for writing "a swell obituary" for him.[1] But we writers are like that. The poet's wife dies. He writes a poem. And gets paid for it! [. . .]

2. Virgil Thomson composed 140 musical portraits, beginning in 1928. He was inspired by Gertrude Stein's abstract word portraits. Thomson required his subjects to sit for him, and he then spontaneously musically sketched his subject. McBride was sketched on May 9, 1935, and Thomson later said that McBride's interest in tennis is indeed present in the portrait: "Oh yes, so I made a tennis game. You bat the ball forward and smash it and do all the tennis things in there." Quoted in Anthony Tommasini, *Virgil Thomson's Musical Portraits* (New York: Pendragon, 1986), p. 119.

1. "The Death of Gaston Lachaise," *New York Sun,* October 26, 1935. Reprinted in *Flow of Art,* pp. 327–30. Lachaise died after a career supported by a small group of loyal and influential friends, including e. e. cummings, Gilbert Seldes, Lincoln Kirstein, and Edward Warburg. The critical support of his work culminated in an exhibition at the Museum of Modern Art the winter before his death. Financial insecurities plagued Lachaise and were particularly severe at his death, leaving his wife almost destitute.

19 *Portrait of Henry McBride*, May 1935. Virgil Thomson. Courtesy Virgil Thomson estate.

I got a new suit at Brookses. $107.50. A darkish gray. I told the tailor that I had reached the age, when I had to go to funerals a great deal and wanted something I could wear on such occasions. But the tailor didn't work fast enough, and after the Lachaise funeral, I went to him for the final try-on. There was four deaths on successive days—Lachaise, Charles Demuth, Langston Mitchell, and Frankel the *Art News* man, whom I didn't care for, but who was involved in my life.

Monday morning [. . .] I've come to the conclusion, that both Mme. D. and I like acting and if we get some pretty good acting in the course of the play, we call it a good evening but the critics—all of whom are youngsters— were not brought up on acting and do not know what it is. They fall instead, for personal charm—the "Barrymore Charm," etc.—and if they see a discrepancy in the play, which they can spin of for half a column of easy writing, they accordingly damn the works. I know how it is—for I do it myself to pictures. [. . .]

To Malcolm MacAdam
November 15, 1935, Herald Square Hotel, New York

Dear Malc:
[. . .] I believe I prefer the Germans, as a people, to the French, though I shrink at the language. Our newest murder involves a German, as you've been reading, and he seems to have been a nice German and the murder itself has some special features and makes good reading. On the other hand illicit amour is better done by the French, there's no doubt of it. Only Wednesday I had an example of it. My friend Gallatin, who is a bit of a prig, as you have surmised, gave a select cocktail party for Léger, the French modernist who paints pictures that resemble silhouettes of machines, and the mistress of Léger had to be asked, too.[1] She arrived first, and when Gallatin introduced her he had to ask her name. "Herbert is the name," she said, and he thereupon presented, "Mme. Herbert." Léger came later and it was plain to see that he was very much in love with the young lady, and it was equally plain that she was an adorable young minx. Immediately I thought: "They still do these things infinitely better in France." In that country, two things happen, that happen no where else; a man can be a restaurant garçon without loss of self-respect and a woman can be a man's

1. Fernand Léger (1881–1955) made his second trip to the United States in 1935, on the occasion of an exhibition of his work at the Museum of Modern Art, New York.

mistress without suffering an inferiority complex. Mme. Herbert, by the way, had already been to Harlem, she told me, and had already attended one of Father Divine's meetings. It's a wonder the way foreigners hit the high spots. I've always been meaning to go investigate Father Divine, but I never get around to it.

[. . .] Speaking of Drama, I met Beatrice Chanler again Tuesday. She gave a dinner for that fellow that wrote *Black Tents of Arabia* and he came in Arabian costume.[2] There were a lot of convives and we were picturesque and the food was good. You know Beatrice is practically penniless, and the Murray Taylors, who rent her house, allowed her to give the dinner there and probably provided the food. It was all sufficiently odd—if you can read between the lines. And young Mrs. Murray Taylor, who is a dear, lent me a book to take home with me, that made my few remaining hairs stand on end, and which I shall forbid you to read. It is called *Butterfield 8* and it makes *Lady Chatterley's Lover* seem like a Sunday school treatise, in comparison.[3] Really, Sodom and Gomorrah had nothing on New York. [. . .]

To Malcolm MacAdam
December 13, 1935, Herald Square Hotel, New York

Dear Ange:

I've been misbehaving—and I feel somewhat elated. I have the sense of triumph of a little boy, who's been naughty and hasn't yet been found out by his Pa and Ma. This has been going on for some time but the culmination was last night; if you can call it culmination, when I intend going tonight to the Joe Louis fight at the Garden! But last night was THURSDAY night—if you get what I mean—and Louie Delano was determined to go see Elsa Maxwell do her stuff at the Versailles (a swanky club) and equally determined I should, too.[1] And we went, and I escaped alive about 2 a.m., and am still alive. Miss Maxwell, as you must know, has made a career out of amusing the very rich, and she pulls off entertainments that people

2. Carl Raswan, *Black Tents of Arabia: My Life Amongst the Bedouins* (London: Hutchinson, 1935).
3. In 1960 John O'Hara's controversial novel was made into a movie starring Elizabeth Taylor and Laurence Harvey. BUtterfield was a Manhattan telephone exchange.

1. Elsa Maxwell was an international arbiter of society. "THURSDAY night" is a reference to McBride's weekly column deadline.

struggle to attend, and lives in the Waldorf Tower (at minimum rates, because of the réclame) and now has designs, she says, on a movie career. She gets $2000.—per week at the Versailles, and on Tuesday, the day after her début, she came to the Delano luncheon, although she had not gone to bed until five in the morning, and appeared as fresh as a daisy and told all about her experiences back stage, and even did her stuff for us. But Mme. D. felt she had to take a table last night just to honor Elsa, and before that we dined and went to see the Marx Brothers in a new film, *A Night at the Opera*. The "we" included Stark Young and the young fellow that lives with him and Mrs. Armour, the wife of our ambassador to Canada (she is the daughter of a Russian prince, married to one of those Chicago Armours, and very charming).[2] But Elsa was slightly on the "flop" order, as Mrs. D. reluctantly admitted, and will never "make" the movies. But I was thoroughly interested in the goings on, for I had never been in a nightclub before in my life, and probably never will go again, and so resolved to dismiss all thoughts of time and prudence, and collected lots of data for use in possible dinner-table conversations. [. . .]

Last week was remarkable for me, because of a set-to with Frank Crowninshield. Frank sent for me and announced that he and some artists were going to give me a banquet, fifty guests, actresses, speeches, Ina Claire, etc., etc., at the Coffee House. I tried to object, but I left his office with him still thinking I would consent to such a farce. When I got home, I called up, got his girl secretary instead of him, told her the scheme was definitely impossible, and wrote a letter to Frank to the same effect. Here's his reply:

Dear Henry: Your letter was altogether charming and disarming. I cannot even be angry with you. I am sorry we couldn't pull it off, because I think it would have been a gala occasion. Fondly, as ever, Frank

Frank is a dear of course, but he's a trouble maker, just the same.

Zoë Akins was at Mrs. Finley Thomas' dinner Wednesday night and told this story of James Joyce. It seems there "was a nice actress in Paris named Ivy Troutman and Joyce told her he thought Ivy was such a pretty name for a woman. Why don't you call me 'Ivy' then, said she, but Joyce drew back and replied that never in his life had he called any woman save his wife by her first name." This from the author of "Ulysses." [. . .]

---

2. Stark Young (1881–1963), American journalist, essayist, playwright, poet, critic, and novelist. Stark wrote for the *New Republic,* and was briefly drama critic of the *New York Times*.

To Malcolm MacAdam
February 21, 1936, Herald Square Hotel, New York

Dear Malc:

This is Friday the day after a particularly arduous Thursday and I am fatigued to death—but I'll try a little letter. I went up last week to Hartford for the festival and instead of describing it I'll send you the *Sun* tomorrow where you'll find some details—if they don't hash the article.[1] I am a bit nervous over it, for I allowed myself considerable length and when ever I take most of the space for a "special," some big advertisement is sure to turn up to make trouble, or else Keats Speed gets on his ear, because I've been a bit gay—and I was a bit gay this time I confess. Be sure to tell me what you think of the poem I quote, if it gets in, for it's by that young Charles Ford who wrote the novel that I hastily sent off to Clagett Wilson, not wishing to have it found among my effects after my death.[2] And ever since I've been wishing it back, for scandalous as it may have been, it was amusing.

Last Friday I woke up in despair, tired, seemingly ill, and when they phoned at 11 a.m. about the train to Hartford leaving at noon, I said I wasn't able to go, but I did languidly throw some things in my bag, and did finally make the train. The blizzard of the winter was raging and the fields looked marvelous on the way up and the struggles of the trainmen with the storm interested me so much that I more or less forgot my ailments and didn't recollect them again until Wednesday and Thursday on my return, when I had to write the experience up. You complain about people petting me, which is all nonsense, but they do rather make a fuss up in Hartford

1. The Hartford Festival, staged by Chick Austin at the Wadsworth Atheneum, included a performance of Erik Satie's *Socrate*, with a set by Alexander Calder; *Magic*, choreographed by George Balanchine; a program of "Music of Today from the Connecticut Valley"; a program of films; and the Paper Ball, about which Lincoln Kirstein observed, "It was about the last public party in America designed as an illustration of the dominance of a certain scale of grandeur in taste and manners." Kirstein, "The Ballet in Hartford," in *A Director's Taste and Achievement* (Hartford: Wadsworth Atheneum, 1958), p. 72.
2. *The Young and Evil*, written by the American authors Charles Henri Ford (b. 1910) and Parker Tyler (1904–74), was published in 1933 in Paris by the Obelisk Press but was considered too scandalous for publication in the United States and was not published here until the 1960s. It is widely considered America's first candid gloves-off, unapologetically homosexual novel, and Gertrude Stein wrote of it: "*The Young and Evil* creates this generation as *This Side of Paradise* by Fitzgerald created his generation." For a fuller description of the novel's genesis, see Steven Watson's introduction to the 1988 reprinted edition of the Gay Presses of New York.

owing to the write-up I gave that time for *Four Saints.* The hotel proprietor was simply beside himself in the effort to make me comfortable, etc., but the only reference I make this time to the Hotel Heublein, is the leak in the roof when the snow melted. So I probably won't be petted so much on my next visit to the hotel. . . What do you think? I've just been interrupted by a telephone call from young Charles Ford suggesting I use a photo of my costume by Tchelitchew to illustrate my article since the photos of the ball have not yet come but I had to tell him it is too late and that we went to press last night. His voice is simply killing, like Cecil Beaton's—the death-bed voice, you know.

The press-man up in Hartford told me he could get me tickets for broad-casts whenever I wished, and sent me two for Lanny Rose last night at 9:00 so I took Ralph Flint. Lanny Rose, over the air, is adorable and sings to perfection, and the whole thing sounds swell—but the actual broadcasting is different. In fact it's incredible. It's such a vast, unwieldy expensive ma-chine for producing an art effect, that it's typical of the age. About 2000 in the audience, 40 ushers, 100 performers including orchestra and singers, tons of high class experts in the glass, sound proof cages superintending things, and all this to advertise Maxwell House Coffee. And to put the joke squarely on us, we in the hall only got a whiff of it, as they sing and speak demi-voce and the amplifiers, I suppose, make it powerful enough to circle the globe. But the audience was in a fever, mostly women. The Show Boat last night was supposed to be in Texas, so we had our fill of the Alamo, brave citizens, gun-shots, etc., and the women next to me must have been from Texas for they almost got up on the stage and helped. Really the things that go on in this town, and in this world, are past belief.

Some wonderful luck has happened to you, though you don't know it yet. I hear the Santayana novel *The Last Puritan,* is a Book-of-the-Month, and it is magnificent, and after you have read it you will really be educated and can look an Englishman in the eye—even in the Madras Club. I feel myself as though I had attended Harvard, the college scenes being espe-cially vivid. The English won't like it, as oddly enough, the English charac-ters do not pan out as well as the American ones. But it's the first novel to have important American types treated as they really are. It, in fact, is the first novel for gentlemen that we have produced.

MCBRIDE MEETS MAX MILTZLAFF

On a Saturday afternoon in March 1935 Henry McBride was standing in line at the Metropolitan Opera behind a 31-year-old man whom he heard some friends call Max.[1] During the entr'actes the two men casually bowed to one another and had informal conversation. When the opera was over and the two found themselves both walking south on Broadway, the young man touched McBride's sleeve and asked if he could walk with him. McBride said, "Yes, Max, you may." The young man, whose full name was Maximilian Miltzlaff, was surprised that the stranger knew his name. Miltzlaff was en route to a church south of 34th Street, where McBride turned east, heading for the Herald Square Hotel. Miltzlaff, who frequently traveled on business, promised to call him for lunch when he was in town.

In retrospect one can find prophetic details in this casual meeting. Miltzlaff not only became a godfather that day, but he also acquired one. And for the next twenty-seven years the two walked along together. Sixty years later, Miltzlaff wrote, "He was not only my friend but father and trusted adviser."

Max Miltzlaff was born in Germany on September 27, 1903, in Bremerhaven, Germany, the second-oldest of four children. Because his father was a sea captain, Max was widely traveled at a young age. His family moved to Marseilles when Max was four, and he celebrated his sixth birthday in Constantinople. In 1914 his father took Max and his older sister on a trip to the United States, and as they arrived in New Orleans, World War I broke out. The Miltzlaff family and the rest of the Germans aboard were interned on the ship until the United States entered the war nearly two and a half years later. At that point, Max's father was interned in a camp, while the boy and his sister were put on the dock and told to "Do your best." They knew one name, a Dr. Rapp in New Orleans, and the family took them in until the war was over. Miltzlaff didn't want to leave the United States, and when he got a chance to return a few years later, he emigrated in 1922. He found employment with the Dollar Lines, a cruise line, and he rose through his

1. Information about Max Miltzlaff and his relationship with Henry McBride is from Steven Watson interview with Max Miltzlaff, January 1999.

wits and hard work. He spent the remainder of his working life with this company. In the mid-1920s he found another mentor, a Dr. Swift, who gave him encouragement, a set of the Harvard Classics, and a gold-plated shoehorn. When there was a conflict with Mrs. Swift, the friendship sadly ended in the early 1930s. By this time Miltzlaff had become a U.S. citizen.

In some broad outlines, Max Miltzlaff resembles the young men Mc-Bride associated with in the pre–World War I days—Otto, the gentleman on the boat, the traveling companion Rad. Miltzlaff had made his way in life by his own enterprise and energy, and his emigration to a new land was only part of it. And he had the natural qualities of a gentleman, a sense of manners, learned from his mother and his subsequent mentors, which made it possible for him to associate successfully with McBride's friends both in New York and in Marshallton.

In complementary fashion, Miltzlaff was primed to understand the value of a mentor; McBride fit into a position with which Miltzlaff was already familiar. This helps to explain the unlikely longevity of their relationship, for they lived in different worlds. Miltzlaff had no background in art, had little interest in the art world, and didn't read McBride's writings until after McBride's death. Miltzlaff initially found McBride's social world "too flossy." In contrast to McBride's contemplative and historical frame of mind, Miltzlaff's was active—he was constantly thinking of ways to move ahead or renovate a house or plan a trip or make the business run better.

At first they met for meals and an occasional event, and Miltzlaff's job frequently took him out of town. "As the years passed my friendship with Henry McBride became firmer and firmer, each first thinking of what is best for the other," Miltzlaff wrote. "When returning to Callicaste after the winter's work in New York I would drive him home, having been down some time before to cut the grass and see that all was in order. Thereafter during the summer months I would drive to Callicaste every other week to care for him and the place." Miltzlaff was always happy to be able to fix things and to make life easier for McBride.

Because McBride was so much older, Miltzlaff didn't feel that it was proper to call him by his first name, nor did he want to call him Mr. McBride, so he started calling him Fritzie. McBride in return called him "the Maxie." Miltzlaff and McBride grew ever closer, and Miltzlaff became caretaker, son, friend. It was the longest close relationship of McBride's life, and it makes complete sense to describe them as mates, in all but the sexual sense. Miltzlaff did not want Henry McBride to be described as homosexual, saying that he didn't believe it was so, and by the time he met McBride,

20 Henry McBride and Max Miltzlaff at Callicaste, 1939. Photographer unknown.

then nearing seventy, McBride was not a figure one thought of in a sexual sense. The love between these two men included domestic banter and pet names and complete mutual loyalty. It was tested when Miltzlaff was offered the chance to become vice president of the line, but Max immediately knew he would turn it down because he wanted to be near McBride in case of health problems.

To Malcolm MacAdam
March 8, 1936, Herald Square Hotel, New York

Dearest Malc:
[. . .] The fuss they make about Toscanini makes me weary, but that's the way we Americans are, we have to fuss about somebody, but between you and me, a large part of the time the bass drum was thumping in the Ninth Symphony, just like the drum in a village band. However, I won't go into that, especially since we had Beethoven's *Fidelio* yesterday with Flagstad doing "Leonore" and the fuss and enthusiasm was excessive there, too. The opera is a rather terrible opera, in fact it isn't opera, but oratorio, with the principals standing motionless and shouting their heads off for half hours at a time, but the word has gone forth that it is supreme, and so we dutifully fall for it. And Flagstad takes the part of a wife, who dresses in men's clothing to get into the jail, where her husband is confined, and she is so terribly womanly, that she would never have got through the outer gates in real life, but in the opera of course the jail-keeper's daughter thinks she is a real man and falls in love with her—resulting in some situations that would do very well in vaudeville, and which the serious audience took without batting an eye. I thought Flagstad looked very much like Mabel Luhan, who is the most womanly woman I have ever met. She sang the difficult music in a musicianly way, which is enough to stifle the critics, but as for making the role believable. Not at all.

Talk about greatness, I went the other night to see Jimmy Savvo the clown, and he IS great. I was astonished at the way the audience received him. At first he did nothing, but look furtive and scared and darted about as though he were lost, but even then the audience laughed at every gesture of his hands. When he finally branched out into singing "Did you ever see a dream walking, I did," the house went into hysterics. He is as great as Charlie Chaplin was in his great days. One strange thing about him is, that though he is misshapen and a dwarf, yet when he wants to, he can be

21 Henry McBride in the kitchen at Callicaste, 1939. Max Miltzlaff.

positively beautiful. I shall make a point of seeing everything he does, after this. [. . .]

[. . .] What you read in the paper can give you slight idea of the jitters the building strike has flung us into. It's been like Paris in war-time—only worse—for here every hotel and sky-scraper has been in a state of siege. Wednesday I went to Walter Chrysler's to dinner, Park Avenue, and twelve cops lined the hall and gave me the eye, just as those soldiers did when you and I landed in Liverpool in 1918. Even the Herald Square has been locked and bolted and detectives in the doorway to scan you as you enter, and guards riding up and down in the lifts to see that Grant isn't poisoned with communist doctrines—for, of course, the whole thing is a communist effort. We are too soft, with those communists. What would such traitors against the state get in Moscow? You know what they'd get.

To Malcolm MacAdam
April 3, 1936, Herald Square Hotel, New York

Dear Malc:

[. . .] Did I tell you about Max's flat? He is only in town for the week-ends (some kind of traveling Manager for the Dollar Steamship Line) and shares a flat with a fellow who is away week-ends. It is the cutest flat I have seen, with a sort of balcony leading to the bed-room, kitchen and bath, and some steps down to the big sitting room. The kitchen and bath, are the last words in modern science, and I never saw such ingenious economy of space—yet for these luxuries he pays only $75.—per month. It makes me dream that I too, might have a flat some day. [. . .]

Speaking of flats, last week I was asked, at last, to dine at Florine's new sensational apartment, along with Carl Van Vechten and Fania Marinoff.[1] I told you, I think, that the Stettheimer girls broke up their big residence upon their mother's death and separated. Everyone objected to this, and prophesied evil, but Florine, at least, seems to have benefited, and is much entertained having her own way, unmolested, in her new place. It's quite magnificent, with the ideas of the *Four Saints* decorations carried to extravagant conclusions. There are oceans of shiny, transparent cellophane hangings, and the dining room glitters with gold cellophane curtains

1. Following the death of Rosetta Walter Stettheimer in 1935, Carrie and Ettie Stettheimer moved to an apartment in the Dorset Hotel, and Florine moved into her studio in the Beaux Arts Building, which she furnished extravagantly with decor of her own design.

posed against white. The second sitting room, for the big double-decker atelier is also a sitting room, is very patriotic for some reason. It's all in white with bits of red and blue here and there and George Washington portraits everywhere.[2] There is a big, white triangle-cupboard in one corner, with an alcove in it painted vermilion to serve as back ground to the white bust of George Washington. The bedroom upstairs are equally unexpected, but I won't describe them as these words do not give the picture to those who have not seen *Four Saints*. Those who saw that production, however, would know the whimsicalities Florine is capable of.

After the dinner (which was superb, Florine has a masterpiece of a colored female cook) Walter Wanger came in, with that rich Miss Lewisohn, who used to run that Grand Street Theatre for her own amusement, and a young and beautiful Finnish danseuse, whose name I never got.[3] [. . .]

Saturday morning, April 4, 1936 [. . .] and in the *Tribune* this morning which you will read, if you care to, an account of a big fire in the Beaux-Art Studio, where Florine is, as described above. I must telephone to see if her splendors were damaged.[4]

To Malcolm MacAdam
April 17, 1936, Herald Square Hotel, New York

Dear Malc:

[. . .] Did I ever tell you about the Harlem *MacBeth*?" It was not so hot as a production, but as a premiere it was beyond belief—the most spectacular of the year. I went with the Dudensings, Georges Keller and Pavel Tchelitchew, the Russian artist. Pavel told such a funny tale at dinner, that that may have been one reason why *MacBeth,* afterwards, seemed a let-down. I suppose I oughtn't to tell you this indecent story. You must have noticed that I strive to keep my correspondence clean (though you don't make much effort in that direction yourself). But anyway here's his tale, or part of it. It concerned the time Thérèse Bonney, in Paris, tried "to make" him,

2. Florine Stettheimer was patriotic and remarked that George Washington was the only man she wanted to collect.
3. The film producer Walter Wanger was Florine Stettheimer's nephew. The philanthropist Irene Lewisohn (d. 1944) founded the Neighborhood Playhouse on the Lower East Side in 1915 as part of the Henry Street Settlement, where plays by Dunsany, Galsworthy, and Joyce were performed.
4. Ruth Ford, an acquaintance of Florine Stettheimer's, recalled that when firemen arrived at Florine's studio, "they were struck dumb and couldn't move; they thought they were visiting an alien." Quoted in Watson, *Strange Bedfellows,* p. 378.

as they say. Dr. Thérèse Bonney, who is connected with the Bignou Gallery, is, I think, a confirmed spinster, and Pavel, all the world knows, is not deeply interested in women.[1] Anyway, Thérèse gave him a dinner à deux in her apartment and made, he says furious advances to him, so much so, that he became hysterically confused. Thérèse said, "Qu'est ce que c'est? Est-ce que le poulet est mauvais?" "No" said Pavel, "C'est pas la poulet. Je suis malade, Je ne suis pas bien," "Alors" said Thérèse, "reposez vous sur le lit, n'est-ce pas?" "Mon dieu" shrieked Pavel, "Pas le lit, pas le lit. Il me faut de l'air. Il me faut le balcon," and to that comparatively safe refuge he fled. All this told, with terrific excitement and the most sweeping gestures. I think myself, that Thérèse is a perfect lady, and that Pavel was unduly alarmed, but just the same, I laugh every time I think of the story. It may partly be the extravagant and shameless way in which it was told. These Russians you know are born dramatists. But of course, you have to know the tightly corseted and outwardly so correct Thérèse to fully appreciate the affair.

To Malcolm MacAdam
May 8, 1936, Herald Square Hotel, New York

Dearest Malc:

[. . .] This will be playing hooky from Max Miltzlaff, who usually lunches with me Saturdays and whom I see at intervals during the week-end. Generally I go up to his place Sundays, help arrange a swanky lunch and perhaps take the air in Max's Chrysler. He drives his car expertly and thinks nothing of it, and always fetches me home from all of our expedition[s] so that the Herald Square is getting accustomed to having a smart car parked in front of the door. [. . .]

You asked if I ever met Edward Dodge. Yes, of course, once; and long before meeting Mabel. I thought him nice—a decent, unpretending, not especially memorable Bostonian. I thought Mabel did well by him in the book, too.[1] Evidently she respected him, though she thought him no great shakes as a figure in romance; nor was he. No one ever hears of him any more, though he married again, and is presumably happy. Mabel's son John is also married, has a son, so Mabel is a grandmother. Her present husband, Tony, the Indian, has lasted longer than any of the others. The

1. Tchelitchew's two most serious partners were Alan Tanner and Charles Henri Ford.

1. *European Experiences,* the second volume in Mabel Dodge Luhan's memoirs.

book, as you say, leaves one with a bad taste in one's mouth. It's partly because all of Mabel's Florentine friends were so shady. Apparently all the demi-reps of Italy, had access to her doors. She herself is not quite so bad as she seems in her books. She merely aims to tell the truth, and you must have observed, she never spares herself. The chapter about Muriel Draper was the best in the book, I thought; though Muriel is much annoyed about it. I don't quite see why she should be, since Muriel herself is another, who never cares much for the opinions of the hoi polloi.

I must quit this to go up to the Hotel Madison to see a film about *Earth Erosion* done for the federal government, with original music by Virgil Thomson, they say it's Virgil's best music, and all the crowd will be there.[2]

Sat. 9 p.m. [. . .] I might add, in case you're interested, that *Earth Erosion* was punk. Virgil's music wasn't bad, but the film was terrible and a lot more of our government's good money gone to waste.

To Malcolm MacAdam
July 19, 1936, Callicaste, Marshallton

Dear Malc:

The visit of Max Miltzlaff, to Callicaste is something, I think, that should be recorded. I have already told you of the panic into which I fell at the mere thought of his coming, and when I got down here and saw the forlorn-ness of the place (infinitely beyond what you saw in your day) and the painful state of collapse of the two Miss Pughs, I decided it wouldn't do to inflict all these things on the elegant Max. However, he is a willful boy and as he insisted that he was coming to see me, regardless of obstacles I might put in the path of his Chrysler, I tackled the job of putting a touch or two of order into chaos. This really was a task equal to those that were put upon the heroes in Greek mythology, for in addition to the natural decay of an old house such as this, there was the debris of shingles caused by the re-roofing, the accumulation of hideous furniture in the parlor, bequeathed to my cousins by Nell Martin, who left in a hurry, when her brother Dick married, and finally the unprecedented drought, which makes the whole place look like a withered cabin somewhere in Nebraska. I won't catalogue all the disgraceful items in the picture but you are to imagine the woodshed, the

2. The film title was actually *The Plow That Broke the Plains* and is generally considered an important documentary. It was directed by Pare Lorentz, photographed by Ralph Steiner, Paul Strand, and Leo Hurwitz, and funded by the U.S. Resettlement Administration.

w.c., and all the rest. The extraordinary heat we are trying to endure slowed me up some, too, but by going slowly, and planning carefully, I hoped to eliminate some of the eyesores by this particular day of the calendar, which was the earliest possible date by which my visitor could get here, I thought. He would arrive in New York on July 11th and would have to attend to business that week-end, I thought, and perhaps come here this week. But the impetuous Max came last week, immediately on landing. He sent me a telegram, which I didn't get, and so that Friday night a week ago, I went peacefully to bed at ten p.m., and apparently slept soundly, for Max had to toot his horn both front and back of the house, before I finally raised. When I discovered it to be Max I went completely rattled. I shouted for him to go round front and I'd be down but like a person trying to escape from a burning building I couldn't find my shoes, stockings or any respectable garments and eventually descended in my pajamas to give Max a hug and a scolding on the porch. Max was laughing and looking very handsome and paying no attention to my scoldings, thoroughly pleased with his adventure in finding me in this outlandish place and equally pleased in making such fast time from New York (It was only 11 p.m. after all). He had already backed his Chrysler into the orchard, and after we both finished a part of our laughter, we extracted Max's new and enormous suitcase from the car and sneaked as quietly as we could upstairs past the door behind which we knew the Miss Pughs were quivering with curiosity, indignation and perhaps fear. Upstairs the arrangements for a guest were as confused as all the rest of the establishment, for I had been sleeping in the newly painted and restored back room, but the front room (your room) was a phantasmagoria because that very afternoon I had been painting the window sills white, and all the toilet accessories were scattered here and yon and the supply of bathing water was about ½ pint. However, Max had to wash after such a wild ride in the night, and though he is the best groomed person in town when in New York, here he contented himself amiably with the half pint. Then we laughed and gossiped until fully 2 a.m.

In the morning Max appeased the excited Miss Pughs with a single look, although they were previously won to him by my explanation that we, Max and I, would lunch and dine in West-Chester. We also drove over to the Hayeses', where Max was a particular success, since they have a German son-in-law and are trying to think as well of the Germans as they can, and Max has returned from his trip decidedly pro-Hitler. He says he never saw a people so contented and so united as the Germans are now. Max had his first disastrous experience in giving me gifts. He fetched me five new made-to-order shirts (copied from an old one of mine) from Germany and a lot of expensive ties, but when I tried a shirt on it was found to be too small even though it had been made to order. It was impossible to lie about the situation and say the shirt was perfect for Max has very sharp eyes and sees everything and he himself decided it was too small. But I do think I can have them enlarged when I get back to town in the autumn. Max departed early Monday morning seemingly pleased with the week-end and threatening to repeat it soon. With that possibility in view, my labours have been intense in restoring an effect of decency to regions sadly lacking it. (I made Max go to the orchard in the mornings. He rebelled, but I insisted. The other place was outrageous. But it has already been improved.)

It is, I told you, painful to see the Miss Pughs attempt to do anything.[1] Even to get up from a chair seems to require strategy. And Mary, the grenadier one, always the one who made difficulties, managed to deck herself in the most loathsome gown I have ever seen, for Max's visit. It was thin and transparent and unwittingly exposed lengths of leg, that shouldn't have been seen. And so Sunday night my cousin's nephew's family (3 noisy brats) saw fit to visit us. They are more uncouth than the Tennessee mountaineers can possibly be, and feeling this to be the limit, I kept Max upstairs, and we didn't go down at all. But we heard them. In fact, Max distinctly got the low-down on Callicaste. It was precisely as though the fates had decided to put me through every test. [. . .]

To Malcolm MacAdam
September 8, 1936, Hotel Somerset, Boston

Dear Malc:

[. . .] I stopped with Max on my way up, over the Labour Day weekend (Friday to Tuesday) and helped install him in his fine new flat overlooking the Hudson at 186th Street [. . .] I have the blues after quitting Max, as I usually do, for he is such a completely successful young man in his own way, and has such a definite plan of life, knowing so exactly what he wants and how to get it, that my more accidental method seems almost criminal by contrast. Max is extraordinarily orderly, and in two days had his flat looking as though it had been lived in for a year, draperies, pictures, everything in place, and everything giving the effect of elegance. He spends

1. McBride's concerns for the well-being of his aging cousins becomes a theme in the letters of the summer of 1936. The opening of a Friend's Home for the elderly in West Chester in early 1936 prompted McBride to move them there.

money prodigally but simply has to have the best, and when I accuse him of extravagance he always looks surprised. The personal history of Max is as remarkable as that of Santayana's Puritan, and he has some strangeness in his character that are entirely new to me, but beautiful always.

[. . .] and then go on home for the auction of the Misses Pugh's chattels, and spend $50–$100 buying things many of which I gave them. But they are to go to the "The Home," and I shall be a hermit at Callicaste, which I won't like either, for though it was a false and unhappy partnership with my cousins, any company is better than none.

To Malcolm MacAdam
September 20, 1936, Callicaste, Marshallton

Dear Malc:

Great doings at Callicaste! History has been made. It is now, for the moment, actually mine! The Misses Pugh have departed for "The Home"; the sale occurred last Thursday; the rooms were completely dismantled; the endless trash accumulated during fifty years, has been held up to the auction and sold; some of the rooms are quite empty, and the whole house resounds when I walk through it. Tonight it is raining drearily. Doolittle, who came up yesterday morning, departed in a taxi at 4 p.m.[1] He had manfully helped me carry the beds from downstairs, put them together, and reassemble the bed-rooms. My room and yours are now rather nice again. The less said of the downstairs the better. I spent $80.—buying back pots and pans I have given the Miss Pughs but found I was shy many essential items just the same. And as usual, when everything is disorganized it seems as though nature herself takes a hand in making chaos more chaotic. For on Friday when I had to go to West Chester to buy Kitchen tables, a cook-stove, food, and utensils, the terrific hurricane, that you read about in the papers occurred. And to make matters worse it turned out to be Yom Kipper and the store that sold kitchen tables was "closed for the holiday." So I haven't got one yet. And fancy cooking meals for Doolittle with nothing but a chair to work on in lieu of a table! And fancy too, how

1. Edmund Warren Doolittle was one of McBride's oldest friends. During World War I the two men shared an apartment at 358 West 22d Street. Later, while living in a rooming house in Baltimore (where he worked in a store selling religious artifacts), Doolittle made annual summer visits to McBride at Callicaste. A generous gourmet cook, he could usually be depended upon to bring such treats as deviled crab, beaten biscuits, and kidneys cooked in wine.

the new oil stove when it finally came refused to burn except on one burner, so that we were compelled to fry bacon on an alcohol stove. But you can't fancy such miseries. You have no imagination. And you have never been obliged to do things for yourself. You have always been cared for by others!

The sale, however, in regard to prices was an enormous success. People seem to have money again. $105.—for the corner cupboard, $50.—for that old walnut table in the kitchen and so on. I was somewhat reconciled to all the annoyances and embarrassments of the occasion by the fact that one dealer offered $150.00 for my miserable old highboy in the sitting room and I accepted! But the people are such fools. One woman paid $7.50 for six glass plates that I bought for 60 cents in Woolworth's three years ago. She thought them antique! I didn't say anything, though I could have said plenty. For one thing, they were *my* plates, not Mary Pugh's. The Miss Pughs seemed to feel that anything of mine, that had been in the house for three years was theirs. But we had no words. Like Tippy Dudensing, to whom another little girl had been rude at a party, "j'ai fait mien de pas comprende!" And enfin, it's all over. But it does seem funny to be all alone in a country cottage on a dreary, rainy night! [. . .]

To Malcolm MacAdam
October 23, 1936, Herald Square Hotel, New York

Dearest Malc:

Max and I had dinner with Mrs. Harry Payne Whitney au palais on Wednesday night, along with Louie Delano and Rawlins Cottenet, and afterwards we went to John Gielgud's *Hamlet*.[1] How this came about might astonish you, unless you have already learned that the very great live about as casually as the rest of us, most of the time. Mme. Delano, who sails tomorrow on one of her hasty trips to Europe, wanted to go one last time to the theatre, and we fixed upon *Hamlet*. As I had been telling her something about Max, she said ask your young German, too. Then two or three days later I got a postcard saying "Gertrude wanted to come, too, and we'll dine with her first. How about your German?" I thought Max had better keep out of it, or until the ground had been prepared a little better, and telephoned the secretary he wasn't coming; but later that day I got a long-

1. Gertrude Vanderbilt married Harry Payne Whitney in 1896. Rawlins Cottenet was a fashionable florist in the 1930s.

distance call from Louie saying "Oh, no, we want your German," so I said "O.K." Secretly I was pleased, for Max, who is simple and honest as the day is long, nevertheless, has an instinctive longing for elegance, and I thought this would be a chance to show him some, as well as introduce him to *Hamlet,* which he had never seen. The fates tried ineffectually to prevent the affair. I fell ill Saturday, had Dr. Williams Sunday, and was prostrated (and you will say this is running true to form) until Wednesday afternoon, when I began to feel I might sit up and take nourishment and incidentally go to the theatre. And poor Max had to drive all the way down from Hartford on Wednesday, and then drive down to pick me up, and then up to 68th Street again to the palace, and had a heavy cold to contend with, besides. Being young, he managed to conceal fatigue and malady, and looked fit as a daisy, as we marched into Mrs. Whitney's rather splendid upstairs rooms. Unlike you, he is never fussed by servants, nor for that matter, situations; and in a minute it became apparent that both Rawly Cottenet and Mrs. Whitney had decided to like him; and Louise, who was late (She came up town by bus, she said.), also adopted him, and so we had nothing further to worry about, and devoted ourselves wholeheartedly to the small birds and champagne and gossip about the celebrated Mrs. Simpson. Everybody but me seems to be off King Edward. I was the only one to stand by him. They are all convinced he intends to make a morganatic marriage of it—or worse; but I told Louie Delano I would bet my entire fortune against hers (the odds were good, you must admit), that he wouldn't.

Then we went to *Hamlet,* John Gielgud is grand. He is the best Hamlet I have seen since my youth, eclipsing the miserable John Barrymore completely. The production, however, is tawdry. It is by McClintic, the husband of Miss Cornell, and has all the Broadway trimmings that her plays have, and poor Mr. Gielgud must have had an awful time reconciling himself to the silly scenery and cheap stage business.[2] But *Hamlet,* as you know, is 90 percent Hamlet, and once he got the stage to himself, Gielgud was wonderful. A bit too forceful, perhaps, especially in the early scenes with the ghost, but for all that, he knows definitely what *Hamlet* is about.

By the way "definitely" is one of the new slang words. Whether it got here via India, with help from you, or just came straight from England I don't know, but it's all over. One of the worst of the new songs is entitled

2. The actress Katherine Cornell (1893–1974) and her husband, the director Guthrie McClintic, produced many successful plays together after their marriage in 1921.

"But Definitely" and in the chorus you get the line "You are an armful of heaven—but definitely." Try to laugh that off in the Madras Club. [. . .]

To Max Miltzlaff
July 4, 1937, French Line[1]

Dear Max:

[. . .] The boat is not first class, but it is not particularly bad. Its chief fault is that it takes nine days for the trip. If I get safely home again, never again will I take a slow boat—though the chances are that this is my last trip. . . A few people are on board that I know—but I don't see them much. The Ernest Peixottos are here, working the cordiale entente with the French for all it's worth.[2] Peixotto is an artist, who pulls all the ropes, is "decorated," lunches with the Captain, etc., and always praises France to the skies.

In the tourist class is Henry Russell Hitchcock, who is more my style. He is a Boston swell, who goes Tourist for reasons of his own, for he is bound on a lecture trip to England. He is connected with our Modern Museum and is chummy with all my pet artists, including Sandy Calder. . .[3] There is a troupe of dancing girls aboard who do tap-dancing in the salon strenuously all day long. They are a mystery, because they do not seem quite professional and they are in [the] charge of a fierce, grenadier-like woman, who treats them like school girls. They are not pretty, but they all have nice legs. . . This afternoon as I was reading in the smoking room a procession of nuns in heavy black veils, etc., came up single file from the Tourist and went forward. I wondered if they were going to see the tap-dancers.

My two cabin mates are non-aryan, or so I judge from their names. One is Dr. Bierman, going to Vienna to lecture on radio-therapy and the other, a young Englishman is named Lipman. He is not objectionable at all, but he is very disorderly. He strews his things about the cabin so that I seem to be a regular Max Miltzlaff in comparison.

Anyway I wish there were a Max Miltzlaff in the party. I need somebody to take care of me, and above all to scold me. If someone would scold me I might wake up and take more interest in this voyage. But as it is I think it abominable. [. . .]

1. This was McBride's last trip abroad.
2. Literally, a cordial understanding, the Entente Cordiale was a loose alliance signed by France and Great Britain in 1904.
3. Alexander Calder (1898–1976) was living in Paris and working on his famous whimsical kinetic sculptures, which Duchamp called "mobiles," in the mid- to late 1930s.

To Max Miltzlaff
July 14, 1937, Hotel Lincoln, Paris, France

Dear Max:

Last night for the first time since I have been here I had something of a good time. It was the private rehearsal for the press of Jean Cocteau's presentation of *MacBeth,* with a troupe of juvenile actors he has got together. I went to see if I could crash the gate—and I did. The old ticket woman told me to go around to the stage entrance and ask for the secretary, and I went up the dark alley way and into the back of the stage where a lot of actors and stage-hands were still rehearsing. The young secretary, when I found him, said certainly, how many places do you wish, and when I said only one, he gave me about the best seat in the house—second row aisle. Then I asked him where I could eat in that neighborhood, for all the places up where I live are shut by the strikers, and he sent me to the Chien Vert, where the food was really good, and the customers amusing. When I got to the theatre the curtain was already up and the witches were doing their work. The production was very simple; on the order of our *Dr. Faustus* only not so good. But Lady MacBeth was only 17 years old! What do you think of that? When the lights went up for the entre acte, a hand tapped me on the shoulder, and there was the famous Marcel Duchamp and his wife, sitting right behind me![1] (He painted the *Nude Descending the Staircase.*) With him, was the translator of the piece, also about 17, and we were joined by the young secretary, who seemed much impressed to find that I knew Marcel; and then we went out to a bar and proceeded to have a party, being joined by several other artists I knew. After *MacBeth* we had Jean Cocteau's own version of Sophocles' *Oedipe Roi,* done very queerly.[2] Cocteau made a witty speech before the curtain. It was the first time I had ever seen him and I could understand why he is so much admired in Paris. He sure is slick. But it was 12:30 before the final curtain fell, and 1 a.m. before I got home. [. . .]

1. Although Duchamp had married Lydie Sarazin-Levassor on June 8, 1927, they divorced six months later, and Duchamp's second marriage, to Teeny Matisse, did not occur until January 16, 1954. The "wife" to whom McBride refers is probably Duchamp's primary female companion during the 1920s and 1930s, Mary Reynolds, an American war widow who was a book designer and bookbinder.
2. This short play by Cocteau was an adaptation of his libretto for an oratorio in collaboration with Stravinsky, *Oedipus Rex.* One notable outcome of this production was that Cocteau met Jean Marais, an acting school student who auditioned for the play and later became his partner.

PS. I decided today not to go visit Gertrude Stein and wrote to her to that effect. Tonight I received a telegram most affectionately insisting—but it is now too late to make the arrangements; and the fact remains that I am too tired to undertake the trip by train and too nervous to go by air. But it is very disappointing; for a visit to Gertrude would have been something to remember—whereas all my other experiences are things to forget. . .³ [. . .]

To Gertrude Stein
July 15, 1937, Hotel Lincoln, Paris¹

Dear Gertrude:

I can't come after all. The other day, when I wrote to you, I was too optimistic. I was feeling wretched but thought I would get better and the weather would get better in time to come to see you. But neither of us has. To be sure, today *is* a bit warmer—but it is now too late to remedy the slough of despond into which I fell. You see, I'm supposed to be working. I was invited by a lot of dealers, ostensibly to write up the Fair, but in reality to brush up my friendships with the French painters—for of late the publicity in America in regard to French art has fallen off and they wish it accelerated. They do no business here, poor things, and can only sell in America, and yet America has suddenly developed a craze to buy American art!²

But knocked out as I was by the cold and rain, I haven't done the tasks allotted to me, and must do some more of them, before leaving Tuesday or Wednesday for London. I now realize I am too aged and too decrepit for this sort of thing and shall certainly never attempt it again. That's why I am particularly disappointed in not getting down to Belley—for I may not do any more ocean traveling. I did so want to see you and Alice and to see the garden and hear the news. . . But in London I'll ask all about your ballet you may be sure. . .³ The only thing of an amusing nature I've had in Paris was

3. McBride never saw Stein again.

1. McBride's last letter to Stein.

2. In an unpublished letter to MacAdam, November 17, 1937, McBride writes, "My tasks are more numerous and more difficult then ever, owing to the fact that this seems to be the only country in the world where there are money and picture buyers and so all the dealers in the world have offices here and put on shows. My assistant and I had over sixty exhibitions on our list this week. I go to see about twenty of them" (YCAL, McBride).

3. *A Wedding Banquet,* composed by Gerald Hugh Tyrwhitt, Lord Berners, based on Stein's play *They Must. Be Wedded to Their Wife,* choreographed by Frederick Ashton, premiered at Sadlers Wells Theatre, April 27, 1937.

the répétition générale of the Jean Cocteau *MacBeth* and *Oedipe Roi*. Marcel Duchamp sat right behind me and lots of people joined us during the entre actes and we had a party. . . Both plays had their oddities in the performance. Lady MacBeth was only seventeen years old for instance! And Jocaste had a marked Russian accent. However Cocteau in a curtain speech warned us not to ask "pour quoi?" and so none of us did.

And I wanted to know about *Everybody's Autobiography,* too!

With love and despair,

To Malcolm MacAdam
November 26, 1937, Herald Square Hotel, New York

Dear Malc:

[. . .] Tomorrow I have a ticket for the Rachmaninoff concert which some one sent me. I am astonished at myself for not having heard him before this, for when we have acknowledged great people in our midst, one might as well get the good of them. But I am careless that way. There are one or two great artists in Paris, such as Maillol and Despiau, the sculptors, and I never stirred hand nor foot to meet them, last summer, as I easily could have.[1] I prefer to judge my artists from their work and not from their persons—but just the same one ought to meet the really good ones in the flesh. Here in America there are no longer any artists who interest me greatly. I sometimes think art is going out entirely, giving place to the Movies.

My only social event this week was a private lunch by Bernard Faÿ, the French writer, in Mrs. Murray Crane's house, attended by the very great.[2] I fell in with Rachel Crothers, the playwright, and told her I was fed up with the hysterics and frights of people in general and that I for one refused to worry about the world which, in my opinion, was just about the same as it

1. Aristide Maillol (1861–1944) and Charles Despiau (1874–1926) were pioneers of a modern French sculptural form that was seen as oppositional to Rodin in its concern with preserving the classical ideal. Despiau was an inheritor of Maillol's formal beauty, and both men were primarily sculptors of the figure.
2. Bernard Faÿ (1893–1978) was a professor of American history at the University of Clermont-Ferrand, and a close friend and translator of Gertrude Stein's. Mrs. Murray Crane conducted discussions about cultural and intellectual matters, often with a featured speaker, at her home at 820 Fifth Avenue, beginning in the late 1920s and continuing for three decades. She was also one of the founding board members of the Museum of Modern Art.

always had been.[3] She agreed heartily. The imaginary woes of the public are due, we both said, to the alarmists in the newspapers and the new school of croakers on the Radio, who recite current events as though the end of the world were scheduled for tomorrow. People act as though it were sensational to discover poverty here and there in our midst, but poverty isn't so hard to bear as the college-boy orators think. I've been poor all my life and reasonably happy as well. If you could make politicians honest and surpress the Jew merchants and lawyers, particularly the Jew lawyers, it would be difficult to tell this earth from heaven.

I find I am writing an essay, so I'll call it off. You want news not thoughts. I met the Countess Pecci-Blunt at Mrs. Crane's. She's a fabulously rich Italian fascist, about to open an art gallery for fun. She has good things to say about Mussolini. Among other things, she pays less taxes in Italy than we Americans pay here. Personally I'm for fascism, Hitlerism, and anything but Communism—and Russia is the source of most of the disorder at present rampant—and war between Japan and Russia would do more to fix things up than a war between Japan and China. . . N'est-ce-pas?

To Malcolm MacAdam
March 18, 1938, The Coffee House, New York

Dear Malc:

If you were here tonight you could hear *Otello* and sit in the Harriman box along with Georgia O'Keeffe, Mabel Dodge and Sybil Walker. Instead Vincent Price, the actor will take your place. Max also. Max will be paralyzed to meet Mabel Dodge, though she is not so formidable as you might think. Particularly just now. She is up here staying with Dr. Brill, the psychiatrist, and probably taking treatment. She behaves like a good little girl and speaks in a meek little voice and is frightfully womanly and sympathetic and Ralph Flint says you had better watch out for something always happens when Mabel gets to acting like that. She says she is coming back to New York next winter, and establish contact with the young people. Whether she is going to do something for them or have them do something to her she doesn't say. She intends to bring Tony, also. Her last two books have not been successes. Nobody could read them. Perhaps that's the real trouble. [. . .]

Did you read the terrific news in paper today about Frankie Parker marry-

3. Rachel Crothers (1878–1958) a playwright interested in portraying the role of women in American society. For three decades, beginning with her first success in 1906, Broadway saw, on average, a new Crothers production every year.

ing Mrs. Beasley who has a daughter as old as Frankie? Apparently Frankie has Max's peculiarity and likes them old.

All the news lately is terrific, but I refuse to get as excited as most of my acquaintances, about the doings in Europe. To hear their passionate declamations, you'd think America was deeply involved. I dined with Ettie and Florine Stettheimer last night and of course, for racial reasons, they are more weepy than most. I have to disguise my sentiments generally, just as I did during the great war, for somehow I never agree with the intellectuals. At present, the chief danger to decency is the Soviet, with its subtle incessant propaganda to destroy democracies, and anything that stabs at communism has my approval. Consequently, I'm not so upset by the disasters in Spain as my friends are. But apparently the Jews have control of most of the newspapers and most of the radios, and all you hear is the "wurra wurra" they are shrieking. I have yet to meet a Jew who can explain the attraction communism has for the Jewry, and I don't know one who acknowledges that attraction, yet in every outburst of communism you usually find a Jew at the bottom of it.

To Carl Van Vechten
November 18, 1938, *The Sun*

Dear Carlo:

The photographs came promptly and were much admired and I am a palsied villain of a hack-writer to be so slow in thanking you. That's what I am—a hack-writer and the difficulties I have had lately in making myself write a single word—let alone a combination of them—is past belief.

I liked the Charles Demuths very much and am grateful to have them. It surprises me that he could be done for I had thought him like myself, non-camera. Georgia, of course, is a natural born movie-queen so that's not so much credit to you as it might otherwise seem. And I saw at Dudensing's the one you did of Lachaise and I thought it marvelous.

I thought of you the other night at Elizabeth Thomas' dinner, for Gertrude Atherton made dramatics the moment she arrived by falling ill and yet refusing to go home and when she finally appeared in the drawing-room at 11:30 p.m. In a dress extremely décolleté with gold spirals running all over the black I thought she was a motif worthy of your talents.[1] She is 82 years old you know. "Look at her shoulders," Maimie Howland said

1. Gertrude Atherton (1857–1948), prolific historical novelist who married into the wealthy Atherton family based in San Francisco. A friend and supporter of Gertrude Stein's and Carl Van Vechten's.

to me, "aren't they wonderful for a woman of 82?" I thought they were too, but all the same, Gertrude was going strong when I left the party at midnight.

You should look into this.

With best thanks and affection

To Malcolm MacAdam
January 29, 1939, Coffee House, New York

Dear Malc:

[. . .] Last night Georgia O'Keeffe took me to the Toscanini broadcast—one of the sensational high spots of the winter activities—and for some reason I thought of you particularly—not being at all sure you would get it, musically, but certain you would be amused, and perhaps irritated by the swank that attends these affairs.[1] You know, under the skin, we are all just as snobbish as the English ever thought of being, though we go about it in different ways. But the high-incomed business men throughout the country know that a symphony orchestra costs millions to support and that Toscanini gets a fabulous salary and that in general it is the top thing in its line. So when in New York they all use their pull to get tickets, and the crush is so great to attend, that only the most privileged get them—and hence the snobbism. All the ones who get balcony tickets dress in tails and white ties and the ladies put on their most sensational togs and they behave as though they were in church. In fact, they behave better than that. But this is only for the Toscanini broadcasts. Earlier in the season, when Rodzinsky of Cleveland, conducted, the hall was only three quarter full and the swank had diminished till you could scarcely notice it. It all takes place at Radio City up on the 9th floor and all the arrangements are different from anything previously known. I hope Toscanini lasts till you get back to New York, and that I also last and am able to take you. Last night among the celebrities was the famous Emma Eames, sitting quite near us, and alas looking fat and placid and totally unlike a prima donna.[2] Going out, Georgia and I followed her through the corridors, admiring her mink coat and the way she progressed with her lady companion to the doors, leaning on a cane. I told Georgia that when her time came, I hoped she would put on as good a show of elderly royalty as Emma Eames did, and

1. Arturo Toscanini (1867–1957) served as principal conductor for NBC radio for seventeen years, beginning in 1937.
2. Emma Eames (1865–1952) American opera soprano who sang mainly in London and New York.

Georgia said she was going to begin right now to practice. Georgia has some job in Honolulu and departs for there tomorrow.[3] I dined with Georgia and Alfred Stieglitz before going to the concert. She took my flippant review of her show in good part.[4] She has the sense to know that it is all to the good in the way of publicity. Alfred maintains a stoical attitude about Hitler and the Jews and I admire him for it.[5] All my other Jewish friends are completely hysterical. He did read me, however, a poetical letter of protest about the fall of Barcelona written by Mrs. Steichen the wife of the photographer. I suppose they all try and lean on Alfred for support, he being a sort of patriarch among them.

I heard the Chamberlain broadcast Saturday afternoon and envied the English, as usual, for having such gentlemanly politicians. His voice and manner were very appealing, though at the same time I suspected he was a completely discouraged and bewildered man. I'm afraid the English aren't up to the situation. Of course, I'm pleased at the taking of Barcelona, as I'm against communism; and if Mussolini can restrain his officers, when Spain is conquered, then I think we may hope for some quiet in Europe. The trouble is that conquerors never do restrain themselves and are never satisfied with enough. That was the trouble with Napoleon, Alexander and all the great ones, who have gone before and I suppose history will repeat.

All the communists now call themselves socialists. Apparently there is no longer any difference.

To Marianne Moore
February 4, 1939, 116 West 34th Street, New York

Dear Marianne Moore:
What a lovely book, inside and out![1] I think *you* are very fortunate to have written it and to have had it so beautifully printed (I like Mr. Plank's

3. O'Keeffe had been commissioned to produce illustrations of tropical fruits and flowers to be used in illustrations by the Dole Company.
4. "Georgia O'Keeffe Accused of Misdemeanor," *New York Sun,* January 28, 1939. In her show, which ran from late December 1937 to January 1938, O'Keeffe exhibited for the first time her abstracted images from the Southwest, including floating skulls and bones against landscape backgrounds. Many critics disapproved of O'Keeffe's new direction.
5. Stieglitz's feelings about the rise of Nazism in Germany are reflected in his first show of a European artist in almost a decade, an exhibition of the overtly political and harshly critical work of George Grosz, a German refuge, in early 1935.

1. *The Pangolin and Other Verse,* with drawings by George Plank, was published in an edition of 120 copies by Curwen Press, London, in July 1936.

decorations—they are exactly suited) and *I* am very fortunate to have received it at last. I have read it all with profit. I thought at first *The Pangolin* was going to be a self-portrait—the creature was too well armoured—but then I read on and found myself included and practically all my acquaintances. Do you flatter us? I wonder! But as you say, the sun recurs and it does recur purposelessly.

I hope your mother mends rapidly for I should like to come and see you both. I have thought of such a thing many times but was held back by the notion—I don't know what suggested it—that you were not trafficking much with the world. It was not until I met Monroe Wheeler and found that he was seeing you ad lib that I realized a visit was possible, and when it is possible I shall bring both my volumes along to have "something written in them" for I do not intend ever to part with them. They are quite all that T. S. Eliot said they were![2]

To Malcolm MacAdam
March 10, 1939, Herald Square Hotel, New York

Cher Malc:

I used to pride myself on not bothering about politics but of late I think of nothing else. . . Some weeks ago, Muriel Draper asked me over the phone, would I come to a Congress of Youth banquet at the Hotel Murray Hill, pay $3.50 and hear Mrs. Roosevelt speak. Muriel is an old friend, brilliant, witty, and sometimes mixed up with shady doings, but always good fun—so I said yes. Besides, I had never heard Mrs. Roosevelt speak. Well, I went, and got several shocks from which I have not yet recovered.

The whole thing proved to be a thinly disguised communism and Jewish war propaganda. It was a rather rough looking mob, 300 or so, and one third of them negroes, and only a small percentage in dinner dress. At our table, with Muriel, the air was thick with conspiracy, and they all have that especial exhilaration, that people have, who are engaged in war. It's very contagious. I half envy them the fun of it. You remember what we all went through in 1914. Muriel warned the young lady next to me not to tell me too much as I was not "one of them," but the young lady just the same filled me full of her exploits in placing the Jewish émigrés from Germany in good Quaker families all through the country. I didn't tell her I was a Quaker myself, but picked up enough to fill the Hayes family with horror

2. Eliot wrote the introduction to Moore's *Selected Poems,* which was published in New York by Macmillan in 1935.

when I go back to Marshallton. I felt just like a spy being there. Your friend Heywood Broun was busy whooping things up and Rockwell Kent, another firebrand, came up to me beaming and shaking hands and asking "are you a Radical?"[1] I said "Heavens, no. I got here by mistake. I'm a capitalist except that I have no capital" and then Rockwell Kent dropped me like a shot.

Then the speeches began, all of them leveled at Hitler and preaching what they call socialism, but which is in reality communism. Mrs. Roosevelt was really rather wonderful. She is the best woman speaker I have ever heard, though it is true I have not heard many. She is absolutely self-possessed, her voice is clear, unforced and easily heard, and her manner is gracious and winning. She actually looks handsome, too, as she speaks. But it is apparent that she is now deeply involved with communism. You never see, I suppose, the article she published every day in a chain of newspapers, called "My Day," but in it she frequently of late inserts pleas for Loyalists in Spain—and those Loyalists were supported by Russia, as you know.[2] I thought in the beginning of Roosevelt's reign, that he was using socialist stuff to combat the menace of socialism and communism—taking the sting out of it, as it were—but long since it has become apparent, that the real communists have out smarted him and have got him in their clutches. I was reminded of this again as Mrs. Roosevelt spoke. She generalized and didn't go into details, but when she said that the administration's tactics had not solved the problem of saving civilization but had given us time in which to think how to save it, a glitter of fear came into her eyes as she said that civilizations had died before this, and this one would die if we didn't use our brains to prevent it—all of which is true enough, of course—even if you do know that socialism is not the way to do it.

What she said was general, and not actually incriminating, but there she was sitting at a table with agitators making inflammatory speeches against a country with which we are not at war—and preaching ideas which, if put in practice, would destroy our own country. The entire evening was anti-Germany and anti-Italy and not a word was said against the totalitarianism of Russia. Russia, evidently, was their ideal. Certainly, Russia, as you can imagine, was definitely back of the movement.

1. Rockwell Kent (1882–1971) American painter of the Maine coast and Canada, was a student of Robert Henri and Abbott Thayer and was a boisterous and outspoken communist, vegetarian, and womanizer.
2. Eleanor Roosevelt's six-days-a-week syndicated column "My Day" first appeared in 1935.

The Soviet plays the game wonderfully I must admit, and if it has genius for nothing else, it has genius for propaganda. The negroes are being played in every way. You should have seen how they beamed at the banquet. Two days later came the Marian Anderson incident in Washington, with Mrs. Roosevelt again taking the prominent stand.[3] Then came the "Swing" *Mikado* performance, with Mrs. Roosevelt and Mayor La Guardia blessing the performance (It was amusing). And over the radio, you are not safe a minute from the subtle insinuations meant to color opinion in favor of Communist Spain and against Germany. Only last night, I tuned in to hear some music, and the artists turned out to be Jewish refugees, and there was a blood-curdling speech asking employment for them, etc. . . and then there followed a long speech by an Irishman, telling of the history of the Irish in America, but ending up with a plea for them all to join the labor organizations. Of course, the theatres are full of communists plays, and the newspapers are all sold to the Jews. The *Tribune* is unbearable, as you must notice, and I am about ready to switch to the *Times,* for, though it is Jewish run, it is not nearly so partisan. The only thing that stops me is that I hate to give up the cross-word puzzles. The *Tribune* does have the best.

But Roosevelt now is in bad. When Billy Bullitt came back from France and Kennedy from England we all knew they would fill the President full of war frenzy and they did. When Roosevelt said the American frontiers were on the Rhine, the country gasped, and Roosevelt sealed his own doom and the party's, as well. He denied the remark afterward, but everyone knows he said something like that. Anyway he is done for. However, he seems determined to wreck the dollar even if he cannot immediately wreck the country. [. . .]

To Malcolm MacAdam
May 7, 1939, Herald Square Hotel, New York

Dear Malc:

[. . .] You told me not to talk politics but there is nothing else in my mind, nor in any of our minds. We talk of nothing else. That is the whole trouble. All of the half-educated people in the world think they know how

3. Marian Anderson (1902–93), who later became the Metropolitan Opera's first African-American singer, was denied permission to rent Constitution Hall in Washington, D.C., by the Daughters of the American Revolution, the owners of the building. In "My Day," Eleanor Roosevelt announced her resignation in protest from the DAR. She then went on to help arrange for Anderson to sing at the Lincoln Memorial, and seventy-five thousand people attended.

to run a perfect government and they cannot run their own little houses. What cheers me a little is the definite reaction against Roosevelt, and the slight discouragement that even the *Tribune* has in trying to get us to war with Germany. You get the *Tribune* don't you? Then you must notice the perpetual propaganda, and the featuring on the front page of continual attacks vs. Hitler; but you can have no conception of the incessant Jewish warfare vs. Germany that hits you from every direction; from the radio, from the theatre, from the movies. The Jews control all those things, and if they had real sense they'd pipe down, but they are determined on destroying Germany, and in doing that, they'll destroy all of us. One big bank asked me to be on a jury to award a prize in a poster competition they were fostering, and at the luncheon in the Union League Club the president of the bank was far more outspoken than I dare to be. He said, among other things, that there would be "some shooting here, too, before the Jewish question was settled." But it was also clear that he knew of no line of defense against the encroaching communists. He said, too, that in every nest of communists there was a Jew bossing the campaign. Muriel Draper asked me to a secret meeting at her house Thursday night, to hear an "escaped" German tell how the revolutionaries were working inside Germany to "get Hitler." But I could not go, although I should have liked to have "spied." I am caught in the red web myself this week, somewhat to my amusement, for Picasso's big mural called *Guernica* is here being shown for 50 cents admission fees, for the benefit of the Spanish refugees. I had to say the picture was remarkable, for it is, but the money, of course, is to go to the bad little communists, who will all be smuggled into this country, where we have too many of them already.[1] Of course the German Jews are smuggled in by battalions.

I've seen a few things at The Fair but I am not wild about the show.[2] The populace is, however, and doesn't mind the second class sculpture and second class everything. They do say it is something to see at night, however. The Soviet Building is one of the best. It cost $10,000,000.—and you can figure out how many million peasants starved to pay for it. But the Japanese building is good, too, which balances the account somewhat. It's hot. How can I ever get packed up, and away, Especially since the Fair has piled a lot of jobs upon me?

1. "Picasso's Guernica," *New York Sun*, May 6, 1939. Reprinted in *Flow of Art,* pp. 367–69.
2. The 1939 World's Fair opened in Queens in March with the theme "Building the World of Tomorrow."

To Malcolm MacAdam
January 28, 1940, Herald Square Hotel, New York

Dear Malc:

I'm very tired. Dined last night at the Kirk Askews' and there was the usual large party afterward of the so-called brilliant set, very talky naturally, and if there is one thing more than another that wears me down it's being brilliant. Yet you have to, at the Askews'. [. . .] I believe there's a war going on somewhere, but at the Askews' it wasn't mentioned. We were all too busy being brilliant. As I recall it, though, that's the way it was during the other war. Everybody had a lovely time, except the actual boys who lost their legs and eyes. Yet our silly president is determined to send a lot more of our youngsters over to lose their legs and nobody knows how we can circumvent him. For my part, as I must have told you before, I'm persuaded there would have been no war if Roosevelt had not led the English to think we would have joined in. I don't so much mind the boys losing their legs and eyes, I suppose they would anyway, but it's quite clear to all of us that every day the war is prolonged means one day nearer to communism. [. . .]

To Marianne Moore
February 16, 1942, Herald Square Hotel, New York

To Marianne Moore:

I am so deep in disgrace by this time that there is nothing left me but to confess all. I liked *What Are Years* too much and admired you too much to say so simply![1] Can you understand that? Do you know how a genuine inferiority complex really works? It flinches in the presence of a great light. I flinched when I tried to tell you I thought *What Are Years* great. I did it in lead pencil first so that it should be exactly right but when I read it over I found, to my horror, it was exactly wrong. You remember what Victoria said about Gladstone (whom she disliked)? That he always addressed her as though she was a public meeting? That's the way I caught myself addressing you—just in time! The next morning I tore it up and wondered why writing people must always be literary. A whole week went by, I being most wretched all the time, and then I tried again, at much greater length, trying

1. Moore sent McBride a copy of her new book *What Are Years* (New York: Macmillan, 1941) with the inscription, "October 7, 1942, To Mr. McBride with gratitude for his refusing to be tragic."

to explain my bad manners, and getting more literary even than I was the first time and then reading it over and saying "No, I can't send that."

If you can't believe all this I still have the two wretched attempts in lead pencil to prove it. This one has not been tried out in lead-pencil and I think, to be safe, I won't re-read it, and I think I'll wait until you ask me over to tea with your mother, before I tell you what I feel about *What Are Years*. Somehow, when actually face to face with you I don't seem to mind so much your being an Immortal.

Shall I be asked over, I wonder, after all this?

Abjectly yours,

To Malcolm MacAdam
July 22, 1942, Callicaste, Marshallton, Pennsylvania

Dear Malc:

[. . .] What a ninny you are to quarrel with John and Max about the war. I should think you old enough to know better. They are exactly the age that prevents them from appreciating military service. Boys, with their craze for parades, and a lack of imagination that suggests the cost, are all for it—but not the men of forty. I remember very well in 1918, when you were approximately their age, that you were no more eager to join the army than John is now. So *can* the recriminations! Your crack about Lord Haw-Haw was probably as unjust as anything they said. That's the way it is—in war talk—mostly hot air. [. . .]

To Ettie Stettheimer
July 14, 1944, Callicaste, Marshallton, Pennsylvania

Dear Ettie:

Not only grieved, but deeply troubled. For a long time after reading your letter I sat looking out the window incapable of thought. It was as though my brain were refusing to accept the news that Carrie was no more. Even now, a day after, I cannot make myself believe it. It seems incredible, that one who seemed so firm and secure a short time ago should have vanished.

I am glad now that I managed to make that call, for at the time I was very uncertain of myself and unequal to anything, but somehow, once at the Dorset, I picked up courage from you two.[1] It seemed to me I had never

---

1. Carrie and Ettie Stettheimer lived at the Dorset from 1935 until their deaths.

seen you so resolute, or as I said, "secure"; and I thought it quite wonderful the way both of you banished emotion from the little interview. As I was going away, and as we three stood, standing in the hall, I looked at Carrie particularly and I remember a moment of surprise at seeing that her head scarcely came above my shoulder. I had become used to thinking her actually as tall as she always appeared in Florine's pictures, and it was strangely moving to see that the tallness was really a tallness of spirit, rather than the body. Florine made me think of Emily Dickinson. That day of parting, which I did not know to be a parting, you and Carrie reminded me of the other Emily, Emily Brontë—and largely because you were facing fate so staunchly. I remember well what you both said then and it has new meaning, when recalled now.

Carrie's tallness reminds me, that she smiled a little indulgently, when I said the likenesses in the family portrait were exact. "Exact," I suppose, is not the exact word. I might better have said truthful, for truth and exactness are not always the same. People who do not mind my way of writing know that I mean to provoke thought rather than to define it. When I said "exact," I was thinking of the little portrait of your mother in the group. It does seem to me exact in some strange way—more like her than any photograph could have been.

I will write again soon. I'm glad Kirk is looking after the pictures.[2] I will try to write to him, too. I am better than I was on coming down here, but am still shaky and the slightest task tires me. But probably the extreme simplicity of my way of living is good for me. Nothing else is possible at any rate. [. . .]

To Ettie Stettheimer
October 20, 1944, Herald Square Hotel, New York

Dear Ettie:

Sorry to hear you have a cold—but it is the price we pay for living in a city. We have to have them and the only thing to do is what you are doing—stay in bed until the medico permits you up again. That will probably be next week, when I shall hope to see you and have a quiet talk. I have seen Kirk and was disgusted to learn that Chick Austin has been fired from

2. Shortly before she died Florine considered destroying all of her paintings. She did not, and as director of the Durlacher Gallery, Kirk Askew handled the work in Florine Stettheimer's estate.

the Athenaeum.[1] In a way it was curious he lasted so long there, for he ran the museum with a verve that amounted to genius, and the surprises he managed for us so enchantingly would, naturally, confuse and infuriate the stodgy trustees. A museum is never an easy berth for a genius. [. . .]

To Ettie Stettheimer
November 16, 1944, Herald Square Hotel, New York

Dear Ettie:

I don't believe in telepathy yet something very like it happens all the time. On my always busy Tuesday I made a special trip to see Kirk to inquire about you—to find out if you were seeing people again—for I wanted to see you. He told me you had gone off to the hospital for a check-up and he persuaded me that it was a wise move and that there was nothing to be alarmed about.

Then I went home and later in the afternoon a package came from Georgia O'Keeffe with the reading-glass of Florine which she said you wished me to have—and it touched me very much, for I remembered seeing Florine using it often. It will be a mute reminder of times past, and although I don't actually need a magnifier, just because it is there on my desk I have already employed it several times. So you see, at the two ends of our telepathic wire, we were somehow related. [. . .]

I wanted to talk to you, among other things, about *Grey Eminence* by Aldous Huxley, a book that has thrilled, horrified and amused me. What a terror that Aldous Huxley must be.

To Max Miltzlaff
August 15, 1945, Callicaste, Marshallton, Pennsylvania

Dear Maxie:

[. . .] Just as I was finishing my peaches last night Burnelle crashed in the door and said "Come on over" and I did. They had been to West Chester taking Lulu the colored maid home, and as I passed through it I said "Oh what an immaculate kitchen," and Mrs. C. replied, "That's because Lulu has been here." Then I said, "I suppose I shouldn't have said that, then," and both replied, "No you shouldn't have." . . They proceeded to have

1. Austin officially resigned January 1, 1945, having served as director of the Wadsworth Atheneum for nearly seventeen years; his tenure at the museum combined modernist art, theater, music, film, and magic in unprecedented ways.

their supper on the terrace, and just then we heard faint whistles from various distant places and Mrs. C. said, "Do you suppose the Japs have signed?" and Burnelle rushed to the radio, turned it on, and found out they had.

So the war is over!

It's going to be very queer, and quite evidently the peace is going to be just about as nasty as the war was. Somehow I can't be enthusiastic about it. There was little noise here. One or two cars rushed by tooting their horns after I had gone to bed, but that was all.

Clarence says he will cut the grass Friday. The routine goes on, war or no war.

To Ettie Stettheimer
September 22, 1945, Callicaste, Marshallton, Pennsylvania

Dear Ettie:

In fifteen minutes the postman comes. T'was ever thus. You might think, having been jailed indoors by a hurricane for four successive days, that I might have found time to scribble a note to an old friend, but on the first of the days, in the midst of the downpour, Malcolm MacAdam arrived unexpectedly to pay me a visit, and then stayed the whole four days. Malcolm is no cook. Somebody had to cook so I did. Did you ever cook for two, for four days, Ettie? If so you will understand easily enough why no letter writing was attempted. But we had pretty good meals, and we played cribbage in front of the fire on the hearth, and were not too afflicted by the storm.

I was glad to hear that you had been away to the New England coast—for any change of scene helps—even though asthma trails its victims everywhere.

It's nice about Florine and Westpoint. Charles Ford has never sent me proofs of my article but I presume it must be due shortly.[1] I had no sooner sent the Ms. to him, than Harry Bull of *Town and Country* wrote wanting such a "piece."[2] I'm almost sorry I had not sent him it instead. It might have had more readers! [. . .]

Virgil is in Paris.

1. Charles Henri Ford was the editor of *View* magazine, where McBride's article "Florine Stettheimer: A Reminiscence" appeared in October 1945. Stettheimer's painting of c. 1917 (current whereabouts unknown) appeared on the cover of the May 1945 issue of *Town and Country* magazine.
2. McBride's article "Artists in the Drawing Room: Looking in on the Stettheimers at Home" appeared in *Town and Country* 100 (December 1946).

22 Henry McBride and Malcolm MacAdam, undated. Photographer unknown.

To Georgia O'Keeffe
July 16, 1946, *The Sun,* New York, New York[1]

Dear Georgia:

I was shocked and astonished to hear last night that Alfred had finally finished his task—the more astonished because we had so often thought him at the end of his resources only to find him the next day as alive as ever. That gradually got me to thinking he could go on indefinitely. I certainly thought he would outlive Marin and me, and that he hasn't, gives me a curious sense of guilt.

But I won't go on talking words and I won't say anything about condolences. I don't know what condolence is.

I am alarmed at the problems you now face (Marin, the gallery, your work) and powerless to offer suggestions, but you must know that all of us will be thinking of you and for you and maybe some wisdom will come out of it. [. . .]

To Ettie Stettheimer
August 12, 1946, Callicaste, Marshallton, Pennsylvania

Dear Ettie:

Are you still at Marblehead? I'll chance a letter. I should have written sooner but I have been laid low by one of my nervous crack-ups, from which I am not yet released and hence this letter won't be a letter but a "note." My illness was humiliating because it is disgusting to be ill alone and at last I have to admit I must not attempt this sort of thing again. . . In fact it is likely that several things have come to an end with me, including possibly my winter's work. But the autumn may benefit me. It often has in the past.

The procession of deaths, under the circumstances was not a help, either. At intervals of a few days portraits of old friends appeared in the newspapers accompanied by proper obituaries. I couldn't help but think that Paul Rosenfeld's was somehow attached to Stieglitz's.[1] And after that I

1. In May 1946 McBride, along with the architect and designer Le Corbusier and several other select guests, had attended a private dinner for the opening of O'Keeffe's retrospective at the Museum of Modern Art, the first retrospective the museum had devoted to a woman. Stieglitz did not attend the opening. He died July 13, in New York City.

1. Rosenfeld wrote two articles on Florine Stettheimer, one in *The Nation* ("The World of Florine Stettheimer," May 4, 1932) and one in *Accent* ("Florine Stettheimer," Winter 1945).

said, "Three are enough"; for country people say that disasters come in threes; but Gertrude's collapse made a fourth.[2]

Do give my love to Bobby.[3] I must write him next. I owe him a letter anyway.

I wonder what effect my Florine piece will have upon you. I am uncertain about it, especially the end of it, for I was already breaking up at the time of writing, and had every imaginable difficulty to confuse me (including the suspicion that my eyes were going wrong); and I may have dissipated some of the fog, as you hope, but I wonder! . . I was better pleased with the *Town & Country* thing though it was distinctly frivolous and you won't like it, but it seemed to do what it started out to do.[4] Harry Bull liked it; but he sends me no proofs. I wonder if the Museum will. Has proof reading gone out of fashion? For that matter Charley Ford never let me see a proof of the *View* article—though they, happily did nothing to it. [. . .]

To Ettie Stettheimer
October 8, 1946, Callicaste, Marshallton, Pennsylvania

Dear Ettie:

So you went to the reception after all! I hope it didn't do you up. . . My neighbor Earle Miller (an artist) in New York that night went to the show and had you pointed out to him but didn't dare speak to you because you were surrounded by people congratulating you.[1] He liked the show. Did you? I rather think Monroe as a showman for Florine would be preferable to Duchamp. Marcel might be too fantastic, and Florine has enough fantasy of her own without adding his to it.[2]

My chances of being comfortable in New York are slim.[3] The Hotel

2. Stein died July 27, 1946.
3. Robert Locher.
4. "Artists in the Drawing Room: Looking in on the Stettheimers at Home," *Town and Country* 100 (December 1946), pp. 74–77, 336–37.

1. On Earle Miller see Biographical Sketches.
2. Duchamp was notorious for his installation ideas. At the 1917 exhibition of the Society of Independents he proposed hanging works alphabetically (he also proposed that instead of the normal twenty-five-cent admission fee, critics should be charged fifty cents to enter). His installation of the "First Papers of Surrealism" in 1942 included a mile of string.
3. As Max Miltzlaff describes the course of events: "When World War II ended other troubles started. The Herald Square Hotel changed management and the new people had no interest in accommodating an old patron who had lived there over 25

Woodward turns me down although a room had been promised. Marie Sterner's Laurelton also says "No."

Earle Miller returned with the news that Teeny Matisse knew a rich old lady who lived "in a house" and would take me in for a small fee which would be given to charity, as she was a very charitable woman and had a lot of charities on her list. I phoned Teeny Monday, who said it wasn't an old lady at all, but a young one, but a rather odd youngish woman; rather dotty in fact. I said that would be O.K. with me, I didn't care how dotty she was. But since then no news, though much telephoning. I plan to come up next Sunday and will call you up at the earliest moment. . . I hope you weathered the party all right.

To Ettie Stettheimer
June 24, 1947, Callicaste, Marshallton, Pennsylvania

Dear Ettie:

[. . .] I was glad to hear about the Stieglitz show and was on the point of writing to inquire, when your letter came.[1] Georgia, I knew, wouldn't write, for she is cross because I didn't stay on in town for it—but that is impossible. Just now the *New Yorker* arrives and I am pleased with the way Coates handled the job. He was apparently not wildly enthusiastic about the photography, but looked on Alfred as I do, principally as a promoter and teacher. One word in his review would have annoyed Alfred excessively—he referred to him as a "dealer"—a term he always rejected furiously—yet the fact remains, that he ran a gallery and sold pictures! I wonder how Dorothy Norman is coming along with her memorial number of *Twice a Year*.[2] I wrote a little piece for it last autumn in the midst of my arriving in town, and after a while corrected the proofs of it—and then

---

years. On his first trip to the city in the fall of 1946 he remained with me at the Wentworth Hotel for a few days, and then through Mrs. Matisse, located a lady and a daughter who had a large apartment on Park Avenue at 93rd Street. . . . After two months a change was made and a small room was found in the Woodward Hotel, east of Broadway on 55th Street. He remained there through the spring of 1946" (unpublished, YCAL).

1. An exhibition of Stieglitz's art collection and his photographs, which O'Keeffe helped to organize, was held at the Museum of Modern Art from June 10 to August 31 and later traveled to the Art Institute of Chicago.

2. Dorothy Norman, *Twice-a-Year*, no. 14–15 (1946–47). Norman worked at the Museum of Modern Art, and became close to O'Keeffe and Stieglitz when she assisted in the preparation of O'Keeffe's 1946 retrospective at the museum.

silence. I must write Georgia and try to pacify her. I can't resist the feeling that the passing of Alfred, makes a stoppage in her career that she hardly yet realizes. And that entire winter given up to business and the estate still seems to me a mistake. You've heard the phrase prize-fighters use about "making a come-back" and you may know that the prizefighters regard it as practically impossible. Well, in art, as in all other career, it is just as difficult to resume after a lay-off. There, is a gap where the germ of defeatism creeps in! [. . .]

To Everett and Alice Barr
December 9, 1948, The Hotel Winslow, New York

To Dr. and Mrs. Dr.:[1]
 There was some swanky Tiffany writing paper in my bedroom at Glenway Wescott's where I was doing the long weekend last week and I thought of stunning you with some of it, and also of describing Glenway's house for you, for it is a gem,—but somehow there was too much social activity and I didn't get round to it.[2] And now I forgot the details.
 But the house is perfect for a writer, not big, and on several levels, with a large library that is for public usage, and a smaller one off from it and so hidden that Glenway can write there no matter what uproar is occurring in the other rooms. The pictures and the furniture are ultra-smart. You wouldn't at all approve of the pictures for Glenway and Monroe Wheeler (who shares the house with him at intervals) are thick with the wildest of our painters and buy their most daring efforts on principle—but you would like the furniture, for most of it came over from France when Glenway's sister-in-law gave up residence there.[3] Although classic it looks early American enough to suit you.
 Glenway's brother Lloyd, you may have heard of, for he is a Guernsey

1. Dr. and Mrs. Everett Barr, see Biographical Sketches.
2. Glenway Wescott (1901–87) was a novelist, poet, critic, and essayist *(The Grandmothers, The Apple of the Eye)* whose output decreased after the 1920s. In the early 1940s Wescott moved permanently to Stone-blossom, the estate in western New Jersey which he had shared with Monroe Wheeler (see Biographical Sketches) and George Platt Lynes.
3. Barbara Harrison, married to Wescott's brother Lloyd, founded Harrison of Paris in 1930. This small press, managed by Wheeler, continued until 1934 and published thirteen lavishly produced books by such authors as Katherine Anne Porter and Glenway Wescott, illustrated by such artists as Alexander Calder and Pavel Tchelitchew.

23 Henry McBride and Chester Dale, in the Dale apartment at the Plaza Hotel, New York, 1948. Rudy Burckhardt.

specialist and has a farm of 1000 acres.[4] Naturally the cream we had in our morning coffee rivaled yours.

He is also a social reformer, and one of the sponsors of a penal institution for bad girls where they are put on parole, no gates, no locks, and where the girls get to be good again speedily, so they say. It is a few miles off, and in the afternoon we went over there to see the dedication of a new

4. Guernsey cows were a special interest of Dr. Barr's.

organ in the little chapel. Ellabelle Davis, the next best colored lady singer after Marian Anderson, was featured on the program, but I was chiefly fascinated by the bad girls in the choir (one of them a murderess), who sang thrillingly and with great piety. [. . .]

To Ettie Stettheimer
March 25, 1949, *The Sun,* New York

Dear Ettie:

You continue to surprise. Georgia O'Keeffe telephoning to me about something the day after you left for the south, mentioned your flight, and added: "Isn't that the most astonishing thing you ever heard?" and I agreed. I think both of us expected disaster to come of it, but here you are actually enjoying Florida and boasting of it with the enthusiasm of an early Spaniard. Just the same you can have it. I don't seem to be enticed into trying it myself. I hear a lot about Florida winds. You mention them yourself. I don't like winds. Also I don't enjoy the spring in America. I tried it once in Europe and got through it happily enough to conclude that, "Oh to be in England now that April's here," is true poetry. But April in New York always lets me down and gives me the blues. I've been having them this week for it has been astonishingly mellow and warm.

I've seen no one and have no gossip for you but the newspapers will be telling you that our "cold war" with Russia is warming with the weather. The arrival of Churchill, to make an important speech is balanced by the coming of Shostakovitch, the Russian, to attend a "cultural" assembly at the Waldorf. Zealous Catholics and war veterans by the thousand are milling about that hotel at this very moment in protest and these rival factions are making such a fuss that the trial of the Communist party leaders is passing almost un-noticed and will probably end in a "no verdict."[1] I may saunter down this evening to see the picketers show, for, as far as the young people are concerned that is what it is. In spite of the terrifying implications of the affair they seem to think it an entertainment. The Hearst newspaper printed the list of the sponsors of this cultural meeting and I found quite a few of our friends on the list. On the whole I think it's wonderful the world gets along as well as it does—we're so irrational. [. . .]

1. In early 1949 growing Cold War fears of the "red menace" resulted in the conviction of eleven American communists for urging an overthrow of the government.

To Everett and Alice Barr
October 21, 1949, The Hotel Winslow, New York

To Dr. and Mrs. Doctor (both of you doctor me wonderfully):

You must think all that bread-and-butter completely wasted, unappreci-ated, unthanked and unlettered. Anyway it really was appreciated and per-haps this will turn out a letter—but if it should be punctuated peculiarly it will be the telephone's fault. It rings continually; due to this cursed "honor" the Knoedler Galleries are putting on me because of my great age. They are celebrating Prof. John Dewey's 90th birthday this week up at Columbia and that philosopher has been quoted as saying "I'm damned if I see the sense of rejoicing because I've reached 90." And he is used to these public hysterics and I am not. Miss Wittler (of Knoedlers) has just phoned to say that she has arranged with the Associated Press man to interview me on November 15.[1] Yesterday she told me she was ogling the *New Yorker* in an effort to get them to do a "profile" of me. I called that off peremptorily. I told her my private life wouldn't bear being looked into. I've called off, too, the banquet Holger Cahill was arranging and the cocktail party Ettie Stett-heimer planned. The game of publicity is not for me. It's not to my taste, and for me it always flops necessarily because I don't play up to it. [. . .]

1. Lelia Wittler was the director of the Knoedler Galleries and was responsible for the arrangements made in conjunction with the gallery's exhibition "To Honor Henry McBride."

CHANGES IN THE 1950s

In the 1950s McBride's personal and professional life changed significantly. With the closing of the *Sun* and a move to writing for the monthly magazine *Art News,* McBride's schedule and the frequency of his name appearing in print slowed considerably. Personally, his lifelong habit of living alone in hotels during the New York season ended when he took up apartment living, residing with his close friend Max Miltzlaff. By the middle of the decade McBride was nearing ninety, and health problems and estate considerations made him decide, in 1955, that it was time to sell both Callicaste and his art collection. In 1957 McBride's oldest friend, Malcolm MacAdam, died.

After more than thirty-five years of writing art criticism, McBride received a long list of awards and honors throughout the decade, beginning with a tribute exhibition at the venerable Knoedler Galleries in late 1949 and culminating in his receipt of the Legion of Honor in September 1958 for his contributions to the success and fame of French artists.

The tribute arranged by Knoedler Galleries, held from November 29 through December 17, 1949, was called "An Exhibition of Paintings, Drawings, and Watercolors to Honor Henry McBride." The show featured works by thirty-one artists McBride had championed over the course of his career, including Henri Rousseau, Pablo Picasso, Joan Miró, Winslow Homer, Paul Cézanne, Thomas Eakins, Constantin Brancusi, Joseph Stella, Juan Gris, Chaim Soutine, John Marin, Augustus John, Georgia O'Keeffe, Charles Demuth, Alexander Calder, Florine Stettheimer, and Gaston Lachaise. The cover of the catalogue for the exhibition featured the Pascin woodblock print of McBride made in 1918 for the cover of the private printing of "Have They Attacked Mary. He Giggled." The inside cover featured Virgil Thomson's 1935 musical portrait of the critic. Lincoln Kirstein wrote the introduction, called "A Quasi-Preface."

In January 1950 the *New York Sun* was sold and became the *World Telegram-Sun*. McBride was not asked to continue writing for the new publication, and his thirty-six-year weekly writing career came to an abrupt end. McBride wrote to his Marshallton friends the Barrs about the fallout of the *Sun*'s collapse and the end of McBride's page: "I received a hundred letters, at least, and an organized group including Charles Henschel, Head of Knoedler, Nelson Rockefeller, Dorothy Shaver, Head of Lord & Taylor, etc. etc. wrote to *The Telegram* asking to have the art-page continued there, but were snubbed bluntly. As for me, I wasn't at all sure I wanted to join *The Telegram*, for it does seem a measly paper, and after playing about town for a fortnight, going to dinners every night in the week, I finally signed up with Dr. Alfred Frankfurter to write for *The Art News*, the official art magazine of America."[1] In February 1950 McBride's first monthly column appeared in the *Art News*, where it continued to appear until 1955. McBride also occasionally accepted a commission to write an essay or catalogue preface. He wrote the catalogue for the 1950 exhibition at the Museum of Modern Art of his old friend Charles Demuth. He also continued to make the rounds of galleries and museums, writing appreciatively of the new developments in American art by Tomlin, Rothko, and Pollock. Although McBride's life and era were drawing to a close, he remained receptive to the next phase.

In the fall of 1950 McBride returned for a third year to the Hotel Winslow, where he had taken up residence in October 1948 "in a small but comfortable room on the 12th floor."[2] In 1951 McBride and Max Miltzlaff moved to a large apartment at 17 West 54th Street, overlooking the garden of the Museum of Modern Art. McBride enjoyed the apartment on 54th Street, writing to the Barrs in October 1951, "I have finally moved into the palace. . . . I have not yet grown accustomed to the grandeur. I feel as though I were visiting rich friends, and in a way that is how it is. I told you, I think, that Ettie Stettheimer was getting out of storage for me the bedroom furniture of her sister Carrie, and it turns out to be overpoweringly magnificent."[3]

In the early part of the decade, McBride continued to spend the summer and early fall months at Callicaste and often visited Appetite Hill, Miltzlaff's country home in Oxford, Connecticut. In 1955, after suffering a slight stroke, he decided to sell Callicaste, as McBride and Miltzlaff considered it unsafe for the eighty-eight-year-old McBride to spend the summer months alone in the country house.

In February 1956 McBride and Miltzlaff moved downtown to Peter Cooper Village. The inconvenience of the location made it increasingly

1. January 25, 1950 (YCAL, McBride).
2. McBride to Dr. and Mrs. Everett Barr, October 10, 1948 (YCAL, McBride).
3. October 19, 1951 (YCAL, McBride).

difficult for McBride to make the rounds of galleries, though he did keep abreast of the younger artists, telling Peter Miller in a letter of February 3, 1956, that a mutual friend had "considered having her portrait painted by the young Larry Rivers. Not a bad idea! He's the best of the new group."[4] McBride saw fewer of his friends after the move, but O'Keeffe, Lelia Wittler, and Maynard Walker remained regular visitors. Many weekends were spent at Appetite Hill.

In 1954 the American Federation of Fine Artists awarded McBride its annual prize as best magazine critic. In keeping up with the ebbs and flows of art, McBride wrote to his friend Maynard Walker in 1955, "Childe Hassam means little to a Monet fan, and Jackson Pollock still less to a disciple of Picasso."[5] By the end of 1955 McBride had retired from writing. His last piece was a 1959 essay called "Those Were the Days," which was a contribution to an exhibition of *The Dial* Collection. Correspondence with his friends continued until January 1962, two months before his death.

In 1959 the first attempts were made to bring McBride's writings together in book form. This project was finally realized with the publication of *The Flow of Art* in 1975, republished in 1997 by Yale University Press.

To Ettie Stettheimer
July 13, 1950, Callicaste, Marshallton, Pennsylvania

Dear Ettie:
Not shocked, as you seem to have been, by the Leo Stein revelations, but confirmed in my worst suspicions.[1] You see, I didn't expect much. I always thought him a confused, bewildered, ineffective person,—something on the order of what we call a stuffed shirt—all on the outside, nothing inside—but I had no idea his frustrations were so complete as he himself says they were. His entire life seems to have been devoted to a study of his physical disorders and if he had been in the slightest degree an artist he might have shaped his account of them into a monument to himself. But he was never an artist. That was his trouble. That was the secret of his maniacal preoccupation with Gertrude's success. He thought he taught her all she knew and he could not understand why the world turned to her and away from him. She was not a thinker, as Leo takes pains to insist, but she was an artist.

4. YCAL, unpublished.
5. Maynard Walker Gallery Files, Archives of American Art, July 9, 1955.

1. Leo Stein's self-revelatory *Journey into the Self* (New York: Crown), edited by Edmund Fuller, was published posthumously in 1950.

You don't say what shocked you. Was it the undressing in public, or the fatuousness of the philosophy? In a way the lapses in good taste were scarcely Leo's fault since, after all, he didn't edit the book, and they should be charged up to the wretched psycho-analysts with whom he had so many dealings. They demand such confessions, but there is no warrant for publishing the stuff. In poor Leo's case they were partly saved by being so tiresome. I confess I had to skip those intolerable letters to Dr. Boas.[2]

But what a colossal ego. Leo rated himself, it seems, on a par with William James and Santayana!! Thanks just the same for the book. You do keep me au courant. . . Hope you recovered from the dentistry. [. . .]

To Everett and Alice Barr
January 19, 1951, Winslow Hotel, New York

Dear Mrs. and Dr. Barr:

[. . .] Here, all luxuries are fading out of sight and the people, who used to have them, do nothing but shake their fists at Harry Truman and do nothing else. What can they do? An individual protest means nothing and we defeated ones are not organized. I did hear about a week ago that Eleanora Sears of Boston was advancing on New York in an effort to start a party opposing the high cost of governments and I cheered up and immediately decided to marry Miss Sears, or at least, sign her petitions and get everybody else to sign them, but since then not a word has been heard of this enterprise and again I begin to get discouraged.

One good thing happened. The Claude Rains play, *Darkness at Noon,* is a great artistic success and a fine political document.[1] It could win the war for us, if properly exploited. It could do for our war what *Uncle Tom's Cabin* did for the Civil War. Frances Rains called me up on the telephone, the Thursday previous to the opening, to say there was a dress rehearsal that night, and would I come? So Max and I went and were simply petrified by the play, which is devastating. If such a play had been put on three or four years ago we would not be in the mess we now are in. I'd give anything to have it performed in Boston where all those measly Harvard students could get the idea. As it was, half the audience at the private view, mostly

2. Franz Boas (1858–1942), anthropologist and ethnologist, authority on languages of the native North Americans.

1. Based on Arthur Koestler's 1941 best-selling anticommunist novel, *Darkness at Noon* describes the inherent conflicts between the individual conscience and totalitarianism.

actors, were unquestionably "pink" and were laid low by the performance. During the entr'acte, a well-known youngish actor of my acquaintance came up to me to shake hands, and when I said, "What do you think of it?" he gave the shiftiest looks imaginable, and began talking in French, "Je ne peux pas parler," etc., and just then the bell rang and I rushed back to my seat with the strong conviction that the young man ought to be investigated by the F.B.I.

Claude Rains does a first-rate job. [. . .]

To Malcolm MacAdam
April 12, 1951, Hotel Winslow, New York

Cher Malc:

[. . .] Things have been going along placidly until yesterday, when Harry Truman's bomb-shell of a dismissal for General MacArthur knocked us all to pieces again. The immediate effect was that of awed terror, just like Sunday broad-cast of the Pearl Harbor affair, and everybody in the hotel downstairs talked in whispers and then cursed Harry Truman once they recovered their breaths. Today people have subsided and begin to see plainly, that it was a choice of a world war or MacArthur, but the president is so much in disrepute, that there is still extreme annoyance. Somehow we feel he did the break with unnecessary roughness and that the whole affair plays as usual into the Soviet's hand. The inflammatory newspapers, such as the *Journal* and the *Evening Telegram,* indulged in a riot of hatred for Truman, but the *Tribune* and the *Times* this morning soberly acknowledged MacArthur had to be chained. Going all out to war with China means another world war, and another world war means our finish. [. . .]

To Everett and Alice Barr
October 19, 1951, 17 West 54th Street, New York

The dear Barrs:

[. . .] I told you, I think, that Ettie Stettheimer was getting out of storage for me the bed-room furniture of her sister Carrie, and it turns out to be overpoweringly magnificent. Very quietly elegant bed-stead, commode, bench, night-table, etc., decorated by hand in dull blue on parchment-colored wood; with window hangings to match; but Ettie's lawyer had me sign a paper to say that at my death these treasures were to be returned to Ettie's estate. This, of course, presents a nice little embarrassment to Max at

my demise, which must occur shortly, for I simply cannot keep up the exaggerated pace, which all this implies. However, this does not bother Max
much. He is so in love with splendor that he doesn't care how he gets it.

But I am more infatuated with the kitchen which, I don't mind telling
you, is about three times handsomer than Agnes's. It has a dark blue floor,
nicely waxed and all the rest is glistening white enamel and chromium,
with countless cupboards and closets. It leads directly into the big front
bay-window, where we breakfast and dine, and from which we look down
on the garden of the Modern Museum and see, off to the east, St. Patrick's
Cathedral, and the church of St. Thomas. The chimes of St. Thomas we
hear all day long. Fortunately, I like them. After having been pinched for
three years in a tiny cell at the Winslow Hotel you can imagine how strange
all this is to me. Several big trunks of mine, which had been stored at Max's
for five years have been brought here, and it astonishes me greatly to
recover things I forgot owning. [. . .]

To Everett and Alice Barr
November 12, 1952, 17 West 54th Street, New York

Dear Neighbour and friend:

Perhaps I can jiggle on my type-writer a letter in the midst of the uproar
that comes to me from across the street. At last they have started building
the Whitney Museum.[1] Whilst still at the breakfast table this morning I was
amazed when something shining red in the sunshine darted by the window. It was the giant derrick, the highest I have ever seen, and it reached
two floors higher, to the eleventh, and this I think carries ostentation to the
extreme, for although we all know that Flora Whitney is the richest girl in
the world, there really was no occasion to use an eleven-story derrick for a
four story building, which is all that the Whitney Museum is going to be. I
sound cross. Perhaps I am. It's the noise; and besides, apart from the derrick
I've always liked Flora Whitney. [. . .]

Max has just had what amounts to a ten-day vacation in Miami. It was a
convention of travel agents, which sounds awful but Max enjoyed it. He

1. In 1949 the Whitney Museum accepted from the Museum of Modern Art a plot
of land at 22 West 54th Street and began to build a new museum to replace their old
building on 8th Street. It opened in late October 1956. The 54th Street site of the
Whitney Museum lasted less than ten years before the institution moved to its current home at Madison Avenue and 75th Street.

brought back a lovely after-dinner story about an old man who lived to be 92 and told how he did it. Tell it to Dr. Everett for he could use it on some of his more fidgety patients. The old man said, "When I sit, I sit loose. When I work, I work easy, and when I worry I just go to sleep." It sounds better if you tell it with a Southern accent; "When Ah sit, Ah sit loose," etc.

I took over to the *Art News* this morning my contribution for the December issue. It's a very personal account of Chester Dale, whose vast art collection is about to become part of the National Gallery in Washington. Perhaps they'll print with it, a photo of Chester and me, for the photographer took a lot of shots in which I have no confidence whatever. Tom Hess, who saw the proofs, said that I looked just like a minister in them.[2] So, naturally, I fear the worst. [. . .]

To Alice Barr
March 17, 1953, 17 West 54th Street, New York

Dear Mrs. Barr:
    [. . .] It was good of you to phone those banks and locate the trust officers. . . I am ashamed of every part of my behavior in regard to my relatives.[1] Not so much ashamed of my behavior, but of the circumstances which compelled it, for if I were to do it again it would have to be the same way. Most people think it a sin to abandon one's relatives, and so it is, but in this case it happened automatically, for when the family broke up, at my age of fifteen, it was the family, such as was left of it, that abandoned me. But I think I told you all this before. But I never had any rancours, nor discomforts and, on the contrary, a singular amount of luck. . . But I had embarrassment when I had to transmit the news of the death of my sister-in-law to my niece in the West, for I had not seen her but once when she was a baby-in-arms, fifty years ago, at least, and I had not been writing her, and was not even sure of her address. So to such a stranger I couldn't even sign my letter with the conventional "your loving uncle." And yet here in New York there are at least fifty youngish people who call me Uncle Henry!!

All very queer, don't you think.

2. Thomas Hess was editor of *Art News*.

1. In early 1953 Sadie McBride, the wife of Henry McBride's brother John, died. On her death her husband's trust was willed equally to Mary Nicolas, a niece, and Henry McBride.

To Alice Barr
May 7, 1953, 17 West 54th Street, New York

Chère Madame Barr:

[. . .] I am just finishing my June essays for the *Art News* and feel so tired of the winter that it will take me all summer to recuperate. My social life doesn't work anymore. I'm through with it. I actually dread dressing for dinner and get out of it whenever I can. A few weeks ago I went to a big, stuffed shirt dinner of twenty or thirty people, the only such thing I have done this year. I have done a few small dinners and a few cocktail parties and that's all. The old-timers, who used to give such wonderful parties, can't do it anymore, and the nouveau riche I have not got acquainted with as yet—and I don't want to be bothered with them anyway. I much prefer idling the evenings away at home with Max. I went to the opera only once, and until this last week had not been to the theater since the French players were here. But a queer poet I know named Parker Tyler wrote a play and had it produced by the Artist's Society in a small theater and sent me tickets.[1] It was an outrageously bad play but wildly entertaining just the same. And the night after that Lincoln Kirstein's Civic Opera Company did a revival of Rossini's *Cinderella* and we went to that and loved it.[2] The singers were not quite good enough for the music, which was extraordinarily difficult, but they acted so well we forgave them. And the costumes, stage sets and management were beyond anything we have had here lately. [. . .]

To Earle and Peter Miller
March 12, 1954, 17 West 54th Street, New York

To Mr. and Mrs. C. Earle Miller:

I seem to continually pelt you with missives—but there is news—and you don't have to answer until after the 16th, when you'll be telling me who slammed your show and why—or perhaps praised it to the skies and made you so vain you wouldn't write to any mere New Yorker at all.

But anyway—I dined with the bride and groom Tuesday evening.[1] Quite

1. Parker Tyler was a poet, essayist, art critic, movie critic, and playwright. He wrote the first book on homosexuality in the movies *(Screening the Sexes)*, the first critical history of underground film *(Underground Film)*, eight art monographs, six volumes of poetry, more than five hundred essays, and some four hundred art reviews. He appears as a prominent character in Gore Vidal's *Myra Breckenridge*.
2. For Kirstein see Biographical Sketches.

1. Marcel and Teeny Duchamp.

wonderful and queer. The flat is at 327 East 58, a walk-up four stories. Marcel had a chair at two landings for me to repose in on the way up. Furniture grandiose, explained because it was too big to be extricated from the flat, when Peggy Guggenheim's husband moved out.[2] There was a cook, ebony colored; Rufino Tamayo and Olga for guests; exotic food hopefully thought to be Mexican I think and Teeny, Duchamp's daughter, lovelier than ever, helped the 100% African with the service. . .[3] After dinner other guests climbed the stair. Janet Flanner (Genet, of the *New Yorker*) and a Mr. and Mrs. Lewin (magnates from Hollywood cinema industry), and the conversation became more lively and international than ever.[4] Teeny is radiantly happy and Marcel has an air of extreme contentment. More of this anon. [. . .]

To Marianne Moore
Callicaste, July 7, 1954

Dear Marianne Moore:

Two nights before I came down to this retreat (now, more than a month ago) I dreamed of you—probably for the first time in my life. Then, just at my departure, they brought me your sumptuous book of fables; yours and, I think, La Fontaine's.[1]

Do you telepath? Or credit dreams? For the moment of my dream must have been the precise moment when you were wrapping up the parcel for me.

And the dream was a nightmare. There were personages present in it whom I didn't quite identify but who were probably among our dearest friends and all were attacking you. What they said I don't recall exactly but I had the feeling it was vicious—something about nobody having the right to do what you were doing—and just when the diatribes were at the wildest

2. The flat formerly belonged to the surrealist Max Ernst (1891–1976), Peggy Guggenheim's second husband.
3. Rufino Tamayo (1899–1991) was a self-taught Mexican painter, muralist, and graphic artist. His style fused elements of European modernism—cubism and surrealism—with the native traditions of Mexican and pre-Columbian art. Teeny (Alexina) married Duchamp in 1954; McBride is perhaps referring to Jacqueline, her daughter by Pierre Matisse.
4. Janet Flanner (1892–1978) was an American journalist based in Paris who wrote a "Letter from Paris" twice a month, under the pseudonym Genêt, until 1974. After 1934 she also wrote a "Letter from London."

1. Moore published her translation of *The Fables of La Fontaine* in 1954.

who should come walking around the corner in my dream but YOU—and then everybody hurriedly scrambled into the obsequious behavior they usually lavish upon you. But at that I awoke, overwhelmed with terror at the suspicion that you might have heard some of it and would be including me among those guilty wretches. And I felt particularly guilty because I did have something to confute them with and didn't use it. If you had delayed your entrance but a moment I might have, but you didn't and so I didn't. I'm not a man of action in my dreams it seems.

For what I had was sure-fire rebuttal. I had had pre-publication knowledge of one of the two fables—that one of Renard et Maître Corbeau—and liked it. I felt sure everyone would like it, including La Fontaine himself. Curt Valentine, in some clever way had got hold of it and used it in the catalogue of one of his exhibitions.[2] What pleased me most in it was the cajollerie addressed by Brer Fox to "Sir Ebony." That, it struck me, was pure Marianne Moore and also, in some strange way, pure La Fontaine. Not that La Fontaine thought of such a phrase but that he would have liked it mightily if he had.

When I get back home to 54th Street, if I ever do, I'll be delving into the volume for more rebuttals and no doubt finding plenty—although I don't propose re-dreaming that dream under any condition. I came down here for a week and have been a month and may linger yet another. It's a matter of getting rid of this house, my library and goods and chattels in the effort to simplify my life and make it more livable than it has been lately.

How long has it been since we have met! And how famous and famouser you get! I seem to like it for you but know very well I wouldn't like it for myself. Which is just as well since the fates don't seem to be insisting upon it.

Best congratulations and thanks.

2. Curt Valentine, owner of the Valentine Gallery.

MCBRIDE'S COLLECTION

On the evening of Wednesday, January 19, 1955, most of Henry McBride's collection of modern works of art was sold at auction at the Parke Bernet Galleries on Madison Avenue. The sale, which also included items from the estate of Millicent A. Rogers, consisted primarily of works on paper in various media. Most of the works had been gifts that McBride had acquired over the course of long friendships with artists. Highlights of the sale included five mixed-media works on paper and an etching by Miró; five watercolors by Marin; five works by Demuth; single works by Léger, Lachaise, Tamayo, Tchelitchew, and Pascin; and print editions by Matisse, Braque, and Modigliani.[1]

McBride wrote an essay, "Good-Bye My Collection," that was published in an edited form in the auction catalogue. The essay opens: "But parting with the watercolors of John Marin, Charles Demuth, Joan Miró, Fernand Léger, Jules Pascin, and Pavel Tchelitchew is more than parting with my pictures, it is like parting with my youth, for we all grew up together, and the pictures are relics of friendships as well as of prophecies that have now come true."[2]

Many of the pieces sold that winter evening had been part of McBride's life for twenty years or more; some of them had hung at his house in Callicaste, where, on at least one occasion, he had reason to worry whether or not two ladies visiting from a Quaker Friend's Home might not be shocked by the work. McBride gives his reasons for giving up his collection in the catalogue: "Most unwillingly, I part from my pictures. But quitting my New York apartment (because it has become offensively co-operative) and also quitting my house in the country (because it has become difficult to run)—leaves me no alternative. To hide them indefinitely in a storage warehouse would be as much of a wrench as selling them outright and would, I

1. The Demuths included an important gladioli watercolor, sold that evening for $1,100 and now in the collection of the Pennsylvania Academy of Fine Arts (see Haskell, *Charles Demuth*, plate 79, p. 165). Haskell dates the work c. 1923.
2. "Foreword by Mr. McBride," *Modern Paintings, Drawings, Prints, and a Few Sculptures Belonging to Henry McBride, the Estate of the Late Millicent A. Rogers, and Others*. New York: Parke-Bernet Galleries, 1955.

am sure, run counter to the intention of the artists who gave them to me long years ago and who most certainly painted them to be seen."[3] We know from his letters that McBride was also concerned that his companion, Max Miltzlaff, not be left with the burden of responsibility for the valuable works of art after his death.

In an itemized list McBride made for himself after the auction, we learn that the sale brought in a total of $19,045. McBride noted the sale price for each lot, and also noted the total value of the collection as $14,135 "when given to me." The biggest jump in price was for a Modigliani aquatint, *Madonna,* which McBride valued at $40 when he received it and sold for $360. Several works sold for less than their original values, including a Marin, *Small Point,* which sold for $1,600, and is listed as worth $2,000 when it was given to McBride. The list is certified at the bottom as an accurate appraisal of the collection by McBride's longtime friend the gallery owner Maynard Walker.[4] With sales prices ranging beginning at a low of $30 for a Miró etching of *Sea Life,* the most expensive items sold that evening were two watercolors by John Marin and *The Negro Jazz Band* by Charles Demuth, each of which fetched $1,600.[5]

Many of the works in his collection were affectionately dedicated to McBride, including John Marin's *From the Cape,* which was given to him on April 4, 1944, and inscribed "An American Place, 509 Madison Ave.—, N.Y. With love from The Place."[6] Also inscribed were pieces by Miró ("Hommage d'Amitié à Monsieur McBride très sincèrement, Miró, 7.34"); and a 1944 Léger work on paper called *The Bicyclists* was dedicated "à Henry McBride cordialement F. Léger." McBride's India ink and gouache portrait by Pascin, which was the illustration for the frontispiece of the private printing of "Have They Attacked Mary. He Giggled," sold that evening for $275. Also sold was a signed and numbered Matisse aquatint *La Sultana,* printed by Jacques Villon, after a watercolor by the artist in an edition of

3. "Foreword by Mr. McBride."
4. McBride's personal, annotated copy of Parke-Bernet catalogue, including inserted notes. Collection of Max Miltzlaff.
5. Demuth's watercolor *The Negro Jazz Band* had perhaps the most exciting provenance. One of several related studies the artist made of the subject, it was left by McBride at the offices of *The Dial* and mistakenly assumed to belong to the magazine. Only through the intervention of Marianne Moore and her lawyer was the work eventually returned to McBride.
6. This and all the following lots are illustrated in the Parke-Bernet catalogue, p. 15, lot 41.

two hundred. The print, which sold for $500, was a gift to McBride from Scofield Thayer, who had purchased the edition in Vienna in 1927.

To Max Miltzlaff
January 19, 1955, 17 West 54th Street, New York

Dearest Maxie:

[. . .] Tonight's the night. Of my sale, I mean. I'm going with Lelia Wittler. Louie Delano had a dinner party on (which I escape) and is furious not to be able to attend. The Millers phoned this morning they couldn't come. The Barrs wrote to say they were thrilled by the newspaper items. Quite a few telephone calls wishing me luck. All of which leaves me calm. Somehow I don't care ——. For I don't ever count on luck and am already prepared for the worst. I am especially bored by the publicity which, after all, will do the sale no good, for it comes out after it is over. But Tuesday Aline Loucheim (who is very nice) of *The Times,* interviewed me for an hour, taking copious notes, but her piece won't appear until Sunday.[1] And yesterday a young man from *News Week* came and talked for an hour and a half, also taking notes, and his piece comes out on Saturday!!! And on Monday the *Life* photographers had me up at the galleries from 4 till half-past five, taking photos. It was excruciating, and I know the photos will be awful. A whole forest of bright lights! I was seated in the midst, burning with shame, and also from the heat of the lamps. When I sat down, they said, "That's good. Hold it," and they went on adjusting the lights until I nearly went crazy, and they'd return, and say, "Now, Hold it, lift up the head a little, look straight at the camera, etc., etc.," and this sort of thing went on for at least fifty shots. When Peter Miller phoned this morning I told her to tell Claude Rains that I thought he earned every penny he ever got in Hollywood.

I probably won't have any time tomorrow to tell you about the sale, but maybe there'll be a little note in the newspaper to say that the Henry McBride Collection sold for twenty-eight cents, and if so, I'll clip it out and enclose it, for this letter has to be mailed tomorrow morning.

Thursday a.m., January 20, 1955. Only time for a word. It was a great success. Lots of fun. Too bad the Maxie wasn't there. A great crowd, and Lelia Wittler said it was an important crowd. Every seat taken and two

1. Loucheim was art writer and columnist for the *Times.*

hundred "standees"!! Walter Chrysler came over and gave me an affectionate greeting. Ruth Ford, the actress, (Charlie Ford's sister) gave me a kiss in
full public view.[2] She and her husband bought the Tchelitchew drawing of
the horse for $325.—The Marin over the fireplace brought $1,600.—The
Demuth "Jazz Band" brought $1,600.—My total for the sale was $19,000.—
The galleries charge 22%. Also government taxes for "capital gain" etc.
Still, there'll be something left for me.

To Maynard Walker
West Chester, Rt. 4, Pa, July 13, 1955

Dear Maynard:[1]

Where was I when I broke off the other day? Pierre Matisse? But I guess
you know all that. And the Millers were a bit vague. "$250,000. for aliena-
tion of affections and $250,000. for tricky business dealings." "Whose af-
fections and whose business?," I asked. But they were vague. But they said
they saw it on the front page of a Philadelphia newspaper! Very flattering,
on the whole, to be sued for $500,000; and good publicity, don't you
think? But what kind of a chance has Matta of getting any of it![2] And what
a nice, old-fashioned scandal that would be to have the whole picturesque
tale unfolded in court! The Jelke trail would be nothing in comparison![3]
How Bibi Dudensing, who hated Pierre with a fifteenth-century hatred,
would have enjoyed all this!

2. Ruth Ford was a model and actress; her husband was the actor Zachary Scott.

1. New York gallery owner Maynard Walker was an important dealer in American
art, supporting such artists as Thomas Hart Benton in the 1930s. McBride and
Walker were close friends and correspondents in the 1950s, when Walker was a frequent guest at Callicaste.

2. Echaurren Roberto Matta (b. 1912), a Chilean born surrealist painter of bio-
morphic abstractions. Matta emigrated from Paris to New York in 1939 and his
work had a significant influence on the development of Abstract Expressionism,
particularly the work of Gorky. In July 1955 Matta sued his ex-wife, Patricia, who
had since married Pierre Matisse, charging illegal possession of his artworks and
works of art that he owned by other artists. The Matisses refused to return the works
in question, and Matta's suit asked for $250,000 in damages and either the sur-
render of the property or an additional $250,000.

3. Minot (Mickey) Frazier Jelke III was sentenced on two counts of compulsory
prostitution. The heir to an oleomargarine fortune, he was convicted on one count
in 1953 and on a second in April 1955. According to the *New York Times,* Jelke was
found guilty of "inducing one woman to live a life of prostitution and had attempted to induce a second to do the same" (*New York Times,* April 29, 1955).

The career of Matta is a curious affair. It seems to have completely collapsed. For a time there was a potent group who were convinced he was a genius of the first order, although I, sitting and waiting and watching on the side-lines, had my doubts. Now no one makes such claims and he is seldom mentioned. I myself dated his decline and fall from the moment he began to follow the teachings of Marcel Duchamp. Perhaps Marcel is really the one he should sue.

And about Francis Taylor.[4] Nice writer, of course, but I was disappointed not to get something definite about the French response to the American "Salute to France." Naturally, they wouldn't care much for our newer artists, but what did they actually say? And how about the Thornton Wilder play with Helen Hayes (who is less of an actress than Matta is a painter) doing the role in which Tallulah was so superb. . .[5] If you have clippings as to these matters, send 'em along, for I am very unhappy this summer and want to be amused. Everything here goes wrong and at times I yearn for a nice mad-house.

So long,

To Alice Barr
February 24, 1956, 17 West 54th Street, New York

Dear Alice:

I'm not writing letters, it seems. Everybody says so, so there must be some truth in it. Lelia Wittler every other day asks me if I have written to Alice Toklas yet, and I say, "no, but I solemnly promise to do it tomorrow," and here it is tomorrow and here I am writing to you instead of the other Alice. Isn't that awful? Knoedler's are trying to inveigle Alice into lending the entire Stein collection to them for a show next autumn with Alice coming along as their guest for the duration of the show, and then the pictures are to be returned and placed again just as before in Alice's abode. I'm supposed to be coaxing her to say "yes."

4. Francis Taylor was named director of the Metropolitan Museum of Art in 1940. McBride wrote to Walker on July 9, 1955, "Here's a quick thank you for the Francis Taylor piece which I hurl back to you enclosed. It's not so hot as you pretend and I refuse to yield my toga to him. Smooth writing but means anything you wish to have it mean. Why should he hate so to actually say that in European eyes our art is corny? It always has been so and still is" (Maynard Walker Gallery Files, Archives of American Art).
5. *The Skin of Our Teeth* by Thornton Wilder (1942).

But with all the distractions of moving ourselves (Max et moi) to another apartment where we don't want to go, it's hard to concentrate on any of the Alices. We move next week, March 1, to No. 2 Peter Cooper Road, New York, 10 N.Y.[1] Mrs. Smith is quite right. She did see Max last Thursday. The new flat is larger than this one, with an extra bedroom and *two* baths, so Max drove all the way down and back on one day, to get my old desk, a table, chairs, a bookcase, etc., etc., and you can readily see (perhaps) why he had no time for visiting. . . If you love comedy, you should have been here last Sunday afternoon, for the new owner of our lovely apartment, telephoned in the morning to know if he could come in for a short visit of inspection and we had to say "yes." We knew him to be Hebrew but had no suspicion he would be quite so Hebrew as he turned out to be, and he brought two friends with him, who were more so than he, and so the general effect of the visit was quite Biblical. I had given strict instructions to Max to remember that he was a gentleman and he did remember. We behaved just the way the English are going to behave when Khrushchev comes to see them. But after the visit was over, we laughed and laughed. We are villains, I suppose. [. . .]

To Earle and Peter Miller
October 5, 1956, 2 Peter Cooper Road, New York

Dear Peter and Earle:

The news? Do you wish to hear it? Then brace yourselves for a surprise. The house sold at public auction last Saturday for $12,750 and the odds and ends of furniture we didn't want, brought $605 more. The whole affair was a great success and not at all the ordeal I expected. The Barrs put us up "for the duration," which was a great help, and besides they cut the grass in the lot for parking space, and supplied us with two of their husky young employees to lift the bureaux and tables, etc., out on the lawn. We had advertised in the Wilmington, Coatesville and West Chester papers and a great crowd of eager buyers assembled. The ladies of the Marshallton Fire Auxiliary served luncheon. Pretty good, too! But the people were most astonishing. Two of them hobbled around on crutches. I got the impression they would buy anything. I paid little attention to the progress of the sale, and retired to the fire place for a rest, when a lady approached and

1. This was McBride's final address. The move was precipitated by the conversion of the rental apartment building on 54th Street to co-ops. McBride balked at the $5,000 price tag on the apartment he and Max shared.

said, "There's a school-room slate upstairs on the window sill. Is it for sale?" When I said, "of course," she dashed upstairs, got it, handed it out and it brought $1. That ridiculous settee you used to sit on brought $27, and the little student lamp brought $18. The most surprised person present was Maxie Miltzlaff. When it was all over, he sighed and said, "Now I've seen everything." The sale began promptly at noon and was over by 3 p.m.

The buyer was Wm. Doherty, a real-estate man from Coatesville. He seemed enchanted to get it, and says he intends to live in it himself. But we suspect he'll sell it again after he gets it restored. We thought him a nice, simple man, but we were not so certain of his architectural taste as we were of Kenneth Stoner's. So it seems, definitely, good-bye to Callicaste. [. . .]

To Peter Miller
July 5, 1957, 2 Peter Cooper Road, New York

Dear Peter:
[. . .] Considering everything, we did a daring thing yesterday. We drove to Coney Island! In the heat. Camera-laden! But we stayed only ¾ of an hour. The *Tribune* says 1,750,000 others were there. They were too much for the Maxie. He had no trouble in India but plenty at Coney. But he took ten shots. For my part I got tired but was enraptured by the bathers. I came to a number of conclusions. For one thing people stripped are better looking than dressed. Those on the boardwalk, clothed, were hideous beyond belief. One could imagine them purposely caricaturing humanity. Those parading on the sands, semi-naked, on the contrary were, 90% of them, ideal material for an artist. Even the little girls with pony-cut hair-dos (hitherto my abomination) were altogether charming and natural. But it sure was hot. And today is a repeat. An old-fashioned summer I suppose! [. . .]

To Earle and Peter Miller
July 22, 1957, 2 Peter Cooper Road, New York

Dear Peter and Earle:
Bad news! Last Thursday morning Freddy Powells, Malcolm MacAdam's friend and companion, phoned me that Malcolm had passed away in the middle of the night. Freddy, who is the reserved and quiet type of Englishman, was almost hysterical in his account of the ending, and of course left me in the same state. Max had gone off to Hoboken to attend a ship-sailing and would not be back till midnight, and so I had nothing to do all day but

think of the disaster and I got through the day somehow but considerably shaken. By this time I have drifted back into routine but have had it made clear to me that I have very few friends left of my generation. But, but. [. . .]

To Peter Miller
January 17, 1958, 2 Peter Cooper Road, New York

[To Mrs. C. Earle Miller]

After being a recluse for two years and seeing nobody suddenly this week I have been to parties each day and now I have seen everybody. At Mary Callery's on Tuesday I resumed relationships with the George Henry Warrens, Theodate Johnson (Philip's sister), Mme. Martin of Brazil, and sixty others. Last evening at the Delanos' there was Mercedes de Acosta calling me Henry as in times past and saying; will you come to see me; Mrs. August Belmont; and William Astor Chanler, who is now in his fifties and a father of two boys!![1] Also a burly man I didn't know who kept calling me by name and when I finally said, "What is your system of remembering names," he said, "Why shouldn't I remember yours. You have been an important item in my life for forty years!!!" I still don't know who he is; and some how am highly suspicious of him. [. . .]

To Alice Barr
May 8, 1958, 2 Peter Cooper Road, New York

Dear Alice Barr of Como:

Felling more than usually decrepit this rainy morning, and knowing myself totally unequal to writing you the proper Hallelujah style letter I should, (in celebration of the miraculous recovery of your eye-sight), I have suddenly hit upon the wild idea of copying for you a letter by Hilaire Belloc, printed along with some others by him, in this week's London *Times*.[1] It was written to the Hon. Mrs. Mervyn Herbert, and runs thus:

1. Strikingly beautiful Mercedes de Acosta (1893–1968), a screenwriter in the early 1930s, is best known for her affairs with Greta Garbo and Marlene Dietrich, among others. She wrote a memoir, *Here Lies the Heart* (1960). Eleanor Robson married banker August Belmont (1816–90), who was also an art connoisseur and a minister to the Netherlands. William Astor Chanler was the son of Beatrice Chanler.

1. Joseph Hilaire Pierre Belloc (1870–1953), prolific Anglo-French poet, essayist, historian, novelist, and satirist. A book of his letters was published posthumously in 1958.

Pixton Park, April 24, 1940
"It is all due to Old Age which is, I assure you, the most horrible, lingering
(and incurable) disease ever pupped or calved. It's funny that the books lie
so terribly about it. To read the books one would think that old age was a
lovely interlude between pleasures of life and the blaze of Beatitude. The
books represent Old Age seated in a fine old dignified chair, with venerable
snowy locks, and fine, wise, thoughtful eyes, a gentle but profound smile
and God-knows-what-and-all! But the reality *is quite other. Old Age is a*
tangle of Disappointment, Despair, Doubt, Dereliction and everything else
that begins with a D. Avoid it."

For years I have been holding up to public admiration the letter on Old
Age written by Henry Adams to his brother Brooks, but now I think I'll
have to cede the palm to Hilaire Belloc, for you know all the time he was
writing those D's he was smiling. And you know equally well that Henry, in
writing his, wasn't. Henry was only fifty at the time, and bitter as gall. So
the moral is, Alice, that bitterness too, is something to be avoided. It gets
you nowhere. [. . .]

To Georgia O'Keeffe
August 6, 1958, 2 Peter Cooper Road

Dear Georgia:
  It was greatly disappointing not to see you during your recent stay in
town for it becomes part of the general frustration that seems to be mine
now that I live in Peter Cooper Village. I seldom see anyone anymore. I am
as much isolated from the world as you are in Abiquiu and the list of
intimate friends remaining for me can almost be counted on the fingers of
one hand. This is partly because of my advancing years which oblige me to
take taxis rather than the buses I used to patronize and raises the cost of a
visit to 57th Street to $3 or more. And those ardent friends of mine up there
say they want to see me awfully but hesitate just as I do at the long taxi
rides involved. So I become more and more a hermit and my disposition is
considerably soured. You, being a hermit of a superior order, surrounded
by nice mountains and sunsets and that sort of thing no doubt avoid my
kind of acidity and could have cheered me up had we met. But alas, it was
not to be.
  The other day your catalogue of Alfred's exhibition at the National Gallery in Washington with Doris Bry's fine essay came to me—and I congratu-

late you both most heartily.[1] I have not forgotten the long months during which you organized the chaos of Alfred's estate, and I see now, that it has paid off superbly for you both, for everything you did was wisely planned and most effective. Nothing could have been happier for Alfred's reputation than this show in Washington and Doris' appraisal of it is first class. I have always liked that young lady but I had no idea she was so clever as all that! . . Tell her that a small French review called *Le Point* has recently appeared, celebrating the photography of Adolphe Braun, and in it, a new critic Claude Roy, raises a brilliant argument for the defense of photography *as an art* much along the line Doris uses, and incidentally slaying Baudelaire who said it wasn't art![2] The sub-title of the essay is "Le Second Empire Vous Regarde." Tell her to search the public libraries for it. She will find it interesting. [. . .]

To Everett and Alice Barr
March 26, 1959, Peter Cooper Road, New York

Dear Everett and Alice Barr:

Each day I say I'll write the Barrs—and don't. It's mostly because of what happened Monday, the night of the opening of the Miró show at the Modern Museum.[1] I don't go to dinner parties any more, so I say, but when Mrs. George Henry Warren asked me to dine with them and go with their guests to the private view I weakened and said "yes." I had hesitated at first, pleading that I already had a half-way engagement to dine with two country neighbors of mine who were lending one of their Mirós to the show and were coming to New York to see how their prize picture looked in New York, but Mrs. Warren blocked that maneuver by saying "Why can't they dine with us. The Johnson Sweeneys are coming and the Marcel Duchamps

1. *Exhibition of Photographs by Alfred Stieglitz.* Text by Doris Bry. Washington, D.C.: National Gallery of Art, 1958.
2. Adolphe Braun (1811–77) a nineteenth-century pioneer of large-scale photographic reproduction. His still lifes, landscapes, and portraits won high praise. His large-scale photographs of flowers were compared to seventeenth-century Dutch still-life painting.

1. The show, organized by James Thrall Soby, chairman of the Department of Paintings and Sculpture at the Museum of Modern Art, opened March 18 and ended May 10. Miró arrived in the United States on April 21 to see the show, then traveled to Washington to receive the 1958 Guggenheim International Award from President Eisenhower.

and a dozen others, do ask your friends to come, too."[2] And realizing how much the Earle Millers would be intrigued by meeting these important arbiters of just the kind of art they themselves liked, I added, "Well, both are artists" and the lady cut in with "That's perfect, do ask them," and I did. . . I had no idea they'd accept but Peter promptly phones "Yes, they'd love it." However this astonishingly casual party didn't come off as planned.

On the Friday before, Peter telephoned me again, but this time to say they couldn't come. Her brother had died, and she would have to stay with her mother in Hanover until her mother could adjust herself to the loss. They had known for a long time that the brother was in a precarious heart condition, but death is death and always a surprise and the mother was in a state of collapse.

So I went alone to the Warrens, and with them afterwards to the museum where there was a jubilant mob, all of them in evening dress, coming from dinner parties and acting with the hilarity of people who have just won the election. I got kissed by an unusual number of young women and hugged by an unusual number of men. I was in the act of being embraced by Glenway Wescott when I became aware of another affectionate arm on my other shoulder, and whose do you suppose it was? No less than that of Earle Millers. All alone at the farm, he decided he couldn't stand it, and at the last minute dashed off to see how his picture was faring. I presented him to Mrs. Warren and her sister Miss Urquhart—and they made dates for future meetings.

But the next day was the next day—and I was a wreck. I still am, as you can see by this ragged writing. I am a little cheered by a telegram just received from Daniel Catton Rich of the Worcester Museum, saying my piece about the *Dial* art collection, which they are about to show, is "just what they wanted."[3] For a year I had not written anything, finding myself

2. James Johnson Sweeny, highly respected curator and critic who specialized in European modernism. Sweeny served briefly as the director of painting and sculpture at the Museum of Modern Art.

3. Daniel Catton Rich (1904–76) was educated at the University of Chicago and Harvard and joined the staff of the Art Institute of Chicago in 1927 as the editor of its *Bulletin*. Named director of the institute in 1938, he held the post for the next twenty years. During his tenure in Chicago, Rich curated shows on Delacroix, Toulouse-Lautrec, and Rembrandt and his circle. In 1958 he was named director of the Worcester Art Museum. Rich met McBride in 1934. Their friendship culminated in Rich's editing of McBride's published writings in *The Flow of Art*.

McBride's last article, "Those Were the Days," was published in the catalogue for

quite our of practice, and I rewrote my little piece four or five times before I got it into reasonable shape. [. . .]

To Peter Miller
March 29, 1959, 2 Peter Cooper Road, New York

[To Mrs. C. Earle Miller]

Last evening at supper time the door-bell rang and a young colored man handed me a heavy package and what do you think it was? Nothing less than the series of Miró Constellations, not only signed but with a kind message on the first page!!![1] I phoned to thank Pierre but he and Patricia had already flown to Europe.

Aren't they lovely though! Max wants them immediately on the walls but I hesitate. They are so pristine I want to keep them that way. What do you do with yours? I don't think I'll ever tire of them.

To Marianne Moore
July 17, 1959, 2 Peter Cooper Road

Dear Marianne Moore:

I spare you me—when I can—but this time I cannot. The word "courtesy" is too small for what you two have done;—the unknown lady who bequeathed me her hoard of clippings from my ancient writings and you who shepherded them so carefully across the river to me.[1] "Benevolence" comes nearer to it, and benevolence IS the word since unmistakably the clippings have bettered in the process. I look at them in astonishment and ask myself "did I write those?" and then blush a little and try to suppress the tide of vanity I feel surging within though not entirely defeating the thought that those things are not "too bad" and might do, in a book. And

---

The Dial collection, which was exhibited at the Worchester Art Museum, April 30–September 8, 1959.

1. Miró approached Pierre Matisse about publishing a series of facsimile editions of the twenty-two gouaches of the *Constellation Series,* 1940–41. Matisse suggested that André Breton write a text. An exhibition of the facsimiles, along with a number of the originals opened at Galerie Berggruen, Paris on January 20, 1959. The show traveled to the Pierre Matisse Gallery, New York, where photographs from the book *The Miró Atmosphere* were also included. The New York show ran from March 17 to April 11.

1. These clippings were probably given to McBride in connection with the exhibition of *The Dial* Collection at the Worcester Art Museum.

Manley Hopkins, you know, said it was not a vanity but a right, his argument being "that pictures are painted to be seen and writings are written to be read." But you've read those marvellous letters to Canon Dixon—so I must stop right here. I am being too literary. This note was intended to be a thank you note.

So, thank you VERY much. It was a kind deed. . . .

Henry McBride died at home on March 31, 1962, at the age of ninety-five, and his body was cremated. Max Miltzlaff wrote of the disposition of McBride's ashes:

> *In the fall of 1963 I drove to California with the urn and on the return went via Santa Fe to Abiquiu seeking Georgia O'Keeffe, thinking she would know of a suitable place. . . . On the road north from Santa Fe to Abiquiu I saw a high promontory on the left and thought the place ideal. I climbed up the mountain side and must have climbed high. My breath came in short gasps and the car standing below looked so small. At the first crest, I stopped, opened the urn and studied the direction of the wind to allow the ashes to drift over the country side, I thought I had sensed the right direction, but as I let the ashes flow, suddenly the wind current changed and the ashes whirled around me as if in a final embrace of Good-bye . . .*

24 Endpiece, *Finis,* 1892. Henry McBride.

BIOGRAPHICAL SKETCHES

These notes provide a background to some of the people and families frequently referred to during the course of McBride's correspondence. Individuals who appear only infrequently are identified in footnotes. Cross-reference to another entry in this section is indicated by SMALL CAPITALS.

ALDRICH, Mildred (1853–1928), was an American expatriate who settled first in London and then, around the turn of the century, moved permanently to France. Born in Providence, Rhode Island, Aldrich had a long career as a writer, editor, critic, and occasional literary agent. She was an early contributor to *Atlantic Monthly* and wrote criticism for the *Boston Evening Transcript*. McBride met Aldrich in Paris through BRYSON and EDITH BURROUGHS. Aldrich may have been responsible for introducing McBride to GERTRUDE STEIN, for Stein had met Aldrich in Paris in 1904. On meeting her, Stein noted that Aldrich was very interesting, smoked cigarettes, and looked like George Washington. In 1914 Aldrich moved to Huiry, a rural area south of Paris, where she spent the rest of her life. Her best-selling and often-reprinted book *Hilltop on the Marne* (1915) is an account of her experiences in the French countryside during World War I. This was the first of several autobiographical historical works for which she became known. Thanks in part to Stein's lobbying efforts, Aldrich was awarded the Legion of Honor for her aid to refugees and children during the war. In her later years, her health failing, Aldrich was supported by a fund established by Stein, ALICE TOKLAS, and Janet Scudder. McBride was one of many friends and supporters who contributed to the fund.[1]

ASKEW, Kirk (1904–74), and Constance were most prominently remembered for their cocktail parties, held weekly from about 1930 to 1942, first on Sunday afternoons, then on Saturday nights. The Askews provided a gathering place for the circle of Harvard modernists who dictated taste for artists, writers, and a few musicians. It was alcoholic, up-to-date, fast moving, and socially fluid. McBride attended these events but was not a regular, as he found their brilliance wearing. Kirk Askew was the director of the New York branch of Durlacher Brothers. He introduced important

1. Kellner, *Gertrude Stein Companion*, pp. 139–40.

exhibitions of Baroque art to this London-based blue-chip gallery. His wife, Constance (née Atwood), had been married previously to America's leading writer on Baroque art, Arthur McComb.

BARNES, Albert (1873–1951), assembled one of the world's finest collections of French impressionism and postimpressionism. Notorious as a boor, a bully, and a braggart, Barnes was nonetheless a brilliant collector, acquiring masterpieces by Cézanne, Matisse, Monet, Renoir, Degas, Van Gogh, Gauguin, and Picasso. Barnes was a millionaire businessman who came into his own as a collector before the Armory Show and America's burgeoning interest in European modernism. His altercations with those in the field who disagreed with him—he prohibited, among other things, any alterations to the collection's salon-style installation, the loan of any artwork in the collection, and any photographs of the collection—is the stuff of legend. His writings on art and the disposition of his collection added to his infamy in the social history of modernism. He set up the Barnes Collection as a private museum in his home in Merion, Pennsylvania. McBride had his own run-ins with Barnes (one of which involved rumored threats about setting two boxing champions loose upon the critic), but ultimately the collector welcomed the critic into his circle of friends. In an obituary ("Dr. Barnes R.I.P.," *Art News,* September 1951) McBride wrote, "The paralyzing terror which the amazing Doctor managed to put upon the entire American art world of this generation is something that will not fade quickly from the memory, and the chances are that in the final story it will assume the importance and an interest comparable to that of the great collection which he assembled, remarkable as that collection is."

BARR, Dr. Everett Spary and Alice, were friends from Marshallton, Pennsylvania, who were a part of the familial support system McBride established for himself in his later years. Dr. Barr owned a sanitarium in nearby West Chester, and in 1944 he bought "the old Martin Farm," which abutted Callicaste, renaming it Penn Grant Farms. By 1950 the Barrs had also purchased a larger adjoining farm and renamed their now-large estate and working cattle farm Como, after the old stone house on the property. Floorboards from McBride's own barn, which he sold to the Barrs, were used in the renovation of the Barrs' manor home. Beginning in the late 1940s the Barrs became a regular part of McBride's summer retreats to Callicaste, sharing dinners, Sunday drives, ice cream cones, and local gossip. McBride stayed with the Barrs in Marshallton when he sold his own home there. Much of McBride's late correspondence, written from New York after selling Callicaste and moving in with MAX MILTZLAFF, was addressed to the Dr. and Mrs. Barr.

BONI, Albert (1892–1981), was a pioneering publisher and bookstore owner. He was a member of the illustrious Harvard class of 1910 (which included John Reed, Walter Lippmann, and T. S. Eliot). Boni was an instrumental figure in the rise of Greenwich Village bohemia and the dissemination of modernist trends in writings, especially Imagist poetry. With his brother Charles (1894–1969) he founded the Washington Square Bookshop at 135 MacDougal Street in 1913. The shop became a headquarters for Greenwich Village bohemians, published *Des Imagistes,* and offered a setting for the founding of the Washington Square Players, the Theatre Guild, and the Provincetown Players. The brothers joined forces with Horace Liverwright in 1917, becoming the publishing firm Boni and Liverwright. One of the most adventurous of mainstream publishers, at one time Boni and Liverwright could claim five Nobel Prize winners on their list, including Hemingway, Faulkner, and Eliot. When Boni and Liverwright broke up, the toss of a coin left the Boni brothers without a publishing house. From 1923 to 1928 they worked under the name Boni and Boni.

BURROUGHS, Bryson (1869–1934) and Edith (d. 1916), were long-term friends of McBride. A painter and curator of painting at the Metropolitan Museum of Art, Bryson worked both jobs part-time after assuming the curatorship left vacant by Roger Fry in 1906. An open-minded and progressive museum administrator and curator, Bryson made history when he bought the Metropolitan Museum its first Cézanne, *Le Colline des Pauvres,* from the Armory Show in 1913. He was also instrumental in acquiring work by American painters for the Met through the Hearn Fund. Not committed only to modernism, Burroughs considered the culmination of his curatorial career the museum's acquisition of Van Eyck's diptych *The Crucifixion; The Last Judgement* from the Hermitage. He also persuaded the board to buy a painting attributed to Pieter Brueghel, which was discovered after cleaning to be a signed work; *The Harvesters* remains one of the museum's prized paintings. Burroughs showed his own paintings throughout his life and is perhaps best known for creating the frescoes at the Century Club during World War I. Burroughs married the American sculptor Edith Woodman in 1893 and both were close friends of McBride's; they had a daughter, Elizabeth, nicknamed Bett. The Burroughses provided many introductions for McBride, including HENRI MATISSE, Roger Fry, MILDRED ALDRICH, and, through her, GERTRUDE STEIN. Bryson married Louise Guerber in 1928. He succumbed unexpectedly to tuberculosis in November 1934.

CAMPBELL, Beatrice (1865–1940), was born Beatrice Stella Tanner in London, began her acting career in 1886, and worked until 1938. Performing Shakespeare, Shaw, and Barrie, Mrs. Pat, as she was known to friends, required six columns in *Who's Who in Theater* to list all of her performances at the time of her death. She married Patrick Campbell at nineteen. In search of a better climate to treat his tuberculosis, her husband moved to South Africa and was killed in the Boer War. In 1912 while recuperating from a long illness, she began to correspond with George Bernard Shaw. Some of the correspondence from Shaw appeared in his 1922 book *My Life and Some Letters*. Shaw wrote his play *Pygmalion* for Campbell. As a social maven in New York and Europe, Campbell made frequent visits to the United States; her first was in 1901 and her last in 1938.

CARPENTER, Dudley, was an early friend of McBride's and a fellow teacher at the Educational Alliance about whom little is known. Carpenter was one of the regular recipients of McBride's earliest letters from Europe, though the two lost touch after McBride became a critic. Some intimacy with McBride's family is implied by the fact that McBride often seems to have written his earliest letters (1894–1913) to either Carpenter or his cousins MARY and MARIA PUGH with the knowledge that they would be shared among the three. Carpenter later settled in California and, except for a brief visit east in early 1930, did not see McBride.

CHANLER, Beatrice (d. 1946), was active in European war relief during both world wars. She received the Legion of Honor for her service in World War I and was a posthumous recipient of the Greek Decoration for her work during World War II. She married William Astor Chanler, an explorer in Africa and a Democratic member of the House of Representatives (and grandson of the original John Jacob Astor) in 1903. Beatrice Chanler founded and was president of the Lafayette Preventorium, the first institute in France devoted to the care of pretubercular and frail children during World War I. Following the war Chanler lived in Paris until 1939, when she returned to New York, settling at 59 East 54th Street. McBride referred to Chanler as "a conspicuous woman in society, and also president of the N.Y. Stage Society" in a letter about their meeting in 1915. Before the turn of the century Chanler was a well-known actress under her maiden name, Minnie Ashley. She was convinced by McBride of the necessity of producing Stein's plays. Although this did not come to pass, a lifelong friendship grew between Chanler and McBride, based on their common love of the stage and art. Following her career in the theater, Chanler took up sculpture, making bas reliefs and portrait busts under her married name. In her later years, when ill health made it impossible to sculpt, she wrote such books as *Cleopatra's Daughter, Queen of Mauritania* (1934). According to MAX MILTZLAFF, Beatrice Astor Chanler was a survivor of the

Titanic sinking. McBride summered with the Chanler family at their home in Maine in 1924 and socialized with Mrs. Chanler in New York. McBride noted that Mrs. Chanler fell on hard times economically after the death of her husband in 1934.

CORTISSOZ, Royal (1869–1948), was a conservative critic for the *New York Tribune* whose record for bad calls was alarmingly steadfast. Cortissoz wrote with the eye of a man out of touch with his time. Inspired by the neoclassical traditions of the nineteenth century, Cortissoz spent more time in Rome than in Paris and as a result developed an early bias against modernism and all art that he saw as lacking in commitment to the traditional standards of idealized beauty and technical facility. In criticism written over a span of almost sixty years, the Cortissoz point of view often acted as a foil for McBride's promodern stance. His most famous decree was delivered during a toast at the celebratory dinner following the opening of the Armory Show: "It was a good show, but don't do it again." McBride's personal fondness for Cortissoz weathered whatever differences of opinion they had in print. Both members of the Coffee House Club, McBride and Cortissoz socialized frequently and seem to have had a genuine affection for each other. McBride wrote a touching obituary of his friend.

CROWNINSHIELD, Frank (1872–1947), was best known as the editor of *Vanity Fair,* the stylish magazine that purveyed the doings of café society, modernism, and amusement. A friend of McBride's until Crowninshield's death, he was also a member of the founding committee of the Museum of Modern Art, a collector of "primitive art," a founding member of the Coffee House Club, and one of the bon vivants of the interwar period who served as a vital connector between society, the arts, and entertainment. At McBride's prompting, "Crownie" published Stein's "Have They Attacked Mary. He Giggled," sometimes called a word portrait of McBride, in *Vanity Fair* in 1917.

DALE, Chester (1886–1962) and Maud (1882–1952), assembled an art collection that became the backbone of the National Gallery of Art's nineteenth-century paintings collection. Chester made his fortune in railroad bonds, Western Canadian municipal bonds, and public utility holding companies. He made millions fast and retired to a life of private financial managing at the age of thirty-five. It was rumored that the stock market crash made him $50 million dollars poorer, leaving him with a net worth of less than $10 million. The setback didn't curtail his collecting interests. Maud Murray, whom Dale married in 1911, had trained in Paris to be an artist. She was several years older, several inches taller, and infinitely more knowledgeable about art than her wealthy husband. With her guidance, "Chesterdale" turned his attention from the American painting he had been acquiring and began building a collection focused on French painting of the nineteenth and twentieth centuries. Dale's second wife, the former Mrs. Mary Tower Bullard, had been his personal secretary.

DELANO, Louie, one of several "women of society" with whom McBride maintained long-lasting, gossip-filled friendships, based on visits to the theater, luncheons, and the dinner parties that made up so much of McBride's life into the 1950s. McBride was close to both Louie and her husband, William A. Delano, and was a guest at their vacation home in Syosett, Long Island. The Delanos resided in a townhouse at 136 East 36th Street, where McBride was often included in dinners, parties, and receptions.

DEMUTH, Charles (1883–1935), was a native of Lancaster, Pennsylvania, where McBride often visited him at his family home. Demuth was known for his watercolors and oil paintings, his naturalistic still lifes, and his abstract poster portraits. In 1912 he told GERTRUDE STEIN that writing was of greater interest to him than painting.[2] He had two works of fiction published in little magazines in the teens. By the twenties his writing was limited to art-related pieces. A diabetic who struggled with the disease in the days before the use of pharmaceutical insulin, Demuth lived primarily with his mother in Lancaster. He also associated with the Provincetown Players, the STETTHEIMER circle, the Society for Independent Artists, and the STIEGLITZ circle. McBride was one of his early and loyal supporters. McBride was also very fond of Demuth's mother (and her famous Fourth of July green turtle soup), who outlived her son and bequeathed to McBride in Charles's memory a first edition of James Joyce's *Ulysses,* as well as a cash inheritance of $10,000.

DRAPER, Muriel Saunders (1886–1956), was best known as a high bohemian hostess in New York and London, as a mentor of creative young men (including the balletomane LINCOLN KIRSTEIN, the painter Mark Tobey, and the composer George Antheil). Her couture was outlandish, her monologues were considered to be among the wittiest of the day, and her politics were left wing. Her memoir, *Music at Midnight,* was published in 1929 and became a best-seller. She wrote about interior decoration in the *New Yorker* (as Leirum Repard, her name spelled backward) and lectured widely on the radio on such varied subjects as women's rights, the Spanish Civil War, exploitation of African Americans, her memories of Henry James, and charm.

DUCHAMP, Marcel (1887–1968), was one of the most revolutionary and influential artists of the twentieth century, associated with Dada in

New York and Paris. He largely avoided the art world, and he surfaced in New York during both world wars. Among his most important works are two of the iconic and controversial works of the early avant-garde: *Nude Descending a Staircase,* which was exhibited at the Armory Show in 1913; and *Fountain,* which was the unexhibited pseudonymous scandal of the first Independents Exhibition in 1917. McBride admired both the man and his art, and Duchamp considered McBride the most important critic of the era and collaborated on the production of the pamphlet *Some French Moderns, Says McBride.* Their relationship, although not consistently intimate, spanned several decades, and McBride was one of the few people invited to celebrate Duchamp's second marriage.

FORCE, Juliana (1876–1948), began her career as secretary to GERTRUDE VANDERBILT WHITNEY but quickly became the driving force behind the Whitney Studio Gallery and Club and the subsequent development of the Whitney Museum of American Art. In purchasing and displaying contemporary American art, her efforts enabled numerous modern artists to continue their work. McBride socialized with Force, visiting her homes in England and New York.

GALLATIN, Albert Eugene (1881–1952), an early collector of modern art and one of the first (along with Katherine Dreier) to found museumlike institutions devoted to modern collections. McBride encouraged Gallatin's idea of opening a public gallery for his art, and the Museum of Living Art was opened at New York University on December 12, 1927.[3] Gallatin's collection was dominated by the work of the Europeans Picasso, Miró, Gris, Léger, Braque, Arp, and Mondrian, as well as the Americans DEMUTH and MARIN. Gallatin's important collection is now part of the permanent collection of the Philadelphia Museum of Art. Gallatin wrote books on Vermeer, Demuth, Sloan, Braque, and Lachaise, most of which were issued in limited, private editions of a few hundred copies. Gallatin was also an avid amateur magician. McBride and the famously reticent and socially prominent Gallatin were both members of the Coffee House Club, where they met and socialized frequently in the 1920s.

KIRSTEIN, Lincoln (1907–96), possessed a combination of drive, intelligence, and family money that helped him accomplish a great deal very quickly. While an undergraduate at Harvard (1926–30), he started the important magazine *Hound and Horn* (1927–34) and was the main force behind the Harvard Society for Contemporary Art (founded 1929). He brought George Balanchine to America in 1933 and formed the School of American Ballet, as well as the other succeeding dance organizations that culminated in the New York City Ballet. Kirstein wrote poetry, memoirs, and dance history and collected art, and his role as cultural entrepreneur left an indelible stamp on the twentieth century.

LACHAISE, Gaston (1882–1935), was a sculptor, frequently of monumental female figures. Born in France, he fell in love with the married Bostonian Isabel Dutaud Nagle and followed her to the United States in 1906. Settling in New York, Lachaise spent the remainder of his life making his heroic, highly exaggerated, and often sexually explicit female nudes. Lachaise had many important and loyal supporters during his lifetime. McBride was an early supporter of the sculptor. Critically acclaimed yet frequently destitute, Lachaise also made portraits, including one of his champion and friend Henry McBride, now in the collection of the Museum of Modern Art.

LEVY, Julien (1906–1981), left Harvard without a degree after three and a half years. He subsequently traveled to Paris to make movies. While working in a bookstore, he organized an Atget exhibition and then decided to start an art gallery, using money inherited from his mother. The Julien Levy Gallery (1931–49) was a pioneering and influential modern gallery, serving as New York's primary source for surrealism, neoromanticism, and photography. Among those he exhibited during his first two years were Walker Evans, Joseph Cornell, Max Ernst, Salvador Dalí, Pavel Tchelitchew, and George Platt Lynes. Levy's first wife, Joella, was the daughter of the poet Mina Loy, and Loy served as the gallery's Paris contact. Levy knew McBride not only through professional contact but through the Askew salon, and McBride was often a guest at the Levys' parties.

LOCHER, Robert (1888–1956), was an illustrator for such little magazines as *Rogue* who also designed book covers (including Max Ewing's *Going Somewhere* and CARL VAN VECHTEN's *The Blind Bow Boy*). He was best known as a stylish interior decorator and stage designer. Locher was close to CHARLES DEMUTH from boyhood on and was named Demuth's primary heir.

LUHAN, Mabel Ganson Evans Dodge Stern (1879–1962), was known for the environments she created, both physically and socially, and for her all-encouraging silence as a hostess. As Mabel Dodge, her first salons were staged at the Villa Curonia in Florence (1906–12). Her influential evenings at 23 Fifth Avenue (1913–16) facilitated general conversation on such subjects as psychoanalysis, the IWW, free love, cubism, and imagist poetry among the coalescing Greenwich Village bohemia. She moved to Taos, New Mexico, in 1918, and there met a Tiwa Indian, Antonio Luhan, whom she married in 1923, living with him until her death in her grand home, Los Gallos. She returned to New York each fall and continued to organize salon gatherings. Her memoirs (four volumes were published as *Intimate Memories,* and other volumes remained unpublished), as McBride's letters note, are remarkable for their frankness and their vivid evocation of her life.

MacADAM, Malcolm (1872–1957), and Henry McBride were confidants, correspondents, and travel companions over the course of a forty-year friendship that began one New Year's when they met in a New York City restaurant. MacAdam's career as an auditor for Standard Oil gave him extensive opportunity to travel, and he spent many years in Asia. In the 1920s and 1930s, McBride wrote many of his most unguarded, witty, and insightful letters to his closest friend MacAdam, whose position as an art world outsider must have freed McBride's hand. In later years the two men spent less time together but made a ritual of lunching together on Sundays.

MARIN, John (1870–1953), a trained architect, spent the years 1905–15 in Europe, where he studied painting, specifically cubism and the work of Cézanne. A painter of delicately abstracted seascapes of the Maine coast and Manhattan cityscapes who excelled in the medium of watercolor, Marin was a part of the STIEGLITZ circle, showing at 291, the Intimate Gallery, and An American Place. A friend and loyal supporter, McBride wrote frequently on Marin's career, and the artist gave the critic several works on paper as gifts.

MATISSE, Henri (1869–1954), the French master of color, was one of the most influential artists of the twentieth century. His earliest work grew out of impressionism, and much of his work retains a traditional aspect, but Matisse's genius was to be found in his decorative use of color and pattern. His earliest postimpressionist style was dubbed fauvism and was noted for the abandon and energy of his color canvases. After 1920 he lived mostly in Nice, where he worked in a naturalistic style. Matisse was also accomplished as a sculptor and illustrator. His last and most intensely colored works were the Cut-Outs, in which he composed simple yet highly decorative compositions from collaged pieces of brightly colored paper. After his first meeting with Matisse in 1910, McBride recorded his own bewildered response to the work, but quickly thereafter he became a staunch and lifelong supporter.

MATISSE, Pierre (1900–1989), son of HENRI, became a dealer of modern art, first in Paris and then on 57th Street in New York. Pierre was married to Alexina "Teeny" Sattler, who later married MARCEL DUCHAMP. McBride was a frequent visitor to the Pierre Matisse Gallery and spent time with both father and son when the French master visited the United States.

MILLER, Earle and Peter, were friends and neighbors of McBride's from Marshallton who painted and showed locally and were active in the art communities of the Philadelphia area. In the post–World War II period, as McBride slowly withdrew from the active social life he had once cultivated, the Millers took on an increasingly important role in McBride's life.

MILTZLAFF, Maximilian (b. 1903), met the sixty-eight-year-old McBride in 1935 and soon became the older man's closest companion. Born in Germany, Miltzlaff immigrated to the United State in 1922. Like MALCOLM MACADAM, Miltzlaff was not a member of McBride's art-related social circles, which seems to have provided a zone of comfort for McBride. Like MacAdam in earlier decades, Miltzlaff's work for the Dollar Steamship Lines took him on extended trips abroad, again affording McBride the opportunity to pen candid, warm, and full letters. After 1951 McBride and Miltzlaff shared an apartment, first on West 54th Street, in an apartment overlooking the garden of the Museum of Modern Art, and later in McBride's last home, in Peter Cooper Village in downtown Manhattan. Miltzlaff helped care for McBride during his final years.

MOORE, Marianne Craig (1887–1972), was one of the most highly regarded American poets of the twentieth century. She first published in such little magazine of the 1910s as *Others,* the *Little Review,* and *Poetry,* and her first book, *Poems,* was published in 1921. She continued to write and publish poetry and essays for the rest of her life. In 1925 she was named acting editor of *The Dial,* soon became editor, and continued in this capacity until the magazine ceased publication in 1929. McBride's relationship with her was initially based on their professional association, but it continued for decades, grounded in mutual respect.

NICKLI, Otto, was a private detective, amateur artist, music lover, and early friend who introduced the titillated McBride to the seedier side of life in New York City in the period 1909–10 in exchange for drawing lessons. The friendship seems to have foundered when McBride unsuccessfully attempted to introduce Nickli into Robertson Trowbridge's more highbrow social circle.

O'KEEFFE, Georgia (1887–1986), was one of America's best known early modern artists. Focusing on abstracted natural forms, O'Keeffe began showing at Alfred STIEGLITZ's 291 in 1916, and they were married in 1924. A lifelong friend and intimate of McBride's, she was probably introduced to McBride by Stieglitz in the early 1920s. O'Keeffe made her first visit to

New Mexico in April 1929, spending four months with MABEL DODGE LUHAN. In honor of their friendship, MAXIMILIAN MILTZLAFF chose an area near O'Keeffe's home to spread McBride's ashes in 1963.

PASCIN, Jules (1885–1930), born in Bulgaria and trained as an artist in Munich, was in many ways the quintessential romantic Parisian artist of the 1920s: international, manic, extravagant, and prolific. Pascin spent six years in the United States, becoming a citizen in 1914 before returning to Paris in 1920. He participated in some of the most important exhibitions of the day, including the Berlin Sezession of 1911, the Cologne Sonderbund-Ausstellung of 1912, and the New York Armory Show of 1913. Pascin made the woodblock portrait of McBride that graced the cover of the privately printed edition of Gertrude Stein's "Have They Attacked Mary. He Giggled."

PHILLIPS, Duncan (1886–1966), was a wealthy Washingtonian from an industrialist family. His interest in modern art began inauspiciously when, as a neophyte collector and conservative art critic, he denounced the Armory Show. His appreciation of experimental modernism, particularly abstraction, grew during the years he bought work for his museum of modern art, which he had begun to plan as early as 1918. The Phillips Collection now ranks among the finest small museums of modern art in the country. After some initial public disagreements over the commercial end of the art world, Phillips and McBride forged a cordial professional relationship.

PUGH family—Caleb (d. c. 1906); his wife, Martha (d. before 1906); and their daughters, Mary (d. 1937) and Maria (d. 1937), were McBride's closest family. Caleb Pugh was the brother of McBride's mother, Sarah. Caleb, a generous man, and aunt Martha, an apparently extravagant woman, had been farmers in Embreeville, Pennsylvania. McBride spent his summers with them after moving to New York just before the turn of the century. In 1906, after Martha's death, the financially strapped family lived at Callicaste, McBride's home in Marshallton, Pennsylvania. Caleb died soon after these new living arrangements had been made. Mary and Maria stayed on, cooking and keeping house, until 1936, when they moved to the nearby Hickman Home for Aged Quakers, leaving McBride alone at Callicaste for the first time. Mary and Maria were McBride's earliest correspondents.

RADCLIFF/RATCLIFF, Walter, a travel companion of McBride's in Italy, France, and England in 1906 and 1907. An architect from Berkeley, California, possibly of English origin, he was twenty-six during the period he traveled with McBride. McBride later spent time with Radcliff and his family, camping in California.

RAINS, Claude (1889–1967) and Frances (1918–65), were Marshallton neighbors of McBride's. Rains's first major film role was as H. G. Wells's *Invisible Man*. Nominated for four Academy Awards, Rains was the first actor to receive $1 million for a single role, playing Julius Caesar in Shaw's 1944 *Caesar and Cleopatra*. His 1951 role in *Darkness at Noon* won him acclaim on the stage. Rains and his sixth wife, Francis (he was her third husband), owned a 350-acre farm in Bucks County, where they met and socialized with McBride in the late 1940s and the 1950s.

STEIN, Gertrude (1874–1946), was, in the estimation of some, herself included, the most creative literary mind of the twentieth century. She wrote tirelessly, beginning in 1903 and continuing until a few weeks before her death. Her early works include *Three Lives* and *The Making of Americans*. ALICE B. TOKLAS moved into Stein's home at 27, rue de Fleurus in August 1910, and their domestic relationship lasted until Stein's death. Until *The Autobiography of Alice B. Toklas* became a best-seller in 1933, Stein was published infrequently, usually in small editions. With the *Autobiography*, the 1934 production of her opera (with VIRGIL THOMSON) *Four Saints in Three Acts*, and her five-month lecture tour (1934–35), Stein became a celebrity in her native land. Stein's relationship with McBride was abiding and loyal. Along with CARL VAN VECHTEN and Jane Heap, McBride was one of her key lieutenants in America. Stein, along with her brother LEO, was among the first collectors of the early modern work of Picasso, HENRI MATISSE, Cézanne, Braque, and Gris. Stein's Paris salon mingled the worlds of the Continental and expatriate Americans and spotlighted writing, music, and the visual arts.

STEIN, Leo (1872–1947), was a seminal collector and aesthetician of modern art, purchasing Cézannes and Picassos early in the century. He broke off his close relationship with his sister GERTRUDE in 1913, and the break was never mended. Leo's book *The A-B-C of Aesthetics* was published by Boni and Liverwright in 1927 to negative reviews and incomprehension. In February 1929 he gave a series of lectures at the New School in New York, where he broke down and forswore writing.

STEIN, Michael (1865–1938), like his siblings LEO and GERTRUDE, settled in Paris around the turn of the century. All three, as well as Michael's sister, Sarah "Sally" Samuels (1870–1953), collected art. Michael and Sarah focused on HENRI MATISSE, who became particularly close to Sarah.

STEPHENS, James (1882–1950), was a poet and Irish nationalist who befriended McBride in Paris in the teens, after they were introduced, perhaps by MILDRED ALDRICH or by Mr. and Mrs. Spicer-Simpson. He was also a friend of GERTRUDE STEIN's. Stephens supposedly shared his birth date (February 2, 1882) with James Joyce, who once described Stephens as "my rival, the latest Irish genius."[4] As a writer for the periodical *Sinn Fein*, Stephens came to the attention of A.E. (George Russell) and the other members of the Irish literary movement often called the Irish Renaissance. An active political writer, in addition to championing a free Ireland, he also wrote in support of women's suffrage.

STETTHEIMER family: The three Stettheimer sisters, Carrie (c. 1870–1944), Florine (1871–1944), and Ettie (Henrietta, 1874–1955), conducted a transatlantic modernist salon from 1915 to 1935, the longest running gathering of its kind in New York. Henry McBride was one of its most regular members beginning in about 1920, and he provided the fullest accounts, including the catalog for Florine's retrospective exhibition at the Museum of Modern Art in 1946. Carrie designed a doll house that included artworks by her friends, Florine painted throughout her life (including a portrait of McBride), and Ettie wrote two novels and some short pieces. Two other siblings, Walter and Stella, lived on the West Coast. McBride's long friendship with the three sisters included summer visits to their house in Atlantic City and intimate dinners in New York. Their salons, held in their rooms at the Alwyn Court, wedded an avant-garde guest list to an Old World style of entertaining that depended on elaborate table settings and six-course meals. Florine's paintings hung on the walls. After her death, Ettie's bedroom set was loaned to McBride, who used the set for the rest of his life.

STIEGLITZ, Alfred (1864–1946), was an American photographer, a vociferous propagandist, and the most influential modern gallerist in the years before World War I (the Little Galleries of the Photo-Secession, also called 291, 1905–17). He published the seminal magazine *Camera Work* (1903–17), notable for the beauty of its gravure images and the modernist aesthetics of its criticism. With the opening of the Intimate Gallery (1925–29) and An American Place (1929–46), which he conceived as a "laboratory center" for new art, rather than simply a gallery, Stieglitz continued the representation of his small circle—O'KEEFFE, MARIN, Dove, Hartley, DEMUTH, and Strand. Throughout his life he continued to take photographs. He was married twice, to Emmeline Obermeyer from 1893 to 1924, and to GEORGIA O'KEEFFE from 1924 to 1946. McBride's relationship with Stieglitz fluctuated from professionally distanced in the early years of the century to personal and intimate during the last years of Stieglitz's life. The earliest connection between the two men is an article McBride wrote on Stieglitz for *Camera Work* in 1917.

THAYER, Scofield (1890–1981), was born to a prominent Worcester, Massachusetts, family, graduated from Harvard, where he studied with George Santayana, and subsequently went to Oxford, where he was involved with the progressive politics of Sidney and Beatrice Webb. He became the editor of *The Dial* in 1919 and was the key influence at the magazine in its first years, but he suffered increasingly from psychological problems and spent more time in Europe in order to be a patient of Sigmund Freud's. During his time in Europe he assembled an important art collection of late-nineteenth- and early-twentieth-century European and American art. By the mid-1920s his paranoia and psychological disabilities prevented him from functioning as *The Dial*'s editor, and thereafter he communicated with the world mostly through a guardian, until his death at age ninety-two. The art collection he built while editor of *The Dial,* held by the Worcester Museum from 1931 until 1981, was willed to the Metropolitan Museum. His personal art collection was given to the Fogg Museum at Harvard.

THOMSON, Virgil (1896–1989), was a pioneering composer and music critic who wrote music that superficially appeared homespun and American. After graduating from Harvard in the mid-1920s, Thomson moved to Paris, where he lived until the outbreak of World War II. In 1926 he met GERTRUDE STEIN, and a year later the two began collaborating on the opera *Four Saints in Three Acts*. Thomson's critical writings in the *New York Herald* and elsewhere earned him the reputation as the most readable and accurate music critic of his era. McBride met Thomson at a private performance of *Four Saints in Three Acts* at the home of the STETTHEIMER sisters, and the art critic was struck by the composer's complete self-confidence.

TOKLAS, Alice B. (1877–1967), was GERTRUDE STEIN's domestic partner and an exceptional cook, and a favorite of the epicurean McBride. Toklas's voice and pithy sense of humor are reflected in Stein's popular book *Autobiography of Alice B. Toklas*. Toklas herself wrote *The Alice B. Toklas Cookbook* (New York: Harper, 1954) and *Aromas and Flavors of Past and Present* (New York: Harper, 1958).

TROWBRIDGE, Robertson, conducted a salon near Washington Square that played a key role in McBride's transformation from teacher to writer. Trowbridge introduced McBride to Lafcadio Hearn. In 1937 he self-published a book called *Forty-Eight Years: Anecdotes and Other Oddments Collected from Original Sources, 1884–1932*. He also wrote *Thirty Sonnets by Robertson Trowbridge, 1919–1929* (Harbor, 1930).

VAN VECHTEN, Carl (1880–1964), was an American novelist and critic of dance, music, and drama, later a photographer. Van Vechten worked as an assistant music critic for the *New York Times* from 1906 to 1908 and also served as the paper's Paris correspondent. An early supporter of African-American culture, Van Vechten was influential in literary circles in the 1920s. His novels included *Peter Whiffle, His Life and Works* (1922), *The Tattooed Countess* (1924), and *Nigger Heaven* (1926).

WHEELER, Monroe (1899–1988), was the director of Harrison of Paris, founded in 1930 by Barbara Harrison. The press specialized in fine hand-crafted editions of poetry and fiction by such authors as Thomas Mann and Katherine Anne Porter. In 1935 Wheeler began a thirty-year career at the Museum of Modern Art as the museum's first director of exhibitions and publications. As a curator, writer, member of the museum's library and advisory committees, and finally a member of the board of directors, Wheeler oversaw the production of more than 350 museum publications.

WHITNEY, Gertrude (1875–1942), the founder of the Whitney Museum of American Art and a sculptor in her own right, was born into the Vanderbilt family and married into the Whitney family. McBride wrote in a letter dated December 10, 1932, "They look with awe on Gertrude Whitney's position in the world, and regard her invitations as royal commands. . . . I suspect on the other hand, that Gertrude herself would cut 'society' absolutely, if she quite dared. She apparently yearns to have real relationships with people and seldom accomplishes it."

SELECTED BIBLIOGRAPHY

Berman, Avis. *Rebels on Eighth Street: Juliana Force and the Whitney Museum of American Art.* New York: Atheneum, 1990.

Bloemink, Barbara. *The Life and Art of Florine Stettheimer.* New Haven: Yale University Press, 1997.

Bramsback, Birgit. *James Stephens: A Literary and Bibliographical Study.* Cambridge: Harvard University Press, 1959.

Brinnin, John Malcolm. *The Third Rose: Gertrude Stein and Her World.* Boston: Little, Brown, 1959.

Brown, Gaye L., ed. The Dial: *Art and Letters in the 1920s, an Anthology of Writing from* The Dial *Magazine, 1920–1929.* Worcester: Worcester Art Museum, 1981.

Brown, Milton. *American Painting from the Armory Show to the Depression.* Princeton: Princeton University Press, 1955.

———. *The Story of the Armory Show.* New York: Abbeville and the Joseph Hirshhorn Foundation, 1988.

Burns, Edward, ed. *The Letters of Gertrude Stein and Carl Van Vechten, 1913–1946.* New York: Columbia University Press, 1986.

De Zayas, Marius. *How, When, and Why Modern Art Came to New York.* Ed. Francis Naumann. Cambridge: M.I.T. Press, 1996.

The Dial and the Dial Collection. Worcester, Mass.: Worcester Art Museum, 1959. Exhibition catalogue for the exhibition held April 30–September 8, 1959.

The Dial and the Dial Collection: A Special Loan Exhibition of Paintings, Sculpture, and Graphics by Thirty American Artists at the Downtown Gallery, September 22 to October 17, 1959. New York: The Gallery, 1959.

Draper, Muriel. *Music at Midnight.* New York: Harper, 1929.

Elderfield, John. *Henri Matisse: A Retrospective.* New York: Museum of Modern Art, 1992.

Ellmann, Richard. *James Joyce.* New York: Oxford University Press, 1965.

Fields, Armond. *Le Chat Noir.* Santa Barbara: Santa Barbara Museum of Art, 1993.

Four Americans in Paris: The Collections of Gertrude Stein and Her Family. New York: Museum of Modern Art, 1970.

Frank, Waldo, Lewis Mumford, Dorothy Norman, Paul Rosenfeld, and Harold Rugg, eds. *America and Alfred Stieglitz: A Collective Portrait.* New York: Doubleday, Doran, 1934; rpt. New York: Aperture, 1979.

Gallup, Donald Clifford, ed. *The Flowers of Friendship: Letters Written to Gertrude Stein.* New York: Knopf, 1953.

Gee, Malcolm. *Art Criticism Since 1900*. Manchester: Manchester University Press; New York: St. Martin's, 1993.

Gelb, Arthur, and Barbara. *O'Neill*. New York: Harper, 1960.

Greenough, Sarah, and Juan Hamilton. *Alfred Stieglitz: Photographs and Writings*. Washington, D.C.: National Gallery of Art; New York: Callaway, 1983.

Haas, Robert Bartlett, and Donald Clifford Gallup. *A Catalogue of the Published and Unpublished Writings of Gertrude Stein*. New Haven: Yale University Press, 1941; rpt. Folcroft Library, 1971.

Hapgood, Hutchins. *A Victorian in a Modern World*. New York: Harcourt Brace, 1939.

Haskell, Barbara. *Charles Demuth*. New York: Whitney Museum of American Art and Harry N. Abrams, 1987.

——. *Marsden Hartley*. New York: Whitney Museum of American Art and New York University Press, 1980.

Homer, William Innes, gen. ed. *Alfred Stieglitz and the American Avant-Garde*. Boston: New York Graphic Society, 1977.

——. *Avant-Garde Painting and Sculpture in America, 1910–1925*. Wilmington: Delaware Art Museum, 1975.

International Encounters: The Carnegie International and Contemporary Art, 1896–1996. Pittsburgh: Carnegie Museum, 1996.

James, Henry. *A Little Tour in France*. New York: Farrar, Straus, and Giroux, 1983.

Joost, Nicolas. *Scofield Thayer and* The Dial: *An Illustrated History*. Carbondale: Southern Illinois University Press, 1964.

Kellner, Bruce, ed. *A Gertrude Stein Companion: Content with the Example*. New York: Greenwood, 1988.

Kleeblatt, Norman L., and Susan Chevlowe, eds. *Painting a Place in America: Jewish Artists in New York, 1900–1945, a Tribute to the Educational Alliance Art School*. New York: Jewish Museum, 1991.

Kluver, Billy, and Julie Martin. *Kiki's Paris: Artists and Lovers, 1900–1930*. New York: Abrams, 1989.

Lanchner, Carolyn. *Joan Miró*. New York: Museum of Modern Art, 1993.

Lipchitz, Jacques, with H. H. Arnason. *My Life in Sculpture*. New York: Viking, 1972.

McBride, Henry. *Florine Stettheimer*. New York: Museum of Modern Art, 1946.

——. *The Flow of Art: Essays and Criticisms*. New York: Atheneum Publishers, 1975; rpt. New Haven: Yale University Press, 1997.

Mellow, James. *Charmed Circle: Gertrude Stein and Company*. New York: Praeger, 1974.

Mellquist, Jerome. *The Emergence of an American Art*. New York: Scribner's, 1942.

Moore, Marianne. *The Complete Prose of Marianne Moore*. Ed. Patricia Willis. New York: Viking Penguin, 1986.

——. *Predilections*. New York: Viking, 1955.

Olson, Arlene. *Art Critics and the Avant-Garde, New York, 1900–1913*. Ann Arbor: UMI Research Press, 1980.

Pohorilenko, Anatole, and James Crump. *When We Were Three: The Travel Albums of George Platt Lynes, Monroe Wheeler, and Glenway Wescott, 1925–1935*. San Francisco: Arena, 1998.

Powys, Llewelyn. *The Verdict of Bridlegoose*. New York: Harcourt, Brace, 1926.

Preato, Robert. *Impressionism and Post-Impressionism: Transformations in the Modern American Mode, 1885–1945*. New York: Grand Central Art Galleries, 1988.

Pyle, Hillary. *James Stephens: His Life and an Account of His Life*. London: Routledge, 1965.

Rose, Barbara, ed. *Readings in American Art, 1900–1975*. New York: Praeger, 1972.

Schwarz, Sanford. *The Art Presence*. New York: Horizon, 1982.

Secrest, Meryle. *Being Bernard Berenson: A Biography*. New York: Holt, Rinehart, and Winston, 1979.

——. *Between Me and Life: A Biography of Romaine Brooks*. New York: Doubleday, 1974.

Sheehy, Eugene P., and Kenneth A. Lohf. *The Achievement of Marianne Moore: A Bibliography, 1907–1957*. New York: New York Public Library, 1958.

Stavitsky, Gail. *The A. E. Gallatin Collection: An Early Adventure in Modern Art*. Philadelphia: Philadelphia Museum of Art Bulletin 89, nos. 379–80 (1994).

Stein, Gertrude. *Geography and Plays*. Madison: University of Wisconsin Press, 1993.

Strachey, Barbara, and Jayne Samuels, eds. *Mary Berenson: A Self-Portrait from Her Letters and Diaries*. London: V. Gollancz, 1983.

Sutherland, Donald. *Gertrude Stein: A Biography of Her Work*. New Haven: Yale University Press, 1951.

Turner, Elizabeth Hutton. *In the American Grain: Arthur Dove, Marsden Hartley, John Marin, Georgia O'Keeffe, and Alfred Stieglitz, The Stieglitz Circle at the Phillips Collection*. Washington, D.C.: The Phillips Collection, 1995.

Tyler, Parker. *Florine Stettheimer: A Life in Art*. New York: Farrar, Straus, and Giroux, 1969.

Vollard, Ambroise. *Paul Cézanne: His Life and Work*. Trans. L. Van Doren. New York: Crown, 1937.

Watson, Steven. *Strange Bedfellows: The First American Avant-Garde*. New York: Abbeville, 1991.

Zilczer, Judith. *"The Noble Buyer": John Quinn, Patron of the Avant-Garde*. Washington, D.C.: Hirshhorn Museum and Sculpture Garden, Smithsonian Institution Press, 1978.

INDEX

Dodge, Edward, 285
Dodge, Mabel. *See* Luhan, Mabel Dodge
Dodge, William De Leftwich, 35, 36
Doolittle, Edmund Warren, 289
Dorr, Charles Henry, 86
Downes, Olin, 249
Draper, Muriel, 136, 168, 170–71, 185, 217, 218, 230, 245, 286, 300, 303, 346
Dreier, Katherine, 152, 163, 183, 235
Dressler, Marie, 194–95
Dry Goods Economist, The, 18
Duchamp, Alexina "Teeny" Matisse, 293n, 312, 325, 349
Duchamp, Marcel, 1, 15, 110n, 130, 136, 139n, 144, 163, 293, 295, 311, 325, 331, 346–47
Dudensing, Bibi, 203, 330
Dudensing, Valentine, 188, 190, 194
Duncan, Anna, 187
Duncan, Isadora, 31, 80n, 238
Dunsany, Edward John, Lord, 128
Dürer, Albrecht, 56
Duse, Eleanor, 72
Duveen, Joseph, 257, 258

Eakins, Thomas, 13, 56n, 90, 162, 317
Eames, Emma, 298
Ecudero, 227
Eddy, Arthur Jerome, 86
Eddy, Frederick W., 86
Educational Alliance, 22–25, 26
Edward VII, King, 43, 77
Edward VIII, King, 291
Ehrich, Benjamin, 246
Eight, The, 83, 255n
Eliot, T. S., 300, 343
Elliot, Maxine, 248
Elliott, Gertrude, 44
Ellis, Mary, 187
Emperor Jones (opera), 227, 229
England, 199–200. *See also* London (England)
Epstein, Jacob, 23
Eugene, Prince of Sweden, 197
Ewing, Max, 217

Fabbri, Mrs. Ernesto, 269
Fairbanks, Douglas, 133–34, 135
Faulkner, William, 213
Fauvism, 83
Fay, Bernard, 295
Feder, Abe, 252
Fitch, Clyde, 75
Fitzgerald, F. Scott, 17
FitzGerald, James, 86, 89
Flagstad, Kristin, 282
Flanner, Janet, 325
Flint, Ralph, 4, 231, 247, 259, 267–68, 277, 296
Florence (Italy), 66, 69–74
Florentine Painters (Berenson), 73
Flow of Art, The (McBride), 1, 319
Forain, Jean-Louis, 52
Force, Juliana, 158, 199–200, 206, 222, 229, 234, 347
Ford, Charles Henri, 5–6, 27, 276, 277, 308, 311
Ford, Ruth, 330
Fourmier, Alice, 259
Four Saints in Three Acts (Stein and Thomson), 91, 178, 244–45, 247–53, 255, 256, 259, 263, 354
France, Anatole, 99
France: Artamarie, 174, 179; Belley, 172–75, 179; Caen, 143–44; Nantes, 52; Pont-Aven, 50–51; Rouen, 144; Tours, 51–54. *See also* Paris (France)
Frank, Waldo, 86
Frankfurter, Alfred, 318
French Academy, 81
Fry, Roger, 31, 32, 70–71n, 78, 79, 185
Fuller, Margaret, 32, 122

Galantière, Louis, 246
Gallatin, Albert Eugene, 156, 158, 177–78, 183, 192, 193, 198, 199, 222, 273, 347
Galleries: in New York, 83, 106–7, 128n, 188n, 205–6n, 231, 312, 316, 317; in Paris, 110–11, 198, 205–6, 294
Gambarelli Villa, 73, 74
Garbo, Greta, 194
Gardner, Isabella Stewart, 54n, 68n